FAITH-BASED ACT FOR CHRISTIAN CLIENTS

Faith-Based ACT for Christian Clients balances empirical evidence with theology to give mental health professionals a deep understanding of both the "why" and "how" of acceptance and commitment therapy (ACT) for Christians. The new edition includes updated discussions in each chapter, more than 20 new and updated exercises, and new chapters on couples and trauma.

The book includes a detailed exploration of the overlap between ACT and the Christian faith, case studies, and techniques that are explicitly designed to be accessible to both non-Christian and Christian (including evangelical Christian) counselors and therapists. Chapters also present the established research on Buddhist-influenced mindfulness meditation and newer research on Christian-derived meditative and contemplative practices and lay a firm theological foundation through the use of engaging biblical stories and metaphors.

Joshua J. Knabb, PsyD, ABPP, is the director of the PsyD program in clinical psychology and a professor of psychology in the College of Behavioral and Social Sciences at California Baptist University. He also serves as the editor for the *Journal of Psychology and Christianity*.

FAITH-BASED ACT FOR CHRISTIAN CLIENTS

An Integrative Treatment Approach

Second Edition

Joshua J. Knabb

Routledge
Taylor & Francis Group

NEW YORK AND LONDON

Cover image: © Getty Images

Second edition published 2023
by Routledge
605 Third Avenue, New York, NY 10158

and by Routledge
4 Park Square, Milton Park, Abingdon, Oxon, OX14 4RN

Routledge is an imprint of the Taylor & Francis Group, an informa business

© 2023 Joshua J. Knabb

First edition published by Routledge 2016

Library of Congress Cataloging-in-Publication Data
Names: Knabb, Joshua J., author.
Title: Faith-based ACT for Christian clients : an integrative treatment approach / Joshua J. Knabb.
Other titles: Faith-based acceptance and commitment therapy for Christian clients
Description: Second edition. | New York, NY : Routledge, 2023. | Includes bibliographical references and index.
Identifiers: LCCN 2022000795 (print) | LCCN 2022000796 (ebook) | ISBN 9781032018812 (paperback) | ISBN 9781032018874 (hardback) | ISBN 9781003181941 (ebook)
Subjects: LCSH: Acceptance and commitment therapy. | Psychotherapy--Religious aspects. | Psychotherapy patients--Religious life.
Classification: LCC RC489.A32 K53 2023 (print) | LCC RC489.A32 (ebook) | DDC 616.89/1425--dc23/eng/20220121
LC record available at https://lccn.loc.gov/2022000795
LC ebook record available at https://lccn.loc.gov/2022000796

ISBN: 9781032018874 (hbk)
ISBN: 9781032018812 (pbk)
ISBN: 9781003181941 (ebk)

DOI: 10.4324/9781003181941

Typeset in Baskerville
by Deanta Global Publishing Services, Chennai, India

THIS BOOK IS DEDICATED TO JESUS, THE
"SUFFERING SERVANT," WHO MODELED LOVE
IN THE MIDST OF SUFFERING AS HE CARRIED
OUT HIS EARTHLY MISSION.

CONTENTS

CONTENTS

CONTENTS

ILLUSTRATIONS

Figures

Tables

FOREWORD

Keeping the Faith:
ACT and the Role of Process-Based Psychotherapy
in Living a Faith-Based Life

Suppose you were wandering in a dark forest trying to find light. Periodically you saw glimpses of sky or the glow of sunlight in the tops of the forest canopy. The way forward initially was blocked, but with effort you found a path and began heading more continuously toward the light. Sometimes it was not clear to you that you were moving forward, but you kept on moving and finally a vast clearing opened up. As you entered it, you were surprised to find people in various corners of the clearing. Some were praying or meditating. Some are wearing monks' robes. Others were dressed as priests, ministers, or rabbis. There were therapists there as well, and artists, novelists, and wise historical figures. The paths they took to get there differed and the specific ways they used did as well, but they shared an illuminated space.

I think faith and science bear a similar relationship.

This elegant and wise book lays out in a very point-to-point fashion how acceptance and commitment therapy or "ACT" (said as a single word, not initials) can be understood and used by Christians, and how faith can foster greater psychological flexibility.

I was raised a Christian, and this overlap does not surprise me. ACT was instigated over 40 years ago by me and the first article I ever wrote about it back in 1984 was on the need to take spirituality seriously in behavioral science.

It was not that ACT set out to create a system that fits with Christianity or any other religious tradition. Rather, I recognized that the very fundamental process-based approach being taken by ACT toward such questions as why it is so hard to be human necessarily overlapped with faith-based traditions and Christianity as I knew it (up to and including four years of Jesuit training at Loyola-Marymount University). There is enormous scientific wisdom in all of our great religions, and that is very clear in what we are learning in behavioral science about how to foster peace of mind and purpose.

The science behind the book you are holding is voluminous and expanding rapidly. When I wrote the foreword for the first edition of this book, there were about 125 randomized trials on ACT and several hundred studies of other kinds. Today, just a few years later, there are over 825 randomized controlled trials on ACT (bit.ly/ACTRCTs) and several thousand other studies on the underlying model and basic processes, or on outcomes in less well-controlled studies. I think we can now say with great confidence that all six elements of psychological flexibility matter. With every study, I feel more confident that this wing of behavioral science and the major religious traditions are sharing the light of a common clearing.

This book shows it. Joshua Knabb dances back and forth in a seamless way between well-chosen scriptural quotes, careful explanation, and what the science shows. Even more than in the first edition, he dances that dance with elegance, utility, accuracy, and ease. Anyone reading this book will see how deep the links are between Christianity and ACT. Every one of the six processes in psychological flexibility are carefully explored, and, in every case, Joshua shows that there is good scriptural support for their importance.

That is true of the Old and New Testaments; it is true of all of the Abrahamic religions. That means that it is simply not true that people of faith must choose between scientific evidence and their faith convictions.

I am not arguing that all religions are the same, nor that science and faith are indistinguishable. I am not arguing that Christianity and science are the same thing. What I am arguing is that it is wonderful and empowering when science and faith find common ground and we should build on those opportunities by very seriously pursing the overlap.

That is precisely what Joshua has done in this volume, even more skillfully than in its first edition. With careful quoting and unpacking, this book proves beyond any doubt that there is an important overlap between ACT and the deepest messages inside the Christian faith. That overlap was not imposed; it is not artificial. It is there because the light falls there. It is there because sometimes knowing by faith and knowing by experimental evidence are windows into a common reality.

Compared to Christianity, the world of therapy is the new kid on the block, and the world of evidence-based therapy is even newer—perhaps only 60 or 70 years old. Over the last several decades, we as a culture began to think of human struggles in the language of illness and health. It would be hard to argue that the shift has been positive in all respects. For example, the dominance of psychiatric syndromes has increased the ease with which clients and therapists alike can fail to see meaning in human suffering. There is no real meaning in a "disease" that you "have," other than to wish you "did not have it."

It was not always like that. As a child when I was struggling with something, my mother used to say, "offer it up, dear, offer it up." What she meant by that was that I was supposed to find some connection between my own suffering and the suffering of others—and then offer it to God as a kind of sacrifice, asking God to use it to help me develop greater wisdom, kindness, and compassion.

Frankly, that seems far wiser than wishing you did not have pain to deal with in the first place. Joshua carefully unpacks such moments in this book. He shows how the "pain of absence" that comes when we put life on hold while waiting for the pain of anxiety, depression, and the like, to go away is very much like waiting for pain to go away before embracing faith in God.

This book wisely asks Christian therapists and clients alike to see if their journey can be empowered by the use of scientifically validated mental and behavioral health principles and methods. In the case of ACT, he arrives at a clear and compelling answer: Yes, it can. This book shows how.

For a Christian, this book is a wonderful opportunity. Almost every paragraph interweaves the Christian faith and psychological flexibility processes together. There is a shared clearing in this book—let's build on this opportunity by seriously pursing that overlap in the interests of the lives of those we love and serve.

Steven C. Hayes
Foundation Professor of Psychology, University of Nevada, Reno
Originator and Co-Developer of ACT and author of
A Liberated Mind: How to Pivot Toward What Matters

ACKNOWLEDGMENTS

To start, I want to acknowledge my wife, Adrienne, who has supported me throughout this writing project. Also, I would like to thank the reviewers, who offered valuable feedback on the proposal for this revised book. Moreover, I would like to thank Steve Hayes and the rest of the ACT community for their tremendous contributions to the clinical psychology literature over the last several decades. Furthermore, I would like to acknowledge Anna Moore at Routledge, who asked me to write a revised edition. Finally, I would like to thank God, the author of love, who generously offers his perfect, benevolent care from moment to moment on the road of life.

PERMISSIONS

ABOUT THE AUTHOR

Joshua J. Knabb, PsyD, ABPP, is the director of the PsyD program in clinical psychology and a professor of psychology in the College of Behavioral and Social Sciences at California Baptist University. He also serves as the editor for the *Journal of Psychology and Christianity*.

INTRODUCTION

The English word *suffer* means to feel physical, emotional, or mental pain, especially when these experiences are unavoidable in life (Merriam-Webster, 1995b). Beyond the feeling of pain, suffering captures the ability to endure, allow, or permit pain (Merriam-Webster, 1995b). The Latin root of suffer, *sub-ferre*, is commonly defined as bearing under (Osborne, 2005). This is a book for mental health professionals (e.g., professional counselors, psychotherapists) to more effectively work with Christian clients who are "bearing under" psychological pain in the 21st century, drawing from both the Christian tradition and *acceptance and commitment therapy* (ACT), an evidence-based treatment approach within the broader family of cognitive and behavioral therapies designed to help clients who are experiencing ongoing mental suffering (Harris, 2019; Hayes, 2019; Hayes et al., 2012; Luoma et al., 2017). In the pages that follow, I explore psychological suffering in the Christian life, including the ways that counselors and therapists can help Christian clients to make better sense of difficult thoughts, feelings, sensations, memories, situations, and relationships, as well as how to help followers of Jesus walk with him in love (Ephesians 5:2) down a road toward meaning and purpose in the midst of the daily psychological struggles that simply will not go away on this side of heaven.

The "Fork in the Road"

For Christian clients, with each and every one of life's steps, whether large or small, there is a "fork in the road" (Hayes et al., 2012), or "choice point" to use more precise ACT language (Harris, 2019), with two distinct traveling options. The first road (i.e., "choice") involves walking with God, enduring psychological suffering, and, ultimately, heading toward the life God has called them to live, anchored to love as *the* requisite moral behavior. Along this road, Christian clients are communing with God (Knabb & Wang, 2021) and loving both God and others (Matthew 22:36–40), recognizing that God, as the author of love (1 John 4:7–21), is with them as a friend and trustworthy traveling companion from moment to moment. In fact, for Christian clients, love, defined as an "unselfish,

DOI: 10.4324/9781003181941-1

loyal, and benevolent intention and commitment toward another person," is a central theme, with the love of God "deeply rooted in the Bible" (*Holman Bible Dictionary*, 2004, p. 222). Conversely, the second road (i.e., "choice") involves fruitlessly attempting to walk alone, futilely striving to avoid psychological suffering, and, ultimately, heading away from the life God has called them to live. See Figure 0.1 for a visual depiction of these two differing roads, one leading toward, and the other leading away from, a meaningful life of love (adapted from Harris, 2019; Hayes et al., 2012).

Succinctly put, this book is about helping Christian clients in counseling and therapy to regularly take the first, not second, road—intentionally choosing to walk with God, step by step and moment by moment, so as to more effectively endure difficult thoughts, feelings, sensations, memories, situations, and relationships and live the life God is offering, tethered to love as *the* crowning virtue for effective behavioral action. Indeed, if the word *acceptance* simply means to "receive willingly" (Merriam-Webster, 1995a), with the help of ACT, Christian clients can learn to "receive willingly" the life that God is offering—even in the middle of psychological suffering—as they steadily walk with him in love on the road toward meaning and purpose.

The "Fork in the Road" for Christians

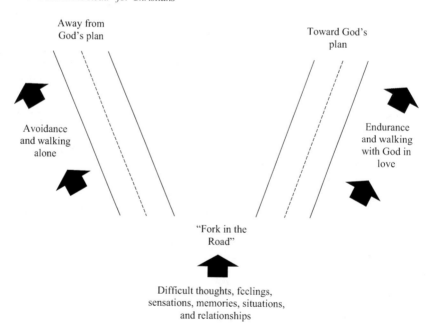

Figure 0.1 The "Fork in the Road" for Christians. *Note.* Adapted from Harris (2019), Hayes (2019), and Hayes et al. (2012).

Combining ACT and Christianity at the "Ground Floor"

Whether Christian clients are experiencing depression, anxiety, trauma-related symptoms, relationship distress, or other recurrent psychological struggles, this book presents an important body of research in the field of clinical psychology on a well-developed strategy for accepting the inevitable pains of life so as to prioritize pursuing a set of values (see, e.g., Bai et al., 2020), integrating these emerging psychological insights from ACT with the Christian tradition in order to help Christian clients follow Jesus—their rabbi (John 3:2) and Suffering Servant (Isaiah 53)—in a counseling or therapy environment.

When working with Christian clients, this type of an exploration inevitably begins and ends with Jesus, given that Christians believe he is the Word of God who took on human form (John 1), revealed the meaning of suffering (1 Peter 4), and modeled how to respond to suffering (1 Peter 2:21) when the aches and pains of life simply will not subside. Because of this, rather than trying to present the Christian faith as merely a culturally sensitive "add-on" to primarily an ACT treatment guide, my goal is to offer a truly integrative treatment approach, with an *Unterbau*, or common infrastructure. Worded differently, ACT and Christianity will be combined at the "ground floor," offering an intervention for Christian clients suffering with recurrent distress. After all, the Christian faith elucidates the "ultimate concerns of human beings," providing a foundation for daily living and offering a solution for the human condition, rooted in virtuous action (Wright, 1992, pp. 122–139). So, too, does ACT, helping clients to effectively respond to suffering so as to engage with life again in a meaningful, vibrant manner. Presented side by side, ACT and Christianity have many points of overlap, revealing the unique fit between the two, which includes a very different understanding of pain when compared to a surrounding Western culture that often typifies a life of hedonism, overindulgence, and superficiality, not value-based purpose.

Two Types of Psychological Pain

At the risk of sounding overly simplistic, Christian clients in counseling and therapy are typically faced with two types of pain within the God-given time they have on this planet. One type of pain, the *pain of presence*, involves distressing psychological experiences, which clients repeatedly try to get rid of in life (Hayes, 2005). For example, chronic worry may get in the way of maintaining healthy relationships, negatively affect work life, and diminish Christian clients' relationship with God. Chronic worry, moreover, can lead to a range of other symptoms, including fatigue, sweating, difficulty sleeping, and a constant "on edge" experience, resulting in a diagnosis of *generalized anxiety disorder* (GAD) (American Psychiatric Association [APA], 2013). Because of this, some Christian clients may understandably try to get rid of chronic worry—including all of its accompanying symptoms—through distraction, drug and alcohol abuse, working overtime, or some other strategy that seemingly helps to avoid the troublesome thoughts that linger for days on end. This strategy—experiential avoidance, which involves attempts to reduce, eliminate, avoid, or distract from difficult inner events (e.g., thoughts, feelings, sensations, memories), as well as their corresponding outer events (e.g., challenging situations, relational conflicts) (Hayes et al., 1996; Hayes, 2019)—seems to make sense, given that chronic worry causes so much pain.

On the other hand, the *pain of absence* captures the life that Christian clients would someday like to cultivate as a follower of Jesus, engaging in authentic, value-based living in some distant future; this life, though, appears to be just out of reach because of the pain of presence, leading to additional pain (Hayes, 2005). Unfortunately, it seems as if Christian clients are faced with only two narrow options—*either* struggle with the pain, trying desperately to make it go away through avoidance strategies and waiting until they are symptom-free to serve God, *or* follow Jesus (i.e., walk with God), free of pain. Yet, continuously wrestling with the pain of presence inevitably leads to the pain of absence because Christian clients erroneously believe they cannot follow Jesus in the midst of pain, leaving them stuck without the life they envisioned having, disconnected from their values.

For instance, each Sunday morning an individual with depression, Jason, may hear a powerful, inspirational sermon that challenges him to serve within his community. Leaving the sanctuary, Jason may feel particularly called toward truly living a life devoted to following Jesus, deciding he will fully surrender to Jesus's teachings on helping the underserved (Matthew 25:35–40). When the pain of presence inevitably begins to surface, though, following Jesus seems to be an unrealistic endeavor. "It is just not possible to follow Jesus when I am hurting so much," Jason may tell himself with an attitude of defeat and hopelessness. Because of this, he may find himself delaying action, waiting for the pain to go away before he can successfully devote his life to God. This decision most certainly leads to a deep-seated sense of loss, beyond the psychological pain that initially weighed Jason down. It is almost as if Jesus is approaching Jason, a potential disciple, on the shore of the Sea of Galilee, similar to Simon and Andrew, stating "Come, follow me" (*New International Version Bible*, 2011, Matthew 4:19). In return, Jason tells Jesus that he will catch up with Jesus as soon as the depression goes away. Yet, standing on the shore, watching Jesus walk away, Jason may feel additional pain beyond the depression he was initially trying to avoid. The reality begins to set in—Jason has missed the opportunity to live the authentic Christian life he always wanted.

Herein lies the dilemma. The more Christian clients futilely try to liberate themselves from the pain of presence through avoidance strategies, the more they end up experiencing the pain of absence because of a perpetual delay in following Jesus. In other words, as Christian clients focus all their effort on getting rid of the psychological pain, believing they can only follow Jesus when the pain goes away, they are not walking with God from step to step and moment to moment—God seems to be absent from their life. Instead, their energy tends to be devoted to getting rid of painful struggles, avoiding the road toward meaning and purpose that Jesus has called them to walk with him on. Struggling with psychological pain that will not go away takes up all of their time, leading to a sort of "wait-and-see" approach to picking up their cross and following Jesus (Matthew 16:24). As a result, Christian clients may end up with both the psychological suffering that will not go away and a missed opportunity to radically follow Jesus and fulfill their purpose on this planet. The main issue for Christian clients, though, is whether the pain of presence or pain of absence causes more suffering in life.

In this book, consistent with ACT, I argue that the pain of absence leads to more suffering than the pain of presence. Therefore, life is about shifting the focus, accepting the pain of presence in order to ameliorate the pain of absence. Indeed, there is a third option, a "both/and" rather than "either/or" solution for Christian clients, beyond *either* wrestling with psychological pain, waiting to live life until it somehow goes away, *or* following Jesus, free of pain. As a third scenario, Christian clients can learn to *both* follow Jesus *and* experience psychological pain, rather than waiting for it to permanently subside in vain. In other words, Christian clients can work toward accepting the pain of life, following Jesus in the midst of inner and outer struggles. If this is the case, counselors and therapists can play a salient role in helping Christian clients embrace this "both/and" approach to psychological pain. Ultimately, letting go of the false dichotomy of "pain/cannot follow Jesus" versus "no pain/can follow Jesus" serves as a major premise of this book.

Psychological Pain and the Rich Ruler

A biblical example of psychological pain—which, of course, has been a ubiquitous experience throughout human history—involves a rich ruler in the first century who had the opportunity to talk directly and authentically to Jesus about the meaning of life. Apparently, he was young, wealthy, and powerful, all attributes celebrated both in his time and our contemporary society (Bock, 1996; Luke 18:18–30). The ruler asked Jesus how he could achieve eternal life, confidently mentioning that he had followed a range of biblical commandments since he was a child. Still, Jesus pointed out that the ruler had not yet given all of his possessions to the poor in order to follow Jesus. Of course, the ruler's famous response involved walking away sad and grieved because he was unwilling to let go of his material wealth, a ubiquitous, scary notion regardless of the time, geographic location, or culture in which people live.

Walking with God is an important theme within this story presented in Luke's gospel. The ruler was saddened by the reality that following Jesus involved letting go of the possessions that seemingly offered him a sense of safety, security, and comfort. Unfortunately, in an effort to guard against the sadness and anxiety that may emanate from a radical shift from walking alone and self-reliance to walking with God and reliance upon God, the ruler experienced both the pain of presence and the pain of absence. Faced with a similar decision today, many Christian clients would walk away saddened as well, concluding that a life fully dedicated to walking with, and relying upon, God is too risky or painful. To be sure, how often do Christian clients attempt to avoid the pain of presence through the pursuit of material wealth, drug and alcohol abuse, or some other numbing behavior and, unfortunately, end up experiencing both the pain of presence and pain of absence?

Overall, this rich young man was faced with a poignant decision—walk with God (i.e., follow Jesus) or walk alone, with the latter involving unilaterally attempting to numb the pain of life through the accumulation of personal wealth. Of course, the former, selling all his material goods to follow Jesus, would have likely involved some sadness, uncertainty, worry, anxiety, and conflict, which he apparently guarded himself from by clinging to self-reliance. Yet, following Jesus the rabbi would have also led to a life worth living.

This story can help to understand the daily decision Christian clients are faced with, including those who come to counseling and therapy. Are they going to follow Jesus the rabbi in the midst of psychological pain or attempt to avoid pain, which leads to an inability to fulfill their God-given purpose? Will they follow Jesus as he, according to the Bible, teaches them, guides them, and prepares a place for them in heaven (John 14:3)? Or will Christian clients turn to avoidance in an effort to distract themselves from the challenges inherent in following Jesus? When they embrace the latter, they will likely face both the psychological pain of the ups and downs of daily living and a deeper sadness and loss because they have declined the invitation to walk with their rabbi and learn directly from him.

Jesus the Rabbi

Understanding Jesus as the *rabbi* may help to more deeply reflect upon the literal calling Christian clients believe in, obediently walking with Jesus as his disciple, regardless of Christian clients' inner and outer struggles. In other words, for Christian clients, following Jesus requires behavioral action in the midst of psychological pain. The term *rabbi*, meaning "great" in Hebrew, was synonymous with "teacher" during Jesus's time (Koessler, 2003, p. 151). Around the time of Jesus's ministry, a student of a rabbi, referred to as a *talmid*, was to learn from this special teacher in order to eventually become a rabbi himself (Koessler, 2003). The student walked behind his rabbi, rather than next to him, so as to fully absorb the rabbi's way of life (Koessler, 2003).

In the gospel of Luke, Jesus stated, "Whoever wants to be my disciple must deny themselves and take up their cross daily and follow me" (*New International*

Version Bible, 2011, Luke 9:23). It was common for disciples of a rabbi to follow him around on a daily basis, walking closely behind him in order to learn his teachings (Koessler, 2003). They were also called to obediently act on his teachings (Koessler, 2003). In fact, not only were Jesus's disciples to follow him as their rabbi, they were also to "take up their cross" to follow him, which was a symbolic way of saying they were to fully commit to him by symbolically carrying a heavy cross (Gundry, 2011). Consisting of two beams, a cross was used to crucify someone sentenced to death in the first century (Gundry, 2011). The sentenced individual was required to carry his own cross to the place of execution, with a crowd typically gathering around him to hurl insults and slurs as he painfully walked to his own death (Gundry, 2011). Therefore, Jesus was instructing his disciples that following behind him would require extreme sacrifice and self-denial (Gundry, 2011).

An Antidote for Psychological Pain

In the pages that follow, I present an integrative approach—grounded in ACT and the Christian faith—to help Christian clients follow Jesus the rabbi (i.e., walk with God) in the midst of psychological pain. Although the pain of presence may not go away—Christian clients will definitely experience uncertainty, distress, conflict, and other difficult inner and outer struggles in their efforts to follow Jesus—counselors and therapists can help Christian clients to cultivate what Harris (2019) referred to as a "rich, full, and meaningful life" (p. 61). Notice, here, that the word "happy" is not embedded within this inspirational quote.

Instead, I explore ways for Christian clients to relate differently to psychological pain, accepting that inner and outer struggles in the Christian life are a given. To live a "rich, full, and meaningful life" entails accepting that life is painful. For Christian clients, the rewards of following Jesus the rabbi, though, surpass mere pleasure or happiness, elusive experiences in the 21st century. Certainly, the Christian experience of a deeper, longer-lasting *contentment*, with God at the center, not surface-level, fleeting human pleasure, is prioritized in the Christian life.

In the Bible, *contentment* comes from the Greek word *arkeo*, meaning "Internal satisfaction which does not demand changes in external circumstances" (*Holman Illustrated Bible Dictionary*, 1998, p. 335), with the Apostle Paul famously declaring that he had "learned to be content whatever the circumstances" (*New International Version Bible*, 2011, Philippians 4:10). In the psychology literature, moreover, recent research has revealed that Christian contentment is positively linked to key mental skills (e.g., attention, present-moment awareness, acceptance), life contentment, and daily spiritual experiences among Christian adults (Knabb et al., 2020). Can counselors and therapists help Christian clients to experience this biblical concept of contentment in the face of psychological suffering? The integrative approach presented in this book can assist counselors and therapists

7

in applying an evidence-based approach, ACT, to clinical work with Christian clients so as to answer this question with a resounding, confident "yes."

In Christian clients' efforts to follow Jesus, avoiding psychological pain is the problem, whereas accepting the reality of psychological pain is the solution, even when they believe that suffering is unjust or unfair. The New Testament is filled with examples of this two-step solution to the human condition—accepting psychological pain in order to follow Jesus. In one of the Apostle Peter's letters, for example, he stated the following: "To this [suffering unjustly] you were called, because Christ suffered for you, leaving you an example, that you should follow in his steps" (*New International Version Bible*, 2011, 1 Peter 2:21). In this passage, Peter highlighted the theological importance of Jesus's suffering—it is a powerful example for Christian clients to emulate because of his atoning work on the cross, as revealed in the pages of the Bible (Marshall, 1991). Therefore, when Christian clients suffer, even unjustly, they are to patiently endure because Jesus first suffered for them (Marshall, 1991).

To illustrate this point, "There may be many possible ways to the summit of a mountain. But the guide chooses the particular path which he himself takes, and his followers must go the same way" (Marshall, 1991, p. 93). As the guide who is paving the way for Christian clients, Jesus clearly presented an example of how to respond to suffering—a hopeful endurance. Because of Jesus's mission—to reconcile God with humankind (2 Corinthians 5:18)—his eyes were focused on the task at hand. Although he undoubtedly felt the pain of presence, he was unwilling to also experience the pain of absence; that is, Jesus refused to walk away sad, disappointed, and grieved, like the rich ruler. He simply would not allow himself to experience "pain on top of pain" and "suffering on top of suffering" (Hayes, 2005, p. 17) because of his deliberate choice to walk on the road his Father chose for him, enduring pain along the way.

When more closely examining Jesus's life, the Passion narrative, which explicates Jesus's tremendous suffering, seems to best capture his willingness to patiently endure pain in order to fulfill his purpose. Shortly before his crucifixion, Jesus prayed to his Father in Gethsemane, with Matthew's gospel revealing that Jesus was "overwhelmed with sorrow to the point of death" (*New International Version Bible*, 2011, Matthew 26:38). On the cross, Jesus cried out to his Father, "Why have you forsaken me," possibly experiencing a deep sense of loneliness and separation from God (*New International Version Bible*, 2011, Matthew 27:46). Isaiah, too, revealed Jesus's purpose on this planet—he was the "Suffering Servant" who was "a man of suffering, familiar with pain" (*New International Version Bible*, 2011, Isaiah 53). Because of Jesus's example, Christian clients believe they are to follow him in his suffering, embracing psychological pain as they faithfully walk with God to fulfill their own divine calling. In fact,

> When you shall have come to the point where suffering is sweet and acceptable for the sake of Christ, then consider yourself fortunate, for

you have found paradise on earth. But as long as suffering irks you and you seek to escape, so long you will be unfortunate.

(Kempis, 2003, p. 43)

A Hopeful Endurance

Interestingly, the New Testament word *hupomone*, meaning steadfastness or a hopeful, joyful, faithful, patient, constant, active, forward-looking endurance in the midst of persecutions and tribulations, seems to best capture a Christian view of enduring psychological pain when following Jesus (Barclay, 2000). This term is emphasized throughout the current book, drawing from the life of Jesus, in order to combine the willingness to accept difficult inner (e.g., thoughts, feelings, sensations, memories) and outer (e.g., challenging situations, relational problems) experiences with value-based behavioral action, something Jesus modeled for Christian clients to do. In other words, a hopeful endurance is about "bearing under" life's struggles in order to "stay the course," steadily walking with God through (not around) life's trials and drawing upon God's strength to persevere in the midst of hardship.

Used approximately 30 times in the New Testament, *hupomone* has been described as an extremely noble New Testament concept (Barclay, 2000). Within the classical Greek language, this word seems to capture a plant growing despite harsh environmental conditions (Barclay, 2000). As a result, a parallel can be drawn between plants that continue to grow in the midst of the storms of life and a Christian client who follows Jesus, enduring psychological pain with a sense of hope and perseverance because there is a destination (i.e., future glory) in sight on the road ahead (Barclay, 2000).

The following definition seems to best capture the definition of *hupomone*: "It is not the patience which can sit down and bow its head and let things descend upon it and passively endure until the storm is passed. It is the spirit which can bear things, not simply with resignation, but with blazing hope" (Barclay, 2000, p. 144). As one final example, a hopeful endurance points to someone who keeps their feet firmly planted, despite the winds of life, holding on to hope and pursuing glory during trials, hardships, and suffering (Barclay, 2000).

With this word, referred to as the "queen of virtues," the fulfillment of Jesus's mission on earth seems to be clearly articulated (Barclay, 2000, p. 145): Continuing to walk forward in life, despite the harshness of a long, sometimes-treacherous road, to achieve the end result—yielding to God's will in order to carry the pain of presence through life's most difficult climates, obstacles, and conditions. To be sure, *hupomone* seems to be quite unique in its focus on the present unfolding into the future. In other words, suffering can be patiently and joyfully endured because there is a future goal in mind, which, for Christian clients, is to grow in their ability to be more like Jesus as they travel with him on the road of life to their final destination—being face-to-face with God in heaven. Of course, with this hopeful endurance of pain comes an ability to ameliorate experiencing the pain of absence because Christian clients are "in the game," rather than "watching from the sidelines," to use a sports metaphor. If life is painful, and this reality is truly accepted, then the Bible suggests Christian clients are to cultivate strength, fortitude, and contentment to grow in spite of an unfavorable soil that will not change. Like the plant that steadily grows toward the sun, the Bible explicates that Christian clients, too, are to follow Jesus wherever he wishes for them to go, regardless of the painful terrain of the world.

Strengthening Christian Endurance: A Faith-Based Strategy

Within subsequent chapters of this book, I explore *hupomone* (i.e., endurance) alongside several other Greek words—*nepsis* (i.e., watchfulness), *hesychia* (i.e., practicing God's presence in order to cultivate inner peace and stillness), and the *nous* (i.e., an awareness of the contemplative self for shifting from an "earthly-minded" to "spiritually-minded"/"heavenly-minded" perspective[1]—within Christianity that capture the ability to face painful experiences with more openness and acceptance and, ultimately, a more acute awareness of God's loving presence. These words, which are drawn from the Christian contemplative tradition and overlap with ACT terminology, can help Christian clients relate differently to psychological pain, with Christian contemplation succinctly defined as a present-moment awareness of God's perfect love (Knabb & Bates, 2020).

With parallels to the millennia-old mindfulness literature that is now ubiquitous in contemporary Western society and focuses on several key mental skills (e.g., attention, present-moment awareness, acceptance) (Feldman et al., 2007), the contemplative tradition has a long history in Christianity, built upon love as its cornerstone (Burton-Christie, 1993; Foster, 1998; Merton, 2015). Beginning with Jesus and John in the gospels, then moving on to the early desert Christians in the third and fourth centuries and the *Sayings of the Desert Fathers*, followed by the teachings within the *Philokalia*, Medieval writers (e.g., John of the Cross, Theresa of Avila, the *Cloud of Unknowing*, Brother Lawrence, Thomas à Kempis), and contemporary presentations of earlier works (e.g., Thomas Merton's writings on meditation and contemplation, Thomas Keating's centering prayer) (Foster, 1998; Knabb, 2021), contemplative Christianity has quite a bit to offer as an incisive psychospiritual response to human suffering, grounded in an awareness of God's love, which can help Christian clients to better love God and others in a suffering, broken world.[2]

In fact, reminiscent of the more recent focus on interpersonal mindfulness in the psychology literature that emphasizes the role that "being aware and attentive as well as accepting and responsive (i.e., not thoughtlessly reactive) during conversations" can play in deepening relational encounters with others (Pratscher et al., 2019, p. 1045), Christian contemplation is, by definition, interpersonal, given that a loving awareness of God is at the core of the practice and being a vehicle for God's love serves as the *telos*, extending formal practice to daily life. Undeniably, by practicing God's loving presence, Christian clients are better prepared to love both God and others in each unfolding moment of life. Gradually, through regular contemplative practice, Christian clients can learn to "think in threes," practicing the presence of God in their most salient relational exchanges with others (i.e., God is active and present, the Christian client is active and present, and the other person is active and present), reminiscent of the skills developed with interpersonal mindfulness, which involves "thinking in twos" (i.e., the client is active and present and the other person is active and present).

Theoretically, I believe that contemplative Christianity, when combined with New Testament teachings on following Jesus, overlaps well with ACT as an evidence-based form of counseling and therapy for a range of psychological problems, conditions, and disorders (Harris, 2019; Hayes, 2019; Hayes et al., 2012; Luoma et al., 2017), especially since Christian contemplation can serve as a Christian-sensitive alternative to mindfulness-based conceptualizations and practices (Knabb, 2012). In fact, in recent years, ACT has even been modified for use among clergy working with religious populations (Nieuwsma et al., 2016), demonstrating its flexibility in addressing religious and spiritual needs. Empirically, moreover, I believe contemplative Christianity overlaps well with ACT, given the emerging research on Christian meditative and contemplative practices as Christian-sensitive alternatives to mindfulness meditation for psychological suffering (Knabb & Vazquez, 2018; Knabb et al., 2017, 2020a, 2020b, 2021).

Another way I present the overlap between ACT and the Christian contemplative tradition—especially when it comes to the dynamic, reciprocal relationship between inner psychological experiences and outer value-based living—comes from the story of Mary and Martha in Luke's gospel (Luke 10:38–42). This story, often emphasized within contemplative writings, is used throughout the book to highlight both the contemplative and active life, which parallels the balance between acceptance and action in ACT. In other words, Mary's example of patiently sitting at the feet of Jesus is used to help Christian clients accept difficult inner experiences, while Martha's example of activity and service is used to help Christian clients follow Jesus in the midst of psychological pain. As Bernard of Clairvaux revealed, "Mary and Martha are sisters and they should dwell together in the same household in peace" (quoted in Merton, 1969, p. 32). Thus, I explore a "both/and" approach to Christian living—both the acceptance of inner pain and the commitment to behavioral action in Christian clients' efforts to follow Jesus the rabbi.

Moving forward, the main goal of this book is to help counselors and therapists work more effectively with Christian clients to cultivate a hopeful endurance—*hupomone*—in order to follow Jesus (i.e., walk with God) in the midst of psychological pain, guided by love as *the* Christian virtue. I attempt to accomplish this by combining secular psychological (i.e., the main goal, three pillars,

11

and six processes of ACT) and Christian (e.g., love and the Christian contemplative tradition, Jesus's example of suffering, the story of Mary and Martha in Luke's gospel, other stories and teachings in the Bible) insights so that counselors and therapists can more effectively work with Christian clients in counseling and therapy.

To mention one final point of overlap, ACT emphasizes the importance of psychological flexibility as the main goal, formally defined as "the ability to contact the present moment more fully as a conscious human being and, based on what the situation affords, to change or persist in behavior in order to serve valued ends" (Luoma et al., 2017, p. 24), with love as the vehicle through which the pains of life are converted into a purposeful life (Hayes, 2016). In a similar vein, the faith-based version of ACT presented in this book is about walking with God from moment to moment so as to live the life God has called Christians to live, anchored to love as the beginning and ending point, with psychological flexibility as a byproduct of this deeper, more loving communion with God.

Counseling and Therapy, Psychological Suffering, and the Christian Faith in Context

Before transitioning to a general overview of the integrative strategy expounded upon in this book, I would like to embed this discussion within a broader context, drawing briefly from prior integrative efforts that combine counseling and therapy, religion, and spirituality. Specifically, over the past several decades, a plethora of integrative writings have emerged that combine psychological science with the Christian faith in order to help Christian clients in counseling and therapy. For example, the *Journal of Psychology and Theology*, the *Journal of Psychology and Christianity*, *Mental Health, Religion & Culture*, *Psychology of Religion and Spirituality*, and *Spirituality in Clinical Practice* all regularly publish theoretical and empirical articles on the intersection between psychology, religion, and spirituality. Moreover, a variety of textbooks have been published in the past decade on counseling and therapy, religion, and spirituality. As a recent example, Worthington et al. (2013) published an edited volume on evidence-based therapies that integrate Christianity. Within this work, interventions and strategies are elucidated for Christian clients with anxiety, depression, trauma, and relationship distress, among other problems, conditions, and disorders. Moreover, Knabb et al. (2019) recently published a book on a distinctly Christian approach to counseling and therapy, which starts with a Christian worldview as the foundation, then assimilates the "common factors" in psychotherapy outcome research.

Yet, very few, if any, professional clinical guides have emerged in the academic literature that focus on helping Christian clients in counseling and therapy to follow Jesus in the midst of psychological pain based on a set of well-defined values—a central feature within both ACT and many historic Christian writings, contemplative and otherwise. ACT, one of the most popular and

well-researched contemporary therapies, combined with a Christian understanding of suffering, can offer an effective strategy for counselors and therapists to help Christian clients ameliorate avoidance tendencies that keep them
stuck, relate differently to symptoms, and pursue deeply held values.

Balancing Acceptance and Action: A Main Goal, Three Pillars, and Six Processes

The six processes presented in this book—which combine the psychological
science of ACT (Harris, 2019; Hayes, 2019; Hayes et al., 2012; Luoma et al.,
2017) with the Christian contemplative tradition (Coniaris, 1998; Cook, 2011;
Foster, 1998; Harmless, 2004; Laird, 2006; Paintner, 2012; Smith, 2013)—
emanate from one main goal and three pillars. Table 0.1 offers the main goal,
three pillars, and six processes (and corresponding definitions) of both traditional and faith-based ACT, with Figure 0.2 providing a visual depiction of the
overlap between the six processes of ACT and Christian faith, separated into
mindfulness/contemplative processes and action-based processes based on the
story of Mary and Martha in Luke's gospel.

As a reminder, psychological flexibility is the central aim in traditional ACT,
with love as the bridge from pain to purpose (Hayes, 2016). With faith-based
ACT for Christian clients, psychological flexibility is a byproduct of walking
with God and manifests from an awareness of God's active, loving presence (see
McGinn, 1991), which is the main goal when working with Christian clients. As
another reminder, traditional ACT utilizes mindfulness to capture four of the
six processes (i.e., the first four processes that focus on accepting psychological
pain; Hayes et al., 2012, pp. 91, 203). For faith-based ACT, I emphasize Mary
and the contemplative Christian life, which has some overlap with mindfulness,
to enhance the four acceptance-based processes, as well as Martha and the
active life to strengthen the remaining two action-based processes.

To summarize, with faith-based ACT, Christian clients are learning to relate
differently to psychological pain with four integrative processes (i.e., "watchfulness" with thoughts [*nepsis* in Greek], "endurance" with emotions [*hupomone*
in Greek], shifting from "earthly-mindedness" to "spiritual-mindedness" via
the contemplative self [the *nous* in Greek], and "practicing God's presence"
to maintain inner stillness and peace [*hesychia* in Greek]) in order to, with two
integrative processes, "follow Jesus" via "biblical virtues" (with love as *the* cornerstone of virtuous living).

ACT Condensed: One-Sentence, Three-Word, and One-Word Versions

Although understanding and practicing ACT (both its traditional and faith-
based versions) certainly requires a working knowledge of *all* its requisite

Table 0.1 The Main Goal, Three Pillars, and Six Processes of Traditional and Faith-Based ACT

Traditional ACT	Faith-based ACT
Main goal	
Psychological flexibility	Walking with God in love
Pillar/process	
"Opening up"	"Watching and enduring"
Defusion	Watchfulness (*nepsis* in Greek)
Watching thoughts with distance, detachment, and flexibility	Watching thoughts with alertness, soberness, and vigilance
Acceptance	Endurance (*hupomone* in Greek)
Accepting thoughts, feelings, sensations, and memories with openness, curiosity, and nonjudgment	Enduring thoughts, feelings, sensations, and memories with patience, steadfastness, and hope
"Being present"	"Noticing and shifting"
The transcendent self	The contemplative self (the *nous* in Greek)
Noticing the inner world from a spiritual and observing (not "verbal") sense of self	Noticing the inner world from a "spiritually-minded"/"heavenly-minded" (not "earthly-minded") perspective
Present-moment awareness	Practicing God's presence (*hesychia* in Greek)
Maintaining a flexible awareness of each unfolding moment, not being preoccupied with the past or future	Maintaining a flexible awareness of God's presence in each unfolding moment, not being preoccupied with the past or future
"Doing what matters"	"Committing and following"
Values	Biblical virtues
Being anchored to personally chosen qualities that guide life	Being anchored to moral behaviors, drawn from the Bible as God's Word, that guide a life devoted to following Jesus
Committed action	Following Jesus
A dedication to taking effective behavioral action, regardless of difficult thoughts, feelings, sensations, memories, situations, or relationships, anchored to personally derived values	A dedication to taking effective behavioral action by following Jesus wherever he would have Christians go, regardless of difficult thoughts, feelings, sensations, memories, situations, or relationships, anchored to biblically derived virtues

Note. Adapted from Coniaris (1998), Cook (2011), Foster (1998), Harmless (2004), Harris (2019), Hayes (2019), Hayes et al. (2012), Laird (2006), Luoma et al. (2017), Paintner (2012), and Smith (2013).

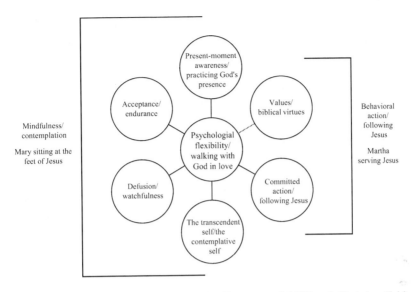

Figure 0.2 The Relationship Between the Six Processes of ACT and Christian Faith.
Note. Adapted from Hayes et al. (2012).

building blocks (i.e., the main goal, three pillars, and six processes), a condensed, one-sentence version of traditional ACT can be succinctly defined as "open up, show up, and move forward toward what we deeply care about" (Hayes, 2019, p. 387), with the faith-based version requiring Christian clients to "endure with, walk with, and follow God from moment to moment."

As a three-word, even more compact version, traditional ACT is all about courageously shifting from "fear to love" (Hayes, 2019) in each unfolding moment of life, as is the faith-based version, given "God is love" (*New International Version Bible*, 2011, 1 John 4:7–21), Christian clients are learning to "walk in the way of love" (*New International Version Bible*, 2011, Ephesians 5:2) with God, not alone, and "perfect love drives out fear" (*New International Version Bible*, 2011, 1 John 4:18) in Christian clients' relationship with God (Marshall, 1978).

Finally, in a bold, much more ambitious attempt to reduce ACT to merely one word, a one-syllable, four-letter description of traditional ACT is "love" (Hayes, 2016, 2019), as is the faith-based version. In fact, in faith-based ACT, "love" will serve as *the* "prayer word," which is a short "reset word," "surrender word," or "acceptance word" used among Christian contemplatives over the last two millennia to gently shift the mind's focus from distracting, compulsive thoughts to God's active, loving presence whenever they noticed it had inevitably drifted (Bangley, 2006; Gillet, 1985; Laird, 2006). In other words, for Christians, given the fallen nature of the inner world, when gently repeated in daily life, "love" as a "monologic" form of prayer can help to settle, simplify, and unify the mind (Ware, 2014). "Love" is also a powerful reminder for Christian clients to get back on the road of life when they have veered off course, with God, the author of love, leading the way.

Ultimately, enduring difficult thoughts, feelings, sensations, memories, situations, and relationships is necessary to live a life of love, with love as the "hinge point" that helps Christian clients pivot from self-preoccupation to God, who is the source of love. Because "God is love" (*New International Version Bible*, 2011, 1 John 4:7–21), learning to love is an outside-in to inside-out process, with Christian clients functioning as a conduit for God's love, which, in turn, is reciprocated to God and extended to others as the *telos*, or ultimate purpose, of life (Matthew 22:36–40). Worded another way, faith-based ACT is meant to help Christian clients learn to be a dwelling place for God to display his perfect love in a fallen, broken world, ACTing on God's love from the inside-out. After all, God modeled his perfect love in the birth, life, death, and resurrection of Jesus, with Jesus as the "Suffering Servant" (*New International Version Bible*, 2011, Isaiah 53) enduring suffering so as to reconcile humans to God. With Jesus as their exemplar, Christian clients, too, can endure suffering, with God's indwelling love as the *telos* for walking through, not around, psychological pain in this fallen world.

ACT and God's Dwelling Place: A House of Enduring Love[3]

For Christian clients, the Old and New Testaments of the Bible reveal that God actively pursues a relationship with humankind, dwelling among and within his people at different points in time and in different ways. In fact, within the pages of the Bible, the various Hebrew and Greek words for "temple" actually mean a dwelling place for God, not simply a place for worshiping God at a designated period in time. In the Old Testament, prior to the fall of humankind, God dwelled with Adam and Eve in the Garden of Eden. In turn, he dwelled with his people in the tabernacle, which was a "portable temple" after their exodus from Egypt. Finally, the first temple served as God's dwelling place until the time of Jesus.

Fast-forward to the New Testament, and Jesus signifies the return of God's presence, following a lengthy departure after the first temple was destroyed in the Old Testament. Then, following Jesus's resurrection, the Holy Spirit dwells in God's people, rather than a human-made tabernacle or temple. Overall, because Jesus now serves as the "Great High Priest" (*New International Version Bible*, 2011, Hebrews 4–10), Christian clients can walk with God as a friend and traveling companion on the road of life, with God's Holy Spirit dwelling within them. As God dwells within Christian clients, he offers his perfect love from moment to moment from the inside out, which has salient ramifications for how Christian clients live their short life on this planet, both spiritually and psychologically, especially in the context of hope.

16

Within traditional ACT, counselors and therapists work with clients to develop a variety of requisite skills for cultivating psychological flexibility. In doing so, clients strive to live out their values, intentionally and confidently, with the hope that the cultivation of this newfound flexibility will help them to build a life of purpose, rather than getting sidetracked by cognitive fusion and experiential avoidance. Within faith-based ACT, Christian clients are the dwelling place of God's perfect love, which means they can draw upon God's active, loving presence to help them from moment to moment and step to step on the road of life. In fact, as the dwelling place of God, Christian clients have an "ultimate purpose," which involves an outside-in to inside-out process of psychological and spiritual change. In other words, because of Jesus's enduring work as the "Great High Priest" (*New International Version Bible*, 2011, Hebrews 4–10), God's Holy Spirit comes to dwell within Christian clients' inner world, which means they can prioritize God's love as *the* guiding principle, characteristic, or quality, living a life of hope because God is within them each step of the way as they walk home with him to their final destination. On this road, traveled with God, not alone, Christian clients are moving from justification (i.e., being declared righteous by, and reconciled to, God through Jesus), to sanctification (i.e., becoming more like Jesus), to glorification (i.e., being face-to-face with Jesus), which is central to their mental health on this side of heaven (Grudem, 1994). Thus, throughout the book, the idea that Christian clients are God's dwelling place will be a foundational theme, with contemplatives throughout the ages stressing the importance of God's presence within (Nguyen, 2020).

ACT and God's Dwelling Place: A Guiding Metaphor

With this understanding that Christian clients are a dwelling place (e.g., vessel, vehicle, conduit, medium) in mind, I would like to present a metaphor for this relationship, which will serve as a guide for faith-based ACT with Christian clients throughout the book. The inner world, from a faith-based ACT perspective, is like living with multiple roommates, several of whom are noisy, inconsiderate, and selfish. These roommates make up the inner world, including the wavering, constantly changing thoughts, feelings, sensations, and memories that often guide life. Yet, the God of love would like to take up residence within every room, not just merely be consigned to a guest room. Similar to living with several roommates, one of whom is God, in each step of life, Christian clients have a question to answer: "In this very instance, who will be the 'head of the house,' my roommates or God." After all, God, as the author of love, is seeking to make his presence known in each and every room, whether the bedrooms, living room, family room, kitchen, or garage. The noisy roommates, too, want to make their presence known, occupying every space in the house. Because of this, the purpose of faith-based ACT is to help Christian clients allow the God of love to take up residence in every square inch of the house. When this happens, God's perfect love can be the guiding principle for daily life, whether inviting guests into their proverbial home or going out into the world to share God's love with others.

Conclusion: The Road Ahead

Overall, the book is organized into 12 chapters. The first three chapters highlight the challenge of mental disorders and relational problems in both contemporary society and the Christian church, focusing on depression, anxiety, trauma, and relationship distress with an intimate partner in the DSM-5 (APA, 2013). Understanding this challenge includes reviewing a common, yet futile, response—attempting to avoid psychological pain. Experiential avoidance, unfortunately, does not work and is often inconsistent with Scripture. The fourth chapter outlines a way to help Christian clients ameliorate unhelpful tendencies to avoid inner struggles; these attempts, exacerbated by an over-reliance on language, only end up serving as a barrier to following Jesus. In the fifth chapter, the story of Mary and Martha is viewed through the lens of the Christian contemplative tradition. Mary represents the contemplative life and an attitude of acceptance, whereas Martha captures the active life, servanthood, and self-sacrifice—both are necessary for helping Christian clients to follow Jesus in the midst of psychological pain.

After laying the foundation for this integrative approach, the sixth, seventh, and eighth chapters help counselors and therapists to assist Christians in living a life devoted to following Jesus, rooted in biblical teachings and behavioral action. This way of living is very different from trying to avoid psychological pain and accomplished by combining the six processes of ACT with overlapping concepts in the Christian contemplative tradition, as well as biblical examples of Jesus's life and other teachings in Scripture.

In the final four chapters of the book, an integrative approach, combining ACT with Christianity, is applied to depression, anxiety, trauma, and relationship distress with an intimate partner, respectively, so that Christian clients can relate differently to these experiences in order to follow Jesus. Although ACT has been utilized with a range of mental problems, conditions, and disorders, applying ACT to a wide variety of DSM-5 labels is beyond the scope of this book. Instead, I focus on two of the most common diagnostic categories for counselors and therapists working with Christian clients, depression and anxiety. In this revised edition, I have also added chapters on trauma and relationship distress with an intimate partner, given these challenges are common among clients, both Christian and non-Christian, presenting for counseling and therapy.

Throughout the revised book, updated exercises, strategies, metaphors, and research support are provided for counselors and therapists, along with examples from Scripture (e.g., the life of Jesus) and a plethora of sayings, writings, and experiences of Christians from the contemplative tradition, to combine ACT with the Christian faith. In addition, *hupomone*—a hopeful endurance, patience, and steadfastness—serves as the Christian equivalent to acceptance, which is a highly popular term in the 21st-century psychology literature. This parallel concept can help counselors and therapists more effectively work with Christian clients in making room for psychological experiences within the inner world in order to live out a set of well-defined values in the outer world.

To conclude, I write from an Evangelical Christian perspective, "thinking evangelically" about traditional ACT, the Christian contemplative tradition, and Scripture (Goggin & Strobel, 2013). Comprising about a quarter of the U.S. population (Pew, 2015), Evangelical Protestant Christians believe that the Bible, as God's divine revelation to humankind, is authoritative and a personal, sanctifying relationship with Jesus is necessary in daily life (Goggin & Strobel, 2013; Larsen, 2007). Evangelical Christianity also affirms the meta-narrative of the Bible, namely that God created humankind in his image, but, due to humans turning away from him, sin and suffering entered the world (Wolters, 2005). Yet, God offered his Son to redeem humankind, and God will eventually restore all things (Wolters, 2005). In this life, from an Evangelical perspective, Christians are made righteous before, and reconciled to, God through Jesus (i.e., justification), attempt to be more like Jesus (i.e., sanctification), and will eventually be face-to-face with Jesus (i.e., glorification) (Grudem, 1994). Ultimately, for Evangelical Christians, Scripture is prioritized as *the* main source for beliefs and practices, although secular sources of knowledge that do not conflict with Scripture are often drawn from to navigate this fallen, broken world (Goggin & Strobel, 2013).

Notes

1 Throughout the book, I have drawn the terms "earthly-mindedness," "heavenly-mindedness," and "spiritual-mindedness" from several Puritan authors (Burroughs, 2010, 2014; Owen, 2016; Rowe, 1672). The Puritans were a group of devout English Christians in the 16th and 17th centuries who attempted to apply an orthodox reading of Scripture to all of life. Although the Puritans are not typically associated with the Christian contemplative tradition (Foster, 1998), I believe the contrast between "earthly-mindedness" and "heavenly-mindedness" (or "spiritual-mindedness") is helpful for understanding the contemplative self. For a more detailed review of contemplative themes in Puritan writings, see Schwanda (2012).

2 As a possible mechanism of action, as an indirect, relational method (Ware, 2001), contemplation may help Christian clients learn to gently and flexibly shift from unpleasant inner experiences to a sustained awareness of the love of God, rather than futilely striving to reduce, eliminate, avoid, or distract from psychological pain on their own. In other words, with contemplative practice, Christians are developing the ability to relate differently to difficult thoughts, feelings, sensations, and memories and rely on God's loving presence to persevere in the midst of inner and outer trials.

3 The summary of God dwelling among his people is from Hays (2016).

References

American Psychiatric Association. (2013). *Diagnostic and statistical manual of mental disorders* (5th ed.). American Psychiatric Publishing.

Bai, Z., Luo, S., Zhang, L., Wu, S., & Chi, I. (2020). Acceptance and commitment therapy (ACT) to reduce depression: A systematic review and meta-analysis. *Journal of Affective Disorders, 260,* 728–737.

Bangley, B. (Ed.). (2006). *The cloud of unknowing: Contemporary English edition.* Paraclete Press.

Barclay, W. (2000). *New Testament words.* The Westminster Press.

Bock, D. (1996). *Luke: 9:51–24:53.* Baker Academic.

Burroughs, J. (2010). *Heavenly-mindedness recommended: In a discourse on Colossians 3:2.* Gale ECCO.

Burroughs, J. (2014). *A treatise on earthly-mindedness.* GLH Publishing.

Burton-Christie, D. (1993). *The word in the desert: Scripture and the quest for holiness in early Christian monasticism.* Oxford University Press.

Coniaris, A. (1998). *Philokalia: The Bible of orthodox spirituality.* Light & Life Publishing Company.

Cook, C. (2011). *The philokalia and mental wellbeing.* Pickwick Publications.

Feldman, G., Hayes, A., Kumar, S., Greeson, J., & Laurenceau, J. (2007). Mindfulness and emotion regulation: The development and initial validation of the Cognitive and Affective Mindfulness Scale-Revisited (CAMS-R). *Journal of Psychopathology and Behavioral Assessment, 29,* 177–190.

Foster, R. (1998). *Streams of living water: Essential practices from the six great traditions of Christian faith.* Renovare.

Gillet, L. (1985). *On the invocation of the name.* Templegate Publishers.

Goggin, J., & Strobel, K. (Ed.). (2013). *Reading the Christian spiritual classics: A guide for Evangelicals.* InterVarsity Press.

Grudem, W. (1994). *Systematic theology: An introduction to biblical doctrine.* Zondervan.

Gundry, R. (2011). *Commentary on Luke.* Baker Academic.

Harmless, W. (2004). *Desert Christians: An introduction to the literature of early monasticism.* Oxford University Press.

Harris, R. (2019). *ACT made simple: An easy-to-read primer on acceptance and commitment therapy* (2nd ed.). New Harbinger Publications.

Hayes, S. (2005). *Get out of your mind and into your life: The new acceptance & commitment therapy.* New Harbinger Publications, Inc.

Hayes, S. (2016, February). *Psychological flexibility: How love turns pain into purpose* [Video]. TED Conferences. https://www.youtube.com/watch?v=o79_gmO5ppg

Hayes, S. (2019). *A liberated mind: How to pivot toward what matters.* Avery.

Hayes, S., Strosahl, K., & Wilson, K. (2012). *Acceptance and commitment therapy: The process and practice of mindful change* (2nd cd.). The Guilford Press.

Hayes, S., Wilson, K., Gifford, E., Follette, V., & Strosahl, K. (1996). Experiential avoidance and behavioral disorders: A functional dimensional approach to diagnosis and treatment. *Journal of Consulting and Clinical Psychology, 64,* 1152–1168.

Hays, J. (2016). *The temple and the tabernacle: A study of God's dwelling places from Genesis to Revelation.* Baker Books.

Holman Illustrated Bible Dictionary. (1998). *Contentment.* Holman Bible Publishers.

Holman Illustrated Pocket Bible Dictionary. (2004). *Love*. Holman Bible Publishers.

Kempis, T. (2003). *The imitation of Christ*. Dover Publications.

Knabb, J. (2012). Centering prayer as an alternative to mindfulness-based cognitive therapy for depression relapse prevention. *Journal of Religion and Health, 51*, 908–924.

Knabb, J. (2021). *Christian meditation in clinical practice: A four-step model and workbook for therapists and clients*. InterVarsity Press.

Knabb, J., & Bates, M. (2020). "Holy desire" within the "Cloud of Unknowing": The psychological contributions of medieval apophatic contemplation to Christian mental health in the 21st century. *Journal of Psychology and Christianity, 39*, 24–39.

Knabb, J., & Vazquez, V. (2018). A randomized controlled trial of a two-week Internet-based contemplative prayer program for Christians with daily stress. *Spirituality in Clinical Practice, 5*, 37–53.

Knabb, J., & Wang, K. (2021). The communion with God scale: Shifting from an *etic* to *emic* perspective to assess fellowshipping with the Triune God. *Psychology of Religion and Spirituality, 13*, 67–80.

Knabb, J., Frederick, T., & Cumming, G. (2017). Surrendering to God's providence: A three-part study on providence-focused therapy for recurrent worry (PFT-RW). *Psychology of Religion and Spirituality, 9*, 180–196.

Knabb, J., Johnson, E., Bates, M., & Sisemore, T. (2019). *Christian psychotherapy in context: Theoretical and empirical explorations in faith-based mental health*. Routledge.

Knabb, J., Pate, R., Sullivan, S., Salley, E., Miller, A., & Boyer, W. (2020a). "Walking with God": Developing and pilot testing a manualized four-week program combining Christian meditation and light-to-moderate physical activity for daily stress. *Mental Health, Religion & Culture, 23*, 756–776.

Knabb, J., Vazquez, V., & Wang, K. (2020). The Christian Contentment Scale: An *emic* measure for assessing inner satisfaction within the Christian tradition. *Journal of Psychology and Theology*. Advance online publication.

Knabb, J., Vazquez, V., Garzon, F., Ford, K., Wang, K., Conner, K., Warren, S., & Weston, D. (2020b). Christian meditation for repetitive negative thinking: A multi-site randomized trial examining the effects of a four-week preventative program. *Spirituality in Clinical Practice, 7*, 34–50.

Knabb, J., Vazquez, V., Pate, R., Garzon, F., Wang, K., Edison-Riley, D., Slick, A., Smith, R., & Weber, S. (2021). Christian meditation for trauma-based rumination: A two-part study examining the effects of an internet-based four-week program. *Spirituality in Clinical Practice*. Advance online publication.

Koessler, J. (2003). *True discipleship: The art of following Jesus*. Moody Publishers.

Laird, M. (2006). *Into the silent land: A guide to the Christian practice of contemplation*. Oxford University Press.

Larsen, T. (2007). Defining and locating evangelicalism. In T. Larsen & D. Treier (Eds.), *The Cambridge companion to Evangelical theology* (pp. 1–14). Cambridge University Press.

Luoma, J., Hayes, S., & Walser, R. (2017). *Learning ACT: An acceptance and commitment therapy skills training manual for therapists* (2nd ed.). Context Press.

Marshall, I. (1978). *The epistles of John*. William B. Eerdmans Publishing Company.

Marshall, I. (1991). *1 Peter*. InterVarsity Press.

McGinn, B. (1991). *The foundations of mysticism: Origins to the fifth century*. The Crossroad Publishing Company.

Merriam-Webster's Desk Dictionary. (1995a). *Acceptance*. Merriam-Webster, Incorporated.

Merriam-Webster's Desk Dictionary. (1995b). *Suffer*. Merriam-Webster, Incorporated.

Merton, T. (1969). *Contemplative prayer*. Doubleday.

Merton, T. (2015). *Choosing to love the world: On contemplation*. Sounds True.

New International Version Bible. (2011). Zondervan. https://www.biblegateway.com/

Nguyen, J. (2020). *Christian contemplation: Theological foundations and contemporary practice*. Wipf & Stock.

Nieuwsma, J., Walser, R., & Hayes, S. (Eds.). (2016). *ACT for clergy and pastoral counselors: Using acceptance and commitment therapy to bridge psychological and spiritual care*. Context Press.

Osborne, E. (2005). *Vocabulary from Latin and Greek roots: A study of word families* (2nd ed.). Prestwick House, Inc.

Owen, J. (2016). *Spiritual mindedness*. GLH Publishing.

Paintner, C. (2012). *Desert fathers and mothers: Early Christian wisdom sayings*. SkyLight Paths Publishing.

Pew Forum. (2015). *America's changing religious landscape*. The Pew Forum on Religion & Public Life.

Pratscher, S., Wood, P., King, L., & Bettencourt, B. (2019). Interpersonal mindfulness: Scale development and initial construct validation. *Mindfulness, 10*, 1044–1061.

Rowe, J. (1672). *Heavenly-mindedness and earthly-mindedness: In two parts*. Francis Tyton.

Schwanda, T. (2012). *Soul recreation: The contemplative-mystical piety of Puritanism*. Pickwick Publications.

Smith, A. (2013). *Philokalia: The eastern Christian spiritual texts: Selections annotated & explained*. SkyLight Paths Publishing.

Ware, K. (2001). *The inner kingdom*. St. Vladimir's Seminary Press.

Ware, K. (2014). *The Jesus prayer*. Catholic Truth Society.

Wolters, A. (2005). *Creation regained: Biblical basics for a reformational worldview* (2nd ed.). William B. Eerdmans Publishing Company.

Worthington, E., Johnson, E., Hook, J., & Aten, J. (Eds.). (2013). *Evidence-based practices for Christian counseling and psychotherapy*. InterVarsity Press.

Wright, N. (1992). *The New Testament and the people of God*. Fortress Press.

1

PSYCHOLOGICAL PROBLEMS IN THE 21st CENTURY

Introduction

In this chapter, psychological problems, conditions, and disorders are reviewed, with particular attention paid to depressive, anxiety, and trauma-related disorders, along with problems related to the primary support group. As revealed by the *Diagnostic and Statistical Manual of Mental Disorders*, Fifth Edition (DSM-5) (American Psychiatric Association [APA], 2013), I discuss symptoms of depression, anxiety, trauma, and relationship distress with a spouse or intimate partner, prevalence rates, and common approaches used in society, the Christian church, and counseling and therapy to respond to psychological problems, conditions, and disorders. Unfortunately, many of these well-intentioned strategies are rooted in attempts to reduce, eliminate, avoid, or distract from psychological suffering. These efforts often do not work in counseling and therapy, leaving Christian clients feeling discouraged, hopeless, distracted, and exhausted in their attempts to follow Jesus. Overall, a central question emanates from these strategies that falls short: "What do counselors and therapists do when Christian clients' psychological suffering will not go away?" Ultimately, my hope is to make the case for an alternative to avoidance—acceptance—which can help Christian clients to more confidently walk with God through, not around, psychological suffering.

Psychological Problems, Conditions, and Disorders in the 21st Century

In the 21st century, a sizeable number of adults currently struggle with depressive, anxiety, and trauma-related disorders, as well as relationship distress. For adults aged 18 to 64 in the United States (U.S.), the lifetime prevalence rate is 21% for any type of *mood disorder* (e.g., major depressive disorder, bipolar disorder), 34% for any type of *anxiety disorder* (e.g., panic disorder, generalized anxiety disorder, social anxiety disorder), and 8% for *posttraumatic stress disorder* (PTSD) (which was previously classified as an anxiety disorder in the DSM-IV-TR,

DOI: 10.4324/9781003181941-2

but is now considered a trauma-related disorder in the DSM-5) (Kessler et al., 2012). In a recent survey among adults in the United Kingdom (U.K.), almost one in five who were married or living with a partner reported relationship distress (Sserwanja & Marjoribanks, 2016).

With mood disorders, a single episode of depression is experienced by 6% of the U.S. adult population (aged 18 to 64) in their lifetime, whereas recurrent depression occurs among 15% of adults (aged 18 to 64) in the U.S. in their lifetime. Combined, about 21% of the U.S. adult population—or one in five individuals aged 18 to 64—will experience either a single or multiple episodes of depression in their lifetime (Kessler et al., 2012). According to more recent data, from 2013 to 2016, about 8% of U.S. adults (aged 20 or over) reported experiencing symptoms of depression over a 14-day period (Brody et al., 2018).

For anxiety disorders, 13% of the U.S. adult population (aged 18 to 64) will suffer from social anxiety in their lifetime, along with 5% and 6%, respectively, for panic disorder and generalized anxiety disorder (Kessler et al., 2012). More recently, survey data collected in 2019 revealed that about 16% of U.S. adults (aged 18 or over) reported anxiety symptoms over a 14-day period (Terlizzi & Villarroel, 2020).

With PTSD, now considered a trauma-related disorder in the DSM-5, almost one in ten adults (aged 18 to 64) will meet diagnostic criteria at some point in their lifetime (Kessler et al., 2012). As revealed by more recent survey data collected in 2017, about 7% of U.S. adults (aged 18 to 70) met *International Classification of Diseases*, 11th Revision (ICD-11), criteria for either PTSD or complex PTSD, based on self-reported symptoms over the previous month (Cloitre et al., 2019).

For relationship distress, in a recent survey among U.K. adults, roughly one in ten who were married or living with a partner stated they at least occasionally thought about divorce or separation or had regrets about originally entering into the relationship (Sserwanja & Marjoribanks, 2016). What is more, in a recent survey among U.S. adults, only about one in two who were married or living with a partner stated the relationship was going "very well" (Pew Research Center, 2019). In a follow-up survey, about one in ten U.S. adults who were married or cohabitating with a partner reported "their relationship [was] going not too or not at all well" (Barroso, 2021).

With regard to specific symptoms, an episode of depression is characterized by a depressed or low mood that occurs over at least a two-week period (APA, 2013). This depressed mood can be reported by the client as hopelessness, extreme sadness, or a feeling of emptiness or noticed by friends, family, or a mental health professional via direct observation (e.g., crying spells) (APA, 2013). In addition to low mood, *anhedonia*—a loss of interest in activities that used to be pleasurable to the client—may be present (APA, 2013). Along with one or both of the above symptoms, at least several others among a longer list of symptoms need to be present to warrant a diagnosis of *major depressive disorder*

24

(MDD), including weight loss or gain, trouble sleeping, a disruption in psycho-motor functioning, diminished energy, extreme guilt or recurrent feelings of worthlessness, trouble concentrating or focusing, and suicidal thoughts (APA, 2013). Finally, the aforementioned symptoms need to lead to a struggle or ina-bility to carry out day-to-day functioning in one or more major life domains, including work or interpersonal relationships (APA, 2013).

In terms of anxiety disorders, common general symptoms include an intense or overwhelming fear that is linked to some sort of present danger, anxiety that is associated with a perceived future catastrophe or threat, and behavio-ral problems that emanate from recurrent fear or anxiety (APA, 2013). Stated more succinctly, fear is rooted in the present moment, often associated with a fight-or-flight response within the sympathetic nervous system to prepare for immediate action in response to a current threat, whereas anxiety involves symptoms such as worry and tension when anticipating or predicting a future doomsday scenario that may or may not come true (APA, 2013). When con-sidering a current or future danger, anxiety disorders differ from normal reac-tions to these real or imagined events in that the experience is usually excessive, with clients overreacting to day-to-day stressors by way of avoidance behaviors (APA, 2013).

Amid the most common anxiety disorders, *social phobia* involves excessive fear or anxiety linked to social interactions, with clients likely preoccupied with being negatively judged, evaluated, or rejected by others (APA, 2013). Along with these recurrent concerns, clients may believe they will display some sort of embarrassing behavior in a social context; thus, a range of interpersonal events and encounters are avoided so as to eliminate the likelihood of rejection, embarrassment, and, ultimately, anxiety (APA, 2013). Of course, given that the anxiety is excessive, it impairs day-to-day functioning (APA, 2013).

Panic disorder, on the other hand, includes episodes of extreme fear, often sur-prising to the individual and fairly regular in terms of frequency or occurrence (APA, 2013). Within these distinct instances of panic, a range of symptoms may be experienced, including excessive sweating, a sudden increase in heartbeat, thoughts about dying or losing control, and extreme shaking (APA, 2013). To receive a diagnosis of panic disorder, clients must experience an ongoing pre-occupation with additional episodes, worrying that an unexpected attack will occur in the future, along with avoidance behaviors, in an attempt to ward off subsequent symptoms of panic (APA, 2013).

As one more anxiety disorder to consider, *generalized anxiety* involves recurrent worry, with clients struggling to ameliorate the experience of catastrophic pre-dictions about a range of topics (APA, 2013). In addition to the central theme of worry, generalized anxiety consists of at least three more symptoms, such as decreased energy, trouble focusing or concentrating, irritable mood, difficulty sleeping, and an "on edge" feeling because of worry (APA, 2013). Similar to the aforementioned disorders, generalized anxiety impairs day-to-day functioning in one or more life areas, including work and interpersonal relationships (APA, 2013).

Concerning trauma-related disorders, PTSD involves being exposed to a serious, violent, life-threatening situation, followed by a variety of symptoms in response to the event (APA, 2013). More specifically, PTSD symptoms may include intrusive, distressing memories, dreams, flashbacks, or reactions to reminders about the traumatic event, the avoidance of internal and external reminders about the traumatic event, impaired thoughts (e.g., cognitive distortions) and feelings (e.g., extreme anger) about the traumatic event, and hyperarousal after the traumatic event (e.g., hypervigilance). Consistent with depressive and anxiety disorders, PTSD impairs daily living in relational, occupational, or other major areas of functioning (APA, 2013).

Turning to the "Relationship Distress with Spouse or Intimate Partner" V code in the "Other Conditions That May Be a Focus of Clinical Attention" section of the DSM-5 (APA, 2013), this designation is used when "the major focus of the clinical contact is to address the quality of the intimate (spouse or partner) relationship or when the quality of that relationship is affecting the course, prognosis, or treatment of a mental or other medical disorder" (p. 716). To warrant this V code assignment, the reported relational distress commonly impairs cognitive (e.g., recurrent negative evaluations of a partner's behavior), affective (e.g., recurrent anger directed toward a partner), or behavioral (e.g., recurrent withdrawal from a partner during conflict) functioning (APA, 2013).

Unfortunately, major depressive disorder commonly co-occurs with social phobia, panic disorder, generalized anxiety disorder, and PTSD, referred to as *comorbidity* (APA, 2013). Also, relationship quality is negatively associated with depressive, anxiety, and trauma-related symptoms (McShall & Johnson, 2015), with relationship distress commonly impacting the "course, prognosis, or treatment" of many diagnoses, including depressive, anxiety, and trauma-related disorders (APA, 2013, p. 716). As an example, among a recent national sample in the Netherlands, 67% of individuals with a depressive disorder also had an anxiety disorder, with this rate increasing to 75% when considering the lifetime prevalence of anxiety disorders (Lamers et al., 2011). On the other hand, 63% of those with an anxiety disorder also had a diagnosis of depression, with this percentage rising to 81% when taking into consideration depression over their lifetime (Lamers et al., 2011). As another example, when studying PTSD and depressive symptoms among a clinical sample of adults who recently experienced a traumatic event, researchers concluded that "the bulk of psychopathology in the aftermath of trauma is best conceptualized as a general traumatic stress factor" (O'Donnell et al., 2004, p. 1395), not independent diagnoses. From a theoretical perspective, this type of overlap between depression, anxiety, and PTSD may be due to each disorder occurring as a different, isolated psychiatric disorder, interaction between the disorders, or the disorders being experienced along a continuum that is anchored to the same underlying neurobiology

(Hranov, 2007). What is more, because of the likelihood of impaired social functioning with depressive, anxiety, and trauma-related disorders, relationship distress with a spouse or intimate partner may often occur in the midst of these DSM-5 diagnoses. Ultimately, relational distress can either exacerbate (with a bidirectional relationship) or emanate from these diagnoses.

Interestingly, many psychological problems, conditions, and disorders, including those previously mentioned, have in common attempts to avoid psychological pain, utilizing unhelpful strategies in an effort to eliminate the ensuing distress. For example, MDD typically involves social withdrawal, whereas panic disorder with agoraphobia includes isolation so as to seemingly avoid another panic attack in public. What is more, social anxiety involves an ongoing struggle with interacting with others, avoiding social events based on a fear of being embarrassed or scrutinized, whereas PTSD includes the avoidance of trauma-related stimuli, whether internal or external. Finally, intimate partners struggling with relational problems may withdraw as a short-term strategy to avoid relationship distress, which may lead to long-term problems with satisfaction, intimacy, commitment, longevity, and so forth.

Thus, frequently embedded within these diagnoses and V codes is a struggle with avoiding unpleasant inner (e.g., thoughts, feelings, sensations, memories), as well as corresponding outer (e.g., challenging situations, relational problems), experiences, given the possibility of additional psychological pain when faced with unrelenting environmental demands. In addition to the avoidance that is inherent within many of these psychological problems, conditions, and disorders, society often utilizes a range of strategies to reduce, eliminate, avoid, or distract from an array of psychological challenges, which often do not work in the long run.

Contemporary Responses to Psychological Problems, Conditions, and Disorders: Common Avoidance Strategies

The Biomedical Model[1]

In response to the prevalence of depressive, anxiety, and trauma-related disorders, along with relational problems in contemporary society, many well-intentioned attempts to ameliorate suffering involve trying to reduce, eliminate, avoid, or distract from psychological pain. Disappointingly, a plethora of these efforts do not provide the relief that clients hope for, leaving them feeling discouraged, frustrated, and hopeless. As one of the most common strategies, the field of psychiatry commonly utilizes a biomedical understanding of psychiatric symptoms to eliminate "disease" via psychotropic medication. Thus, individuals struggling with symptoms of depression, anxiety, or trauma may receive a prescription for an antidepressant from a primary care physician or board-certified psychiatrist, with the overarching goal of eradicating abnormal, distressing inner states. This approach seems to make sense if symptoms of depression, anxiety, and trauma, such as low mood, a loss of interest in pleasurable activities, worry, tension, intrusive memories, and hypervigilance, are viewed as aberrant human experiences.

With the biomedical model, psychiatrists tend to view symptoms of depression, anxiety, and trauma as rooted, at least in part, in abnormal neurobiological processes (e.g., structural and functional deficits within the brain). Similar to other specialty areas in medicine, symptoms such as low mood, worry, and intrusive memories are conceptualized as primarily biologically rooted and, thus, in need of medicine to ameliorate these atypical physiological experiences (Casey, 2009). As a common example, within the biomedical model, mood is associated with the neurotransmitter serotonin, with the understanding that antidepressants ameliorate depressive symptoms by blocking the reuptake of serotonin, leading to the availability of more serotonin within the synapse. From this perspective, an increase in serotonin within the brain is linked to improved mood; because of this, psychotropic medicine is a vital, necessary intervention when someone experiences prolonged low mood or anhedonia, especially when depressive symptoms are severe and debilitating. As another example, PTSD is associated with structural and functional deficits in the *prefrontal cortex* (e.g., decreased activity), *amygdala* (e.g., increased activity), and *hippocampus* (e.g., decreased volume), with antidepressants possibly increasing hippocampal volume and, thus, improving memory among those with a PTSD diagnosis (Bremner, 2006).

In the past several decades, a large portion of the U.S. population has turned to antidepressant medication for the treatment of psychological symptoms, problems, conditions, and disorders. Between 2005 and 2008, for example, 11% of individuals aged 12 or older were taking antidepressant medication (Pratt et al., 2011), with this percentage increasing to about 13% among those aged 18 or older between 2015 and 2018 (Brody & Gu, 2020). Moreover, for women aged 40 to 59, about one in five were taking this type of medication from 2015 to 2018, with this number increasing to about one in four for women aged 60 or over for the same time period (Brody & Gu, 2020). When considering antidepressant use and depression symptom severity from 2005 to 2008, 8% of the sample (aged 12 or older) was taking this medication with no reported depressive symptoms, whereas almost 50% reported mild to moderate symptoms and 34% indicated they were experiencing severe symptoms of depression (Pratt et al., 2011).

Within this same time period of 2005 to 2008, about 14% of individuals aged 12 or older who reported taking an antidepressant medication stated they had been doing so for at least a decade, and more than half of those surveyed during this period indicated they had been taking an antidepressant for at least two years (Pratt et al., 2011). Also worth noting, among participants aged 12 or older who reported taking one antidepressant between 2005 and 2008, only

29% indicated they met with a mental health professional over the course of the previous year, whereas slightly less than half of individuals taking two or more antidepressants had an appointment with a mental health professional in the past 12 months (Pratt et al., 2011). Indeed, as the use of antidepressant medication steadily rose from 6% to 10% between 1996 and 2005, counseling and therapy declined from 32% to 20% during this same period (Olfson & Marcus, 2009).

Regarding the efficacy of antidepressant medication, a meta-analysis of six studies submitted to the Food and Drug Administration (FDA) revealed that the effect of antidepressants increased based on the severity of clients' ratings of depression, with the authors of the study concluding that antidepressant medication may be no more beneficial than a placebo for mild to moderate symptoms of depression (Fournier et al., 2010). Still, Fournier et al. noted that there was a clinical benefit, beyond placebo, for antidepressants among clients who reported more severe symptoms. In a similar vein, Kirsch et al. (2008) conducted a meta-analysis of 35 randomized trials submitted to the FDA on the efficacy of antidepressants, revealing that the difference between placebo and antidepressant groups increased based on the severity of the depression, with "virtually no difference" for individuals with moderate depression and "a relatively small difference" for those with more severe depression (p. 260). More recently, in a meta-analysis that reviewed 522 randomized trials on the efficacy of 21 different antidepressants, Cipriani et al. (2018) concluded that antidepressants were more efficacious than a placebo, although Munkholm et al. (2019) reanalyzed these same data and concluded that "it is unclear whether antidepressants are more efficacious than placebo" (p. 1). Despite some of these inconsistent findings, overall, these data elucidate that at least some clients with more severe depression may benefit from psychotropic medication to reduce their depressive symptoms, although those with mild to moderate symptoms may not fully reap the rewards of this type of a biomedical intervention.

In an effort to shed additional light on antidepressant use, longitudinal data from the Baltimore Epidemiologic Catchment Area Study have emerged that reveal important trends among adults in the U.S. (Takayanagi et al., 2015). Based on survey data from approximately 1,000 adults between 1981 and 2005, results illuminated that 13% of the study participants were taking an antidepressant; within this group, just over two-thirds did not report experiencing the necessary symptoms to warrant a diagnosis of major depressive disorder and more than one-third had never received a diagnosis of major depressive disorder, panic disorder, social phobia, generalized anxiety disorder, or obsessive-compulsive disorder (Takayanagi et al., 2015). Overall, these data reveal that "antidepressants are commonly used in the absence of clear evidence-based indications" (Takayanagi et al., 2015, p. 40).

In the past few decades, several authors have presented concerns about this purely biomedical conceptualization of mental disorders, noting that focusing solely on biochemistry fails to address a range of complex factors contributing to human functioning. For example, Engel (1977) highlighted that the biomedical model has become "the dominant model of disease in the Western world," with "its limitations easily overlooked" (p. 130). As a result, Engel advocated for a biopsychosocial, rather than entirely biomedical, model that preserves a biological understanding of mental disorders, but adds psychological and social contributing factors, too, when considering client treatment. In other words, Engel argued that a purely biological account of disordered functioning is too reductionistic, failing to take into consideration a more multifaceted picture of mental health and holistic client care that involves the client's beliefs, attitudes, and emotions, along with their culture and environment.

As another example, over a decade ago, Kiesler (2000) summarized the biomedical model, including its approach to treating psychiatric "disease," as involving three main steps. To begin, psychiatrists attempt to understand a list of symptoms by organizing them into a syndrome, which is followed by an effort to identify the underlying biological mechanisms responsible for the abnormal functioning (Kiesler, 2000). Finally, in that the explanation is rooted in a biological understanding, treatment involves medicine to ameliorate the symptoms (Kiesler, 2000). Still, from Kiesler's perspective, the view that psychological problems, conditions, and disorders emanate purely from biological "disease" prevents a variety of other mental health professionals (e.g., psychologists, marriage and family therapists, social workers) from being part of a client's holistic care, disallowing a broader understanding of the inner world of the suffering individual that honors the unique thoughts, feelings, sensations, memories, and behaviors that contribute to the current problem.

To offer one final illustration, in the acceptance and commitment therapy (ACT) literature, Hayes et al. (2012) offered reservations about the "biomedicalization" of American society, noting that unpleasant inner experiences have been converted to "symptoms," which are clustered together to arrive at a diagnosis that points to a "disease." From a biomedical perspective, health is viewed as the absence of disease, similar to other branches of medicine (Hayes et al., 2012). As a result, inner distress is commonly labeled as "abnormal," rather than a normal, ordinary part of the human condition (Hayes et al., 2012). Based on a biomedical viewpoint, then, human beings should be free of distress, that is, disease, which constitutes a baseline for day-to-day functioning (Hayes et al., 2012). When this does not happen, medicine is utilized to eliminate the diseased, abnormal state (Hayes et al., 2012). Yet, according to Hayes et al., life is about much more than feeling "happy" and efforts to fully eradicate distress are unrealistic and unattainable, distracting individuals from finding a deeper meaning in life by developing and pursuing a set of well-defined values.

In summary, the biomedical model in contemporary society commonly views depressive, anxiety, and trauma-related disorders as "disease," similar to other physiological conditions (e.g., cancer) that must be removed, with psychotropic medication serving the purpose of eliminating distressing, abnormal symptomatology. This conceptualization of mental disorders is popular within the U.S., especially given the number of adults currently taking antidepressants. Yet, unfortunately, antidepressants do not always work, sometimes only benefiting those with more severe symptoms. What is more, some individuals are taking psychotropic medication without actually meeting the criteria for a psychological problem, condition, or disorder, suggesting that biomedical interventions may be administered for psychological struggles that do not rise to a clinical level. Because of this, some authors have recently offered concerns that the biomedical model is too reductionistic, failing to take into consideration a more holistic understanding of human functioning. Still, a variety of other efforts within contemporary society, beyond medicine and the biomedical model, have been employed to reduce, eliminate, avoid, or distract from depressive, anxiety, and trauma symptoms, along with relationship distress, and are explored in several of the following sections of this chapter. Similar to antidepressants, many of these strategies do not ultimately work, leaving clients feeling exhausted, demoralized, and uncertain about how to proceed in life.

The Internet

In addition to psychotropic medication, contemporary society has increasingly turned to the internet to cope with the pain of daily life. By entering into a world of fantasy, many adults utilize the internet to avoid psychological suffering (Young et al., 2011). When examining excessive internet use, some estimates suggest that between 6% and 15% of individuals may struggle with internet addiction, with emerging studies revealing that internet addiction is correlated with depression and anxiety (Cheng & Li, 2014; Young & Nabuco de Abreu, 2011). What is more, a recent study of online community adults revealed a positive correlation between symptoms of PTSD and problematic smartphone use (Contractor et al., 2019). Although there may be an initial pleasant feeling when using the internet, this euphoria may turn into numbness over time (Young et al., 2011). Among other activities, users commonly turn to the internet—often accessed in the 21st century via smartphones—for social networking, shopping, gaming, movies/music, and pornography.

In a survey of more than 15,000 internet users, three in four men and almost half of women reported they viewed pornography online (Albright, 2008). Although the consumption of pornography on the internet has likely increased during the past few decades, some researchers have noted that this body of research is difficult to define and measure, especially in terms of what constitutes pornography and the behaviors that are associated with its usage (Short et al., 2012). Even so, a study among U.S. adults found that certain internet activities were more strongly associated with problematic internet use, including "general surfing," shopping, and pornography (Ioannidis et al., 2018). What is more, several authors, as well as empirical studies, have revealed that internet pornography consumption may be a way to avoid psychological pain (Crosby & Twohig, 2012).

In a community sample of adult males, findings revealed that those who reported more time using pornography had a higher likelihood of attempting to avoid difficult inner experiences, including unpleasant feelings such as sadness and anxiety, through the use of pornography (Reid et al., 2011). In addition, among a sample of male college students, results revealed that the tendency to avoid unpleasant inner experiences was positively correlated with problems consuming pornography, along with depression, anxiety, and stress (Levin et al., 2012). In this same study, when attempting to avoid difficult private encounters reached a clinical range, this variable moderated the association between consuming pornography and anxiety symptoms (Levin et al., 2012). Moreover, in a combined sample of college students and community adults, findings revealed a positive association between the length of time consuming pornography and a tendency to avoid difficult inner experiences (i.e., experiential avoidance) (Wetterneck et al., 2012). Furthermore, among a sample of women in substance abuse treatment, experiential avoidance mediated the relationship between PTSD symptoms and compulsive sexual behavior, with compulsive sexual behavior likely including the online consumption of pornography (Brem et al., 2018). Also, among a combined sample of male and female college students who reported viewing pornography, results revealed a positive relationship between problematic pornography use and experiential avoidance (Borgogna & McDermott, 2018). Finally, in a combined sample of male and female college students, a study found that interpersonal sensitivity and hostility mediated the relationship between experiential avoidance and problematic internet use (Chou et al., 2017). Overall, this body of research suggests that internet use generally, and viewing pornography in particular, may be used as a way to avoid psychological pain, including depressive, anxiety, and trauma symptoms and relationship distress, given the correlation between these variables.

The "Prosperity Gospel"

Interestingly, religion, too, may be employed as a form of avoidance. In the U.S., a large portion of the population identifies as belonging to the Pentecostal/ Charismatic Christian tradition, including individuals within specific denominations (e.g., Church of God in Christ, Assemblies of God), referred to as Pentecostals, and Charismatic Christians, who believe in the "gifts of the Holy Spirit" and are connected to evangelical, mainline, Catholic, and Orthodox Christianity (Pew Forum, 2006, p. 1). Defined in part by their emphasis on the power of the Holy Spirit, the "Renewalist" movement represents almost one-quarter of the U.S. population (Pew Forum, 2006). What is more, Renewalists constitute 28% of all Protestants in the U.S. (Pew Forum, 2006). Worldwide, some estimates suggest about one-quarter of Christians identify as Pentecostal (Pew Forum, 2006).

Inspired by the gifts of the Holy Spirit mentioned in Acts 2 and the Apostle Paul's list of the gifts of the Holy Spirit in 1 Corinthians 12, many Renewalist Christian teachings emphasize speaking in tongues, healing, prosperity, and wealth (Pew Forum, 2006). Among Renewalists in the U.S., about one in two report they have personally observed divine healings pertaining to injuries or illnesses, with between one-third to one-half stating they speak in tongues at least weekly and about two-thirds believing that God will bless them with "material prosperity" and "good health and relief from sickness" if they possess sufficient faith (Pew Forum, 2006, p. 30). In fact, many Renewalists adhering to prosperity theology emphasize divine healing, linking the amelioration of illness, poverty, and sickness to "God's divine intention" (Bowler, 2013, p. 141). To be sure, the vehicle through which Christians can be healed, according to prosperity theology, is faith in God, with the power of healing emanating from Jesus's atoning work on the cross (Bowler, 2013).

Yet, the Bible appears to speak frequently about the inevitability of suffering, rather than the total elimination of pain, guaranteed health, and the accumulation of wealth. In fact, God seems to have suffered in the Old Testament (Fretheim, 1984; Hall, 1986), the psalmists appeared to have commonly suffered in the Old Testament (Brueggemann, 1984), Jesus suffered a violent death (Moltmann, 1993), and Christians are commonly taught to suffer with Jesus (Hall, 1986). As Hall revealed, "Biblical faith does not flinch or cloak in pretty phrases its assumption that being human means suffering" (p. 32). Therefore, although well intentioned, for Christian clients, utilizing faith in God to completely heal from physical, psychological, and social pain may be unrealistic, as well as inconsistent with the experience of many biblical figures.

Traditional CBT

As one final trend in contemporary society that involves attempting to eliminate psychological pain, some forms of *cognitive behavioral therapy* (CBT), commonly referred to as "traditional" CBT, help clients to understand that events happening to them in life do not inevitably lead to depressive, anxiety, and trauma-related disorders and relational problems. Instead, clients' interpretations of life events contribute to psychological problems, conditions, and disorders. In other words, cognitive distortions, or thinking errors, commonly lead to psychological suffering. As a result, some traditional CBT counselors and therapists work with their clients to change thinking patterns—automatic, passing thoughts; more rigid, entrenched intermediate beliefs; and core schemas/beliefs (Beck, 2020)—so as to reduce a range of forms of psychological suffering, including those related to depression, anxiety, trauma, and relational problems. Overall, at its most basic level, one of the main goals is to modify thinking in order to reduce or eliminate symptoms and distress (Beck, 2020).

Still, in my own professional experience, many clients walk away from counseling and therapy feeling exhausted and discouraged when they cannot fully rid themselves of thinking "errors." Moreover, because these patterns are not permanently "repaired," they do not seemingly reap the benefits of rational, balanced cognitions that inevitably lead to "feeling good" (Burns, 1999; Greenberger & Padesky, 1995). This clinical observation—symptoms and distress are not entirely eliminated by simply disputing distorted thought content—is also confirmed via studies that suggest depressive, anxiety, and trauma-related disorders and relational problems may be sometimes chronic in nature.

The Recurrent Nature of Psychological Pain

Regrettably, many clients with depressive, anxiety, and trauma-related disorders will continue to struggle with recurrent symptoms. Also, a portion of clients will frequently suffer from relationship distress with a spouse or intimate partner. For depressive disorders, up to four out of five individuals who have received treatment may have a subsequent episode, with the presence of residual symptoms increasing the chances of depression relapse (Nierenberg et al., 2003; Thase, 2003). With anxiety disorders, too, there is a likelihood of additional episodes, along with lower recovery rates (Bruce et al., 2005). In particular, in a 12-year study, most of the individuals with an anxiety disorder, including social phobia, generalized anxiety, and panic with agoraphobia, during an intake in the first year were still suffering from some of the same symptoms 12 years later (Bruce et al., 2005). Also in this 12-year study, those with social phobia, panic disorder with agoraphobia, and generalized anxiety exhibited anxiety symptoms at least three-quarters of the time (Bruce et al., 2005). For PTSD, a recent review of 54 studies on civilian trauma/accidents revealed four types of trajectories following a traumatic event, including "resilience," "recovery," "chronic," and "delayed onset," with a "chronic" trajectory pooled prevalence rate of about 11% of the total sample (Galatzer-Levy et al., 2018). The results of this study suggest that, although "resilience" was the most common trajectory, with a pooled prevalence rate of about 66%, a sizeable portion of the combined sample struggled with chronic PTSD symptoms after a traumatic event (Galatzer-Levy et al., 2018).

When considering treatment approaches to prevent relapse, in a review of 31 randomized controlled trials, researchers revealed that the rate of depression relapse for those taking an antidepressant medication was 18%, whereas those taking a placebo experienced a relapse rate of 41%, although the authors noted that many studies were only a year long, and thus, they could not determine the long-term impact of antidepressants on depression relapse prevention (Geddes et al., 2003). In a separate study of 11 trials, findings revealed that participants relapsed roughly a quarter of the time when taking an antidepressant, whereas individuals taking a placebo relapsed about half of the time (Williams et al., 2009). Finally, Casacalenda et al. (2002) analyzed six randomized trials for clients experiencing mild to moderate depression, with results revealing a remission rate of 46% for antidepressants.

More recently, based on a detailed review of several large-scale studies on antidepressants, Pigott et al. (2010) concluded, "Meta-analyses of FDA trials suggest that antidepressants are only marginally efficacious compared to placebos and document profound publication bias that inflates their apparent efficacy" (p. 267). Specifically, when critically examining results from the Sequenced Treatment Alternatives to Relieve Depression (STAR*D) study, a comprehensive study on the efficacy of antidepressants, the authors explicated that 37% (calculated as a "weighted mean relapse rate") of individuals who initially achieved remission went on to experience relapse (Pigott et al., 2010, p. 275).

It is worth mentioning that other authors have also highlighted a possible publication bias with antidepressant research, making it difficult to fully ascertain the benefits of antidepressant medication. In particular, when reviewing FDA data on 74 studies, Turner et al. (2008) noted that studies with positive findings had a much higher likelihood of being published in the literature than studies with negative findings. Of course, this discrepancy may lead to a less than fully accurate understanding of the long-term efficacy, including relapse rates, for adults taking antidepressants. Based on their review of the data, Turner et al. concluded, "the efficacy of this drug class is less than would be gleaned from an examination of the published literature alone" (p. 256).

As another type of critique, Hengartner (2020) recently argued that the placebo group in antidepressant trials for relapse prevention may actually be experiencing withdrawal symptoms because of the abrupt discontinuation of treatment, not depression relapse. Because of this, the interpretation of drug-placebo comparisons may be especially difficult in antidepressant research.

Upon examining counseling and therapy for depression, Vittengl et al. (2007) reviewed 28 studies on CBT for depression relapse prevention. Findings revealed that the relapse rate was almost one in three at the 12-month mark following the end of treatment, with roughly one in two participants relapsing after 24 months of treatment discontinuation (Vittengl et al., 2007). Yet, adhering to continuation treatment after the acute phase of CBT did lead to a 14% reduction in the likelihood of relapse (Vittengl et al., 2007). However, overall, after reviewing eight (out of 28) studies that actually tracked continued treatment, participants still experienced a relapse rate of 42% upon completion of the continued treatment beyond the acute treatment (Vittengl et al., 2007).

In a more recent study, over 400 participants completed a "low intensity" version of CBT for depression and anxiety, then completed monthly measures for a year after treatment concluded (Ali et al., 2017). Findings revealed that about half of participants relapsed during the 12-month monitoring period, whereas the remaining participants did not (Ali et al., 2017). In another recent study, Zhang et al. (2018) reviewed 16 randomized trials on CBT for depression relapse prevention, with results revealing that "in the first 12 months, CBT was more efficacious than control in reducing the risk of developing a new episode of depression for [major depressive disorder] patients in remission" (p. 1).

When investigating data on recurrent depressive, anxiety, and trauma-related disorders, including the relapse rates for those receiving antidepressant medication and/or traditional CBT, empirical findings suggest that a portion of adults will continue to struggle with psychological symptoms, despite well-intentioned efforts to eliminate disordered functioning via medication and counseling and therapy. And although less empirical data are available on the potentially chronic nature of relationship distress with a spouse or intimate partner, some survey data elucidate that a portion of adults in the U.S. and U.K. struggle with interpersonal problems in a committed relationship (Barroso, 2021; Sserwanja & Marjoribanks, 2016), whether acute or chronic. Because of this, additional treatment approaches are needed that focus on the recurrent nature of such mental disorders and relational problems so that clients can respond to these experiences in a more realistic way—accepting, rather than constantly fighting against, the inevitability of psychological pain. In other words, many clients will not achieve complete remission, whether from psychotropic medication or one of the leading forms of counseling and therapy—traditional CBT. Also, other efforts to reduce, eliminate, avoid, or distract from psychological pain, including pornography consumption and the embrace of prosperity theology, will likely fall short of their goal, especially if depressive, anxiety, and trauma symptoms and relationship distress are an understandable reaction to the ubiquitous challenges of the human condition—life is difficult, painful, and unpredictable, filled with loss, disappointment, current and future danger, and interpersonal conflict. Because of the aforementioned findings, some researchers have started to explore alternative ways to help clients accept psychological pain, recognizing that there may be a common thread that links some of these experiences of suffering.

The Transdiagnostic Movement

In the past few decades, researchers have increasingly emphasized a transdiagnostic, rather than diagnosis-specific, approach for understanding and treating depressive, anxiety, and trauma-related disorders in counseling and therapy, especially given the comorbidity of mental disorders, common neurobiological underpinnings of many disorders, and the need for more acceptance-based strategies because symptom elimination is not always realistic or attainable (Clark & Taylor, 2009; Dalgleish et al., 2020; Rector et al., 2014). Therefore, a variety of psychological constructs have been explored in the research literature, some of which have even been embedded in cognitive behavioral treatment approaches.

As an example, *repetitive negative thinking* (RNT), which includes recurrent, problematic rumination and worry, has been positively linked to symptoms of depression, anxiety, and trauma (Ehring & Watkins, 2008; Mathes et al., 2020; McEvoy et al., 2013), possibly contributing to the high rate of comorbidity between these diagnostic categories. Also, perfectionism has received attention in the research literature. For instance, Egan et al.'s (2011) literature review revealed that perfectionistic thought content (e.g., high standards, a preoccupation with mistakes, the experience of critical parents) is positively linked to anxiety and depression separately, along with comorbid anxiety and mood disorders, and a recent study of participants in treatment for PTSD revealed a positive link between perfectionism and trauma symptoms (Egan et al., 2014). Furthermore, *intolerance of uncertainty* (IU), defined as "a dispositional characteristic resulting from negative beliefs about uncertainty and its implications," has been researched as a transdiagnostic construct, with one study revealing that individuals with depression and anxiety reported higher IU than community adults/undergraduates (Carleton et al., 2012, p. 468). In a separate study with a clinical sample, IU was positively linked to symptoms of trauma (Oglesby et al., 2017). Based on this type of empirical support, the IU construct has also been embedded with a more traditional CBT protocol that helps clients with generalized anxiety to accept uncertainty, rather than use approach or avoidance strategies to futilely pursue certainty (Dugas & Robichaud, 2007). Finally, struggles with intimacy have been identified as a transdiagnostic target within the cognitive behavioral intervention literature (Wetterneck & Hart, 2012), beyond the almost ubiquitous emphasis on individual functioning.

In the CBT literature, there are at least two different types of transdiagnostic approaches to treat recurrent psychological symptoms, problems, conditions, and disorders—generic CBT and acceptance-based strategies (Craske, 2012). The rationale behind this movement toward transdiagnostic protocols includes the comorbidity of many DSM-5 disorders, including emotional disorders, along with the need for a more streamlined treatment approach that helps counselors and therapists work effectively with clients with multiple diagnoses in order to identify and treat common underlying processes (Craske, 2012). A popular CBT-based approach, Barlow et al.'s (2010) Unified Protocol for Transdiagnostic Treatment of Emotional Disorders (UP) includes 12 sessions to treat emotional disorders, helping clients to, among other goals, understand the utility of emotions, the consequences of emotional avoidance, strategies to cultivate emotional acceptance, and exposure exercises to help clients accept painful emotions. In terms of acceptance-based approaches, both ACT (Hayes et al., 2012), which is a central focus of this book, and *mindfulness-based cognitive therapy* (MBCT; Segal et al., 2012) help clients relate to unpleasant inner experiences with more flexibility, openness, and nonjudgmental compassion. Drawing upon mindfulness, these transdiagnostic approaches allow clients to recognize that fighting against the inner world commonly leads to both relapse and distraction, which prevents them from living a life of values (see, e.g., Craske, 2012).

As a common theme among transdiagnostic approaches, acceptance assists clients in recognizing that their futile efforts to avoid psychological pain commonly exacerbate suffering and lead to relapse. As an example, Sauer-Zavala et al. (2012) investigated the efficacy of UP among a sample of 37 adults—the majority exhibiting comorbid anxiety disorders—with a focus on accepting, rather than avoiding, emotions, along with exposure exercises to cultivate a willingness to accept a range of emotional experiences. Discussing their findings, the authors concluded that "psychological health depends less on the frequency of negative emotions and more on how one relates to these emotions when they occur" (Sauer-Zavala et al., 2012, p. 551). This understanding of the problem of emotional avoidance, including the importance of emotional acceptance, seems to go against the grain within contemporary Western society, especially given the tendency to try to reduce, eliminate, avoid, or distract from psychological suffering via medication, pornography, and prosperity theology, among other ineffective strategies. Of course, many of these attempts do not work in the long run, leaving clients feeling exhausted, discouraged, and fatigued.

In a similar vein, about a quarter of a century ago, Hayes et al. (1996) argued that many of the major therapies, including Freudian psychoanalysis, Rogerian therapy, Gestalt therapy, and existential therapy, aim to help clients accept, rather than avoid, psychological pain. With existential therapy, for example, existential anxiety is viewed as an entirely normal experience that should not automatically be reduced or eliminated (Iacovou & Weixel-Dixon, 2015). Certainly, from an existential perspective, the removal of anxiety is not fully possible, given that anxiety emanates from freedom, choice, uncertainty, and, ultimately, the human condition (Iacovou & Weixel-Dixon, 2015). In addition to this literature, the Old Testament of the Bible offers guidance regarding how Christian clients can effectively respond to suffering.

Lamenting to God: An Alternative to Avoidance

In the Old Testament, the Book of Psalms is a collection of songs and poems, many of which are historically attributed to King David. According to Brueggemann (1984), the psalms can be arranged in a particular sequence, paralleling the human condition, with these poems and songs focusing on three major life phases—orientation, disorientation, and new orientation. Specifically, some of the psalms capture themes of joy, celebration, and well-being, with the psalmists celebrating God's blessings through the use of music and poetry (Brueggemann, 1984). In addition, the psalms of disorientation, also called lament psalms, capture the suffering that is inherent within the human condition, including experiences of agony, pain, loneliness, and rejection (Brueggemann, 1984). Quite frequently, these laments are "over the top," in terms of the ways in which the psalmists expressed themselves, helping them to effectively communicate a deep sense of hurt toward God (Brueggemann, 1984). Finally, psalms of new orientation point to the experience of God's blessings following a period of despair, hurt, and loneliness (Brueggemann, 1984). Because God is sovereign, according to the Christian tradition, this is a time of celebration to give thanks to God for helping to convert suffering into blessings (Brueggemann, 1984). In other words, at their lowest point, the psalmists experienced God's presence, with God responding to their cries for help, leading to insight, a new awareness of the situation, and growth (Brueggemann, 1984).

Interestingly, Brueggemann (1984) suggested that the Book of Psalms is frequently thought of as only a positive, happy collection of poems that celebrate God's blessings, a sort of "cover up" within the Christian tradition because of the "wishful optimism in [contemporary] culture" (p. 51). As Brueggemann revealed, however, the lament psalms are actually "an act of bold faith," given that the psalmists wanted to brutally accept the reality of the human condition, including the pain that emanates from daily living, rather than pretend that life is solely filled with happiness and pleasure. Because of this, the psalmists believed that "all experiences of disorder are a proper subject for discourse with God" (Brueggemann, 1984, p. 52). Stated differently, rather than attempting to reduce, eliminate, avoid, or distract from the pain of the human condition, the psalmists accepted and verbalized their pain to God, something Christian clients may struggle to do in 21st-century America.

In terms of the structure of these laments, they typically follow a consistent pattern, including a plea to God, complaint to God, petition for God to immediately act to remedy the situation, argument for God to act quickly, angry phrase or curse to God, praise to God, and acknowledgment that God has heard the psalmist's request (Brueggemann, 1984). Stated more succinctly, lament psalms involve both a plea and praise on the part of the psalmist (Brueggemann, 1984). For example, apparently experiencing sheer agony, King David lamented the following in Psalm 13:

> How long, Lord? Will you forget me forever? How long will you hide your face from me? How long must I wrestle with my thoughts and day after day have sorrow in my heart? How long will my enemy triumph over me? Look on me and answer, Lord my God. Give light to my eyes, or I will sleep in death, and my enemy will say, "I have overcome him," and my foes will rejoice when I fall. But I trust in your unfailing love; my heart rejoices in your salvation. I will sing the Lord's praise, for he has been good to me.
>
> (*New International Version Bible*, 2011)

Here, it is important to observe that David did not attempt to reduce, eliminate, avoid, or distract from his distressing thoughts or sorrow. Instead, in the midst

39

of his suffering, he accepted these experiences, cried out to God, and thanked God for his blessings, despite the inner turmoil. This, of course, is a very different response than many well-intentioned efforts in the 21st century to eradicate mental "disease." Yet, consistent with acceptance-based strategies within the transdiagnostic movement, David's course of action involved embracing difficult experiences, presenting them to God, and thanking God.

Conclusion

A fundamental question emanates from the information presented in this chapter:

> What do Christian clients do when psychological suffering does not go away, despite their best efforts to eliminate the pain through society's most popular remedies—the biomedical model and psychotropic medicine, distraction and fantasy (e.g., internet pornography), the "prosperity theology" movement and hope of health and wealth, and "coping skills" in counseling and therapy?

In the next chapter, I discuss the difference between symptoms and disorders, arguing that they are not one and the same by drawing upon the psychiatry and psychology literatures, as well as biblical examples of the life of Jesus Christ and the Apostle Paul. Following the second chapter, I review the experiential avoidance literature in detail, which will lay a firm theoretical and empirical foundation for the faith-based ACT model presented in the fourth chapter. Above all else, my hope is that this book offers a strategy for mental health professionals to effectively work with Christian clients to accept, rather than avoid, psychological pain so as to live a life devoted to walking with God and living out a set of well-defined values.

Note

1 It is worth mentioning that ACT is not against psychotropic medicine when it is rooted in well-designed studies that elucidate significant improvements beyond a placebo (see, e.g., Hayes et al., 2012, p. 342). In fact, medication compliance can be viewed as a way to follow values, including taking care of one's physical and mental health. Similarly, contemplative Christianity, presented throughout this book, is not against medication *per se*. As Basil the Great revealed, "God's grace is as evident in the healing power of medicine and its practitioners as it is in miraculous cures" (quoted in Trader, 2011, p. 10).

References

Albright, J. (2008). Sex in America online: An exploration of sex, marital status, and sexual identity in Internet sex seeking and its impact. *Journal of Sex Research, 45*, 175–186.

Ali, S., Rhodes, L., Moreea, O., McMillan, D., Gilbody, S., Leach, C., Lucock, M., Lutz, W., & Delgadillo, J. (2017). How durable is the effect of low intensity CBT for depression and anxiety? Remission and relapse in a longitudinal cohort study. *Behaviour Research and Therapy, 94*, 1–8.

American Psychiatric Association. (2013). *Diagnostic and statistical manual of mental disorders* (5th ed.). American Psychiatric Association.

Barlow, D. Farchione, C., Ellard, K., Boisseau, C., Allen, L., & Ehrenreich-May, J. (2010). *Unified protocol for transdiagnostic treatment of emotional disorders: Therapist guide.* Oxford University Press.

Barroso, A. (2021). *For American couples, gender gaps in sharing household responsibilities persist amid pandemic.* https://www.pewresearch.org/fact-tank/2021/01/25/for-american-couples-gender-gaps-in-sharing-household-responsibilities-persist-amid-pandemic/

Beck, J. (2020). *Cognitive behavior therapy: Basics and beyond* (3rd ed.). The Guilford Press.

Borgogna, N., & McDermott, R. (2018). The role of gender, experiential avoidance, and scrupulosity in problematic pornography viewing: A moderated-mediation model. *Sexual Addiction & Compulsivity, 25*, 319–344.

Bowler, K. (2013). *Blessed: A history of the American prosperity gospel.* Oxford University Press.

Brem, M., Shorey, R., Anderson, S., & Stuart, G. (2018). Does experiential avoidance explain the relationships between shame, PTSD symptoms, and compulsive sexual behaviour among women in substance use treatment? *Clinical Psychology & Psychotherapy, 25*, 692–700.

Bremner, J. (2006). Traumatic stress: Effects on the brain. *Dialogues in Clinical Neuroscience, 8*, 445–461.

Brody, D., & Gu, Q. (2020). *Antidepressant use among adults: United States, 2015–2018.* https://www.cdc.gov/nchs/data/databriefs/db377-H.pdf

Brody, D., Pratt, L., & Hughes, J. (2018). *Prevalence of depression among adults aged 20 and over: United States, 2013–2016.* https://www.cdc.gov/nchs/data/databriefs/db303.pdf

Bruce, S., Yonkers, K., Otto, M., Eisen, J., Weisberg, R., Pagano, M., & Keller, M. (2005). Influence of psychiatric comorbidity on recovery and recurrence in generalized anxiety disorder, social phobia, and panic disorder: A 12-year prospective study. *American Journal of Psychiatry, 162*, 1179–1187.

Brueggemann, W. (1984). *The message of the psalms: A theological commentary.* Augsburg Publishing House.

Burns, D. (1999). *Feeling good: The new mood therapy.* Avon Books.

Carleton, R., Mulvogue, M., Thibodeau, M., McCabe, R., Antony, M., & Asmudson, G. (2012). Increasingly certain about uncertainty: Intolerance of uncertainty across anxiety and depression. *Journal of Anxiety Disorders, 26*, 468–479.

Casacalenda, N., Perry, J., & Looper, K. (2002). Remission in major depressive disorder: A comparison of pharmacotherapy, psychotherapy, and control conditions. *American Journal of Psychiatry, 159*, 1354–1360.

Casey, D. (2009). A psychiatric approach to case formulation. In P. Sturmey (Ed.), *Clinical case formulation: Varieties of approaches* (pp. 93–106). Wiley.

Cheng, C., & Li, A. (2014). Internet addiction prevalence and quality of (real) life: A meta-analysis of 31 nations across seven world regions. *Cyberpsychology, Behavior, and Social Networking, 17*, 755–760.

Chou, W., Lee, K., Ko, C., Liu, T., Hsiao, R., Lin, H., & Yen, C. (2017). Relationship between psychological inflexibility and experiential avoidance and internet addiction: Mediating effects of mental health problems. *Psychiatry Research, 257*, 40–44.

Cipriani, A., Furukawa, T., Salanti, G., Chaimani, A., Atkinson, L., Ogawa, Y., Leucht, S., Ruhe, H., Turner, E., Higgins, J., Egger, M., Takeshima, N., Hayasaka, Y., Imai, H., Shinohara, K., Tajika, A., Ioannidis, J., & Geddes, J. (2018). Comparative efficacy and acceptability of 21 antidepressant drugs for the acute treatment of adults with major depressive disorder: A systematic review and network meta-analysis. *Lancet, 391*, 1357–1366.

Clark, D., & Taylor, S. (2009). The transdiagnostic perspective on cognitive-behavioral therapy for anxiety and depression: New wine for old wineskins. *Journal of Cognitive Psychotherapy, 23*, 60–66.

Cloitre, M., Hyland, P., Bisson, J., Brewin, C., Roberts, N., Karatzias, T., & Shevlin, M. (2019). ICD-11 posttraumatic stress disorder and complex posttraumatic stress disorder in the United States: A population-based study. *Journal of Traumatic Stress, 32*, 833–842.

Contractor, A., Weiss, N., & Elhai, J. (2019). Examination of the relation between PTSD symptoms, smartphone features use, and problematic smartphone use. *Social Science Computer Review, 37*, 385–403.

Craske, M. (2012). Transdiagnostic treatment for anxiety and depression. *Depression and Anxiety, 29*, 749–753.

Crosby, J., & Twohig, M. (2012). A contextual approach to pornography addiction. In S. Hayes & M. Levin (Eds.), *Mindfulness and acceptance for addictive behaviors: Applying contextual CBT to substance abuse & behavioral addictions* (pp. 304–322). New Harbinger, Inc.

Dalgleish, T., Black, M., Johnston, D., & Bevan, A. (2020). Transdiagnostic approaches to mental health problems: Current status and future directions. *Journal of Consulting and Clinical Psychology, 88*, 179–195.

Dugas, M., & Robichaud, M. (2007). *Cognitive-behavioral treatment for generalized anxiety disorder: From science to practice*. Routledge.

Egan, S., Hattaway, M., & Kane, R. (2014). The relationship between perfectionism and rumination in posttraumatic stress disorder. *Behavioural and Cognitive Psychotherapy, 42*, 211–223.

Egan, S., Wade, T., & Shafran, R. (2011). Perfectionism as a transdiagnostic process: A clinical review. *Clinical Psychology Review, 31*, 203–212.

Ehring, T., & Watkins, E. (2008). Repetitive negative thinking as a transdiagnostic process. *International Journal of Cognitive Therapy, 1*, 192–205.

Engel, G. (1977). The need for a new medical model: A challenge for biomedicine. *Science, 196*, 129–136.

Fournier, J., DeRubeis, R., Hollon, S., Dimidjian, S., Amsterdam, J., Shelton, R., & Fawcett, J. (2010). Antidepressant drug effects and depression severity: A patient-level meta-analysis. *JAMA, 303*, 47–53.

Fretheim, T. (1984). *The suffering of God: An Old Testament perspective*. Fortress Press.

Galatzer-Levy, I., Huang, S., & Bonanno, G. (2018). Trajectories of resilience and dysfunction following potential trauma: A review and statistical evaluation. *Clinical Psychology Review, 63*, 41–55.

Geddes, J., Carney, S., Davies, C., Furukawa, T., Kupfer, D., Frank, E., & Goodwin, G. (2003). Relapse prevention with antidepressant drug treatment in depressive disorders: A systematic review. *The Lancet, 361*, 653–661.

Greenberger, D., & Padesky, C. (1995). *Mind over mood: Change how you feel by changing the way you think.* The Guilford Press.

Hall, D. (1986). *God & human suffering: An exercise in the theology of the cross.* Augsburg Publishing House.

Hayes, S., Strosahl, K., & Wilson, K. (2012). *Acceptance and commitment therapy: The process and practice of mindful change* (2nd ed.). The Guilford Press.

Hayes, S., Wilson, K., Gifford, E., Follette, V., & Strosahl, K. (1996). Experiential avoidance and behavioral disorders: A functional dimensional approach to diagnosis and treatment. *Journal of Consulting and Clinical Psychology, 64*, 1152–1168.

Hengartner, M. (2020). How effective are antidepressants for depression over the long term? A critical review of relapse prevention trials and the issue of withdrawal confounding. *Therapeutic Advances in Psychopharmacology.* Advance online publication.

Hranov, L. (2007). Comorbid anxiety and depression: Illumination of a controversy. *International Journal of Psychiatry in Clinical Practice, 11*, 171–189.

Iacovou, S., & Weixel-Dixon, K. (2015). *Existential therapy: 100 key points and techniques.* Routledge.

Ioannidis, K., Treder, M., Chamberlain, S., Kiraly, F., Redden, S., Stein, D., Lochner, C., & Grant, J. (2018). Problematic internet use as an age-related multifaceted problem: Evidence from a two-site survey. *Addictive Behaviors, 81*, 157–166.

Kessler, R., Petukhova, M., Sampson, N., Zaslavsky, A., & Wittchen, H. (2012). Twelve-month and lifetime prevalence and lifetime morbid risk of anxiety and mood disorders in the United States. *International Journal of Methods in Psychiatric Research, 21*, 169–184.

Kiesler, D. (2000). *Beyond the disease model of mental disorders.* Praeger Publishers.

Kirsch, I., Deacon, B., Huedo-Medina, T., Scoboria, A., Moore, T., & Johnson, B. (2008). Initial severity and antidepressant benefits: A meta-analysis of data submitted to the Food and Drug Administration. *PLOS Medicine, 5*, 260–268.

Lamers, F., van Oppen, P., Comijs, H., Smit, J., Spinhoven, P., van Balkom, A., & Penninx, B. (2011). Comorbidity patterns of anxiety and depressive disorders in a large cohort study: The Netherlands study of depression and anxiety (NESDA). *Journal of Clinical Psychiatry, 72*, 341–348.

Levin, M., Lillis, J., & Hayes, S. (2012). When is online pornography viewing problematic among college males? Examining the moderating role of experiential avoidance. *Sexual Addiction & Compulsivity, 19*, 168–180.

Mathes, B., Kennedy, G., Morabito, D., Martin, A., Bedford, C., & Schmidt, N. (2020). A longitudinal investigation of the association between rumination, hostility, and PTSD symptoms among trauma-exposed individuals. *Journal of Affective Disorders, 277*, 322–328.

McEvoy, P., Watson, H., Watkins, E., & Nathan, P. (2013). The relationship between worry, rumination, and comorbidity: Evidence for repetitive negative thinking as a transdiagnostic construct. *Journal of Affective Disorders, 151*, 313–320.

McShall, J., & Johnson, M. (2015). The association between relationship distress and psychopathology is consistent across racial and ethnic groups. *Journal of Abnormal Psychology, 124*, 226–231.

Moltmann, J. (1993). *The crucified God*. Fortress Press.

Munkholm K., Paludan-Müller, A., & Boesen, K. (2019). Considering the methodological limitations in the evidence base of antidepressants for depression: A reanalysis of a network meta-analysis. *BMJ Open, 9*, 1–9.

New International Version Bible. (2011). Zondervan. https://www.biblegateway.com/

Nierenberg, A., Petersen, T., & Alpert, J. (2003). Prevention of relapse and recurrence in depression: The role of long-term pharmacotherapy and psychotherapy. *Journal of Clinical Psychiatry, 64*(Supplement 15), 13–17.

O'Donnell, M., Creamer, M., & Pattison, P. (2004). Posttraumatic stress disorder and depression following trauma: Understanding comorbidity. *American Journal of Psychiatry, 161*, 1390–1396.

Oglesby, M., Gibby, B., Mathes, B., Short, N., & Schmidt, N. (2017). Intolerance of uncertainty and posttraumatic stress symptoms: An investigation within a treatment seeking trauma-exposed sample. *Comprehensive Psychiatry, 72*, 34–40.

Olfson, M., & Marcus, S. (2009). National patterns in antidepressant medication treatment. *Archives of General Psychiatry, 66*, 848–856.

Pew Forum. (2006). *Spirit and power: A 10-country survey of Pentecostals*. The Pew Forum on Religion & Public Life.

Pew Research Center. (2019). *Married adults have a more positive view of how things are going in their relationship*. https://www.pewresearch.org/fact-tank/2019/11/06/key-findings -on-marriage-and-cohabitation-in-the-u-s/ft_19-11-05_marriagecohabitation_ married-adults-more-positive/

Pigott, H., Leventhal, A., Alter, G., & Boren, J. (2010). Efficacy and effectiveness of antidepressants: Current status of research. *Psychotherapy and Psychosomatics, 79*, 267–279.

Pratt, L., Brody, D., & Gu, Q. (2011). *Antidepressant use in persons aged 12 and older: United States, 2005–2008* (vol. 76, pp. 1–8). U.S. Department of Health and Human Services.

Rector, N., Man, V., & Lerman, B. (2014). The expanding cognitive-behavioural therapy treatment umbrella for the anxiety disorders: Disorder-specific and transdiagnostic approaches. *Canadian Journal of Psychiatry, 59*, 301–309.

Reid, R., Li, D., Gilliland, R., Stein, J., & Fong, T. (2011). Reliability, validity, and psychometric development of the Pornography Consumption Inventory in a sample of hypersexual men. *Journal of Sex & Marital Therapy, 37*, 359–385.

Sauer-Zavala, S., Boswell, J., Gallagher, M., Bentley, K., Ametaj, A., & Barlow, D. (2012). The role of negative affectivity and negative reactivity to emotions in predicting outcomes in the United protocol for the transdiagnostic treatment of emotional disorders. *Behaviour Research and Therapy, 50*, 551–557.

Segal, Z., Williams, M., & Teasdale, J. (2012). *Mindfulness-based cognitive therapy for depression* (2nd ed.). The Guilford Press.

Short, M., Black, L., Smith, A., Wetterneck, C., & Wells, D. (2012). A review of Internet pornography use research: Methodology and content from the past 10 years. *Cyberpsychology, Behavior, and Social Networking, 15*, 13–23.

Sserwanja, I., & Marjoribanks, D. (2016). *Relationship distress monitor: Estimating levels of adult couple relationship distress across the UK*. https://www.relate.org.uk/sites/default/ files/relationship_distress_monitor_0.pdf

Takayanagi, Y., Spira, A., Bienvenu, J., Hock, R., Carras, M., Eaton, W., & Mojtabai, R. (2015). Antidepressant use and lifetime history of mental disorders in a community sample: Results from the Baltimore Epidemiologic Catchment Area Study. *The Journal of Clinical Psychiatry, 76*, 40–44.

Terlizzi, E., & Villarroel, M. (2020). *Symptoms of generalized anxiety disorder among adults: United States, 2019.* https://www.cdc.gov/nchs/data/databriefs/db378-H.pdf

Thase, M. (2003). Achieving remission and managing relapse in depression. *Journal of Clinical Psychiatry, 64*(Supplement 18), 3–7.

Trader, S. (2011). *Ancient Christian wisdom and Aaron Beck's cognitive therapy: A meeting of the minds.* Peter Lang Publishing, Inc.

Turner, E., Matthews, A., Linardatos, E., Tell, R., & Rosenthal, R. (2008). Selective publication of antidepressant trials and its influence on apparent efficacy. *The New England Journal of Medicine, 358*, 252–260.

Vittengl, J., Clark, L., Dunn, T., & Jarrett, R. (2007). Reducing relapse and recurrence in unipolar depression: A comparative meta-analysis of cognitive-behavioral therapy's effects. *Journal of Consulting and Clinical Psychology, 75*, 475–488.

Wetterneck, C., & Hart, J. (2012). Intimacy is a transdiagnostic problem for cognitive behavior therapy: Functional Analytical Psychotherapy is a solution. *International Journal of Behavioral Consultation and Therapy, 7*, 167–176.

Wetterneck, C., Burgess, A., Short, M., Smith, A., & Cervantes, M. (2012). The role of sexual compulsivity, impulsivity, and experiential avoidance in Internet pornography use. *The Psychological Record, 62*, 3–18.

Williams, N., Simpson, A., Simpson, K., & Nahas, Z. (2009). Relapse rates with long-term antidepressant drug therapy: A meta-analysis. *Human Psychopharmacology, 24*, 401–408.

Young, K., & Nabuco de Abreu, C. (Eds.). (2011). *Internet addiction: A handbook and guide to evaluation and treatment.* Wiley.

Young, K., Yue, X., & Ying, L. (2011). Prevalence estimates and etiologic models of Internet addiction. In K. Young & C. Nabuco (Eds.), *Internet addiction: A handbook and guide to evaluation and treatment* (pp. 3–18). Wiley.

Zhang, Z., Zhang, L., Zhang, G., Jin, J., & Zheng, Z. (2018). The effect of CBT and its modifications for relapse prevention in major depressive disorder: A systematic review and meta-analysis. *BMC Psychiatry, 18*, 1–14.

2

DIFFERENTIATING PSYCHOLOGICAL SYMPTOMS FROM DISORDERS

Introduction

In this chapter, the difference between psychological symptoms and problems, conditions, and disorders is explored, devoting this portion of the book to the notion that the inevitable, normal symptoms of daily life do not automatically lead to a *Diagnostic and Statistical Manual of Mental Disorders,* Fifth Edition (DSM-5) diagnosis or V code. Instead, clients' interpretation of, and response to, a range of psychological symptoms determine whether or not they go on to experience problems, conditions, and disorders in day-to-day living. In other words, if symptoms are simply defined as subjective "indicators" of the presence of ubiquitous, universal psychological processes (e.g., thoughts, feelings, sensations, memories), rather than the "presence of disease or abnormality" (Merriam-Webster, 1995), the unavoidable "symptoms" of the human condition can be more fully accepted as an ordinary part of moment-by-moment experiences.

This distinction between symptoms and problems, conditions, and disorders—the former does not inevitably lead to the latter—can be helpful when treating followers of Jesus, especially when Christian clients' recurring symptoms do not remit or permanently go away. Examples in Scripture of enduring suffering, rather than waiting for it to completely subside, include Jesus's "Passion" narrative, translated "to suffer" (*New International Version Bible,* 2011, Luke 22:1–24:53), as well as Paul's "thorn in the flesh" (*New International Version Bible,* 2011, 2 Corinthians 12:7), which he learned to accept and reinterpret as helping him to lean upon God. Moreover, in this chapter, I include a case vignette to elucidate the distinction between symptoms and problems, conditions, and disorders. A fundamental question in this chapter is as follows: "What if the solution to psychological pain for Christian clients is relating differently to these experiences in order to more effectively walk with God and live out a set of biblical virtues, rather than fighting to get rid of them or make them go away?" Walking on the road of suffering, when guided by biblical virtues, leads to God, who offers a deeper, more satisfying, more permanent rest in each unfolding moment.

DOI: 10.4324/9781003181941-3

The DSM-5: Defining Psychological Problems, Conditions, and Disorders

According to the DSM-5, a diagnosable psychological disorder involves impairment across a range of domains, including disturbed functioning in the areas of cognition, affect, and behavior (American Psychiatric Association [APA], 2013). This, too, goes for DSM-5 problems and conditions (e.g., V codes), which also commonly involve psychological impairment (APA, 2013). Mental disorders, moreover, are generally linked to underlying developmental, biological, or psychological states that deviate from normal processes (APA, 2013). Finally, psychological problems, conditions, and disorders tend to impair daily functioning in the context of relationships, work, or some other life dimension, with the level of impairment or distress subjectively reported by the client and observed by the counselor or therapist (APA, 2013). When considering the aforementioned criteria, though, culturally normative behavior does not typically warrant a formal DSM-5 diagnosis or V code (APA, 2013).

As Lilienfeld et al. (2013) revealed, there are several theories that attempt to draw a distinction between healthy and unhealthy functioning. For instance, the statistical model of disorders separates normal from abnormal based on how frequently disorders occur in society, focusing on their prevalence, whereas the subjective distress model elucidates that psychological pain differentiates diagnosable from nondiagnosable states (Lilienfeld et al., 2013). As another example, the biological model emphasizes evolutionary processes, suggesting that disordered functioning involves biological vulnerabilities that prevent individuals from achieving optimal health and, subsequently, transferring healthy genetic material to their offspring (Lilienfeld et al., 2013). Finally, a "need for treatment" understanding of mental disorders attempts to link diagnoses with interventions, commonly relying on medicine to restore a client's health (Lilienfeld et al., 2013). Although by no means an exhaustive list, these differing theories help to better understand the wide variety of attempts to identify and define what constitutes a "disorder," contrasting atypical and typical functioning in contemporary society.

Among the plethora of diagnoses listed in the DSM-5, symptoms are organized as building blocks that form disorders, which are grouped together under the umbrella of diagnostic categories. Also, V codes are listed at the end of the DSM-5 to bring clinical attention to other problems and conditions that may impair functioning and warrant treatment. For example, low mood and *anhedonia*, occurring alongside several other depressive symptoms over a period of at least two weeks, warrant a diagnosis of *major depressive disorder*, which falls under the heading of depressive disorders (APA, 2013). Moreover, although not a formal diagnosis in the DSM-5, relationship distress with a spouse or intimate partner is considered a relational problem that impairs cognitive, affective, or behavioral functioning and may have an impact on a formal DSM-5 diagnosis (APA, 2013). Yet, because there are currently no biological markers for an array of DSM-5 problems, conditions, and disorders, some of the criteria, gleaned from a client's subjective, self-reported experience, seem to lack a precise rationale for their thresholds, frequencies, and durations.

To illustrate this point, at least five depressive symptoms are required over the course of two weeks to justify a major depressive disorder diagnosis. However, this two-week, five-symptom minimum, although helpful in establishing that clients are suffering with depressive symptoms, does not seem to clearly differentiate health from pathology in the same way that a cancer patient definitively knows, based on a series of medical tests, whether or not malignant cells are present following a period of remission. Although the experience of *more* symptoms, possibly leading to impaired daily functioning, may point toward a disorder, the actual diagnosing process remains somewhat subjective (Francis, 2010), with counselors and therapists relying on clinical judgment along the way.

The DSM-5: Assigning a Diagnosis or V Code

To assign a DSM-5 diagnosis or V code, mental health professionals must attempt to utilize a clearly defined, common strategy for differentiating normal from abnormal behavior, especially given the unavailability of biological markers to discern healthy versus unhealthy psychological functioning (APA, 2013). For instance, whereas a blood test can help a primary care physician to arrive at a medical diagnosis for a variety of abnormal physiological processes, no such test exists for an anxiety disorder. What is more, there is no universally accepted psychological assessment instrument to diagnose or assign a V code within the DSM-5 (APA, 2013), with many of the most commonly used measures cautioning against unilaterally arriving at a diagnosis without the triangulation of data—an intake interview, along with behavioral observations, for example, helps to make sense of an elevated score on a personality assessment instrument in order to more confidently reach a diagnosis. In general, the identification of a cluster of symptoms, rather than symptoms in isolation, is combined with a client's subjective report of distress and impairment in daily life to warrant a formal diagnosis or V code (APA, 2013).

Making diagnosing more complex, culture plays an important role in determining whether a DSM-5 diagnosis or V code is appropriate (APA, 2013). Accordingly, rather than the mere presence of symptoms, counselors and therapists must elucidate whether the symptoms are culturally normative or deviate from the behavioral standard accepted within a client's community. As an interesting dilemma, a particular client may experience an assortment of symptoms. Yet, because the symptoms are widely accepted within their culture, a formal DSM-5 diagnosis or V code may not apply. Interestingly, with other disciplines in medicine, though, culture plays little, if any, role in diagnosing certain conditions, as in the examples of the presence of a malignant tumor or high blood pressure.

As another example, symptoms of narcissistic personality seem to be increasing within contemporary American society, with some authors suggesting narcissism in Western culture has reached an "epidemic" level (Twenge et al., 2014). Given that personality disorders within the DSM-5 must "deviate markedly from the expectations of the individual's culture" (APA, 2013, p. 646), a case could be made that narcissism, at some point, should not be diagnosable because of how common it is within certain parts of the world. In other words, because excessive, individualistic self-expression, as revealed by symptoms such as self-absorption, grandiosity, feelings of "specialness," and the need for continuous validation and praise (APA, 2013), seems to be ubiquitous in many contemporary circles, these seemingly abnormal thoughts, feelings, and behaviors may not actually fall outside of the normal range.

To offer two biblical illustrations, according to the New Testament, Jesus died for the sins of the world, believing that his mission was to suffer for humankind (Mark 8:31–32; 1 Corinthians 15:3). In fact, many Christians suggest that Jesus is the manifestation of the "Suffering Servant," also referred to as the "Man of Sorrows," who was prophesied to experience tremendous pain and suffering while on this planet (*New International Version Bible*, 2011, Isaiah 53). Within Christian culture, followers of Jesus commonly accept, at least on some level, that they will suffer, too, because of their dedication to obeying Jesus's teachings (Mark 8:34–35; John 15:20; 1 Peter 2:21, 5:10). If this is the case, an argument can be made that suffering on the part of Christian clients is culturally normative, based on Jesus's model of self-denial, self-sacrifice, and hardship, along with a plethora of other key New Testament passages on the topic.

What is more, the Apostle James advocated finding joy in suffering, especially when facing hardships and trials (James 1:2–3). Again, a case can be presented that mental anguish is a normal, customary experience within Christianity, especially given the martyr deaths experienced by first-century Christians (Acts 7:54–60) and the teachings of the New Testament on suffering (Philippians 1:29), with these experiences viewed by a variety of Christian communities as an inevitable day-to-day experience when following Jesus. As the DSM-5 disclosed, "The boundaries between normality and pathology vary across cultures for specific types of behaviors" and "thresholds of tolerance for specific symptoms or behaviors differ across cultures, social settings, and families" (p. 14). For Christians who believe they will suffer with Jesus, a DSM-5 diagnosis or V code may not be appropriate, given a culturally normative interpretation that symptoms bring them closer to God via the process of sanctification, surrendering to God's will and trusting that he is in control (2 Thessalonians 1).

Nonetheless, because no biological markers or agreed upon psychological tests exist that unilaterally point to DSM-5 diagnoses or V codes, "clinically significant distress or impairment," often revealed by the client or someone close to the client, is commonly utilized as a dichotomous dividing line for normal and abnormal.[1] In other words, whether or not the symptoms are distressing enough to impair daily functioning, rather than the mere presence of symptoms, tends to serve as a litmus test for a range of DSM-5 disorders and V codes. This decision to include "distress" among the other criteria is based on the notion that psychological dysfunction exists on a continuum, with those at the extreme side easier to identify as warranting a diagnosis (Francis, 2010). Yet, on the other end, with milder symptomatology, it is much more difficult to differentiate normal from abnormal, necessitating a subjective "distress" requirement on the part of the client in order to avoid overly diagnosing (Francis, 2010).

For example, a client may have recurrent depressive symptoms, but still be able to function in daily living, reframing the experience as a necessary, normal part of life that gives rise to psychological or spiritual growth. A formal diagnosis, as a result, would not be justified, given that the symptoms do not cause anguish or get in the way of living life. This, too, goes for relational problems. One couple may view their problems as a catalyst for growth in the relationship, whereas another couple might conceptualize their interpersonal problems as highly distressing and in need of clinical attention. Above all else, clients' subjective, self-derived interpretation of symptoms, including whether they believe the symptoms cause distress and impair daily functioning, plays a vital role in determining if a diagnostic label is employed during instances of prolonged suffering.

The DSM-5: Growing Concerns

Despite the popularity of the DSM-5, including its utility in allowing mental health professionals to use a common language and predict the course of a psychological problem, condition, or disorder (Lilienfeld et al., 2013), several recent authors have offered reservations regarding its ability to accurately define and identify "mental illness." In fact, an increasingly common concern is that the DSM-5 pathologizes what would otherwise be considered normal functioning (Francis, 2013), struggling to accurately differentiate healthy from unhealthy, especially given the high comorbidity among many disorders, lack of biological markers, addition of many seemingly unnecessary new disorders, and unfortunate easing of some diagnostic thresholds (Lilienfeld et al., 2013). More recently, Division 32 (Society for Humanistic Psychology) of the American Psychological Association (APA) has been part of an effort to draw greater awareness to some of these growing concerns (Dean Robbins et al., 2017) and propose guidelines for the development of a paradigm-shifting system for conceptualizing and treating psychological suffering (Society for Humanistic Psychology, 2020). Overall, several salient questions emanate from a variety of these emerging concerns.

First, do the "problems," "conditions," and "disorders" of the DSM-5 actually exist in the real world, similar to diagnoses in other branches of medicine? Asked differently, does the DSM-5 demonstrate *validity*, beyond the *reliability* that is established when counselors and therapists consistently diagnose clients based on symptoms as building blocks, which are embedded within a comprehensive classification system (Phillips, 2013a)?[2] Although DSM-5 field trials have established adequate reliability for many problems, conditions, and disorders, with independent counselors and therapists being able to agree upon whether or not they are present among the same client (Regier et al., 2013), a lack of ample research establishing the validity of the DSM-5 continues to pose challenges for the mental health field (Phillips, 2013b). Rather than pointing to "pathophysiological mechanisms," the problems, conditions, and disorders in the DSM-5 are more useful "for the assessment of clinical course and treatment response of individuals grouped by a given set of diagnostic criteria" (APA, 2013, p. 20).

Also, do DSM-5 symptoms, which serve as building blocks, inevitably lead to "problems," "conditions," and "disorders" observable in day-to-day living? Certainly, as previously noted, many DSM-5 problems, conditions, and disorders are reliable, frequently diagnosed or assigned in both research and practice. Still, a frequent reservation is that there is a dearth of research establishing validity (Lilienfeld et al., 2013). Because of this, in the past half-century, psychiatry has attempted to confirm the validity of psychological problems, conditions, and disorders by focusing on several areas of research (Feighner et al., 1972; Robins & Guze, 1970), including clear-cut distinctions between them and genetic and laboratory findings (e.g., structural and functional neuroimaging, molecular genetic testing), ultimately struggling to achieve this goal (Phillips, 2013a).[3]

Regarding the aim of identifying clear distinctions between symptoms, problems, conditions, and disorders, unfortunately, many DSM-5 diagnoses and V codes overlap with one another (Phillips, 2013a). As an example, the comorbidity rate for depressive and anxiety disorders in adult populations may be as high as 75% (Lamers et al., 2011). This finding illuminates that there may be far too many problems, conditions, and disorders in the DSM-5, which can likely be collapsed into higher-order categories, and a plethora of distinct diagnoses and V codes may actually originate from common underlying processes (Phillips, 2013a). Although comorbid problems, conditions, and disorders can most certainly be linked together because one gives way to another, valid, truly separate diagnoses and V codes do not tend to have "fuzzy" boundaries, overlapping with each other (Lilienfeld et al., 2013). Here, it is important to note that, because of this problem of comorbidity, the transdiagnostic movement mentioned in the previous chapter may help to better understand common underlying processes that link comorbid DSM-5 problems, conditions, and disorders, regardless of whether they are valid. (The next chapter in this book further develops this notion by way of the experiential avoidance construct, which is important when conceptualizing psychological suffering from an acceptance and commitment therapy [ACT] perspective.)

Nevertheless, in terms of biological markers, Paris (2013) highlighted that the DSM-5 has been heavily influenced by research within neuroscience, with the hope that an added understanding of both brain functioning (e.g., neurochemistry) and genetics will elucidate a biological basis for many psychological problems, conditions, and disorders. Yet, this form of reductionism often discounts psychological, social, and environmental experiences that may contribute to mental functioning (Paris, 2013; Society for Humanistic Psychology, 2020). In other words, the inner world–outer world interaction is much more complex, transcending an overly simplified understanding that psychological problems, conditions, and disorders are merely a "brain disease" that are located within the individual and requiring an expanded view of the many variables that contribute to psychological suffering (Society for Humanistic Psychology, 2020).

Although the development of the DSM-5 was strongly guided by neuroscience, Paris (2013) noted that there are currently no biological markers—revealed via neuroimaging or neurochemistry—that unequivocally connect psychological problems, conditions, and disorders to the brain. This finding is also confirmed in the actual pages of the DSM-5, which explain that it may be challenging to separate normal from abnormal processes, especially with mild cases (APA, 2013, p. 21). In fact, as Paris revealed, "We still do not know whether most conditions listed in the diagnostic manual are true diseases. We are no closer to understanding the etiology and pathogenesis of mental disorders than 50 years ago" (pp. 50–51). A supplemental textbook to the DSM-5, too, recently confirmed that genetic testing is unlikely to unilaterally elucidate the actual presence of psychological problems, conditions, and disorders anytime soon (Hyman, 2011).

This reality, of course, is a limitation of a classification system that commonly views psychological problems, conditions, and disorders as "disease," since there are few clear lines that differentiate "normal" from "abnormal," as opposed to, for example, neuroimaging that can uncover a brain tumor within the field of neurology. With this common lack of a dichotomous "yes" versus "no" distinction, there may be a tendency to over-pathologize clients because of the subjective nature of what constitutes abnormal functioning. Stated differently, because many DSM-5 problems, conditions, and disorders are broadly defined, society may be left with a much higher lifetime prevalence, resulting in about 13% of individuals consuming psychotropic medication in the United States (Brody & Gu, 2020). In general, because of the lack of biological markers, along with broadly defined, subjective criteria for psychological problems, conditions, and disorders, much of the population is likely to be assigned a DSM-5 label, leading to a biological intervention for what would otherwise be considered the natural, ordinary, organic ups and downs of daily living (Paris, 2013).

Again, because of some of the aforementioned challenges with validity, including a variety of highly comorbid problems, conditions, and disorders and a lack of definitive biological markers, diagnosing may be especially subjective, possibly resulting in over-diagnosing and -medicating the population. As Francis (2013) illuminated, "The absence of biological tests is a huge disadvantage for psychiatry. It means that all of our diagnoses are now based on subjective judgments that are inherently fallible and prey to capricious change" (p. 12). Quite possibly, many "problems," "conditions," and "disorders" in Western society are actually ubiquitous, normal human experiences, that is, "symptoms" as indicators of everyday psychological processes, rather than "disease" or psychopathology (Francis, 2013; Hayes et al., 2012). Once more, psychological pain may not inevitably lead to disordered functioning for clients in counseling and therapy, especially when considering that some definitions of "normal" and "abnormal," even what constitutes "health" and "happiness," may be wholly inaccurate.

To offer a quick example, major depressive disorder is one of the most common mental disorders in contemporary Western society, with almost one in five adults struggling with depressive symptoms in a recent U.S. survey (Villarroel & Terlizzi, 2020). Yet, Horwitz and Wakefield (2007) argued that what appears to be a large number of individuals struggling with major depressive disorder is actually a misinterpretation of the normal, ubiquitous sadness that has existed throughout human history. Indeed, in prior generations, the sadness–depression dividing line was based on whether or not there was a known "cause," that is "sadness with cause" versus "depression without cause" (Horwitz & Wakefield, 2007). With the former, sadness signified a salient, clearly identifiable loss, with the individual being offered social support to cope with the painful experience (Horwitz & Wakefield, 2007). With the latter, however, given there was no identifiable loss, the depression was thought to be based on some sort of underlying illness and in need of professional help from a trained expert (Horwitz & Wakefield, 2007). Ultimately, according to Horwitz and Wakefield, the overabundance of current major depressive disorder diagnoses stems from unnecessarily combining these two distinct experiences, which were previously distinguished based on whether or not there was a precipitating loss. Therefore, the 21st century client's subjectively evaluated experience, not the presence or absence of an objectively identifiable loss, now determines whether or not sadness has reached a "clinically significant" level.

Interestingly, although "clinical significance" in the DSM-5 is commonly established via a client's subjective experience of distress, the actual word "distress" is not well defined within the manual (Narrow & Kuhl, 2011). Also, it is important to remember that "all forms of distress are locally shaped" (APA, 2013, p. 758), embedded within particular cultures. Unfortunately, distress "is a vague term with no precise markers" (Francis, 2010). As a result, it can be especially difficult to understand what is meant by distress when counselors and therapists work with clients to elucidate their degree of suffering and impairment. This reality, coupled with the notion that "symptom counts" (e.g., a minimum of five symptoms for major depressive disorder) within the DSM-5 may not adequately delineate "normal" and "abnormal," especially with clients on the mild end of the spectrum of psychopathology (Narrow & Kuhl, 2011), can create additional confusion. In sum, distress seems to be a subjective term that lacks exact measurement, defined by the client based on a range of factors (e.g., cultural influences).

Possibly shaping clients' cultural understanding of distress, Harris (2007) presented several myths of happiness, common within American society, including the notion that happiness is a natural, normal state for human beings. Conversely, a lack of prolonged happiness, according to this myth, means that humans are somehow flawed or defective (Harris, 2007). Nested within this possibly misguided viewpoint, the overarching goal in life seems to be to eliminate unpleasant inner and outer experiences, including all forms of distress, so as to achieve a permanent state of happiness, which is both "normal" and intertwined with mental health (Harris, 2007). For Hayes et al. (2012), too, there is an "assumption of healthy normality" circulating within Western culture, which states that "normal" is synonymous with the absence of psychological pain, similar to physical health within the human body being defined as the nonexistence of disease (p. 5).[1] With this understanding in mind, the trend toward diagnosing, labeling, and treating a range of unpleasant inner and outer experiences, reliant upon the subjective notion of distress, seems to make sense, especially when some humans believe that happiness is a permanent, normal state and psychological pain is a clear deviation from this pleasurable, ubiquitous experience.

Even so, if happiness is not the end result and psychological pain is a normal, rather than abnormal, part of the human experience, the task of differentiating symptoms from problems, conditions, and disorders may be a bit easier to accomplish. In other words, if clients resist the temptation to judge psychological pain as "bad," labeling it as a "disease" or "problem," "condition," or "disorder," they are able to move in the direction of accepting its presence and continuing to live their lives. Symptoms functioning as building blocks, therefore, do not end up creating a proverbial castle of "disordered functioning." After all, psychiatry appears to continue to struggle with establishing valid problems, conditions, and disorders that are rooted in the real world. Hence, pursing labels, which tend to reify inner and outer experiences as "pathological," may not be the best use of clients' time and energy in counseling and therapy. In consideration of some of these points, in recent years, many counseling and therapy modalities have set out to help clients differentiate symptoms from problems, conditions, and disorders, accepting, rather than fighting against, the pain that naturally emanates from daily life.

Relating Differently to Psychological Pain: Perspectives from Counseling and Therapy

As a vital goal in counseling and therapy, a plethora of contemporary modalities strive to help clients relate differently to symptoms, recognizing that difficult thoughts, feelings, sensations, memories, situations, and relationships are an inevitable part of the human condition. Within some traditional cognitive behavioral and many acceptance-based literatures, a common strategy for working with suffering clients includes helping them to accept the inescapability of psychological pain. For example, Barlow and colleagues' Unified Protocol (UP), a transdiagnostic cognitive behavioral therapy (CBT) approach, emphasizes treating a range of emotional disorders with a common etiology, helping clients to recognize both the utility of emotions and unhelpful, dysfunctional responses to painful psychological experiences (Wilamowska et al., 2010). Focusing on the link between thoughts, feelings, and behaviors, UP seeks to assist clients in cultivating a greater appreciation for the spectrum of emotions, ranging from pleasant to unpleasant, rather than judging psychological pain as "bad" or "unacceptable" (Wilamowska et al., 2010). To summarize, UP concentrates on helping clients relate differently to symptoms, cultivating acceptance and nonjudgment along the way, so as to prevent psychological pain from derailing daily life (Wilamowska et al., 2010).

With acceptance-based therapies, also referred to as "third wave" cognitive behavioral approaches, accepting psychological pain is also a central tenet (Hayes et al., 2011). By helping clients to make room for distressing symptoms, rather than avoiding or fighting against them, clients are able to ameliorate behavioral disorders. Often, these newer approaches in the cognitive behavioral literature utilize mindfulness as the vehicle for learning to relate differently to the inner and outer worlds, which helps clients to cultivate several key mental skills on the path of acceptance, including attention, present-moment awareness, and acceptance (Feldman et al., 2007).

As a first example, within *mindfulness-based cognitive therapy* (MBCT), clients use mindfulness skills to allow instances of low mood to simply run their natural course, rather than catastrophizing (e.g., "I'm going to be depressed all over again") the experience, which frequently leads to depression relapse (Segal et al., 2012). To be sure, shifting from the "doing mode," which involves trying to "solve the problem" by eliminating the low mood, to the "being mode," which encompasses fully accepting the experience in the here-and-now, allows clients to engage with life again (Segal et al., 2012). As a fundamental assertion within MBCT, clients' unhealthy relationship to symptoms, rather than the symptoms in and of themselves, leads to recurrent depressive episodes (Segal et al., 2012).

As a second example, *dialectical behavior therapy* (DBT) assists clients with emotion regulation difficulties, employing mindfulness-based skills to encourage clients to "radically accept" impermanent psychological pain and drawing upon the notion that clients have the ability to alter their attitude toward distressing thoughts, feelings, sensations, memories, situations, and relationships (McKay et al., 2007). Essentially, "radical acceptance" involves allowing things to be, just as they are, in the present moment, without judging them or wanting them to be different in any way (McKay et al., 2007). Like the "being mode" in MBCT, this skill helps individuals relate to unpleasant experiences with more openness and flexibility, rather than spending vital energy fighting against what clients cannot change. Of course, when change is possible, it may be helpful to focus on areas for improvement. Yet, when it comes to psychological pain, similar to UP and MBCT, trying to eliminate thoughts, feelings, sensations, and memories may create more problems than the original distressing experience.

As a third example, *compassion-focused therapy* (CFT) focuses on helping clients with shame and negative self-judgments to be more compassionate to themselves via a range of mindfulness- and acceptance-based strategies (Gilbert, 2010). More specifically, clients learn how to cultivate a more compassionate mind by accepting their thoughts, feelings, sensations, and memories, utilizing mindfulness as a way to practice nonjudgment and self-soothing (Gilbert, 2010). Overall, by using the technology of mindfulness-based acceptance, clients are able to be more compassionate, kind, and gentle toward themselves, rather than getting lost in rumination and self-criticism, which often leads to shame and disordered functioning (Gilbert, 2010).

As a fourth example, ACT, expounded upon further in the remaining chapters of this book, employs mindfulness- and acceptance-based interventions and metaphors to aid clients in being more accepting of psychological pain. As one particular metaphor that may be helpful for this discussion, the "two-sided coin" captures the vital relationship between psychological pain and values, with the pain of life on one side of the metaphorical coin, which helps clients to elucidate what matters most on the other side (Greco et al., 2008). For instance, on one side of the "coin" may be a middle-aged male client's sadness, which reveals a sense of profound loss emanating from the thought that more than half of life has already passed him by. Still, the other side of the coin reveals what the client values—deeply meaningful and fulfilling relationships that he has missed out on thus far. Therefore, the pain (e.g., sadness, sorrow, loss) helps the client to better understand what matters most—connection with others. Although the low mood is painful, it is also necessary, serving as a signal to illuminate an important reality for the client—pursuing the heartfelt value of loving relatedness is deeply ingrained within his heart.

As a final example, although not a "third wave" CBT approach *per se*, interpersonal mindfulness has grown in popularity in recent years, which can help clients to be more accepting in their relationships with others (Pratscher et al., 2019). Specifically, as a construct, interpersonal mindfulness is defined as "involving an awareness of self and others, accompanied with the qualities of a nonjudgmental and nonreactive presence" (Pratscher et al., 2018, p. 1207). Beyond investigating interpersonal mindfulness as a construct, researchers have developed programs to help practitioners be more mindful in their relationships, with a recent intervention study among healthcare workers revealing an increase in self-compassion and empathy after just over two months of weekly training and supplemental at-home practice (Bartels-Velthuis et al., 2020).

In addition to the above examples, the Bible lends support to the notion that life is painful, emotions serve a useful purpose, and symptoms do not inevitably lead to disordered, problematic functioning. Hence, what follows is a discussion of several biblical examples of the inevitability of psychological pain, along with three biblical figures' reinterpretation of suffering. Paralleling many of the aforementioned counseling and therapy approaches, these characters in the Bible seemed to be able to accept the inevitability of psychological pain as a result of their understanding that suffering is necessary to fulfill their purpose, bringing them closer to God and experiencing joy along the way. Above all else, the proceeding examples can help Christian clients to better understand the distinction between symptoms and problems, conditions, and disorders, especially since the Apostle Paul, Jesus Christ, and the Apostle James did not allow their suffering to impair their God-given purpose, viewing their distress as culturally normative in the context of a burgeoning first-century Christian church that faced persecution and annihilation as they patiently waited for Jesus to return. Certainly, these biblical examples seem to illuminate that suffering does not inevitably lead to disordered, problematic, impaired functioning, a DSM-5 label, and a medical intervention, given that DSM-5 criteria and modern medicine were unavailable 2,000 years ago.

Relating Differently to Psychological Pain: Perspectives from the Bible

Within the pages of the Bible, there are a wide variety of examples of biblical figures enduring psychological pain, persevering with hope and constancy by walking with God in the midst of suffering. Writing to the first-century church at Corinth, the Apostle Paul referenced a "thorn in the flesh" that he could not get rid of, despite praying three times for God to heal him from this ailment (*New International Version Bible*, 2011, 2 Corinthians 12:4–10). Also described as "a messenger of Satan," Paul suggested that the purpose of the "thorn" was to keep him humble, as well as to entirely rely on God's grace to sustain him. In an effort to reinterpret his "thorn," Paul revealed, "for Christ's sake, I delight in weakness, in insults, in hardships, in persecutions, in difficulties" (*New International Version Bible*, 2011, 2 Corinthians 12:10), arguing that this enduring vulnerability made him stronger because of his dependence upon God, finding delight in his suffering.

Interestingly, the "thorn" Paul referred to, the Greek word *skolops*, seems to mean some sort of recurrent annoyance (e.g., a sharp, pointed affliction) in the context of Paul's physical functioning (Matera, 2003). Throughout history, there have been at least three popular interpretations of Paul's "thorn," including a physical ailment, interpersonal conflict, or sexual temptation (Matera, 2003).

In any case, because Paul prayed for this "annoyance" to be removed a total of three times, there is an assumption that the condition, whatever it may have been, was serious (Matera, 2003). Also, in that Paul was not specific about the exact nature of the "annoyance," 21st-century Christians can more generally apply his core message—suffering provides the opportunity to humbly depend on God's grace, accepting and embracing a weak, vulnerable state because of the sustained strength that God provides—to a variety of difficult life circumstances and inner states (Matera, 2003). In other words, like Paul, Christians can learn to walk with God through, not around, suffering. In the context of recurrent psychological problems, conditions, and disorders, Christian clients can work toward accepting that chronic symptoms draw them closer to God, cultivating a deeper relationship with him. After all, if God is sovereign, there may be a divine purpose hidden in the symptomatology. Consistent with Paul's "thorn," maintaining hope and trust in the midst of trials can allow Christian clients to ameliorate disordered, problematic, impaired functioning by living out a set of biblical virtues, with God by their side.

For instance, when Christian clients are struggling with recurrent depressive, anxiety, or trauma-related symptoms or relational problems, Paul's "thorn" can help them to better understand the importance of depending on God during moments of low mood, rumination, worry, intrusive memories, hypervigilance, or relationship distress, recognizing that Paul was able to endure his affliction because of his ability to reinterpret its meaning—the "thorn" was actually a divine gift for the furthering of God's kingdom. Although Paul could have persisted in praying for the "thorn" to be removed, waiting to be healed before continuing on in his ministry, he was able to accept it as necessary, reinterpreting its role in his life and adjusting his attitude. Worded differently, Paul's symptoms did not inevitably lead to impaired, disordered functioning. Rather, placed within a larger, transcendent context, Paul was able to view the permanent "thorn" as a blessing.

Similar to the Apostle Paul, Jesus Christ faced extreme distress shortly before his crucifixion, asking God to "take the cup" of suffering from him (*New International Version Bible*, 2011, Luke 22:39–46). Yet, Jesus endured, recognizing that his mission was to die the next day on a Roman cross. In particular, at the Mount of Olives, on his knees, Jesus prayed before God, with his "cup" representing "calamity and death" (Green, 1997, p. 780). Although he was "in anguish," Jesus was willing to submit to God's sovereign will, drawing strength from an angel who was with him. As Keener (2009) stated, "Matthew's narrative suggests that even in events that seem as hideous and disastrous as Jesus' arrest and execution seemed to his first disciples, God may be preparing his sovereign purposes" (p. 634).

Immediately preceding Jesus's passionate prayer on the Mount of Olives, Matthew's gospel explicated that Jesus experienced "sorrow to the point of death" (*New International Version Bible*, 2011, Matthew 26:38), revealing both his grief and anticipation of violent suffering (Keener, 2009). Here, the Greek word *perilypos* translates as "deeply grieved," likely reflecting a lament reminiscent of one of the psalmists crying out to God in the midst of suffering (France, 1985, p. 372). Overall, according to Keener, this passage reveals that those who serve God are to submit to his plan, despite the suffering that inevitably ensues. For Christian clients struggling with depressive, anxiety, or trauma symptoms or relationship distress, Jesus's submission to God's will, in the midst of both extreme sorrow and the anticipation of a painful death, may help to better understand that God's sovereign, omniscient purposes are at work, even when he does not seem to "take the cup" of suffering. Indeed, despite Jesus's suffering, he continued on toward God's divine purpose, undermining the notion that symptoms automatically lead to disordered, problematic functioning.

As one final example, the Apostle James, writing to a growing first-century church that was facing suffering and persecution, instructed his audience to reinterpret "trials of many kinds" as a source of "pure joy," especially given that suffering helps to cultivate perseverance (*New International Version Bible*, 2011, James 1:1–2). In this passage, "trials," the Greek word *peirasmos*, may refer to either hardships in the outer world or inner temptations (Moo, 2000). As explained by Moo, James' reference to "trials of many kinds" may mean poverty, although the phrase likely elucidates a variety of instances of suffering (e.g., sadness, loss, isolation, ailments). When experiencing such "trials," surely, Christians are to persevere, the Greek word *hupomone*, meaning a hopeful endurance. What is more, Christians are to find joy in suffering, based on the notion that these types of experiences cultivate steadfastness and patience, requisite qualities in the Christian life (Moo, 2000). For Moo, suffering and hardships help Christians to faithfully depend on God, similar to building muscle with resistance training. Essentially, James' instructions can help Christian clients to reframe both difficult circumstances and psychological pain as necessary means to an end—developing perseverance and an attitude of trustful surrender to God.

Within these three biblical passages, the Apostle Paul, Jesus Christ, and the Apostle James reinterpreted their suffering, viewing their painful experiences as necessary because they served a greater purpose. For Paul, his "thorn" helped him lean on God, recognizing that God's grace was enough for him in the midst of weakness. With Jesus's prayer, he accepted that God was not willing to "take the cup," resulting in Jesus's suffering and dying the following day as he yielded to God's will. Finally, James's letter to a persecuted church serves as a reminder that painful experiences lead to perseverance, strengthening Christians' ability to trust in God. Truly, these three instances capture the inevitability of adversity in the Christian life, as well as the idea that symptoms do not necessarily result in disordered, problematic, impaired functioning, especially when they are viewed through the lens of a hopeful endurance. Disproving the perception that recurring, unpleasant psychological experiences are inevitably pathological and warrant a DSM-5 label, Christian clients can develop gratitude for their pro-verbial "thorn," faithfully surrendering to God's will in the midst of suffering and finding joy in their hardships.

Differentiating Psychological Symptoms from Problems, Conditions, and Disorders: A Case Example

Jennifer, a 33-year-old, single, Latina female, presented for therapy because of several recent bouts with recurrent depression. As a child, she reported a strained relationship with her father, who struggled with a terminal illness. Because of this, she constantly felt alone, having a hard time reaching out to him for emotional support. Over time, she became increasingly isolated, view-ing herself as unworthy of love and innately flawed. Although her parents went to church, she found it difficult to understand how God could love her, conclud-ing that God withheld his love because he was punishing her for a yet-to-be-identified moral failure.

When she presented for treatment, she had few friends, along with recur-rent depressive symptoms, which lasted about two months at a time. Despite moments of remission, most of the time she suffered from residual depressive symptoms, including a lack of interest in pleasurable activities, along with exces-sive guilt, low self-esteem, and hopelessness. Based on her own understanding of depression, Jennifer concluded that her symptoms were biologically rooted, emanating from a genetic predisposition to depression based on a family his-tory. This left her with the strong belief that psychotropic medication was the only way to eliminate her suffering.

As Jennifer began to work with her therapist, she soon discovered the dif-ference between her recurrent symptoms and disordered, problematic func-tioning. Without her judging the symptoms as "pathological," they revealed a "sadness with cause," that is, a longing to connect with both her biological father and God, illuminating an understandable reaction to a life filled with isolation and pain. When she started to explore these inner experiences, rather than trying to rid herself of them because they constituted a "diagnosis," she discovered that they served a purpose, reminding her that she desired to be connected to others. Instead of isolating herself and withdrawing because of low self-esteem and guilt, she embraced her symptoms, which served as a signal, reminding her what mattered most in life—deeply meaningful and fulfilling relationships, wherein she could express herself, turn to others for support, and discern God's will for her life. Similar to King David crying out to God in the Book of Psalms, Jennifer was able to reinterpret her pain as a catalyst toward divine connection, hope, and healing.

Over the course of the next few months, Jennifer began to attend church, recognizing that her depressive symptoms actually helped her slow down and lean on God during moments of weakness and fatigue. Although she originally

60

prayed to God quite often to heal her from her depression, concluding that God did not love her because he did not "take the cup" or "remove the thorn," she began to view her pain as a compass, a "sadness with cause" that pointed her to what she valued most in life. What is more, she started to recognize that she could find joy in the midst of pain, especially when she surrendered to God's plan for her life and lived out a set of biblical virtues. Instead of viewing her depressive symptoms as debilitating, automatically warranting a formal diagnosis and medical intervention to eliminate them, she learned to utilize moments of depression as a stepping-stone toward God, persevering in the midst of inner trials.

Conclusion

To summarize, with the assistance of a counselor or therapist, Christian clients have the ability to differentiate DSM-5 symptoms from problems, conditions, and disorders, which can help them to continue to live life, despite recurring psychological pain. Unfortunately, the DSM-5 has yet to identify clearly defined biological markers and agreed-upon psychological tests to unilaterally differentiate normal from abnormal psychological processes. Instead, clients' subjective experience of distress or impairment is frequently utilized to determine whether a DSM-5 label is warranted. When combined with a fixed number of symptoms, these criteria lead to diagnosable mental disorders, as well as the assignment of V codes to draw attention to other problems and conditions. Even so, culture, too, plays a role in determining whether behavior is considered abnormal. As a result, many problems, conditions, and disorders in the DSM-5 may not be as applicable in cultures that view suffering as at least somewhat normative.

More recently, a variety of authors have questioned some of the validity claims of the DSM-5, given the high rate of comorbidity and absence of biological markers. In addition, several myths about happiness seem to permeate 21st-century Western culture, exacerbating an already confusing picture, including the idea that happiness is the "baseline" for healthy functioning, as well as the notion that unpleasant inner experiences constitute pathological processes, leading to the need for a psychiatric label and exclusively medical treatment. Emanating from some of these conclusions, the cognitive behavioral literature has increasingly embraced a range of acceptance-based strategies to help clients relate differently to psychological pain, rather than fighting against normal, ubiquitous psychological experiences.

The Bible, too, seems to embrace the notion that suffering is unavoidable, with pain playing a vital role in helping Christians to cultivate perseverance, leading to a deeper, more trusting relationship with God. For Christian clients, counselors and therapists can help to draw a clear distinction between symptoms—a normal, ubiquitous part of life—and problems, conditions, and disorders—subjectively defined based on clients' reported distress and impaired functioning—which may be a necessary first step toward positive change. Although many Christian clients will still be working with a psychiatrist to ameliorate symptoms via psychotropic medication and, thus, carrying a DSM-5 label along the way, counselors and therapists can help them to view these symptoms with more openness, flexibility, gentleness, and kindness, turning to the pages of the Bible and acceptance-based interventions for guidance.

In sum, the solution to client suffering in the 21st century may involve relating to symptoms with more acceptance, nonjudgment, and compassion, rather than fighting to get rid of them by assigning a pathologizing label and focusing solely on a medical intervention. In the next chapter, I explore experiential avoidance as a transdiagnostic construct, which can assist Christian clients in making better sense of the distinction between symptoms and problems, symptoms, and disorders—unhelpful attempts to avoid symptoms, rather than the symptoms in and of themselves, often lead to disordered, problematic, impaired functioning. Stated differently, rather than utilizing the DSM-5 as the only source for differentiating "normal" from "abnormal," experiential avoidance can serve as a lens through which Christian clients can view the health versus dysfunction distinction. This understanding—psychological pain is inevitable and cannot be fully avoided in life—also aligns quite well with a biblical view of suffering. In the second half of this book, I present an integrative approach to help Christian clients more effectively endure suffering, as revealed in both Scripture and the ACT literature.

Notes

1 See Spitzer and Wakefield (1999) and Wakefield and Schmitz (2010) for a critique of the "clinical significance" (CS) requirement, which was originally intended to reduce the number of "false positive" diagnoses in the mental health field.

2 Diagnostic reliability is defined as "the certainty with which it can be predicted that different clinicians will apply the same diagnosis to the same patient" (Black & Grant, 2014, p. 5), whereas diagnostic validity points to "whether or not an instrument accurately assesses what it sets out to measure" (Paris, 2015, p. 70). For a discussion of the reliability and validity of the DSM, including research/field trials, see Paris (2015). As revealed by Paris, the DSM has limitations with both reliability and validity, which many counselors and therapists are unaware of when using the DSM to assign a diagnosis or V code.

3 For a rebuttal to some of these criticisms, including a defense of the reliability and validity of many DSM-5 diagnoses, see Lilienfeld et al. (2013).

4 Here, it is important to note that ACT is based on functional contextualism, which aims to view client functioning in particular contexts (Harris, 2019). In other words, from this perspective, ACT does not automatically assume the inner world is problematic and in need of being eradicated whenever clients experience distressing thoughts, feelings, sensations, and memories. Rather, from an ACT perspective, psychological pain is problematic when clients engage in cognitive fusion and experiential avoidance, which can undermine authentic, vibrant living. Clients, therefore,

can learn to relate differently to upsetting inner experiences, viewing them with more openness and flexibility, which results in the ability to focus on values and meaningful living. For a more detailed overview of functional contextualism, see Harris (2019) and Hayes et al. (2012).

References

American Psychiatric Association. (2013). *Diagnostic and statistical manual of mental disorders* (5th ed.). American Psychiatric Association.

Bartels-Velthuis, A., van den Brink, E., Koster, F., & Rogier Hoenders, H. (2020). The interpersonal mindfulness program for health care professionals: A feasibility study. *Mindfulness, 11*, 2629–2638.

Black, D., & Grant, J. (2014). *The essential companion to the diagnostic and statistical manual of mental disorders* (5th ed.). American Psychiatric Publishing.

Brody, D., & Gu, Q. (2020). *Antidepressant use among adults: United States, 2015–2018.* https://www.cdc.gov/nchs/data/databriefs/db377-H.pdf

Dean Robbins, B., Kamens, S., & Elkins, D. (2017). DSM-5 reform efforts by the Society for Humanistic Psychology. *Journal of Humanistic Psychology, 57*, 602–624.

Feighner, J., Robins, E., Guze, S., Woodruff, R., Winokur, G., & Munoz, R. (1972). Diagnostic criteria for use in psychiatric research. *Archives of General Psychiatry, 26*, 57–63.

Feldman, G., Hayes, A., Kumar, S., Greeson, J., & Laurenceau, J. (2007). Mindfulness and emotion regulation: The development and initial validation of the Cognitive and Affective Mindfulness Scale-Revisited (CAMS-R). *Journal of Psychopathology and Behavioral Assessment, 29*, 177–190.

France, R. (1985). *The gospel according to Matthew: An introduction and commentary.* Wm. B. Eerdmans Publishing Co.

Francis, A. (2010). *The significance of clinical significance.* http://www.psychiatrictimes.com/diagnostic-and-statistical-manual-mental-disorders/significance-clinical-significance

Francis, A. (2013). *Saving normal: An insider's revolt against out-of-control psychiatric diagnosis, DSM-5, big pharma and the medicalization of ordinary life.* HarperCollins Publishers.

Gilbert, P. (2010). *Compassion focused therapy.* Routledge.

Greco, L., Barnett, E., Blomquist, K., & Gevers, A. (2008). Acceptance, body image, and health in adolescence. In L. Greco & S. Hayes (Eds.), *Acceptance & mindfulness for children & adolescents: A practitioner's guide* (pp. 187–216). New Harbinger Publications, Inc.

Green, J. (1997). *The gospel of Luke.* Wm. B. Eerdmans Publishing Co.

Harris, R. (2007). *The happiness trap: How to stop struggling and start living.* Trumpeter Books.

Harris, R. (2019). *ACT made simple: An easy-to-read primer on acceptance and commitment therapy* (2nd ed.). New Harbinger Publications, Inc.

Hayes, S., Follette, V., & Linehan, M. (Eds.). (2011). *Mindfulness and acceptance: Expanding the cognitive-behavioral tradition.* The Guilford Press.

Hayes, S., Strosahl, K., & Wilson, K. (2012). *Acceptance and commitment therapy: The process and practice of mindful change* (2nd ed.). The Guilford Press.

Horwitz, A., & Wakefield, J. (2007). *The loss of sadness: How psychiatry transformed normal sorrow into depressive disorder.* Oxford University Press.

Hyman, S. (2011). Diagnosis of mental disorders in light of modern genetics. In D. Regier, W. Narrow, E. Kuhl, & D. Kupfer (Eds.), *The conceptual evolution of the DSM-5* (pp. 3–18). American Psychiatric Publishing, Inc.

Keener, C. (2009). *The gospel of Matthew: A socio-rhetorical commentary.* Wm. B. Eerdmans Publishing Co.

Lamers, F., van Oppen, P., Comijs, H., Smit, J., Spinhoven, P., van Balkom, A., & Penninx, B. (2011). Comorbidity patterns of anxiety and depressive disorders in a large cohort study: The Netherlands study of depression and anxiety (NESDA). *Journal of Clinical Psychiatry, 72,* 341–348.

Lilienfeld, S., Smith, S., & Watts, A. (2013). Issues in diagnosis: Conceptual issues and controversies. In W. Craighead, D. Miklowitz, & L. Craighead (Eds.), *Psychopathology: History, diagnosis, and empirical foundations* (2nd ed., pp. 1–35). Wiley.

Matera, F. (2003). *II Corinthians: A commentary.* Westminster John Knox Press.

McKay, M., Wood, J., & Brantley, J. (2007). *The dialectical behavior therapy skills workbook: Practical DBT exercises for learning mindfulness, interpersonal effectiveness, emotion regulation & distress tolerance.* New Harbinger Publications.

Merriam-Webster's Desk Dictionary. (1995). *Symptom.* Merriam-Webster, Incorporated.

Moo, D. (2000). *The letter of James.* William B. Eerdmans Publishing Co.

Narrow, W., & Kuhl, E. (2011). Clinical significance and disorder thresholds: The role of disability and distress. In D. Regier, W. Narrow, E. Kuhl, & D. Kupfer (Eds.), *The conceptual evolution of the DSM-5* (pp. 147–162). American Psychiatric Publishing, Inc.

New International Version Bible. (2011). Zondervan. https://www.biblegateway.com/

Paris, J. (2013). The ideology behind DSM-5. In J. Paris & J. Phillips (Eds.), *Making the DSM-5: Concepts and controversies* (pp. 39–46). Springer.

Paris, J. (2015). *The intelligent clinician's guide to the DSM-5.* Oxford University Press.

Phillips, J. (2013a). The conceptual status of DSM-5 diagnoses. In J. Paris & J. Phillips (Eds.), *Making the DSM-5: Concepts and controversies* (pp. 143–158). Springer.

Phillips, J. (2013b). *DSM-5 field trials: What was learned.* http://www.psychiatrictimes.com /dsm-5/dsm-5-field-trials-what-was-learned

Pratscher, S., Rose, A., Markovitz, L., & Bettencourt, A. (2018). Interpersonal mindfulness: Investigating mindfulness in interpersonal interactions, co-rumination, and friendship quality. *Mindfulness, 9,* 1206–1215.

Pratscher, S., Wood, P., King, L., & Bettencourt, B. (2019). Interpersonal mindfulness: Scale development and initial construct validation. *Mindfulness, 10,* 1044–1061.

Regier, D., Narrow, W., Clarke, D., Kraemer, H., Kuramoto, S., Kuhl, E., & Kupfer, D. (2013). DSM-5 field trials in the United States and Canada, part II: Test-retest reliability of selected categorical diagnoses. *American Journal of Psychiatry, 170,* 59–70.

Robins, E., & Guze, S. (1970). Establishment of diagnostic validity in psychiatric illness: Its application to schizophrenia. *American Journal of Psychiatry, 126,* 983–987.

Segal, Z., Williams, M., & Teasdale, J. (2012). *Mindfulness-based cognitive therapy for depression* (2nd ed.). The Guilford Press.

Society for Humanistic Psychology. (2020). *Regarding the reform and revision of diagnostic systems: An open letter from Div. 32 (Society for Humanistic Psychology).* https://www .apadivisions.org/division-32/leadership/task-forces/diagnostic-alternatives

Spitzer, R., & Wakefield, J. (1999). DSM-IV diagnostic criterion for clinical significance: Does It help solve the false positives problem? *American Journal of Psychiatry, 156,* 1856–1864.

Twenge, J., Miller, J., & Campbell, W. (2014). The narcissism epidemic: Commentary on modernity and narcissistic personality disorder. *Personality Disorders: Theory, Research, and Treatment, 5,* 227–229.

Villarroel, M., & Terlizzi, E. (2020). *Symptoms of depression among adults: United States, 2019.* https://www.cdc.gov/nchs/data/databriefs/db379-H.pdf

Wakefield, J., & Schmitz, M. (2010). The measurement of mental disorder. In T. Scheid & T. Brown (Eds.), *A handbook for the study of mental health: Social contexts, theories, and systems* (2nd ed., pp. 20–45). Cambridge University Press.

Wilamowska, Z., Thompson-Hollands, J., Fairholme, C., Ellard, K., Farchione, T., & Barlow, D. (2010). Conceptual background, development, and preliminary data from the united protocol for transdiagnostic treatment of emotional disorders. *Depression and Anxiety, 27,* 882–890.

3

THE PROBLEM OF EXPERIENTIAL AVOIDANCE

Introduction

In the first two chapters, I outlined the problem of psychological suffering in the 21st century, including the prevalence of DSM-5 problems, conditions, and disorders and common attempts to try to reduce, eliminate, avoid, or distract from psychological pain, many of which do not seem to work for clients with recurrent struggles. Also, I discussed several contemporary concerns about the validity of the DSM-5, highlighting that symptoms do not inevitably lead to problems, conditions, and disorders, especially because there is some debate about the actual presence of many DSM-5 labels in the real world (e.g., a lack of biological markers, high comorbidity between some disorders), as well as because of the subjectivity of a range of DSM-5 labels based on the "distress" and "impairment in functioning" criteria and cultural considerations of what constitutes normality.

In this chapter, in order to better understand the problem of psychological suffering in the 21st century and distinction between symptoms and problems, conditions, and disorders, I review the experiential avoidance construct, which I believe offers a better way to understand the link between symptoms and impaired functioning, especially for clients experiencing ongoing mental struggles. In other words, symptoms do not inevitably lead to DSM-5 problems, conditions, and disorders. Rather, clients' avoidance of difficult inner (e.g., thoughts, feelings, sensations, memories), as well as corresponding outer (e.g., challenging situations, relational conflict), experiences determine whether or not disordered functioning ensues. Although experiential avoidance—a well-defined process for understanding the dilemma of psychological suffering—was only recently established as a psychometrically sound construct, the notion that clients create more problems, beyond their initial pain, when they fight against psychological suffering has been prevalent within the mental health field for some time. Important questions to consider in this chapter include the following: "What if the root of disordered functioning for Christian clients is experiential avoidance, rather than the actual symptoms they present with in counseling and therapy?" "For Christian clients, what if life is about following Jesus, in the midst of pain, rather than waiting for the symptoms to go away?"

DOI: 10.4324/9781003181941-4

The Experiential Avoidance Literature: Theoretical and Empirical Considerations

Almost three decades ago, Hayes et al. (1996) wrote a pioneering theoretical article that explored the link between experiential avoidance, a psychological process, and disordered functioning. In this article, they elucidated that experiential avoidance involves the struggle to stay connected to unpleasant inner events (e.g., thoughts, feelings, sensations, memories), along with recurrent efforts to avoid such distressing inner events and the corresponding outer events (e.g., challenging situations, relational conflict) they are linked to. When clients repeatedly utilize these avoidance strategies, impairment in functioning can often follow, with experiential avoidance bridging the gap between many DSM-5 symptoms and problems, conditions, and disorders.

In terms of the etiology, Hayes et al. (1996) argued that society tends to encourage the avoidance of unpleasant inner experiences, starting in childhood, with common statements such as "don't cry," "don't be a baby," and "be a man." Moreover, because most individuals find success when controlling and managing their outer world, this approach is applied to the inner world of thoughts, feelings, sensations, and memories, leading to an overreliance on experiential avoidance with private events (Hayes et al., 1996). Consequently, because of the aforementioned cultural messages, along with a natural tendency to want to control thoughts, feelings, sensations, and memories, clients may offer reasons for their reluctance to accept the inner world, especially if there are short-term payoffs for such avoidance behaviors (Hayes et al., 1996). For example, a client with anxiety symptoms may state, "I can't go to the party because I'm too anxious." The immediate benefit, of course, involves a reduction in anxiety. Yet, over time, relationships cannot be cultivated, and life seems to pass the client by.

Although experiential avoidance is a ubiquitous strategy in contemporary society to seemingly cope with psychological pain, it can lead to a range of client consequences, beyond the initial distress clients suffer from (Hayes et al., 1996). For instance, attempting to fully eradicate unpleasant thoughts and feelings tends to distract clients from creating a life that matters, especially if the expectation is that they will only be able to live life once the pain goes away (Hayes et al., 1996). Also, expecting to be completely free from inner distress is unrealistic, possibly resulting in discouragement, hopelessness, and fatigue stemming from regularly fighting against the symptoms (Hayes et al., 1996). In addition, many painful emotions are actually helpful, allowing clients to make sense of salient interpersonal events (Hayes et al., 1996). Therefore, when experiential avoidance is used frequently, clients do not learn to utilize emotions as signals, which help them to navigate life (Hayes et al., 1996). Finally, quite often, pain is a requisite step toward psychological growth (Hayes et al., 1996). Because of this, the mere presence of pain does not mean that clients should discontinue their efforts toward progress (Hayes et al., 1996).

Following Hayes et al.'s (1996), theoretical exploration of experiential avoidance as a functional process, Hayes et al. (2004) developed the Acceptance and Action Questionnaire (AAQ) to empirically test this burgeoning construct. With nine items that load onto one scale, the AAQ measures the struggle to follow through with responsibilities when faced with depression or anxiety, negative views about anxiety, and the desire to permanently remove distress from day-to-day living (Hayes et al., 2004). When examined alongside other measures, results have revealed positive correlations with psychopathology in general, along with depression and anxiety in particular (Hayes et al., 2004). As a result, Hayes et al. concluded that the AAQ may hold promise in both clinical and psychopathology research. Several years later, the shorter, seven-item AAQ-II was developed, which demonstrated adequate internal consistency reliability, test-retest reliability, and concurrent validity in the original psychometric study (Bond et al., 2011).

Building on this preliminary research, Gamez et al. (2011) developed an expanded measure of experiential avoidance—the Multidimensional Experiential Avoidance Questionnaire (MEAQ). Consisting of six scales and a total of 62 items, the measure demonstrated adequate internal consistency reliability and was positively correlated with psychopathology in the original psychometric study (Gamez et al., 2011), similar to the AAQ. In terms of the actual scales, the MEAQ includes behavioral avoidance (e.g., avoiding situations that may lead to unpleasant inner experiences), distress aversion (e.g., negatively judging distressing inner states), procrastination (e.g., trying to postpone inner pain), distraction and suppression (e.g., attempting to push away unpleasant inner states), repression and denial (e.g., seeking to block inner distress), and distress endurance (e.g., persevering, doing what matters in the midst of pain), surpassing the AAQ as a nine-item, single-factor scale (Gamez et al., 2011). Worth mentioning, Gamez et al. (2011) recently created a shorter, 15-item version, the Brief Experiential Avoidance Questionnaire (BEAQ), which demonstrated adequate internal consistency reliability and was correlated with the MEAQ within the original psychometric study.

Nevertheless, all six dimensions of the MEAQ seem to be highly relevant and applicable to counseling and therapy clients struggling with depressive, anxiety, and trauma-related disorders and relationship distress with a spouse or intimate partner, along with Christian adults imperfectly striving to live out the Christian life by following the central tenets of their faith. In fact, when working with Christian clients in counseling and therapy, mental and spiritual struggles commonly overlap, leading to the need to focus on a broader understanding of experiential avoidance, applied to Christian living.

Given that several measures (e.g., the AAQ, AAQ-II, MEAQ, and BEAQ) have been developed to assess experiential avoidance, researchers have increasingly investigated the association between this variable and general psychopathology. More specifically, in the last two decades, experiential avoidance has been explored as a direct correlate of psychopathology, as well as a mediating variable linking psychological functioning and psychopathology. To date, data continue to emerge that suggest experiential avoidance can better help counselors and therapists make sense of the problem of psychological suffering—although symptoms are a ubiquitous, unavoidable part of life, impaired functioning often stems from the avoidance of difficult inner (e.g., thoughts, feelings, sensations, memories), along with corresponding outer (e.g., challenging situations, relational conflict), events.

Roughly 15 years ago, Chawla and Ostafin (2007) reviewed the literature and concluded that experiential avoidance appears to be consistently (and positively) linked to psychopathology. Boulanger et al. (2010), too, reviewed the literature, highlighting that experiential avoidance is positively correlated with a range of forms of psychopathology. Around this same time, Hayes et al. (2006) uncovered large (and positive) effect sizes when examining the relationship between experiential avoidance and psychopathology. In a more recent study among almost 25,000 college students, experiential avoidance was strongly (and positively) correlated with symptoms of depression and anxiety (Borgogna et al., 2020). In another recent study, this time among community adults with a history of trauma, experiential avoidance was strongly (and positively) linked to trauma symptoms (Bishop et al., 2018). Finally, in a recent study among military couples, experiential avoidance was moderately (and negatively) correlated with marital quality (Zamir et al., 2018).

Thus far, this growing literature reveals that experiential avoidance is often positively linked to psychopathology in general, as well as depressive, anxiety, and trauma symptoms and relational distress in particular, which is helpful for conceptualizing suffering clients in counseling and therapy. In other words, experiential avoidance can assist counselors and therapists in better understanding the difference between symptoms and problems, conditions, and disorders—although clients' symptoms may persist, attempting to avoid such symptoms can lead to a plethora of forms of psychopathology.

As another type of investigation, experiential avoidance has been examined as a mediating influence, explaining the relationship between a variety of psychological variables and psychopathology. For example, in a review of the literature, Boulanger et al. (2010) found that experiential avoidance mediated the association between pain and psychopathology, emotional reactivity and psychopathology, and environmental stressors and psychopathology. As another example, among a community sample of adult men, findings revealed that experiential avoidance mediated the relationship between gender role conflict and psychological distress (Spendelow & Joubert, 2018). This emerging research base suggests that, beyond merely functioning as a correlate of psychopathology in general, experiential avoidance helps to explain the link between an assortment of psychological variables and disordered functioning.

In addition to studying the association between experiential avoidance and general psychopathology, of late, researchers have examined the relationship between this variable and emotional distress and mental health. Cristea et al. (2013) explored the link between experiential avoidance and emotional distress, revealing a strong correlation among both student and clinical samples. Moreover, the authors investigated experiential avoidance as a mediating variable, with results suggesting that experiential avoidance mediated the relationship between global irrationality and dysfunctional attitudes and emotional distress for both college students and clients with generalized anxiety disorder. Also, in a study exploring the relationship between experiential avoidance and mental health among a clinical population, Fledderus et al. (2010) found that experiential avoidance mediated the association between passive coping and emotional and psychological well-being.

Beyond empirical investigations that link experiential avoidance and general psychopathology, emotional distress, and mental health, several authors have offered theoretical rationales for explaining how the tendency to avoid unpleasant inner experiences is central to psychological suffering, including depressive, anxiety, and trauma-related disorders and relationship distress. Smith and Alloy (2009), for example, recently reviewed several theories of *rumination*, a common feature of depression, highlighting that those with depressed mood may ruminate in order to avoid distressing emotions, ultimately exacerbating an already depressed state. Zettle (2007), moreover, suggested that rumination involves attempts to consistently answer questions about the meaning of depression so as to ameliorate a depressed mood. Presumably, by figuring out the cause of prolonged dysphoria, individuals going through depressive episodes are attempting to evaluate the experience in order to control and remedy it. Yet, this strategy seldom works, only heightening suffering when the low mood does not permanently go away.

On the other hand, *ironic processes theory* captures the role that attempting to suppress negative thoughts, rather than rumination, plays in depression (Beevers et al., 1999; Wenzlaff et al., 2001). In this theory, individuals employ a searching strategy to identify negative thoughts, seeking to shift the focus away from negative cognitions when they arise (Beevers et al., 1999; Wenzlaff et al., 2001). Unfortunately, this process malfunctions, breaking down for depressed clients. Viewed through the lens of experiential avoidance, thought suppression is an attempt to maintain a "happy" state, avoiding negative thoughts that seemingly lead to a depressed mood. Even so, for depressed clients, cognitive resources are limited, which prevents this two-pronged cognitive process from working optimally. Also, clients' distraction efforts are not always effective, undermining attempts to fully avoid negative thoughts (Beevers et al., 1999). Whether clients are engaged in rumination or suppression, the goal appears to be the same—attempting to avoid unpleasant inner experiences.

Along with rumination and thought suppression, some authors have highlighted that drugs, alcohol, social isolation, and, ultimately, suicide may be forms of avoidance, utilized by depressed clients during moments of distress

(Hayes et al., 2012; Zettle, 2007). Of course, drugs and alcohol can serve to numb psychological pain. Still, they create a whole host of additional problems, one of which is that the use of substances prevents the individual from living out a set of well-defined values. With social isolation, depressed clients may be attempting to avoid perceived dangerous experiences (Zettle, 2007). Stated differently, along with seeking to avoid the distressing experience of dysphoria, depressed individuals may shut down, both psychologically and physically, in order to sidestep anticipated risky psychological encounters in their environment. Finally, suicide, viewed through the lens of experiential avoidance, appears to involve attempts to permanently avoid prolonged suffering through the final act of ending one's life (Hayes et al., 2012).

For anxiety disorders, some theorists have conceptualized worry as a form of avoidance. With *cognitive avoidance theory*, for instance, clients tend to employ worry as a way to ameliorate a future threat or catastrophe, utilizing thinking to problem-solve an anticipated doomsday scenario, especially when an effective behavioral strategy to remove the threat is not available (Borkovec et al., 2004). In essence, there is a sense of perceived control in using cognition as a vehicle through which to actively respond to an uncertain future. Also, cognitive avoidance theory suggests that worrying serves the purpose of attempting to reduce the physiological experience of anxiety (Borkovec et al., 2004). As a result, clients try to avoid the unpleasant, somatic feeling of anxiety-related symptoms through repeatedly worrying about the future (Borkovec et al., 2004). This process seems to capture experiential avoidance, given that clients may strive to eliminate the experience of anxiety, rather than accepting its inevitability, through the cognitive exercise of recurrent worry.

On top of cognitive avoidance, recent authors have argued that individuals with anxiety disorders struggle with *intolerance of uncertainty* (Dugas & Robichaud, 2007). In this theory, which has also been applied to depressive disorders (Mahoney & McEvoy, 2012), clients have a difficult time accepting uncertainty, leading to attempts to either obtain certainty (e.g., repetitive checking behaviors, seeking reassurance) or avoid the situation (e.g., withdrawal, procrastination) if attaining certainty is not possible (Dugas & Robichaud, 2007). Of course, this theory seems to point to experiential avoidance, in that clients continuously try to avoid the inevitability of uncertainty, along with the accompanying anxiety, utilizing control as a way to secure a certain, predictable future.

Eifert and Forsyth (2005) argued that avoidance is a core feature of all anxiety disorders, given that these conditions involve efforts to escape from anxiety symptoms. In other words, clients struggle with fear about their symptoms, leading to efforts to avoid the inner (e.g., thoughts, feelings, sensations, memories), as well as corresponding outer (e.g., uncertain situations), world. With generalized anxiety, for example, clients may attempt to employ worry to both reduce the physiological sensation of anxiety and attain certainty and predictability when faced with an unknown future. In terms of *panic disorder*, clients commonly try to avoid future panic attacks, constantly monitoring physiological symptoms and isolating themselves in an effort to reduce the likelihood of panic-related public embarrassment. Finally, for *social phobia*, clients tend to avoid interpersonal interactions because they fear they will be rejected, scrutinized, or embarrassed, believing that withdrawal from the social world will help to manage anxiety symptoms. Certainly, in all of these scenarios, avoidance seems to be a central feature, with clients seeking a short-term solution (e.g., the elimination of inner distress) at the expense of long-term functioning in the real world.

Turning to trauma-related disorders, *posttraumatic stress disorder* (PTSD) often includes avoidance, given trauma survivors commonly attempt to avoid reminders of the traumatic event in both the inner (e.g., intrusive memories) and outer (e.g., environmental reminders) world (Lewis & Naugle, 2017; Walser & Westrup, 2007). In doing so, however, daily functioning can quickly become impaired, which includes the pursuit of well-defined values, given the effort devoted to reduce, eliminate, avoid, or distract from these reminders (Lewis & Naugle, 2017; Walser & Westrup, 2007). Although it certainly makes sense that, given the potentially life-threatening situation the trauma survivor has been through, avoidance seems like the only solution, avoiding psychological pain is prioritized over fully engaging with life and living out a set of values.

With regard to relationship distress with a spouse or intimate partner, couples in conflict may use behavioral avoidance as a way to reduce, eliminate, avoid, or distract from difficult relational schemas (and schema-related emotional pain), which can be defined as the stories that people slowly develop from childhood onward, carry with them throughout life, and use to make sense of their relationships with others (Lev & McKay, 2012). Themes linked to these rigid schemas, which can focus on the self, others, or relationships, may include the notion that the individual will be abandoned, abused, neglected, or viewed as a failure by others (Lev & McKay, 2012). Ultimately, couple conflict may trigger relational schemas, which result in painful emotions, then behaviors to reduce, eliminate, avoid, or distract from the emerging difficult thoughts and feelings (Lev & McKay, 2012). Over time, couples may experience both the initial pain (e.g., relational schemas, painful emotions that emanate from the relational schemas) and additional pain because they are avoiding their relationship and missing out on the intimacy and closeness they long for (Lev & McKay, 2012).

In terms of faith integration, I have published original research on experiential avoidance and psychospiritual functioning, beyond solely focusing on psychological correlates of the experiential avoidance construct. In the first of three studies, I explored the relationship between an unwillingness to tolerate unpleasant inner experiences (i.e., experiential avoidance), orthodox Christian beliefs (e.g., Jesus's divinity, Jesus's virgin birth, Jesus's resurrection, Jesus's atoning work for salvation, the Bible as God's word), and self-sacrificial behaviors (e.g., giving time and money to others, showing love to others, sharing the gospel message with others) among a sample of Christian college students (Knabb et al., 2014). Findings elucidated that experiential avoidance was negatively correlated with orthodox Christian beliefs, which were positively linked to self-sacrificial Christian behaviors. Also, distress endurance, a component of experiential avoidance, was positively associated with faith maturity, suggesting that the Christians in this study who accepted inner distress, pushing forward despite psychological pain, endorsed a higher level of maturity in their relationship with God and others (Knabb et al., 2014).

In a separate study among Christian college students, I found that those who struggled with utilizing God as a source of support during moments of adversity were more likely to experience psychological distress (Knabb & Grigorian-Routon, 2014). This positive link between negative religious coping and psychological distress, moreover, was partially explained (i.e., mediated) by Christians' willingness to tolerate unpleasant inner experiences. In other words, Christians who used negative religious coping strategies tended to report a higher level of depression, anxiety, and stress. Also, Christians who relied on negative religious coping strategies were more likely to employ experiential avoidance. Finally, Christians who reported utilizing avoidance as a coping strategy tended to indicate they suffered from a higher level of depression, anxiety, and stress.

In one more study, this time among community Christian adults, I found a positive relationship between experiential avoidance and communion with God, with the latter defined as a mutual, intimate friendship with God that is pursued and maintained through prayer, meditation, and Bible study (Knabb & Wang, 2021). Although this positive link was initially surprising, it may make sense when examining communion with God as a dependent variable. In other words, when Christians struggle with experiential avoidance, they may turn to God for support, drawing upon this friendship in their time of need.

To offer a concluding example, among a sample of community adults, Dworsky et al. (2016) uncovered a positive link between experiential avoidance and spiritual struggles (e.g., feeling abandoned by God, feeling like life is meaningless). What is more, experiential avoidance moderated the relationship between spiritual struggles and depression and anxiety (Dworsky et al., 2016). These findings suggest that experiential avoidance may play an important role in the spiritual struggles of religious adults.

To summarize, in the past several decades, both theorists and researchers have argued that avoidance plays a central role in the maintenance of psychopathology, with an unwillingness to accept painful experiences in the inner world and corresponding efforts to behaviorally avoid situations and relationships in the outer word, rather than the mere presence of symptoms, leading to disordered functioning. Once psychometrically sound measures (e.g., the AAQ, AAQ-II, MEAQ, and BEAQ) were developed, researchers began to empirically investigate the correlation between experiential avoidance and general psychopathology, along with experiential avoidance as a mediating influence for explaining the link between a range of psychological variables and negative mental health outcomes. Avoidance has also been conceptualized as a central problem for depression, anxiety, trauma, and relationship distress. Unfortunately, avoidance seldom offers a permanent solution, commonly leaving clients frustrated, confused, and hopeless, especially since they have likely exhausted a range of efforts to eradicate psychological suffering.

For Christian clients, experiential avoidance may play an important role in faith-based counseling and therapy, serving as a foundational construct, especially given that the aforementioned research has revealed that this variable is linked to general psychopathology, Christian beliefs, and negative religious coping. To be sure, Christians who endure psychological suffering, despite painful thoughts, feelings, sensations, and memories, may be more likely to live out their faith with God and others, walking with God in love from moment to moment. Therefore, in the next chapter, I present a faith-based, integrative treatment approach to ameliorate experiential avoidance for Christian clients suffering from psychological problems, conditions, and disorders, drawing on acceptance and commitment therapy (ACT) and the Christian faith. In the remainder of the chapter, though, I present clinical and biblical examples of experiential avoidance and a way to conceptualize clients' transition from avoidance to acceptance, all in an effort to deepen an understanding of experiential avoidance in faith-based counseling and therapy.

Desperately Trying to Escape Psychological Pain: A Clinical Illustration of Experiential Avoidance

Rachel, a 46-year-old, divorced, Black female, came to therapy stating she was experiencing overwhelming anxiety at work. Over the years, she had developed a thriving accounting business, making a six-figure salary and living in an upper middle-class neighborhood. For Rachel, growing her business was always a dream, especially after going through a painful divorce about a decade earlier. With no children, Rachel believed she was well on her way to ensuring occupational success. Yet, as her business grew, so did her level of anxiety.

After an intake interview, her therapist diagnosed her with generalized anxiety disorder, given that Rachel reported recurrent worry from one area of life to the next, trouble managing her worry, and a variety of other anxiety symptoms, including muscle tension and fatigue. What is more, she frequently avoided life in an effort to try to control her worry, canceling appointments and isolating herself in her apartment for days on end. Because of her impaired functioning, her primary care physician prescribed an anti-anxiety medication, Klonopin, which seemed to relieve her symptoms for a short period. Still, over time, she built up a tolerance for the medication, needing more and more to achieve the same results. Rachel would frequently run out of pills because she took more than prescribed, desperately trying to achieve the same tranquil, relaxed state she initially experienced when she started her medication regimen. Unfortunately, when out of her medication, she would experience severe withdrawal symptoms, which would further impair her functioning, leading to tremendous suffering. Indeed, over the course of a few months, she experienced compounded distress, including the initial symptoms, coupled with medication withdrawal symptoms and impaired functioning. This experience, of course, led to additional pain, resulting in a sort of snowball effect. Simply put, Rachel felt out of control.

For Rachel, life without medication seemed unbearable. Yet, attempting to numb her anxiety with psychotropic medication and isolation when her symptoms would flare up created a whole host of problems, beyond the initial experience of recurrent anxiety. Because of this, she decided to work with her physician to taper off the medication, as well as find an alternative way to relate to her anxiety—avoidance, whether through medication or behavioral with-drawal, was not working. In therapy, Rachel learned that attempting to avoid her worry was the problem, rather than the mere presence of anxiety symptoms, leading to frantic efforts to eradicate the pain. Turning to medication, she sought some sort of permanent relief, which never came.

Over the course of the next few months, she tapered off the Klonopin and began to relate differently to her worry, recognizing that her anxiety symptoms were a normal reaction to a thriving, though sometimes overwhelming, accounting business. By trying to eliminate the pain via avoidance behaviors, her symptoms led to a formal DSM-5 diagnosis—generalized anxiety disorder—because she originally believed that she could not live life as long as they were present. Also, taking powerful, habit-forming medication, focusing on short-term symptom relief, led to impaired occupational functioning in the long run. On the other hand, slowly learning to accept the ubiquity of anxiety, viewing anxiety-related inner experiences as a normal, natural part of the ups and downs of the business world, helped Rachel to continue to function in spite of her psychological pain.

Covering Up and Hiding in Fear and Shame: Experiential Avoidance in the Bible

In the Book of Genesis, Adam and Eve famously ate from the tree of the knowledge of good and evil, which God had commanded them not to do, leading to the ubiquitous consequences of death, banishment from the Garden, and separation from God (Genesis 2–3). Before partaking of the tree of knowledge, Adam and Eve were naked and innocent and experienced no shame. Yet, when they ate the fruit from the forbidden tree, the "eyes of both of them were opened" (*New International Version Bible*, 2011), leading to the recognition that they were both exposed. As a result, they made clothes to cover up, hiding from God in their state of distress (Hayes et al., 2012; Knabb et al., 2010).

Interestingly, this biblical account of the origin of humankind may help to better understand the dilemma of experiential avoidance, originating from Genesis. For Adam and Eve, hiding seemed necessary because they were afraid, recognizing they were fully exposed and likely leading to the moral evaluation that being naked was "bad" or "wrong." Based on their newly acquired "knowledge," derived from eating the forbidden fruit, they noticed their vulnerable state and reached for a layer of clothing to ameliorate their distress. In other words, this story may capture the first human experience of avoidance as an ineffective coping strategy, responding to painful emotions (e.g., fear, shame) through withdrawing, covering up, and hiding.

Like Adam and Eve, with Christian clients in the 21st century, experiential avoidance may not only involve attempts to withdraw or distract from inner distress, but also efforts to avoid God, hiding from God in the proverbial garden. Yet, from a Christian perspective, the antidote to lonely, isolated suffering involves inviting God into the experience, rather than trying to unilaterally make it go away. Stated differently, surrendering to God's will, recognizing that humans can never truly run from God, may help to relate to suffering in a different way. Overall, for Adam and Eve, God clothed them in their naked, vulnerable state, suggesting that he is compassionate, forgiving, and responsive, even in the midst of human suffering (Bonhoeffer, 1959). This account of the dilemma of human knowledge, derived from eating the forbidden fruit, is further explored in the next chapter. Until then, what follows is a strategy for helping clients to transition from avoidance to acceptance, combining insights from counseling and therapy with a biblical view of surrender.

Creative Hopelessness in the Presence of God: A Strategy for Shifting from Avoidance to Acceptance

Drawing from the ACT literature, Hayes et al. (2012) suggested that *creative hopelessness* involves clients' awareness that attempting to control the inner world, via experiential avoidance strategies, has not worked. For many clients, these efforts to reduce, eliminate, avoid, or distract from psychological pain have not yielded lasting results. Instead, they end up creating additional pain, exhaustion, fatigue, and frustration. When all of their prior avoidance behaviors are systematically explored, clients begin to realize that experiential avoidance is the problem, rather than the solution. Once this paradigm shift in awareness occurs, clients can begin to open up to new, more creative ways of relating to symptoms, which involves experiential acceptance as an alternative strategy. In other words, rather than trying to fight against symptoms in an effort to get the life they want, clients can start to view unpleasant inner experiences as a normal, ubiquitous part of life—inner states wax, wane, come, and go, and relating to them with more gentleness, curiosity, openness, and flexibility can help to shift the focus toward living a life of substance, authenticity, deeper meaning, and values.

Among many Christian clients, creative hopelessness seems to capture a positive shift in the way they relate to symptoms through surrendering to God's providence (i.e., good governance, protective care; Erickson, 2013). Similar to Jesus's teaching in the Sermon on the Mount (Matthew 6:25–34) that emphasized God's sovereign responsiveness as an antidote to worry, Christian clients can begin to recognize that they do not need to fear inner symptoms because God is always present. Worded differently, God is sovereign over humans' intrapsychic world, which suggests that Christian clients can relinquish their own control efforts, by way of experiential avoidance, to futilely eliminate psychological distress. Similar to God providing for the "flowers of the field" and the "birds of the air" (*New International Version Bible*, 2011, Matthew 6:25–34), those who trust in Jesus can surrender to his control, letting go of their own strivings because he is benevolent, sovereign, and actively present in the life of Christian clients.

In sum, with Christian clients, creative hopelessness involves recognizing that efforts to unilaterally control their inner world, apart from God, have led to *both* symptoms *and* disordered functioning. Conversely, accepting the inner world, letting go of fruitless control efforts because God is sovereign, can help to pivot from experiential avoidance to experiential acceptance. In essence, Jesus's teaching on worry elucidates that the antidote to a futile control agenda involves trustfully surrendering to God's protective care (Colombiere, 1983). What follows is a clinical example of moving from avoidance to acceptance, inviting God into the experience.

Learning to Lean on God: A Clinical Example of Experiential Acceptance

Steven was a 38-year-old, married, White male, presenting to therapy because of marital discord, reporting that his wife was threatening to move out of the house because he was emotionally withdrawn and unavailable. In recent years, his drinking had become unmanageable, turning to alcohol to deal with recurrent anxiety, which was related to his perception that his wife would eventually leave him. During moments of escalation with his spouse, Steven would frequently become overwhelmed with anxiety, followed by excessive drinking and withdrawal for days on end. In these instances of despair, Steven would also attempt to hide from God, stopping his daily ritual of prayer and Bible study, believing God was judging him, like his wife.

Growing up, Steven experienced neglect in his household, with his parents constantly devoting time and energy to his younger sister, who had a terminal illness. As a result, he developed low self-esteem, struggling to trust that loved ones would be there for him in his time of need. Over time, Steven also began to experience recurrent anxiety, worrying that his wife would leave him because he was inherently unlovable. Because of these reverberations from childhood, Steven was convinced it was only a matter of time before his world would fall apart and, thus, increasingly used avoidance strategies to try to bury his distress. In other words, to manage his anxiety, he employed unhelpful avoidance behaviors, which only exacerbated his suffering by preventing him from facing his troubled marriage.

In therapy, Steven worked on accepting his anxiety, recognizing that it was a wound from childhood that may never fully go away, inviting God into the experience. A common metaphor used in treatment, Steven referred to the transition from avoidance to acceptance as learning to "walk with a limp," recognizing that the pain helped him to remember what he valued most—authentic, meaningful connections with others, especially his wife. During moments of anxiety, Steven learned to allow the anxiety to simply be, without judging it, recognizing that he did not need to withdraw through alcohol misuse or behavioral isolation. By accepting his anxiety, Steven's symptoms did not inevitably lead to disordered functioning. In fact, when anxious, Steven developed a habit of visualizing himself reaching for God, with God giving him the stability to continue on, supporting him as he walked with a "wounded leg."

Paul in Chains: A Biblical Case of Experiential Acceptance

In Paul's famous letter to the Philippian church, he explained to his audience at Philippi that his imprisonment would actually "advance the gospel," given that the guards knew he was "in chains for Christ" and that other followers of Jesus were able to "proclaim the gospel without fear" because of Paul's predicament (*New International Version Bible*, 2011, Philippians 1:12–30). Originally jailed because of accusations of engaging in "unlawful customs" among Roman citizens (*New International Version Bible*, 2011, Acts 16), Paul seemed to be attempting to provide his audience with a meaning for the suffering he endured in prison, pointing to opportunities to share the gospel message with his captors, along with emboldening those who had received word that Paul was suffering for Christ (Craddock, 1985).

For Paul, imprisonment led to rejoicing, rather than withdrawing or shutting down in the midst of pain and hardship. In other words, Paul saw his experience as an opportunity to "suffer for [Christ]" (*New International Version Bible*, 2011, Philippians 1:29), actively promoting the gospel message, rather than allowing suffering to lead to disordered functioning. Above all else, "how special is the gift of being identified with Christ in suffering" (Craddock, 1985, p. 34), which can help Christian clients to transition from experiential avoidance to experiential acceptance. For Christian clients, experiential acceptance involves recognizing that suffering with Christ allows them to endure, even in the midst of tremendous psychological pain. Just as Paul reinterpreted his suffering as a source of joy, seeking the opportunity to share his message with guards and motivating others to continue on, Christian clients can learn to accept, rather than fight against or distract from, unpleasant thoughts, feelings, sensations, and memories. Instead of letting his suffering turn to disordered functioning, Paul was able to reframe his experience, pressing forward to accomplish his ultimate goal—following and serving Jesus in love.

Conclusion

In this chapter, the experiential avoidance construct was explored, which can help to better understand the link between symptoms and disordered functioning in faith-based counseling and therapy. In other words, the mere presence of symptoms does not inevitably lead to a problem, condition, or disorder. Instead, clients' struggle with making room for psychological pain plays an important role in determining whether or not they go on to experience impairment in functioning. For Christian clients, the Bible is filled with examples of characters who faithfully endured, carrying their distress with them as they pursued God's will. In the remainder of the book, I present an integrative approach, combining ACT and the Christian tradition, to help Christian clients cultivate experiential acceptance in the midst of suffering so as to ameliorate disordered functioning and more effectively follow Jesus.

References

Beevers, C., Wenzlaff, R., Hayes, A., & Scott, W. (1999). Depression and the ironic effects of thought suppression: Therapeutic strategies for improving mental control. *Clinical Psychology: Sciences and Practice, 6*, 133–148.

Bishop, L, Ameral, V., & Palm Reed, K. (2018). The impact of experiential avoidance and event centrality in trauma-related rumination and posttraumatic stress. *Behavior Modification, 42*, 815–837.

Bond, F., Hayes, S., Baer, R., Carpenter, K., Guenole, N., Orcutt, H., Waltz, T., & Zettle, R. (2011). Preliminary psychometric properties of the acceptance and action questionnaire-II: A revised measure of psychological inflexibility and experiential avoidance. *Behavior Therapy, 42*, 676–688.

Bonhoeffer, D. (1959). *Creation and fall.* Touchstone.

Borgogna, N., McDermott, R., Berry, A., Lathan, E., & Gonzales, J. (2020). A multicultural examination of experiential avoidance: AAQ-II measurement comparisons across Asian American, Black, Latinx, Middle Eastern, and White college students. *Journal of Contextual Behavioral Science, 16*, 1–8.

Borkovec, T., Alcaine, O., & Behar, E. (2004). Avoidance theory of worry and generalized anxiety disorder. In R. Heimberg, C. Turk, & D. Mennin (Eds.), *Generalized anxiety disorder: Advances in research and practice* (pp. 77–108). The Guilford Press.

Boulanger, J., Hayes, S., & Pistorello, J. (2010). Experiential avoidance as a functional contextual concept. In A. Kring & D. Sloan (Eds.), *Emotion regulation and psychopathology: A transdiagnostic approach to etiology and treatment* (pp. 107–136). The Guilford Press.

Chawla, N., & Ostafin, B. (2007). Experiential avoidance as a functional dimensional approach to psychopathology: An empirical review. *Journal of Clinical Psychology, 63*, 871–890.

Colombiere, C. (1983). *Trustful surrender to divine providence*. Tan Books.

Craddock, F. (1985). *Philippians: A Bible commentary for preaching and teaching*. Westminster John Knox Press.

Cristea, I., Montgomery, G., Szamoskozi, S., & David, D. (2013). Key constructs in "classical" and "new wave" cognitive behavioral psychotherapies: Relationships among each other and with emotional distress. *Journal of Clinical Psychology, 69*, 584–599.

Dugas, M., & Robichaud, M. (2007). *Cognitive-behavioral treatment for generalized anxiety disorder: From science to practice*. Routledge.

Dworsky, C., Pargament, K., Wong, S., & Exline, J. (2016). Suppressing spiritual struggles: The role of experiential avoidance in mental health. *Journal of Contextual Behavioral Science, 5*, 258–265.

Eifert, G., & Forsyth, J. (2005). *Acceptance & commitment therapy for anxiety disorders: A practitioner's treatment guide to using mindfulness, acceptance, and values-based behavior change strategies*. New Harbinger Publications, Inc.

Erickson, M. (2013). *Christian theology* (3rd ed.). Baker Academic.

Fledderus, M., Bohlmeijer, E., & Pieterse, M. (2010). Does experiential avoidance mediate the effects of maladaptive coping styles on psychopathology and mental health? *Behavior Modification, 34*, 503–519.

Gamez, W., Chmielewski, M., Kotov, R., Ruggero, C., & Watson, D. (2011). Development of a measure of experiential avoidance: The multidimensional experiential avoidance questionnaire. *Psychological Assessment, 23*, 692–713.

Hayes, S., Luoma, J., Bond, F., Masuda, A., & Lillis, J. (2006). Acceptance and commitment therapy: Model, processes and outcomes. *Behaviour Research and Therapy, 44*, 1–25.

Hayes, S., Strosahl, K., & Wilson, K. (2012). *Acceptance and commitment therapy: The process and practice of mindful change* (2nd ed.). The Guilford Press.

Hayes, S., Strosahl, K., Wilson, K., Bissett, R., Pistorello, J., & Toarmino, D., & McCurry, S.M. (2004). Measuring experiential avoidance: A preliminary test of a working model. *The Psychological Record, 54*, 553–578.

Hayes, S., Wilson, K., Gifford, E., Follette, V., & Strosahl, K. (1996). Experiential avoidance and behavioral disorders: A functional dimensional approach to diagnosis and treatment. *Journal of Consulting and Clinical Psychology, 64*, 1152–1168.

Knabb, J., & Grigorian-Routon, A. (2014). The role of experiential avoidance in the relationship between faith maturity, religious coping, and psychological adjustment among Christian university students. *Mental Health, Religion & Culture, 17*, 458–469.

Knabb, J., & Wang, K. (2021). The communion with God scale: Shifting from an etic ot emic perspective to assess fellowshipping with the Triune God. *Psychology of Religion and Spirituality, 13*, 67–80.

Knabb, J., Ashby, J., & Ziebell, J. (2010). Two sides of the same coin: The theology of Dietrich Bonhoeffer and acceptance and commitment therapy (ACT). *Journal of Spirituality in Mental Health, 12*, 150–180.

Knabb, J., Pelletier, J., & Grigorian-Routon, A. (2014). Towards a psychological understanding of servanthood: An empirical investigation of the relationship between orthodox beliefs, experiential avoidance, and self-sacrificial behaviors among Christians at a religiously-affiliated university. *Journal of Psychology and Theology, 42*, 269–283.

Lev, A., & McKay, M. (2012). *Acceptance and commitment therapy for couples: A clinician's guide to using mindfulness, values & schema awareness to rebuild relationships.* New Harbinger Publications, Inc.

Lewis, M., & Naugle, A. (2017). Measuring experiential avoidance: Evidence toward multidimensional predictors of trauma sequelae. *Behavioral Sciences, 7,* 2–11.

Mahoney, A., & McEvoy, P. (2012). A transdiagnostic examination of intolerance of uncertainty across anxiety and depressive disorders. *Cognitive Behaviour Therapy, 41,* 212–222.

New International Version Bible. (2011). Zondervan. https://www.biblegateway.com/

Smith, J., & Alloy, L. (2009). A roadmap to rumination: A review of the definition, assessment, and conceptualization of this multifaceted construct. *Clinical Psychology Review, 29,* 116–128.

Spendelow, J., & Joubert, E. (2018). Does experiential avoidance mediate the relationship between gender role conflict and psychological distress. *American Journal of Men's Health, 12,* 688–695.

Walser, R., & Westrup, D. (2007). *Acceptance & commitment therapy for the treatment of post-traumatic stress disorder & trauma-related problems: A practitioner's guide to using mindfulness & acceptance strategies.* New Harbinger Publications, Inc.

Wenzlaff, R., Rude, S., Taylor, C., Stultz, C., & Sweatt, R. (2001). Beneath the veil of thought suppression: Attentional bias and depression risk. *Cognition and Emotion, 15,* 435–452.

Zamir, O., Gewirtz, A., Labella, M., DeGarmo, D., & Snyder, J. (2018). Experiential avoidance, dyadic interaction and relationship quality in the lives of veterans and their partners. *Journal of Family Issues, 39,* 1191–1212.

Zettle, R. (2007). *ACT for depression. A clinician's guide to using acceptance & commitment therapy in treating depression.* New Harbinger Publications, Inc.

4

FAITH-BASED ACT FOR CHRISTIAN SUFFERING

Introduction

In this chapter, acceptance and commitment therapy (ACT)[1] is presented, which can help clients to cultivate psychological flexibility in order to live a meaningful life, guided by values, rather than psychological pain. More specifically, the six processes of ACT are reviewed for counselors and therapists, including the four mindfulness-based processes—*acceptance, cognitive defusion, the transcendent self,*[2] and *present-moment awareness*—that help clients to develop acceptance of painful thoughts, feelings, sensations, and memories and two action-based processes—*values* and *committed action*. Mindfulness, commonly derived from Buddhist teachings and widely popular in the 21st century psychology literature, is embedded in a variety of newer counseling and therapy approaches and helps clients relate to psychological symptoms with acceptance, nonjudgment, openness, and curiosity. These six processes are integrated with equivalent concepts in Christianity, drawing primarily from the contemplative tradition for the acceptance-based processes and life and teachings of Jesus for the action-based processes. The six Christian processes, which parallel ACT's six processes, are watchfulness (i.e., *nepsis* in Greek), endurance (i.e., *hupomone* in Greek), the contemplative self (i.e., the *nous* in Greek), practicing God's presence (i.e., *hesychia* in Greek), biblical virtues,[3] and following Jesus. These six integrative processes can help counselors and therapists work more effectively with Christian clients to relate to painful inner experiences with flexibility, rather than using unhelpful avoidance strategies, in order to focus on following Jesus (i.e., walk with God in love), a central aim in the Christian life.

Ultimately, the faith-based version of ACT presented in this chapter and further explored in subsequent chapters in this book is about helping Christian clients to ACT on God's love from the outside-in to the inside-out, with Christian clients functioning as a dwelling place (i.e., conduit, channel, vehicle, vessel, medium) for God's love as they interact with God and others to create a life of meaning, purpose, intentionality, and vitality. Worded differently, faith-based ACT is about helping Christian clients to recognize that the God of love is dwelling within their proverbial "house." As a result, the *telos* (i.e., ultimate

DOI: 10.4324/9781003181941-5

purpose, design, aim, end) of life is to be filled with, and guided by, God's perfect love, which, in turn, is extended to others, not wavering thoughts, feelings, sensations, and memories. Like sharing a house with several roommates, some of whom are noisy, inconsiderate, and overly self-focused, a central question is as follows: "Who will be the 'head of the house,' my noisy roommates or God?"

ACT: Preliminary Considerations

ACT emerged roughly four decades ago, initially with a workshop in the early 1980s, followed by the first ACT study in 1986, about a decade of research on its theoretical foundations, and the publication of several *randomized controlled trials* (RCTs) in psychology literature at the turn of the 21st century (S. Hayes, personal communication, December 7, 2014). Since then, ACT has been applied to a variety of psychological problems, conditions, and disorders, especially those that involve some form of avoidance behavior (Gloster et al., 2020). With the launch of the first edition of the textbook by the same name (Hayes et al., 1999), the popularity of this unique combination of acceptance and value-based action in the counseling and therapy room began to grow. Currently, the American Psychological Association's (APA) Division 12 (Society for Clinical Psychology) lists ACT as an evidence-based practice with strong research support for chronic pain and modest research support for obsessive-compulsive disorder, depression, mixed anxiety disorders, and psychosis.[1] Overall, ACT is included in the larger family of cognitive behavioral therapies, with some authors referring to ACT as the "third wave" of cognitive behavioral therapy (CBT)—as opposed to traditional CBT, considered the "second wave"—because of the addition of mindfulness and acceptance-based strategies (Hayes, 2004).

ACT integrates six processes in order to help clients relate to inner experiences with more openness, flexibility, compassion, and kindness, while, at the same time, identify and commit to a set of actions, anchored to values that serve as a guide for daily life. In other words, thoughts, feelings, sensations, and memories tend to fluctuate and change on a day-to-day basis. Because of this, they do not always offer a reliable navigation system for life's adversities. Instead, a set of values, emanating from the heart, can serve as a guide in ways that wavering inner experiences cannot. Unfortunately, when clients experience psychological pain, they tend to lose focus on what matters most in life and rigidly try to avoid this pain through a narrow range of behaviors that are often incongruent with their values. Therefore, having a firm grasp on their values, along with a set of strategies to relate to unpleasant thoughts, feelings, sensations, and memories with more acceptance, rather than avoidance, can help clients to live a fulfilling, meaningful life.

In ACT, clients learn the *ACT* acronym, which is easy to remember and involves accepting thoughts, feelings, sensations, and memories ("A"), committing to a value-based direction ("C"), and taking effective action by engaging in behaviors that help to pursue deeply held values ("T") (Harris, 2007). At its core, ACT seeks to cultivate psychological flexibility, which consists of the ability to be *open* to each and every experience in the inner world (with the acceptance and cognitive defusion processes), *aware* of what is unfolding in the inner and outer world in the here-and-now (with the transcendent self and present-moment awareness processes), and fully *engaged* with life in an effort to live out a set of personally chosen values (with the values and committed action processes) (Walser, 2019). Notice, here, that *happiness* is not emphasized within ACT. Of course, happiness most certainly can be a byproduct of living a life devoted to actions anchored to well-defined values. Still, an enriching, vibrant life is not always synonymous with "happiness" or "pleasure."

In fact, happiness seems to be rather elusive in 21st-century America. From 2017 to 2019, the United States (U.S.) ranked 18th among a list of 153 nations in the *World Happiness Report*.[5] This report used polling and survey data to rank the happiness and well-being of countries from around the world. Despite being the wealthiest, most powerful, and advanced nation on the planet, the U.S. was apparently unable to secure a "top ten" spot. This finding is even more surprising when considering the advancements that have been made with medicine and healthcare, including mental healthcare. For instance, in a recent study, two antidepressants, Sertraline and Fluoxetine, were ranked among the top 20 most prescribed medications in the U.S. (Fuentes et al., 2018).

These results beg a fundamental question asked throughout this book: "What if *happiness*, a pleasant emotion that comes and goes, is not the goal for Christian clients in counseling and therapy?" In this chapter, I present the six processes of ACT, aligning them with the Christian contemplative tradition in an attempt to understand an alternative way for Christian clients to live life, beyond chasing happiness as the proverbial carrot dangling from the end of a stick. In subsequent chapters, I identify specific metaphors, strategies, and biblical examples to apply the six processes of ACT to daily client struggles, including depression, anxiety, trauma, and relationship distress. Before I turn to the actual six processes, though, it is important to first unpack ACT's views on the link between language and human suffering, drawing a parallel with the Christian contemplative tradition.

Language and Human Suffering: ACT and Christian Perspectives[6]

In their seminal ACT textbook, Hayes et al. (1999) devoted several pages to the fall of humankind in Genesis 3, arguing through this narrative that language leads to a sizeable amount of human suffering. Originally, Adam and Eve were both innocent and dependent upon God in the Garden of Eden. Before their banishment from the Garden, Adam and Eve certainly did not suffer in their daily lives. Yet, when tempted by the serpent, they ate from the "tree of the knowledge of good and evil," striving to be like God in knowing good and evil, rather than fully dependent on him. After they ate the forbidden fruit, they recognized that they were naked, covered up and hid from God, and experienced shame because of their separation from him. Through this newly acquired "knowledge of good and evil," Adam and Eve lost both their innocence and connection with their source of life, God.

From an ACT perspective, this ability to apply "knowledge of good and evil" to daily life has both benefits and costs, helping human beings to improve the outer world (e.g., establishing and enforcing societal laws), while, at the same time, exacerbating suffering in the inner world through the constant evaluation of psychological experiences.[7] Because of the cognitive ability to differentiate, prioritize, sort, organize, categorize, label, evaluate, and judge psychological experiences through the use of language, humans tend to add on an additional layer of suffering. Stated differently, not only are humans directly affected by psychological pain, the mind also evaluates these inner experiences through the tool of language. This evaluative function, although helpful in many areas of life, causes additional suffering in Christian clients' day-to-day efforts to follow Jesus while in psychological pain: "I shouldn't feel depressed," a Christian client may say, or "I can't serve in my church because I have social anxiety."

This constant inner dialogue, on top of the actual symptoms, can serve as a barrier to effective action. In other words, the mind uses this "knowledge of good and evil" to evaluate unpleasant thoughts, feelings, sensations, and memories as "good," "bad," "right," "wrong," "normal," "abnormal," "healthy," and "unhealthy." This pattern of perpetual, unrelenting assessment is also employed within the mental health field, wherein counselors and therapists use the *Diagnostic and Statistical Manual of Mental Disorders* (American Psychiatric Association [APA], 2013) to label psychopathology, organizing symptoms into problems, conditions, and disorders, which are arranged into overarching categories.

In the contemplative tradition, though, Christians attempt to sit in loving silence with God, connecting directly to God in love, without an overreliance on language and labels (Foster, 1998). The early desert Christians, extending back to the time of Anthony in the third century in the deserts of Egypt, used silence as a way to cultivate inner stillness and peace. In fact, for contemplatives throughout the ages, the desert landscape represents a place to go to be with God in silence, shedding all obstacles and barriers (Lane, 1998). In the desert, there are no societal distractions, such as advertisements and marketing campaigns encouraging overconsumption, city noise, or the verbal chatter that occurs in public places. Rather, contemplatives are able to strip away all nonessentials, relying solely on God for nourishment, comfort, and connection. In this wordless fellowship with God, "One comes eventually to embrace an *apophatic* anthropology, letting go of everything one might have imagined as constituting the self—one's thoughts, one's desires, all one's compulsive needs" (Lane, 1998, p. 12, italics added).

The word *apophatic*, or *via negativia*, is a term commonly used in contemplative writings that simply means a negative theology of God.[8] In other words, *apophatic* writers suggest that human language and labels, at a certain point, fail to fully capture God (Johnston, 2000). Therefore, it is easier to rule out God's qualities, characteristics, and nature (e.g., "God is *not* malevolent," "God is *not* finite"), rather than employing words and language to fully encapsulate God's essence and being. Pseudo-Dionysius, a theologian in the fifth century, made a large impact on the *apophatic* movement, stating that Christians can know God through either reason or contemplation, preferring the latter, rather than the former (Johnston, 2000). According to Pseudo-Dionysius, "the more we take flight upward, the more our words are confined to the ideas we are capable of forming; so that now as we plunge into that darkness which is beyond intellect, we shall find ourselves not simply running short of words but actually speechless and unknowing" (quoted in Louth, 2012, pp. 140–141). In essence, the *apophatic* spiritual tradition in Christianity emphasizes few to no words, no images, and love when relating to God (Knabb & Bates, 2020). Ultimately, Christian contemplation is an imageless and wordless form of prayer that involves spending time with God in silence, transcending the limitations of language, rational thought, and human-constructed categories and labels (Lane, 1998).

Conversely, the *cataphatic* spiritual tradition, or *via positivia*, relies on words, images, knowledge, and the language of the Bible (i.e., God's special revelation to humankind) to describe God's characteristics and attributes (e.g., "God is omnipotent") and relate to God (Knabb & Bates, 2020). In contrast to the *apophatic* tradition, it is a positive theology of God, given it emphasizes God's qualities, characteristics, and nature, anchored to the Bible as God's Word (Knabb & Bates, 2020). These two ways to experience God—knowing via knowledge and discursive prayer and emphasizing language, images, and symbols and unknowing via love and nondiscursive prayer and de-emphasizing language, images, and symbols—function in a complementary, rather than adversarial, manner (Knabb & Bates, 2020). After all, even contemplatives rely on God's Word, the Bible, to guide Christian living. Indeed, the monastic practice of *lectio divina*, which involves reading Scripture, meditating on Scripture, praying to God, and resting in God in silent contemplation (Guigo II, 2012), integrates *cataphatic* and *apophatic* spirituality, given it is anchored to the Bible as a starting point. Yet, when practicing contemplation, language is de-emphasized in favor of a direct relationship with, and experience of, God.

Throughout the ages, Christian contemplatives have tended to describe God as *ineffable*, beyond mere categories that are constructed through the use of language. Therefore, contemplation involves sitting in silence to experience God directly, in love, transcending reason, language, knowledge, or other proverbial "hooks" Christians tend to hang the concept of God on to understand him. A popular biblical example of God's ineffability comes from the Old Testament, with Moses's experience of God as a burning bush. In his encounter with God,

Moses was instructed by God to keep his distance and take his sandals off because God was present. In addition, when Moses asked for God's name to relay God's message to the Pharaoh, God simply said, "I am who I am" (*New International Version Bible*, 2011, Exodus 3). In this passage, God was beyond verbally constructed categories and simply could not be contained within human words, names, or labels.

To relate the foregoing discussion to psychological pain, sometimes Christian clients can add on an extra layer of suffering by overly relying on language to understand their inner experiences, especially challenging thoughts, feelings, sensations, and memories. Constantly judging, through the use of an imperfect "knowledge of good and evil," can leave Christian clients struggling to directly depend on God, in love. Instead of overly relying on language to interpret psychological pain, "[leaning] not on [one's] own understanding" (*New International Version Bible*, 2011, Proverbs 3:5) can help Christian clients to trustfully surrender to God in silence, without eating from the "tree of the knowledge of good and evil" (Knabb et al., 2010). To sit in God's presence, in a symbolic desert landscape made up of solitude, simplicity, and silence (Lane, 1998), is to accept whatever experiences arise because Christian clients are fully reliant on God's love, beyond words, judgments, labels, categories, and knowledge. Stated differently, Christian clients are a dwelling place for God's love, which fills the inner world experientially, beyond a possible overreliance on language and abstract belief (Benner, 2015). Jesus modeled this total reliance on God when he was tempted in the desert (Matthew 4:1–11). Although Christians can only speculate about many of Jesus's interactions with God the Father during his 40 days in the desert, I wonder if he experientially relied on God's divine, silent, loving presence a lot of the time, transcending an overreliance on language.

Because of the importance of experiencing God directly in silence and love, not just through the medium of words and knowledge, I believe contemplative practices can be helpful for Christian clients to learn a different way of spending time with God, even in the midst of psychological pain. What follows is a review of the mindfulness-based processes of ACT—acceptance, cognitive defusion, the transcendent self, and present-moment awareness—which can help clients accept inner experiences and relate to them in new ways, beyond the limitations of language. In addition, the Christian contemplative tradition is further explored so as to assist Christian clients in understanding a new way of relating to inner pain, inviting God into the process through silence, stillness, and love.

An Introduction to the Four Mindfulness-Based Processes: Accepting Inner Pain

In ACT, clients learn how to accept, rather than avoid, unpleasant thoughts, feelings, sensations, and memories. As discussed in the introductory chapter, avoiding psychological pain leads to both the pain of presence and the pain of absence (Hayes, 2005). In other words, in addition to being unable to get rid of psychological pain through avoidance strategies, clients miss out on a deeply fulfilling life because they are futilely waiting for the symptoms to go away. This day, of course, may never come, as many of us who offer long-term counseling and therapy have quickly discovered when working with clients with recurring psychological disorders.

Acceptance involves helping clients to be with painful thoughts, feelings, sensations, and memories, embracing them, not running from them. ACT helps clients to do this by focusing on the processes of acceptance, cognitive defusion, the transcendent self, and present-moment awareness. Although these four processes have parallels with the practice of Buddhist-influenced mindfulness (Hayes, 2002), they were developed within the framework of the contemporary psychology literature, without Buddhist underpinnings in mind (Association for Contextual Behavioral Science, 2006). Therefore, I review them individually and separately from Buddhist influences in the paragraphs that follow. In addition, I have added in Christian contemplative writings in order to help counselors and therapists work more effectively with followers of Jesus to relate differently to inner experiences. Before starting this discussion, though, I briefly illuminate both the technology of mindfulness, commonly (though not always) emanating from Buddhist philosophy, and contemplative Christianity, which slowly developed over the last 2,000 years. Because many Christian clients may have concerns about some of the Eastern roots of mindfulness practice (whether explicitly Buddhist or secularized with implicit Buddhist influences), comparing and contrasting Buddhism (and Buddhist-influenced mindfulness) and Christianity (and Christian-influenced contemplation) can be a helpful starting point for counselors and therapists when utilizing faith-based ACT with Christian clients.

The Technology of Acceptance: Buddhist and Christian Perspectives

Many evidence-based practices in the 21st century utilize the technology of mindfulness, which functions as both a construct for measurement and meditative practice in the contemporary psychology literature. Often directly or indirectly inspired by the 2,500-year-old Buddhist tradition (Chiesa & Malinowski, 2011), mindfulness in the psychology literature involves nonjudgmental, sustained, flexible, present-moment attention, with an attitude of acceptance, openness, and curiosity toward whatever is unfolding in the here-and-now (Bishop et al., 2004).[9] More succinctly put, the main ingredients of mindfulness often include attention, present-moment awareness, and acceptance (Feldman et al., 2007). To date, mindfulness in the psychology literature has primarily been developed as a construct and practice applied to individuals, although more recent research has extended its use to interpersonal relations (Cohen & Miller, 2009; Pratscher et al., 2018, 2019).

Buddhism, which has roughly 400 million followers around the world, is one of the major world religions and includes several main "streams"—Theravada, Mahayana (e.g., Zen), and Vajrayana (e.g., Tibetan Buddhism) (Maguire, 2001). The "Buddha," or "the awakened one," was born in 566 BCE and had a spiritual awakening in 531 BCE while sitting under a tree (Maguire, 2001).

Based on this experience, he developed the Four Noble Truths: (a) all of life involves suffering, (b) suffering is caused by desire, (c) suffering can be ameliorated, and (d) the way to ameliorate suffering is the Noble Eightfold Path (Maguire, 2001). Included in the Noble Eightfold Path is right-mindfulness, which practitioners are to cultivate within the Buddhist framework (Maguire, 2001). Overall, as an "insight" form of meditation for psychological and spiritual growth (with some "concentrative" elements), mindfulness helps practitioners to gain a greater awareness of the "three marks of existence," that is, life is suffering, everything is impermanent, and there is no independent, separate self (Kok et al., 2013; McCown et al., 2010; Walsh & Shapiro, 2006).

Still, a variety of core Buddhist teachings does not seem to fully align with the Christian faith. For example, Buddhism does not emphasize either a God or individual self, which is very different from the Christian faith, with Christianity suggesting that humans, distinct from God, were created in God's image (Kabat-Zinn, 1990). Also, Buddhists pursue emptiness, letting go of a perceived separate self in order to become one with the world, meditate in order to look within, and view thinking as just another impermanent sensation, similar to seeing, hearing, smelling, tasting, and touching (Maguire, 2001).

Christianity, on the other hand, offers its own meditative and contemplative teachings and practices for psychological and spiritual growth, first inspired by the sayings, writings, and experiences of the early desert Christians.[10] Beginning around the third century, Christians moved to the deserts of Palestine, Egypt, Syria, and Arabia in order to establish monasteries away from the rest of the world. Turning to the barren desert terrain to experience solitude and loving communion with God, these Christians sought to deepen their awareness of him through daily devotion and prayer. Based on these experiences, they compiled teachings that are called the *Sayings of the Desert Fathers*. These recorded ideas and practices, which focus in part on prayer and a deeper relationship with God, served as a catalyst for subsequent contemplative writings (e.g., the *Philokalia*) and reveal deep insights into the human psyche, including ways to relate differently to thoughts, feelings, sensations, and memories so as to cultivate an experiential, present-moment awareness of the God of love. Certainly, because the overarching *telos*, or ultimate goal, for Christian contemplation is to recognize God's active, loving presence, distinctly Christian practices, rather than mindfulness (whether explicitly Buddhist or secularized with implicit Buddhist roots), may better help Christian clients to attain this awareness. Of course, as a more pragmatic endeavor, Christian clients can also utilize contemplation to relate differently to painful inner experiences, similar to the practice of mindfulness.

Ultimately, although many of the skills developed with mindfulness and Christian contemplative practices may be similar (e.g., attention, present-moment awareness, acceptance) (Feldman et al., 2007), the *telos* can be quite different (e.g., gaining "insight" into the "three marks of existence" versus cultivating a loving communion with God) (Knabb, 2021; Walsh & Shapiro, 2006). Also, it is debatable whether mindfulness meditation can be fully disentangled from its Eastern religious roots when working with clients who do not share its originating worldview (Brown, 2016). Nevertheless, what follows is a more detailed review of ACT's six processes and overlapping concepts from the Christian contemplative tradition, beginning with the technology of acceptance.

Acceptance and Endurance

To begin, accepting unpleasant inner experiences means relating to them with more openness, curiosity, nonjudgment, compassion, and kindness. Conversely, with experiential avoidance, there is a sort of adversarial relationship with difficult thoughts, feelings, sensations, and memories. In other words, clients tend to pursue the inner experiences that they like—"happiness" is a notorious culprit—and attempt to reduce, eliminate, avoid, or distract themselves from the thoughts, feelings, sensations, and memories they wish would go away. For example, sadness is a ubiquitous human feeling that tells us we have lost something or someone important in life. As a necessary feeling, sadness helps us to understand the significance of a loss, as well as take the steps necessary to replace what was lost. In addition, sadness, and the accompanying dysphoria, may help us to take a break from pursuing resources that are unavailable or just out of our reach; hence, the feeling of loss and depleted energy (Zettle, 2007). Without sadness, life would not have its richness or depth and we would not have the ability to rest and recover. In fact, the shortest verse in the Bible, "Jesus wept" (*New International Version Bible*, 2011, John 11:35), helps to understand the utility of emotions, including the reality that Jesus allowed himself to feel sadness, despite his apparent awareness that he would raise Lazarus from the dead moments later. In addition, psalmists in the Old Testament often cried out to God, lamenting about pain, sorrow, and heartache (Brueggemann, 1984). I cannot help but think that these passages were included in the Bible, at least in part, to help Christians better understand the God-given nature of emotions, including their healthy expression during moments of uncertainty and confusion.

From an ACT perspective, acceptance does not mean clients necessarily *want* unpleasant emotions (and other challenging inner experiences). Although learning to embrace them is certainly helpful, accepting painful feelings does not mean clients have to be excited about them. Instead, acceptance is pursued because the alternative—experiential avoidance—does not tend to offer a fulfilling, meaningful life. Undoubtedly, sadness, fear, anxiety, and anger will not go away, despite clients' best efforts. Because of this, acceptance strategies are used to allow these recurring experiences to run their natural course, without any deliberate effort to control them. When clients do pursue control strategies, they end up losing vital time and energy because their emotions (and accompanying thoughts, sensations, and memories) will soon return, and all of their attention is focused on numbing and avoiding tactics. Undeniably, acceptance is a way to prevent clients from being distracted from the most important part of life—pursuing values that emanate from the heart. Common language used to describe acceptance includes "expand around it," "allow it to be there," "stop fighting it," "make peace with it," "let it be," and "hold it gently" (Harris, 2019, p. 252). Acceptance has even been described as "putting out the 'welcome mat'" (Williams et al., 2012, p. 128). With acceptance, clients decide to stop arguing with difficult inner experiences or shouting at them to go away.

Although ACT is not rooted in a distinctly Christian view of suffering *per se*, a range of ACT writers have highlighted the importance of the *Serenity Prayer*, secularized in the ACT literature, in understanding acceptance: "Grant me the serenity to accept the things I cannot change, the courage to accept the things I can, and the wisdom to know the difference" (Hayes et al., 2012, p. 270). Interestingly, the original version, written by the American theologian Reinhold Niebuhr in the first part of the 20th century and widely available online, is as follows:

> God, give us grace to accept with serenity the things that cannot be changed, courage to change the things which should be changed, and the wisdom to distinguish the one from the other. Living one day at a time, enjoying one moment at a time, accepting hardship as a pathway to peace, taking, as Jesus did, this sinful world as it is, not as I would have it, trusting that You will make all things right, if I surrender to Your will, so that I may be reasonably happy in this life, and supremely happy with You forever in the next. Amen.

Notice, here, that wisdom involves recognizing the things that cannot be changed, in this case painful emotions and other inner experiences. What is more, in the original version, "hardship" is accepted, as is this world, given there is a hope that God will "make all things right." In other words, there is a willingness to accept psychological suffering because it is impermanent and part of the fall and, consequently, God will eventually restore all things. This more transcendent perspective, tethered to Niebuhr's insights into the human condition, can help Christian clients to endure with a forward-looking, hopeful optimism.

Given human thoughts, feelings, sensations, and memories are impermanent and tend to fluctuate from moment to moment, day to day, week to week, month to month, and year to year, acceptance is a much more fitting alternative to avoidance, on both a micro and macro level. Indeed, acceptance can help clients relate to passing inner experiences, which often "cannot be changed," with more openness, curiosity, nonjudgment, compassion, and kindness, similar to watching a bird perched on a tree branch just outside a bedroom window with simplicity and awe. After all, it is not the experience of sadness, for example, that leads to an unwillingness to have it, but the interpretation of the emotional pain as "bad" through the conduit of language. Yet, in returning to the *Serenity Prayer*, "taking ... this world as it is, not as I would have it" means recognizing the power of language in interpreting the inner world, especially the more unpleasant psychological experiences that are deemed problematic by the human mind.

This distinction—the direct experience of emotional pain versus the mind's interpretation of emotional pain as "bad," "wrong," and so forth—seems to be captured throughout the New Testament of the Bible. As noted in the introduction of this book, the Passion narrative within the gospels (John 18–19) highlights Jesus's experience of suffering for humankind. Because he was keenly aware of his purpose—to die on a cross as the ultimate act of love for the world (John 3:16)—he patiently endured the pain that emanated from this experience, interpreting his suffering as necessary because of his ability to stay connected to God's will.

Within the Christian contemplative tradition, the sayings, writings, and experiences of the early desert Christians highlight the importance of monks staying in their cell to face whatever inner experiences may arise.[11] Apparently, someone once asked Abba Moses, a fourth-century Egyptian monk, for "a word," with Moses replying, "Go sit in your cell, and your cell will teach you everything" (quoted in Paintner, 2012, p. 7). The ability of desert monks to sit patiently in their cells reflects their willingness to patiently endure in order to be mindful of God. The purpose of the cell, which was a small living space, was to help them cultivate a deeper spirituality. Within this room, they were to simply sit with their inner experiences, silently spending time with God, the author of love. Behind the walls of the cell, *hupomone*, or a hopeful, steadfast, longsuffering endurance, captures the willingness of monks to develop an awareness of the interior life in the presence of their loving God.

The "cell" was an actual place, to be sure, but it also symbolized the inner world, that is, the "outer cell" was reflective of the "inner cell" (Paintner, 2012). To patiently sit in the cell, enduring whatever thoughts, feelings, sensations, and memories arise, means to get to know the nature of these fluctuating states—the fact that they arise, linger, and slowly pass away, similar to clouds gently moving to and fro in a bright blue sky on a sunny day. To translate this practice for 21st-century Christian clients, sitting in a "cell" with God involves embracing whatever painful thoughts, feelings, sensations, and memories arise, watching them patiently and getting to know their impermanence. With this practice, "we develop an inner freedom and begin to discover something of the foundation of who we are that endures no matter the constantly shifting tides around us" (Paintner, 2012, p. 8). Moreover, by "staying put," Christian clients are learning to recognize God's active, loving presence in the midst of the inner world, especially during moments of suffering (Paintner, 2012). When Christian clients learn to sit, they develop the ability to safely watch over the inner life, with God by their side, which is further explained via the next ACT process.

Cognitive Defusion and Watchfulness

In addition to acceptance, *cognitive defusion* helps clients relate differently to inner experiences. Whereas acceptance commonly focuses on making room for a broader range of difficult thoughts, feelings, sensations, and memories, cognitive defusion more narrowly captures the ability to watch thoughts with detachment and distance, rather than getting forcefully pulled into the world of language. A helpful way to capture this ACT process is to note the difference between "looking *at* thoughts" versus "looking *from* thoughts" (Harris, 2009a, p. 97). Notice the distinction here. The latter statement highlights the tendency to assume all of our thoughts are true, accurate, or factual, emphasizing whether or not a thought is believable. The former, conversely, captures the ability to apply more curiosity to the entire process of thinking, emphasizing whether or not a thought helps us to live out a set of values and create a meaningful, fulfilling, thriving life. In other words, when looking *at* thoughts, there is less reliance on language to make sense of thoughts, feelings, sensations, and memories. Ultimately, although our thoughts will always have some influence, they do not need to be the "be-all and end-all" of daily life.

Unfortunately, when clients assume all of their thoughts are true, they tend to listen to even their most inaccurate or contradictory verbal messages. The main problem, of course, with believing that all of their thoughts are true is that the mind often leads them in a direction that is inconsistent with their values. As a brief example, a therapy client, Rachel, may decide that she is going to join a church ministry this year, concluding that a major part of her spiritual development as a Christian involves building relationships with others within the Body of Christ. Yet, when she shows up on Sunday to sign up, her mind may jump in to provide a list of reasons this decision will not work out: "It's not the right time," "They won't understand me," or "I can find other ways to grow spiritually." Based on this verbally constructed list, which is reliant on the medium of language, Rachel's mind concludes that she is justified in walking away from the sign-up table. Unfortunately, her mind has just led her down a road that moves her away from what is important to her—fellowshipping with other Christians, with love as a central aim.

As noted previously, language tends to be a "double-edged sword." On one hand, language helps clients to plan, organize, problem-solve, and engage in a range of important interpersonal behaviors. Yet, when it comes to the relationship between inner experiences and values, language often gets in the way of value-based action (Hayes et al., 2012). From a Christian perspective, the desire to "know," like God, led to Adam and Eve's banishment from Eden.[12] To be sure, thinking patterns and habits become especially problematic when they get in the way of deeply held values that enable Christians to follow Jesus. Instead, assisting Christian clients in relating to their judgmental, fallen mind with a bit more openness, flexibility, and distance helps them to walk with God in love, heading in the direction that he would have them go.

Within the sayings and writings of the early desert Christians, "watchfulness," the Greek word *nepsis*, can help to better understand the nature of the mind. Meaning a "calm vigilance" (Paintner, 2012, p. 8), watchfulness captures the ability to stay sober and alert on a daily basis. Contemplative authors likely derived this practice from 1 Peter, which instructs Christians to "be alert and of sober mind" (*New International Version Bible*, 2011, 1 Peter 5:8). Similar to enduring other inner events (e.g., painful emotions), watching thoughts with an inner vigilance and attentiveness helps to notice the fluctuating patterns of the mind.[13] Certainly, "Watchfulness is the antithesis of our ways of numbing ourselves to life, whether through watching hours of television, surfing the internet, shopping, eating, or drinking" (Paintner, 2012, p. 10).

To remain open and present to the inner life helps Christian clients shift their focus to the God of love, who is active and present in each unfolding moment. Evagrius Ponticus, a Christian monk from the fourth century, offered specific instructions on the topic: "Let him keep careful watch over his thoughts. Let him observe their intensity, their periods of decline and follow them as they rise and fall" (quoted in Laird, 2006, p. 99). Here, the purpose of this observant and vigilant attentiveness toward thinking is to get to know inner patterns without clinging to them or pushing them away. From an ACT viewpoint, clients practice cognitive defusion so as to observe verbal events from a more transcendent, spiritual perspective and, consequently, avoid getting bullied around by thoughts that get in the way of values. With contemplative Christianity, watchfulness is utilized in order to guard the contemplative self (the *nous* in Greek), which is the spiritual self that connects directly to God (Bingaman, 2012), as well as practice God's presence so as to cultivate an inner stillness with God (*hesychia* in Greek). Therefore, what follows is a review of ACT's third process, the transcendent self, including its overlap with Christianity's contemplative self.

The Transcendent Self and Contemplative Self

As a mental health professional, reflect for a moment on the "you" that is reading this sentence. Does this "you" consist of your thoughts? How about your feelings? Do your sensations or memories form the building blocks of the "you" that is reading this book? ACT suggests there is a more transcendent, spiritual, stable "you" that is beyond these wavering inner experiences. In other words, there is a "you" that is watching all of this unfold, beyond your impermanent thoughts, feelings, sensations, and memories, similar to the common experience of watching a movie. In the two hours you enjoy a movie, the images and sounds are definitely a part of your experience, but you are also keenly aware that there is a "you" that is not the actual movie.

With the clients we work with in counseling and therapy lies the distinction between the verbal, language-driven self and transcendent self. The verbal self consists of what the mind says via words that form sentences, whereas the transcendent self watches these moment-to-moment experiences unfold, beyond the limitations of language. For clients, there is an observer who recognizes they are not in the actual movie they are watching. This distinction, of course, can be applied to a range of client struggles, including the "mind" concluding they are worthless, unlovable, in danger, or incapable of intimacy with others, with the transcendent self watching all of this rubble roll down the proverbial hill without being pulled into the avalanche of language.

A popular ACT metaphor used by counselors and therapists to describe this distinction for clients involves the game of chess.[14] If a chess game symbolizes the inner workings of the mind, many clients would point to the chess pieces as an accurate representation of their thoughts, feelings, sensations, and memories, which make up their actual "self." The game they are playing, apparently, involves one side getting rid of the other side. The black pieces might capture clients' positive inner experiences, such as pleasant memories and feelings of joy and happiness. Like other board games, the goal seems to be to get rid of the opponent, in this case the white pieces, which represent their distressing inner experiences. However, getting rid of the white pieces does not seem to work. Whenever a white piece is removed, another piece quickly appears on the board. Viewing themselves as the pieces, ultimately, leaves them stuck in a constant game of "win or lose." Yet, the transcendent self captures the ability to watch the game unfold, similar to the actual chessboard steadily holding the pieces. From the perspective of the board, clients do not have to get "caught up" in the "win or lose" battle. Instead, they can just watch the game take place from a place of safety, stability, and curiosity.

In ACT language, we would say that the transcendent self is a perspective clients can always take to relate differently to difficult inner experiences, which often get in the way of value-based action. If they can simply watch their thoughts, feelings, sensations, and memories, rather than getting distracted by them and devoting all of their energy to avoiding them, clients can shift their focus and energy toward living out the values they deeply believe in. In other words, the rules of the game change and clients can just allow these experiences to arise, linger, and go on to do whatever it is that they do, all from a safe distance. The transcendent self is the enduring, stable, spiritual part of psychological experience that does not change, wherein varying thoughts, feelings, sensations, and memories have been watched since childhood.

From a Christian perspective, followers of Jesus may use more "spiritual" language to capture this transcendent part of the self that exists beyond thoughts, feelings, sensations, and memories. For instance, the early desert Christians (along with other contemplatives over the centuries) referred to a contemplative part of the self (the *nous* in Greek, which means "eye of the soul").[15] This is the spiritual part of human functioning that connects with God on a deeper level during moments of contemplation, motivated by love and existing beyond reason, facts, language, and other verbal events within the mind. Accordingly, the contemplative self, which relies upon love, can be contrasted with the "reasoning self" (*dianoia* in Greek), which relies upon knowledge, abstract thought, logic, and so forth.

Interestingly, Thomas Aquinas, a Christian philosopher from the 13th century, offered a similar dichotomy between the reasoning and contemplative parts of the self or mind, referring to the former as *ratio inferior* and the latter as *ratio superior* (Laird, 2006). As a second example, several 17th-century writings among the Puritans, a devout group of Protestant Christians from England, contrasted "earthly-mindedness" and "spiritual-mindedness" (or "heavenly-mindedness"), with the former capturing a preoccupation with the worries of the current world and the latter emphasizing a transcendent, spiritual understanding of reality and heaven as a final destination (Burroughs, 2010, 2014; Owen, 2016; Rowe, 1672). As a third example, the 19th-century monk Theophan presented a contrast between the mind and heart, stating,

> You must descend from your head to your heart. At present your thoughts of God are in your head ... While you are still in your head, thoughts will not easily be subdued but will always be whirling about, like snow in winter or clouds of mosquitoes in the summer.
>
> (quoted in Laird, 2006, p. 27)

Overall, the contemplative self (i.e., the *nous*) seeks to connect directly to God in love, serving as a "little radio" to hear, receive, and understand God's voice (Mathewes-Green, 2011), beyond the abstract concepts that make up the "reasoning self" (i.e., the *dianoia*).

For counselors and therapists working with Christian clients to integrate ACT's transcendent self with Christianity's contemplative self (i.e., the *nous*, "spiritual-mindedness," "heavenly-mindedness"; Burroughs, 2010, 2014; Mathewes-Green, 2011; Owen, 2016; Rowe, 1672), the ability to observe the inner workings of the mind can be conceptualized as a place of safety and distance. For Christian clients, this is the "eye of the soul," which was created in God's image to experience him directly in love, beyond knowledge, thoughts, feelings, and sensations. When experiencing psychological pain, the contemplative self, which is a more spiritual, transcendent sense of self, can help Christian clients to observe so as to patiently endure with the God of love by their side, speaking to them with his "gentle whisper" (*New International Version Bible*, 2011, 1 Kings 19:11–13). As a liberating notion for Christians, there is a "me" that is more than negative thoughts, unpleasant emotions, painful sensations, and intrusive memories. This "me" longs to lovingly connect directly and experientially to God and needs to let go of an overreliance on the "reasoning mind" (i.e., the *dianoia*) from time to time in order to do so. In other words, Christian clients can experience God, with love, rather than merely think about God, with knowledge (Bangley, 2006; Benner, 2015). When Christian clients are struggling with symptoms of depression, anxiety, trauma, or relational distress, they may be especially in need of a direct experience with God, the author of love, rather than eating from the "tree of the knowledge of good and evil." What follows is a review of this experience of present-moment awareness, as revealed via ACT's process and practicing God's presence (*hesychia* in Greek) within the Christian contemplative tradition.

Present-Moment Awareness and Practicing God's Presence

The ability to stay present, in the here-and-now, is a central aim of ACT. Thus far, I have covered acceptance, cognitive defusion, and the transcendent self, which all require the ability to connect to the present moment. Building on these processes, moment-to-moment awareness is the ability to utilize mindfulness to cultivate nonjudgmental, sustained, flexible attention in the here-and-now. A more formal definition of mindfulness is as follows: "paying attention in a particular way; on purpose, in the present moment, and nonjudgmentally" (Kabat-Zinn, 2012, p. 1). To offer one more popular definition in the psychology literature, the two components of mindfulness include "the self-regulation of attention so that it is maintained on immediate experience, thereby allowing for increased recognition of mental events in the present moment" and "adopting a particular orientation toward one's experience in the present moment, an orientation that is characterized by curiosity, openness, and acceptance" (Bishop et al., 2004, p. 232).

Notice that mindfulness typically involves sustained, flexible attention and acceptance in the present moment (Feldman et al., 2007). The reason mindfulness may be helpful within ACT is because of its emphasis on simply allowing thoughts, feelings, sensations, and memories to run their natural course, without clients trying to reduce, eliminate, avoid, or distract from these experiences. When clients practice awareness, they are able to pursue value-based living because the inner world no longer bullies them around. By accepting the impermanence of psychological experiences, clients are able to shift their focus toward creating a life that is connected to their values—what matters deep within the heart.

97

Interestingly, another evidence-based practice—mindfulness-based cognitive therapy (MBCT)—refers to the struggle to stay connected to the moment as "automatic pilot" (Williams et al., 2012, p. 108). For example, try to imagine what your commute is like on the way home from a busy day at the counseling or therapy office. Driving along the freeway, you may notice that you have traveled a great distance, possibly even pulling into your driveway at home, yet you do not remember getting there. Automatic pilot involves getting caught up in your head, letting your thoughts pull you away from present-moment sensory experiences. Instead of focusing on your hands on the steering wheel, the sound of your tires moving along the asphalt, your foot on the gas pedal, and your back against the car seat, your mind is somewhere else. For clients, getting lost in their thoughts, although quite common, seems to best capture their lack of awareness of the life that is unfolding in front of them. Without present-moment awareness, clients are always somewhere else, experiencing something else in their mind, not fully engaging with the world before them.

For Christian clients, present-moment awareness involves practicing God's loving presence in each and every activity, whether exciting or mundane, in addition to connecting to sensory experiences. Reminiscent of the medieval monk Brother Lawrence's (2015) ability to practice the presence of God, God is moving in this very moment, which means washing the dishes, taking out the trash, or talking to a colleague at work all involve God's loving presence. Yet, quite often, Christian clients lose sight of this reality and, instead, get lost in the mind by drifting off into the busyness of a mental "to do list." When this happens, they miss out on the inner stillness, calmness, and peace that come from resting in God's loving presence.

For the early desert Christians, the Greek word *hesychia* captures the ability to rest in God's love within each moment by cultivating a deeper awareness of his presence. Translated as "inner silence," "quiet," or "stillness" (Paintner, 2012, p. 118), the saying of Abba Arsenius, an Egyptian monk of the fifth century, captures this experience: "Be solitary, be silent, and be at peace" (quoted in Paintner, 2012, p. 142). Here, the central ingredients of inner peace include being alone with the "God of love and peace" (*New International Version Bible*, 2011, 2 Corinthians 13:11), as well as sitting in silence. In fact, *hesychia* is the "ultimate goal of the spiritual life" (Paintner, 2012, p. xxviii). In this state, Christian clients are able to notice their inner experiences, including difficult thoughts, feelings, sensations, and memories, without reacting to them. Whereas mindfulness practice typically involves focusing on the five senses or the breath, Christian contemplation usually requires a focus on some sort of "prayer word" (e.g., "God," "Jesus," "love") to calm the mind and symbolically gaze upon God (Bangley, 2006; Gillet, 1985; Jacques, 2001; Laird, 2006; Pennington, 1980).

Among contemplatives, the Jesus Prayer is used as a way to achieve *hesychia*: "Lord, Jesus Christ, Son of God, have mercy on me, a sinner" (the long form) or "Lord Jesus Christ, have mercy on me" (the short form). The goal of gently repeating this prayer, which is apparently based on the Apostle Paul's instructions to "pray continually" (*New International Version Bible*, 2011, 1 Thessalonians 5:17) and reference in Luke to a tax collector asking God for mercy (Luke 18:13), is to focus the mind and attain inner stillness and peace. Constantly pulling the mind back to the Jesus Prayer is a way to cultivate inner quiet, as revealed by Hesychios of Sinai, a monk who likely lived in the eighth or ninth century: "Attentiveness is the heart's stillness, unbroken by any thought. In this stillness the heart breathes and invokes, endlessly and without ceasing, only Jesus Christ who is the Son of God and Himself God" (quoted in Laird, 2006, p. 100).

As another example among contemplatives, the medieval monk Brother Lawrence (2015) advocated "practicing God's presence" throughout the day, which involves "[becoming] accustomed to his divine company, speaking humbly and conversing lovingly with him all the time, at every moment, without rule or measure, especially in times of temptation, suffering, aridity, weariness, even infidelity and sin" (p. 38). To do so, he instructed Christians to "perform [their] actions carefully and deliberately, not impulsively or hurriedly," "[working] gently and lovingly with God" by pairing whatever activity is being carried out in the here-and-now with a short phrase, such as "My God, I love you with all my heart" (pp. 38, 41). The result of this practice, which simply involves the acknowledgment that "all our thoughts, words and actions belong by right to him" (p. 39), is a "sacred fire of love" (p. 45).

Overall, this inner stillness, quiet, and peace, nourished through the Jesus Prayer and practice of God's presence in daily life, can help Christian clients to internally recognize God's loving presence, especially when struggling with depression, anxiety, trauma, and relational distress, then extend God's love to others. If Christian contemplation is succinctly defined as the cultivation of a present-moment awareness of God's perfect love (Knabb & Bates, 2020), it has several points of overlap with mindfulness meditation, including the development of a plethora of mental skills (e.g., attention, present-moment awareness, acceptance) (Feldman et al., 2007). To be certain, although mindfulness meditation differs in some ways from practicing God's presence in order to achieve a deeper, more loving stillness and peace, they both allow clients to rest in the present moment, flexibly focusing on immediate experience so as to fully engage with what is unfolding in the here-and-now. As a result, both practices gradually help the mind to settle, rather than pursue or push away thoughts. When clients sit still, they can relax into a deeper awareness of moment-by-moment experience. Of course, for Christian clients, this awareness is the God of love himself, beyond categories, labels, and images.

With these four processes of ACT, clients are learning to relate differently to the inner world, with more openness, gentleness, kindness, and curiosity. For Christian clients, this also involves an awareness of God's loving presence in order to walk with him through, not around, psychological pain. Rather than getting lost in thoughts or being overwhelmed by emotions, Christian clients are able to simply notice the waves and currents of the sea of the inner world, recognizing that the tide moves in and out and they do not have to chase the ocean away. Relating differently to psychological pain brings up another question, though.

If thoughts, feelings, sensations, and memories do not serve as a trustworthy tour guide for life, what is used, instead, as a reliable navigation system in the 21st century? Values, rather than fluctuating thoughts, feelings, sensations, and memories, offer a stable, reliable road to travel down. Although clients may, from time to time, wander off the road of life, values do not usually lead them in contradictory directions. Instead, value-based action combines deeply held beliefs that come from the heart and a sincere commitment to act on them. What follows are the remaining two processes of ACT, which serve as the other side of the proverbial coin—acceptance of the inner world as "heads" and a commitment to living out values as "tails."

Values and Biblical Virtues

To live a meaningful, fulfilling life, ACT proposes that accepting inner experiences with openness, flexibility, compassion, and kindness helps clients to focus on pursuing values through behavioral action. In other words, rather than being guided by fluctuating thoughts, feelings, sensations, and memories, what matters deep within the heart serves as a tour guide. From an ACT perspective, thoughts, feelings, sensations, and memories commonly lead clients in the opposite direction of their values. Because of this, relating to the inner world with flexibility, rather than viewing these experiences as "facts," helps clients to connect to their values in each moment in order to take deliberate steps toward a valued direction.

From a biblical perspective, virtues emanate from the Bible and serve as the Christian equivalent to ACT's "values," which are "chosen qualities of actions" (Luoma et al., 2017, p. 29). Defined as "moral excellence" (*Zondervan Bible Dictionary*, 2011, p. 1512), "virtue is considered a necessary ingredient in the exercise of faith" for followers of Jesus (*Nelson's Bible Dictionary*, 2005, p. 259) and derived from God's Word. As the psalmist revealed, "Your word is a lamp for my feet, a light on my path" (Psalm 119:105). Therefore, on the road of life, biblical virtues, illuminated within the pages of the Old and New Testaments, are to guide Christians each step of the way. Probably the most famous list of biblical virtues, or "character qualities" (Wright, 2017, p. 134), comes from the Apostle Paul's discussion of the "fruit of the Spirit," which includes "love, joy, peace, [patience], kindness, goodness, faithfulness, gentleness, and self-control" (*New International Version Bible*, 2011, Galatians 5:22–23). Of course, love is the leading virtue, given Christians are to "walk by the Spirit" in love

(*New International Version Bible*, 2011, Galatians 5:13–26). What is more, love is the cornerstone of the Christian contemplative tradition (Foster, 1998), with Christian contemplatives first developing an awareness of God's loving presence, which, in turn, is extended to others as they walk with God along the road of life. Interestingly, walking down this road may quickly send Christian clients in a very different direction than the road their thoughts, feelings, sensations, and memories may lead them down.

One such example that commonly plays out in counseling and therapy involves a client, Aaron, needing to have an open, direct conversation with a coworker about a difficult matter. Quite possibly, in counseling, Aaron frequently discusses someone he does not get along with at his job and is competing with for a promotion. Over the past few months, Aaron has heard that this person is criticizing him in front of other people. When he learns about this, Aaron gets angry, feeling deeply resentful that his coworker has apparently worked to undermine his reputation, which he has actively strived to build. In addition, Aaron may have the thought "I'm going to get back at this person," which he expresses in counseling. These thoughts and feelings may begin to build, turning into "factual conclusions" that his counselor needs to address with him. Within the inner world, Aaron seems to have already confirmed this "reality."

Yet, from both ACT and biblical viewpoints, a set of "qualities" offers Aaron, who is a Christian, a much more stable, trustworthy road to travel down. For example, his counselor might turn with him to Scripture for guidance, reading Jesus's teaching in Luke: "As you are going with your adversary to the magistrate, try hard to be reconciled on the way, or your adversary may drag you off to the judge, and the judge turn you over to the officer, and the officer throw you into prison" (*New International Version Bible*, 2011, Luke 12:58). Or Aaron's counselor may turn with Aaron to Galatians 5 to read about the "fruit of the Spirit" (*New International Version Bible*, 2011). Here, Aaron is faced with a dilemma—follow his thoughts and feelings, which are telling him to retaliate, or attempt to reconcile with his "adversary" and lead with "love" as *the* "character quality" for followers of Jesus. Although his inner experiences definitely seem to be "true," they do not align with the "lamp and light" that are explicated in God's Word, the Bible.

ACT writers commonly present a dichotomy between the inner and outer worlds.[16] The inner world, represented by thoughts, feelings, sensations, and memories, tends to offer a rather unstable road in life that changes each step of the way, filled with potholes, cracks, and loose gravel, whereas our deeply held values lead us down a much different road, consisting of paved asphalt that offers stable footing for the long trek ahead. The challenge, of course, involves heading in a direction that creates a fulfilling life, rather than a life devoted to avoidance strategies to "play it safe." After all, the pain of absence tends to cause much more sorrow and regret than the pain of presence (Hayes, 2005).

ACT suggests that values are "verbally constructed, global, desired, and chosen life directions" (Luoma et al., 2007, p. 131). Values are also intimately connected to action, rather than merely abstract concepts for thinking about life. Stated differently, values, by definition, lead in a particular direction, serving as a verb, rather than a noun (Luoma et al., 2007).

As a common example within the ACT literature, the "compass metaphor" helps clients to understand value-based living. With a compass, clients are able to steadily walk in a particular direction, whether north, south, east, or west. Rather than merely pursuing goals, which can be "crossed off a list," values help clients to head in a meaningful, consistent direction (Harris, 2009a, p. 192). Among other qualities, values are enduring and connected to the present moment, suggesting clients can continuously head down a global, desired, and meaningful road (Harris, 2009a). Values, additionally, are deeply embedded within the heart, beyond wavering thoughts, feelings, sensations, and memories, which tend to fluctuate, change, wax, and wane. Common examples of client values include being a loving and forgiving spouse, pursuing educational opportunities because learning and curiosity are meaningful and enriching, and maintaining physical fitness because health is important and life giving. Again, these qualities that guide action tend to send clients down a very different road than their thoughts, feelings, sensations, and memories, which might try to convince them to avoid risks in life. However, because values emanate from the heart, clients know that pursuing them is their ultimate purpose on this planet.

Although the values in ACT are not typically considered the same as virtues, ethics, or morals, there can be overlap between them, especially when considering that many clients will wish to be guided by virtues that emanate from their own cultural or religious tradition. Because of this, the main point, from an ACT perspective, is that values are freely chosen on the part of the client, rather than forced onto the client by society. In the Christian faith, the teachings of Jesus offer Christian clients a parallel for action-based living, especially given that "God is love" (*New International Version Bible*, 2011, 1 John 4:8) and Jesus is "the way and the truth and the life" (*New International Version Bible*, 2011, John 14:6). In fact, "To speak of God in the Christian context is to become as particular and concrete as the historical person of Jesus and as universal as the power of love to bring forgiveness and reconciliation into human relationships" (Jersild, 2000, p. 21). As a result, Christian clients have a guide, Jesus, who offers specific teachings to lead them in life, modeled by Jesus's life of love. Of course, Christian clients have a choice about whether they want to follow Jesus (i.e., walk with God in love). Thus, similar to freely choosing values within ACT, Christian clients are to make the choice on their own about following Jesus on a daily basis. Certainly, there are a variety of examples in the New Testament of individuals who declined Jesus's invitation, as noted in the introduction to this book.

If Christian clients freely make the decision to follow Jesus, both the Old Testament and gospels and letters in the New Testament offer a moral vision for the Christian life, including laws, commandments, right conduct, principles, and imperatives, with moral behavior defined as "the practices and virtues that are found in the Christian community" (Jersild, 2000, p. 7). Still, Christian clients are to pursue these practices in love, rather than as a rigid obligation, and Christian behavior is to be grounded in the person of Jesus, instead of abstract concepts or a legal moral system (Jersild, 2000). To be sure, Jesus consistently critiqued the Pharisees, Jewish leaders in the first century, who "[looked] beautiful on the outside but on the inside [were] full of the bones of the dead and everything unclean" (*New International Version Bible*, 2011, Matthew 23:27).

What, then, is the moral "compass" of New Testament writings, an ethical "map" for Christian clients to follow? Quite possibly, moral behavior emanates from *freedom, agape love*, and *responsibility*.[17] With freedom, God, through the atoning work of Jesus, has offered Christians grace, as well as the ability to find a true identity in him. Because of the gospel message, or "good news," God has reconciled Christians to both himself and their neighbors. His grace provides Christians with the opportunity for a new life. In addition, *agape* love is the glue that holds together this newly found freedom in relationship with God and others, modeled by Jesus's life, death, and resurrection. Finally, responsibility captures a commitment to God, given Christians have a personal relationship with him. To summarize, biblical virtues are to be guided by an ethic of moral behavior, grounded in a freedom in Jesus, altruistic love for God and others, and commitment to living out these healing relationships. Jesus, of course, modeled this behavior as the "Suffering Servant" and rabbi. Therefore, becoming more like Jesus is central in the Christian life, with the fruit of the Spirit on display for those who walk with God in love along the road of life. Indeed, in the Christian life, followers of Jesus are a dwelling place for God's love, which is extended to God and others as the two greatest commandments (Matthew 22:36–40). Rather than being guided by impermanent inner experiences, Christians can cultivate the psychological and spiritual flexibility to allow God to lead the way.

Because Jesus leads Christians along the road they are to follow, turning to his teachings can help Christian clients develop a proverbial map for life, consistent with value-based action in ACT. Rather than being guided by impermanent, and often contradictory, thoughts, feelings, sensations, and memories, Jesus helps Christian clients to understand the centrality of love in action, including loving one's neighbors (Luke 10:27), forgiving and praying for one's enemies (Matthew 6:14–15), giving to the poor (Matthew 5:42), serving others in the local church (Galatians 6:10; Romans 12:3–8), and ministering to non-Christians through missionary work (Matthew 28:19). Following Jesus (i.e., walking with God in love) involves behavioral action, putting his words into practice, rather than seeing Jesus as someone merely offering teachings or wisdom:

> Jesus summons men [sic] to follow him not as a teacher or a pattern of the good life, but as the Christ, the Son of God ... When we are called to follow Christ, we are summoned to an exclusive attachment to his person.
>
> (Bonhoeffer, 2012, p. 58)

This brings us to the last process within ACT— committed action.

Committed Action and Following Jesus

Without action, values are simply abstract concepts or pleasant ideas. Therefore, in the final process of ACT, action is a central feature. Thus far, I have covered an ACT approach to understanding inner experiences in counseling and therapy and discussed a different kind of "map" that can serve as a guide for clients' actions. Yet, clients will remain stuck with the pain of absence (Hayes, 2005) unless there is a courageous dedication to living out well-defined values, a "step-by-step process of acting to create a life of integrity, true to one's deepest wishes and longings" (Luoma et al., 2017, p. 238). Along the way, clients must develop a willingness to take action, guided by values. ACT writers commonly refer to *willingness* as "being open to the entirety of one's experience while also actively and intentionally choosing to move in valued life directions" (Luoma et al., 2017, p. 38). With this effort, clients are putting one foot in front of the other as they balance acceptance and action, continuing to get back on the road of life when they notice they have lost their way. With a trusted "compass," that is, values, clients can head down the road of purposeful, committed action, despite the geographic changes they might face, such as swamps, mountains, deserts, and other unfriendly landscapes.

Referred to as the "Action pivot," Hayes (2019) proposed the following question to fittingly capture the choice that clients face in life:

> Based on a distinction between you as a conscious being and the story the mind tells of who you are, in this time and situation are you willing to experience your experiences as they are, not as what they say they are, fully and without needless defense, and direct your attention and effort to creating larger and larger habits of behavior that reflect your chosen values? YES or NO?
>
> (pp. 254–255)

Of course, for Christian clients, a similar question is succinctly presented by Jesus as "[Will you] come [and] follow me[?]" (*New International Version Bible,*

2011, Matthew 4:19). Certainly, the "Action pivot" for Christian clients, traced back to the fall of humankind, involves deciding who will lead on the road of life—the self or God.

Nevertheless, ACT's committed action, which "occurs at a particular moment in time and is deliberately linked to creating a pattern of action that serves a value" (Hayes et al., 2012, p. 328), typically involves several major steps, including choosing an area of life clients want to focus on, identifying the specific value they want to connect to, cultivating a set of goals to guide them in pursuing the value, and acting on the value in a way that is compassionate, non-judgmental, and focused on the task at hand in the here-and-now. Within the ACT literature, authors tend to think of committed action in "all-or-nothing" terms (Hayes et al., 2012, p. 280). In other words, there is no middle ground with committed action—clients need to act.

There are clear parallels here for Christian clients following Jesus all the way home to the Father's house (John 14:2), with Jesus calling Christians into an intentional relationship with him. In the gospel of Mark, Jesus stated, "Whoever wants to be my disciple must deny themselves and take up their cross and follow me" (*New International Version Bible*, 2011, Mark 8:34). Here, Jesus is telling Christians to follow his model, including suffering based on his reference to carrying a cross (Witherington, 2001). In the first century, the cross was an "extreme penalty" used to execute the worst of criminals (Witherington, 2001, p. 244). So, Jesus seems to be highlighting the sacrifice required to follow him, which parallels a criminal's death on a cross. Yet, he goes on to state that those who "lose their life for me and the gospel will save it," which is possibly "an editorial word of encouragement by Mark to his Gentile audience under fire" (Witherington, 2001, p. 245). As a result, following Jesus involves suffering and hardship. Still, the journey is well worth it because of the hope Christians have in the gospel message: "That Christ died for our sins according to the Scriptures, that he was buried, that he was raised on the third day according to the Scriptures" (*New International Version Bible*, 2011, 1 Corinthians 15:3–4).

In the gospel of John, Jesus proclaimed, "You did not choose me, but I chose you and appointed you so that you might go and bear fruit—fruit that will last—and so that whatever you ask in my name the Father will give you. This is my command: Love each other" (*New International Version Bible*, 2011, John 15:16–17). In these verses, Jesus personally selected his disciples and called them to their purpose—bearing fruit in love, helping to bring individuals into the faith (Carson, 1991). In other words, "the union of love that joins believers with Jesus can never become a comfortable, exclusivistic huddle that only they can share" (Carson, 1991, p. 523). With virtue-based Christian living, the focus is on demonstrating love for others through behavioral action.

To summarize, ACT's committed action process involves the willingness to apply well-defined values to daily life, regardless of the thoughts, feelings, sensations, and memories that may emerge in the process. For Christian clients, each moment brings with it the opportunity to follow Jesus, in love. With ACT, clients can accept inner experiences through cognitive defusion (traditional)/watchfulness (faith-based), acceptance (traditional)/endurance (faith-based), the transcendent self (traditional)/the contemplative self (faith-based), and present-moment awareness (traditional)/practicing God's presence (faith-based). By accepting these experiences with more openness, flexibility, compassion, and kindness, Christian clients are able to walk with God in love, exemplified by the altruistic sacrifice of a "Suffering Servant" on a lonely cross (*New International Version Bible*, 2011, Isaiah 53; John 15:13).

Psychological Flexibility and Walking with God in Love

As a reminder, combined, the six processes of ACT help clients to cultivate psychological flexibility, which consists of

> the ability [for clients] to feel and think with openness, to attend voluntarily to [their] experience of the present moment, and to move [their] life in directions that are important to [them], building habits that allow [them] to live life in accordance with [their] values and aspirations.
>
> (Hayes, 2019, p. 5)

Or, simply put, psychological flexibility is about clients "turning toward [their] suffering in order to live a life full of meaning and purpose" (Hayes, 2019, p. 5). With faith-based ACT, psychological flexibility is a byproduct of following Jesus, the "Suffering Servant" (*New International Version Bible*, 2011, Isaiah 53), walking with God through, not around, psychological suffering in order to live like Jesus by emulating his self-sacrificial love. Of course, with both the traditional and faith-based versions of ACT, clients have a choice to make in each unfolding moment, a "Choice Point," which can help to clarify and focalize the salience of the decision-making process in the here-and-now.

The "Choice Point" and "Fork in the Road"[18]

As one of the newer developments in ACT, the "Choice Point" tool (Harris, 2019) can help counselors and therapists to conceptualize psychological flexibility in a quick, easy-to-understand manner. In essence, in each unfolding moment, clients are either heading toward or away from a life of meaning, purpose, vitality, and significance. When experiencing pleasant thoughts, feelings, sensations, memories, situations, and relationships, clients may find it rather easy to head toward the life they want to live, relying upon helpful overt (i.e., observable, such as walking and talking) and covert (i.e., unobservable, such as thinking and feeling) behaviors. Yet, when experiencing difficult thoughts, feelings, sensations, memories, situations, and relationships, clients can quickly head away from the life they desire, engaging in unhelpful overt and covert behaviors. Thus, when suffering from psychological pain, clients have a choice to make, that is, there is a "Choice Point." To continue to head toward an intentional life, they must remain "unhooked" by difficult inner (e.g., thoughts, feelings, sensations, memories) and outer (e.g., situations, relationships) events so they can confidently press on, utilizing helpful behaviors that lead toward purpose and vitality. Conversely, when they get "hooked" by difficult inner and outer events, they may end up heading away from an intentional life, getting into the habit of engaging in unhelpful behaviors that undermine the meaning they long for. Overall, ACT's six processes can help clients to head toward, not away from, a vibrant, impactful, intentionally chosen life from moment to moment.

As a parallel process, Christian clients are regularly presented with a "Fork in the Road" in life whenever they experience a difficult thought, feeling, sensation, memory, situation, or relationship. In these ubiquitous, inevitable moments of psychological pain, they can choose to walk with the God of love toward the life he is offering, enduring psychological suffering along the way because God is by their side, or walk alone and away from the life he is providing, avoiding psychological suffering and prioritizing the self above God. Although the latter may certainly seem appealing to Christian clients in the short-term, especially in the midst of difficult thoughts, feelings, sensations, memories, situations, and relationships, in the long-term, Christian clients are not fulfilling their God-given purpose on this planet. To be certain, the *telos* for Christian clients in this short, imperfect life is to commune with the God of love as they move from justification (i.e., being declared righteous by, and reconciled to, God through Jesus), to sanctification (i.e., becoming more like Jesus), to glorification (i.e., being face to face with Jesus) (Grudem, 1994). Along the way, relationships are paramount, given that God, the author of love, desires for humankind to be unified with him and one another (John 17:20–23).

ACTing in Relationships

Before concluding the chapter, I would like to further emphasize the relational nature of ACT in both its traditional and faith-based versions. Although many counselors and therapists might not consider cognitive behavioral approaches to be primarily relational, I believe ACT is inherently so, given its emphasis on love (Hayes, 2016, 2019). With traditional ACT, of course, clients can intentionally choose to walk with other people in life with a shared set of values, as well as align their personally chosen values with those from a surrounding community or culture, whether secular or religious. What is more, the values that clients choose to live by in traditional ACT are often (although not always) applied to human relationships, such as being loving, forgiving, kind, generous, and so forth. Indeed, to date, ACT has been applied to a variety of different relational contexts, as revealed by a plethora of books on the topic (Dahl et al., 2014; Harris, 2009b; Lev & McKay, 2017; McKay et al., 2013; Walser & Westrup, 2009).

With faith-based ACT, Christian clients are learning to walk with God in love, with God's Word, the Bible, offering a set of biblical virtues to guide behavioral action. In both cases, I believe that love is the guiding characteristic for life and loving relationships are key to living a life of meaning and purpose. In fact, I view many commonly identified values in ACT as "offshoots" of love (e.g., caring, compassionate, friendly, forgiving, kind, supportive) (Harris, 2019). Because of this, I firmly believe that the two versions—traditional and faith-based ACT—presented in this book overlap quite well with one another, reminiscent of a Venn diagram with converging circles that share most of their space. The "shared variance" between the two versions, to use the language of statistics, is love, lived out in value-based relationships of care and commitment.

Conclusion

To conclude, both the traditional and faith-based versions of ACT share many similarities, ultimately converging with their emphasis on flexibly accepting the inner world so as to intentionally live a life of love in the outer world. In the chapter that follows, I explore an additional way to help Christian clients understand the acceptance and action processes, as revealed by the story of Mary and Martha in the gospels. Mary represents the contemplative life, that is, patiently sitting at the feet of Jesus and lovingly gazing upon him, whereas Martha points us to the active life, or serving Jesus. With Mary's example, Christian clients can learn to sit at Jesus's feet during moments of difficult thoughts, feelings, sensations, and memories, whereas Martha's devotion to service helps Christian clients to live out their faith. Following this discussion, I transition to chapters that focus on metaphors, strategies, and techniques for the six processes of ACT, along with specific applications of faith-based ACT to depression, anxiety, trauma, and relational distress.

Notes

1 Unless otherwise noted, the main points on ACT in this chapter are derived from Harris (2019), Hayes (2019), Hayes et al. (2012), and Luoma et al. (2017).
2 Throughout the book, I have chosen to use the less common ACT term "transcendent self," in contrast with the more popular "observing self," given I believe the word "transcendent" is a more familiar term in Christianity.
3 Although the general term "values" is used in the ACT literature, for faith-based ACT, I substitute "values" with the more precise language of "virtues," or "moral excellence," to more closely align with biblical teachings.
4 See http://www.div12.org/PsychologicalTreatments/treatments.html for a list of evidence-based practices.
5 See Helliwell et al. (2020) for the full report, which is published annually.

6 See Hayes et al. (2013) for a more detailed review of ACT's conceptualization of the problem of language. Also, see Knabb et al. (2010) for a more detailed review of the overlap between ACT's conceptualization of the problem of language and a biblical viewpoint. Finally, see Knabb and Bates (2020) for a more detailed review of the psychology of *apophatic* spirituality in Christianity, which elucidates the limits of human language.

7 The theory underlying this understanding of language is referred to as *relational frame theory* (Hayes et al., 2012), which is foundational for ACT. Although a more detailed review is beyond the scope of this book, relational frame theory suggests that employing language to solve problems works well in the outer world, but can cause suffering in the inner world, given that human beings are able to create and assign labels to inner experiences, evaluating and judging them and forming contingency statements (e.g., "If … then …") about external events that may or may not happen (Hayes et al., 2012). As an example, the inner experience of anxiety can be labeled as a "disorder" and linked to a future event (e.g., "If I experience anxiety in public, I'll have a panic attack, embarrassing myself in front of others"), resulting in a client staying indoors and isolating themselves.

8 For a straightforward, yet detailed, overview of the similarities and differences between the *apophatic* and *cataphatic* (or *kataphatic*) spiritual traditions in Christianity, see McGrath (2011).

9 It is important to note that, dating back to the 1970s, some researchers have investigated the benefits of meditation for stress and stress-related problems without emphasizing Buddhist philosophy (Benson, 2000).

10 This review of the early desert Christians is based on the summary by Paintner (2012).

11 Some of the main points in this paragraph are from Paintner (2012).

12 Again, see Knabb et al. (2010), along with Hayes et al. (2012), for an expanded account of ACT, language, and the Genesis account of the fall of humankind.

13 Here, it is important to note that "watchfulness" may be slightly different than ACT's defusion process, which helps clients to gently notice thinking, especially because "watchfulness" is also described as "vigilance." Yet, both processes seem to encourage an awareness of thinking, creating some space between a more transcendent, spiritual sense of self and thought content.

14 See Hayes et al. (2012) for the "Chessboard Metaphor."

15 Unless otherwise noted, this discussion on the "contemplative self" is derived primarily from Bingaman (2012), Harmless (2004), Nikodimos (2015), and Smith (2013).

16 For example, Hayes's (2005) self-help book for clients is fittingly titled, *Get Out of Your Mind and Into Your Life*.

17 The main points in this paragraph are from Jersild (2000).

18 This summary of the "Choice Point" tool is based on Harris (2019, pp. 9–17). Moreover, the "Fork in the Road" adaptation is inspired by Hayes et al. (2012).

References

American Psychiatric Association. (2013). *Diagnostic and statistical manual of mental disorders* (5th ed.). American Psychiatric Publishing.

Association for Contextual Behavioral Science. (2006). *New Harbinger's interview with Steve Hayes*. https://contextualscience.org/new_harbingers_interview_with_steve_hayes#

Bangley, B. (Ed.). (2006). *The cloud of unknowing: Contemporary English edition.* Paraclete Press.

Benner, D. (2015). *Surrender to love: Discovering the heart of Christian spirituality.* InterVarsity Press.

Benson, H. (2000). *The relaxation response.* Harpertorch.

Bingaman, B. (2012). Becoming a spiritual world of God: The theological anthropology of Maximus the Confessor. In B. Bingaman & B. Nassif (Eds.), *The philokalia: A classic text of Orthodox spirituality* (pp. 137–162). Oxford University Press.

Bishop, S., Lau, M., Shapiro, S., Carlson, L., Anderson, N., Carmody, J., Segal, Z., Abbey, S., Speca, M., Velting, D., & Devins, G. (2004). Mindfulness: A proposed operational definition. *Clinical Psychology: Science and Practice, 11,* 230–241.

Bonhoeffer, D. (2012). *The cost of discipleship.* Touchstone.

Brown, C. (2016). Can "secular" mindfulness be separated from religion? In R. Purser, D. Forbes, & A. Burke (Eds.), *Handbook of mindfulness: Culture, context, and social engagement* (pp. 75–94). Springer.

Brueggemann, W. (1984). *The message of the psalms: A theological commentary.* Augsburg Publishing House.

Burroughs, J. (2010). *Heavenly-mindedness recommended: In a discourse on Colossians 3:2.* Gale ECCO.

Burroughs, J. (2014). *A treatise on earthly-mindedness.* GLH Publishing.

Carson, D. (1991). *The gospel according to John.* Wm. B. Eerdmans Publishing Company.

Chiesa, A., & Malinowski, P. (2011). Mindfulness-based approaches: Are they all the same? *Journal of Clinical Psychology, 67,* 404–424.

Cohen, J., & Miller, L. (2009). Interpersonal mindfulness training for well-being: A pilot study with psychology graduate students. *Teachers College Record, 111,* 2760–2774.

Dahl, J., Stewart, I., Martell, C., & Kaplan, J. (2014). *ACT and RFT in relationships: Helping clients deepen intimacy and maintain healthy commitments using acceptance and commitment therapy and relational frame theory.* Context Press.

Feldman, G., Hayes, A., Kumar, S., Greeson, J., & Laurenceau, J. (2007). Mindfulness and emotion regulation: The development and initial validation of the Cognitive and Affective Mindfulness Scale-Revisited (CAMS-R). *Journal of Psychopathology and Behavioral Assessment, 29,* 177–190.

Foster, R. (1998). *Streams of living water: Essential practices from the six great traditions of Christian faith.* Renovare.

Fuentes, A., Pineda, M., & Venkata, K. (2018). Comprehension of top 200 prescribed drugs in the US as a resource for pharmacy teaching, training and practice. *Pharmacy, 6,* 43.

Gillet, L. (1985). *On the invocation of the name.* Templegate Publishers.

Gloster, A., Walder, N., Levin, M., Twohig, M., & Karekla, M. (2020). The empirical status of acceptance and commitment therapy: A review of meta-analyses. *Journal of Contextual Behavioral Science, 18,* 181–192.

Grudem, W. (1994). *Systematic theology: An introduction to biblical doctrine.* Zondervan.

Guigo II. (2012). *The ladder of monks* (P. Nau, Trans.) [Kindle version]. Amazon.com.

Harmless, W. (2004). *Desert Christians: An introduction to the literature of early monasticism.* Oxford University Press.

Harris, R. (2007). *The happiness trap: Stop struggling, start living.* Exisle Publishing.

Harris, R. (2009a). *ACT made simple: An easy-to-read primer on Acceptance and Commitment Therapy*. New Harbinger Publications.

Harris, R. (2009b). *ACT with love: Stop struggling, reconcile differences, and strengthen your relationship with acceptance and commitment therapy*. New Harbinger Publications, Inc.

Harris, R. (2019). *ACT made simple: An easy-to-read primer on acceptance and commitment therapy* (2nd ed.). New Harbinger Publications.

Hayes, S. (2002). Buddhism and acceptance and commitment therapy. *Cognitive and Behavioral Practice, 9*, 58–66.

Hayes, S. (2004). Acceptance and commitment therapy and the new behavior therapies: Mindfulness, acceptance, and relationship. In S. Hayes, V. Follette, & M. Linehan (Eds.), *Mindfulness and acceptance: Expanding the cognitive-behavioral tradition* (pp. 1–29). The Guilford Press.

Hayes, S. (2005). *Get out of your mind and into your life: The new acceptance & commitment therapy*. New Harbinger Publications, Inc.

Hayes, S. (2016, February). Psychological flexibility: How love turns pain into purpose [Video]. TED Conferences. https://www.youtube.com/watch?v=o79_gmO5ppg

Hayes, S. (2019). *A liberated mind: How to pivot toward what matters*. Avery.

Hayes, S., Barnes-Holmes, D., & Roche, B. (Eds.). (2013). *Relational frame theory: A post-Skinnerian account of human language and cognition*. Springer.

Hayes, S., Strosahl, K., & Wilson, K. (1999). *Acceptance and commitment therapy: An experiential approach to behavior change*. The Guilford Press.

Hayes, S., Strosahl, K., & Wilson, K. (2012). *Acceptance and commitment therapy: The process and practice of mindful change* (2nd ed.). The Guilford Press.

Helliwell, J., Layard, R., Sachs, J., & De Neve, J. (2020). *World happiness report*. https://happiness-report.s3.amazonaws.com/2020/WHR20.pdf

Jacques, F. (2001). *I say nothing to him, I love him: Contemplative prayer*. Mediaspaul.

Jersild, P. (2000). *Spiritual ethics: Scripture and the moral life*. Augsburg Fortress.

Johnston, W. (2000). *The mysticism of the cloud of unknowing*. Fordham University Press.

Kabat-Zinn, J. (1990). *Full catastrophe living: Using the wisdom of your body and mind to face stress, pain, and illness*. Random House, Inc.

Kabat-Zinn, J. (2012). *Mindfulness for beginners: Reclaiming the present moment—and your life*. Sounds True, Inc.

Knabb, J. (2021). *Christian meditation in clinical practice: A four-step model and workbook for therapists and clients*. InterVarsity Press.

Knabb, J., & Bates, M. (2020). "Holy desire" within the "Cloud of Unknowing": The psychological contributions of medieval apophatic contemplation to Christian mental health in the 21st century. *Journal of Psychology and Christianity, 39*, 24–39.

Knabb, J., Ashby, J., & Ziebell, J. (2010). Two sides of the same coin: The theology of Dietrich Bonhoeffer and acceptance and commitment therapy (ACT). *Journal of Spirituality in Mental Health, 12*, 150–180.

Kok, B., Waugh, C., & Fredrickson, B. (2013). Meditation and health: The search for mechanisms of action. *Social and Personality Psychology Compass, 7*, 27–39.

Laird, M. (2006). *Into the silent land: A guide to the Christian practice of contemplation*. Oxford University Press.

Lane, B. (1998). *The solace of fierce landscapes: Exploring desert and mountain spirituality*. Oxford University Press.

Lawrence, B. (2015). *The practice of the presence of God*. ICS Publications.

Lev, A., & McKay, M. (2017). *Acceptance and commitment therapy for couples: A clinician's guide to using mindfulness, values & schema awareness to rebuild relationships*. New Harbinger Publications, Inc.

Louth, A. (2012). Apophatic and cataphatic theology. In A. Hollywood & P. Beckman (Eds.), *The Cambridge companion to Christian mysticism* (pp. 137–146). Cambridge University Press.

Luoma, J., Hayes, S., & Walser, R. (2007). *Learning ACT: An acceptance and commitment therapy skills training manual for therapists*. Context Press.

Luoma, J., Hayes, S., & Walser, R. (2017). *Learning ACT: An acceptance and commitment therapy skills training manual for therapists* (2nd ed.). Context Press.

Maguire, J. (2001). *Essential Buddhism: A complete guide to beliefs and practices*. Pocket Books.

Mathewes-Green, F. (2011). *Praying the Jesus prayer*. Paraclete Press.

McCown, D., Reibel, D., & Micozzi, M. (2010). *Teaching mindfulness: A practical guide for clinicians and educators*. Springer.

McGrath, A. (2011). *Christian theology: An introduction* (5th ed.). Wiley.

McKay, M., Fanning, P., Lev, A., & Skeen, M. (2013). *The interpersonal problems workbook: ACT to end painful relationship patterns*. New Harbinger Publications, Inc.

Nelson's Student Bible Dictionary. (2005). *Virtue*. Thomas Nelson, Inc.

New International Version Bible. (2011). Zondervan. https://www.biblegateway.com/

Nikodimos, S. (2015). *The philokalia: The complete text*. R. P. Pryne.

Owen, J. (2016). *Spiritual mindedness*. GLH Publishing.

Paintner, C. (2012). *Desert fathers and mothers: Early Christian wisdom sayings*. SkyLight Paths Publishing.

Pennington, M. (1980). *Centering prayer: Renewing an ancient Christian prayer form*. Doubleday.

Pratscher, S., Rose, A., Markovitz, L., & Bettencourt, A. (2018). Interpersonal mindfulness: Investigating mindfulness in interpersonal interactions, co-rumination, and friendship quality. *Mindfulness, 9*, 1206–1215.

Pratscher, S., Wood, P., King, L., & Bettencourt, B. (2019). Interpersonal mindfulness: Scale development and initial construct validation. *Mindfulness, 10*, 1044–1061.

Rowe, J. (1672). *Heavenly-mindedness and earthly-mindedness: In two parts*. Francis Tyton.

Smith, A. (2013). *Philokalia: The eastern Christian spiritual texts—selections annotated & explained*. SkyLight Paths Publishing.

Walser, R. (2019). *The heart of ACT: Developing a flexible, process-based, and client-centered practice using acceptance and commitment therapy*. New Harbinger Publications, Inc.

Walser, R., & Westrup, D. (2009). *The mindful couple: How acceptance and mindfulness can lead you to the love you want*. New Harbinger Publications, Inc.

Walsh, R., & Shapiro, S. (2006). The meeting of meditative disciplines and Western psychology: A mutually enriching dialogue. *American Psychologist, 61*, 227–239.

Williams, M., Teasdale, J., Segal, Z., & Kabat-Zinn, J. (2012). *The mindful way through depression: Freeing yourself from chronic unhappiness*. The Guilford Press.

Witherington, B. (2001). *The gospel of Mark: A socio-rhetorical commentary*. Wm. B. Eerdmans Publishing Co.

Wright, C. (2017). *Cultivating the fruit of the Spirit: Growing in Christlikeness*. InterVarsity Press.

Zettle, R. (2007). *ACT for depression. A clinician's guide to using acceptance & commitment therapy in treating depression*. New Harbinger Publications, Inc.

Zondervan Illustrated Bible Dictionary. (2011). *Virtue*. Zondervan.

5

MARY, MARTHA, CONTEMPLATION, AND ACTION

Introduction

In the gospel of Luke (*New International Version Bible*, 2011, Luke 10:38–42), Jesus came to the home of Mary and Martha. As Jesus arrived, Martha generously invited him in. Yet, she was rather preoccupied and distracted with guest preparations. Conversely, Mary sat at the feet of Jesus, intently listening to him as he spoke. When she observed Mary's apparent inactivity, Martha became upset and complained to Jesus that Mary was not helping her. In Jesus's famous reply, he acknowledged that Martha was "worried and upset about many things" and Mary chose "what is better."

According to the Christian contemplative tradition, this short story in Luke's gospel elucidates both the contemplative and active life, with Mary representing contemplation and Martha capturing action. Both are necessary for Christians, with this portion of Scripture illuminating a balanced life when following Jesus. For Mary, sitting at Jesus's feet was the primary task, whereas Martha focused on serving as a gift to Jesus.

Immediately preceding this story, Jesus told the parable of the Good Samaritan (Luke 10:25–37), wherein the central focus is on compassionate, loving action (Carroll, 2012). In this famous story, a man was badly beaten and left for dead, with several individuals passing him by without helping him. Yet, a Samaritan man had compassion for him, helping him to an inn so as to nurse him back to health. Thus, between these two stories—one about a Samaritan who responded to a wounded man in need and the other about listening to God in an authentic manner—Jesus was drawing out the importance of balancing hearing and doing in the Christian life (Carroll, 2012).

In this chapter, contemplation and action are explored, utilizing the story of Mary and Martha to integrate psychological science and Scripture. In general, drawing a parallel between Mary's mode and acceptance, as well as Martha's mode and action, counseling and therapy can help Christians with recurrent psychological symptoms to be more compassionate toward the inner world, as well as pursue value-based action in the outer world. To be sure, psychological

DOI: 10.4324/9781003181941-6

113

flexibility, the cornerstone of ACT, involves knowing when to accept unpleasant inner experiences, sitting at the feet of Jesus, along with employing a set of well-defined values in daily living in order to serve Jesus.

Characteristics of Mary

In the story of Mary and Martha, Mary focused attentively on Jesus, which is a central theme (Knight, 1998). Also, as she was attuned to Jesus, she intently listened to Jesus's words, sitting at his feet (Knight, 1998). Thus, Mary represents a disciple learning from her rabbi, receiving his words as she submitted to his will, with this position elucidating that she was listening to his teachings (Carroll, 2012; Green, 1997).

Mary's sustained attention is contrasted with Martha's busyness and distraction. Although Martha was clearly serving Jesus, Mary chose "what is better" because she placed Jesus at the center of her world, fully submitting to him based on her position at his feet, rather than focusing on tasks that were inconsequential in comparison to recognizing and responding to Jesus's presence. Overall, Mary's posture is characterized by attentive, sustained listening, along with a willingness to learn as a disciple. Indeed, when reading this passage, there is a sense that she had tuned everything else out, placing Jesus above life itself. Although Jesus clearly articulated that compassionate, loving action is also required of his disciples, emphasizing this requisite behavior in the parable of the Good Samaritan, Mary's inactivity was preferred because she was focused on learning from her master.

Characteristics of Martha

For Martha, the most important part was activity, given that she was showing hospitality to Jesus as she welcomed him into her home (Carroll, 2012). In fact, Martha eagerly accepted Jesus into her house, focusing on meeting Jesus's needs. In this story, Martha's behavior underscored a ministry of service, prioritizing action above all else in order to make sure he was comfortable in her residence (Carroll, 2012). Yet, Jesus clearly preferred Mary's submissiveness and attentive listening, given that Martha was distracted (Green, 1997). As a result, Martha's service and hospitality were undermined by her struggle to focus on hearing Jesus's teachings, submitting to him as a disciple (Green, 1997). In other words, she was preoccupied with herself, rather than Jesus, especially when she proclaimed, "Tell her to help me!" Her focus on herself, instead of submitting to Jesus's will, was the central problem.

Again, Martha's activity is not the main concern in this story, especially since Jesus just finished teaching about the importance of compassionate, loving action in the parable of the Good Samaritan. In fact, hearing and doing are combined in these two New Testament stories. Instead, for Martha, her preoccupied activity ended up distracting her from the most salient task—submitting to Jesus, focusing attentively on him. As a disciple, Mary recognized her primary goal was to listen with a yielding posture, rather than placing her own needs first. By and large, hearing and doing are both integral parts of the Christian life. Still, doing must be based on a firm desire to serve Jesus, rather than to pursue self-interests, rooted in distracted activity. In other words, "This rhythm of listening quietly and acting decisively is the very rhythm Jesus has displayed in his own working" (Carroll, 2012, p. 248). Throughout the gospels, Jesus listened attentively to the will of his Father, engaging in compassionate, loving action as he fulfilled his purpose on earth. In this story, there are clear parallels with ACT's focus on present-moment awareness, a salient component of psychological flexibility. Whether relating to inner events or acting based on a set of well-defined values, staying rooted in the here-and-now is the most important part of daily living. Therefore, Mary's action was preferred because she seemed to have a loving awareness of Jesus's presence, whereas Martha was distracted, unable to anchor herself in the present moment by gazing upon him. Hypothetically, had Martha been serving Jesus with an attentive, sustained, loving awareness of his presence, there might have been a much different outcome.

Theological Interpretations of Mary and Martha within the Contemplative Tradition

Contemplative writers throughout the ages, including Augustine, Bernard, and Teresa of Avila, have interpreted the story of Mary and Martha as representing the contemplative and active life, respectively. For Gregory, a contemplative theologian and Catholic Pope who lived around the turn of the sixth century, the contemplative life, captured by Mary, involves resting, avoiding action, focusing on God's love, and consenting to the will of God (Cutler, 2003). On the other hand, the active life, expressed by Martha, requires loving acts like feeding the poor and helping those who are sick (Cutler, 2003). Interestingly, Gregory explicated that Jesus modeled both lives, at times healing the ailing, while also withdrawing to pray to God in secret (Cutler, 2003). In general, Gregory argued that combining the contemplative and active life—Mary sitting at the feet of Jesus and Martha serving Jesus—is ideal (Cutler, 2003).

As another example, in the *Cloud of Unknowing*,[1] written by an anonymous English monk in the 14th century, the author highlighted that Martha was actively engaged in serving Jesus, which represents the active life (Bangley, 2006). All Christians, to at least some degree, must embrace activity, which is necessary in this world. Conversely, Mary attentively listened to Jesus, drawing in his wisdom, which captures the contemplative life (Bangley, 2006). In fact, for Mary, nothing got in the way of her simple, loving focus on Jesus, sitting in silence as she gazed upon him. Certainly, the contemplative life transcends this world, given that a deeper relationship with God extends into the afterlife (Bangley, 2006).

For the author of the *Cloud of Unknowing*, this story captures the active life, which Christians are to fully embrace while on earth, along with the contemplative life, which involves transcending knowledge and developing a loving gaze upon God, beyond words, images, and any other mental distractions (Bangley, 2006). In moments of contemplation, thoughts, feelings, sensations, and memories are placed beneath a *cloud of forgetting*, given that the *Cloud* author draws a contrast between knowledge and love in moving closer to God (Bangley, 2006). In other words, knowledge is inherently limiting when approaching God, since human cognition can never fully capture God's totality (Bangley, 2006). Thus, contemplatives must let go of a preoccupation with knowledge when cultivating a deeper relationship with their Creator, pursing an *apophatic* form of prayer (Bangley, 2006).

Once this pursuit of knowledge is de-emphasized, placed under a cloud of forgetting, practitioners quickly look up to a *cloud of unknowing*, which symbolizes the place where Christians lovingly interact with God, beyond knowledge (Bangley, 2006). In fact, the obscurity within this cloud represents a "dark" mental space, wherein God is pursued with a simple, present-moment, loving attentiveness, rather than abstract, preconceived notions of God (Bangley, 2006; Knabb & Bates, 2020). For contemplatives who struggle with distraction, the *Cloud* author recommended using a short, simple, single-syllable word (e.g., "God," "love") to attentively focus on God, capturing a loving gaze upon him (Bangley, 2006). According to the author of the *Cloud*, during such moments of silent, passive attention, God will either fully provide or help practitioners to faithfully endure any trial (Bangley, 2006). Because of this, when sitting at Jesus's feet, using a "prayer word" to symbolically gaze upon him, there is nowhere else to be and nothing else to do.

As a side note, as a more contemporary version of contemplation, based in part on the recommendations offered by the *Cloud* author, centering prayer helps practitioners surrender to God's divine presence, cultivating an awareness that he is actively engaging with, and healing, the unconscious (Keating, 2006). Within 20-minute, formal sessions of contemplation, practitioners slowly, softly, and simply repeat a "prayer word" that captures their willingness to yield to God's presence, with the selected word symbolizing a sort of gazing upon God, similar to Mary sitting at the feet of Jesus. Within this present-moment awareness of God's active, loving presence, Christians relate to inner experiences in a passive, accepting manner, gently acknowledging the thoughts, feelings, sensations, and memories that pull their attention away from their "prayer word." In turn, practitioners shift their focus back to their "prayer word" as a symbol of their willingness to repeatedly surrender to God's presence, despite a plethora of distractions that pass through the inner world.

Ultimately, the "prayer word" in centering prayer may just as easily be described as a "surrender word" or "acceptance word," given the purpose is to, like Mary, yield to God's presence within, shifting from self-sufficiency and -reliance to total reliance upon God. Indeed, in this *apophatic* practice, Christians are simply deepening their awareness of what is already present—God is dwelling within, offering his perfect love from the outside-in to the inside-out in each unfolding moment of the day. Stated differently, because Christians become God's dwelling place as they move from justification (i.e., being declared righteous by, and reconciled to, God through Jesus), to sanctification (i.e., becoming more like Jesus), to glorification (i.e., being face to face with Jesus) (Grudem, 1994), the purpose of this type of simple, silent contemplative practice is for Christians to recognize that the God of love is active and present within their inner world, then gradually shed their overreliance on the thoughts, feelings, sensations, and memories that they commonly employ to guide life, apart from God. As Christians continue with contemplative practice, they are cultivating an "adoring, uncomplicated, and enduring attention of the soul to divine things" (de Sales, 2011, p. 46), moving from Mary's contemplation to Martha's action as they apply this present-moment awareness of God's perfect love (Knabb & Bates, 2020) to daily life.

Returning to the story, when responding to Martha's complaint, the *Cloud* author explained that Jesus was, in essence, saying the following:

> Activities, activities, work hard at your merciful business now, but do not interfere with the work of contemplatives. You simply do not understand what they are doing. Leave them alone. Grant them the stillness and quiet of Mary's third and best part.
>
> (Bangley, 2006, pp. 32–33)

Indeed, contemplation and action are two sides of the same coin, with contemplation beginning the process of deepening a loving relationship with God that transcends worldly action. As Christians are better able to yield to God's active, loving presence within the inner word, recognizing that they are a dwelling place for God's love, they are, in turn, able to extend God's love to others in the outer world—an outside-in to inside-out dynamic. Worded another way, by "gazing on God with the inner eye of love" (Pickering, 2019, p. 195), Christians, consequently, can more authentically love others.

As one final contemplative lens through which to view this story, in the *Interior Castle*, Theresa of Avila suggested that Mary and Martha had to work in unison, given that Mary was able to sit at Jesus's feet because of the fact that Martha chose to serve him (Teresa, 2002). In other words, contemplation and action are intermingled and, thus, are not to be seen as adversaries. Certainly, living in the same house, Mary and Martha worked together as they interacted with Jesus. For Christians in the 21st century, there will be moments of action, serving Jesus, the Body of Christ, and the world, along with instances of contemplation, sitting at Jesus's feet in silent, loving submission, discerning God's will, and basking in God's perfect love.

To summarize, Martha represents the active life, including acts of charity, service, and self-sacrifice, which should be grounded in God's love. For Christians, action is a necessary part of faith-based living, just so long as servanthood is linked to an awareness of Jesus in the present moment. In fact, following Jesus as his disciple involves a compassionate, loving response, similar to the parable of the Good Samaritan. In addition, contemplation is a vital, though often overlooked, part of the Christian faith, with Mary capturing a simple, yet profound, attitude of loving submission toward Jesus. Listening intently, focusing entirely on him, Mary was able to learn from Jesus as she blocked out all of the distractions that would have pulled her away from him. These two positions, Mary's hearing and Martha's doing, represent distinct, yet overlapping, modes in the Christian life.

Interestingly, several counseling and therapy approaches in the 21st century seem to also advocate balancing acceptance and action in daily living. What follows, therefore, is a review of three such orientations—mindfulness-based cognitive therapy (MBCT), dialectical behavior therapy (DBT), and acceptance and commitment therapy (ACT)—in order to develop an integrative understanding of an acceptance-action blend for Christian clients struggling with recurrent psychological symptoms. Like Mary and Martha living in the same house, working together to meet Jesus's needs, Christian clients must embrace both acceptance and action in order to cultivate psychological flexibility, the cornerstone of mental health.

Parallels between Mary and Martha and Acceptance-Based Counseling and Therapy

In the story of Mary and Martha, Christian writers throughout the ages have drawn a contrast between the contemplative and active life, with some highlighting the importance of Mary and Martha working together. In a similar vein, several contemporary counseling and therapy approaches advocate for both acceptance and action within daily living, especially when responding to a variety of recurrent psychological symptoms. At times, the acceptance of symptoms is necessary, given the chronic nature of some inner experiences. On the other hand, change may be necessary in order to cultivate a vital, meaningful life. Because of this, Christian clients may benefit from an integrative approach that draws from the best of both worlds, embracing a theologically and psychologically sensitive strategy that amalgamates acceptance and action.

Over a decade ago, Williams (2008) offered an overview of the technology of mindfulness, defining the term and exploring different "modes of mind" for clients struggling with recurrent depression. Based on the central tenets of MBCT (Segal et al., 2012), Williams highlighted that mindfulness involves several salient ingredients, including an awareness of experiences that unfold from minute to minute, gently paying attention to a variety of responses to inner events, and moving forward with a gentle, open, and curious posture. Embedded within this process is an attitude of loving compassion, which helps practitioners respond to inner activity with more flexibility and distance, given that unpleasant thoughts, feelings, sensations, and memories are no longer viewed as negative, debilitating, or harmful (Williams, 2008). In essence, mindfulness is a form of nonjudgmental, present-focused, sustained, flexible attention (Bishop et al., 2004; Segal et al., 2012), leaning into difficult private experiences, rather than attempting to avoid or eliminate them, which can derail life.

In this same article, Williams (2008) laid out a strategy for better understanding two distinct responses to depressive symptoms, including the "being" and "doing" modes. In the "doing" mode, or "discrepancy-based processing," clients are aware that a great distance exists between the current state of affairs and their goal for the inner world, attempting to ameliorate the gap between their present and wished-for psychological state (Williams, 2008). One common strategy for achieving their desired psychological state is avoidance, wherein clients try to get rid of unpleasant inner experiences (Williams, 2008). As a final characteristic, the "doing" mode is typically grounded in the past or future, rather than the present moment, with clients ruminating about a troubled past or worrying about perceived impending doom (Williams, 2008).

In contrast, in the "being" mode, clients accept the inner world as it is, without striving to ameliorate their current mental state (Williams, 2008). Also, the "being" mode is firmly rooted in the present moment, accepting, rather than avoiding, unpleasant inner experiences (Williams, 2008). Here, there seem to be clear parallels with Mary's unassuming, relaxed, sustained attentiveness, given that her primary task was to simply yield to Jesus's presence, devoting her entire attention to him. As Martha strived to close the distance between her actual and desired state, Mary was unencumbered by such demands. Instead, her focus remained on Jesus, disregarding all peripheral distractions and accepting that the place in which she was seated, at Jesus's feet, was exactly where she needed to be.

For Christian clients with recurrent psychological symptoms, shifting from Martha's "doing" mode to Mary's "being" mode may be helpful, especially when relating to difficult, chronic inner experiences. If Mary's submissive posture represents the inner world, Christian clients can work toward simply accepting their unpleasant thoughts, feelings, sensations, and memories, given that Jesus is with them. Certainly, if Jesus is present, there is no other place to be and nothing else to do. Rather than being preoccupied with changing or eliminating distressing inner states, in the Mary mode, Christians can continuously shift their focus from distracting symptoms to Jesus's loving instructions. To be a disciple, sitting at Jesus's feet, involves present-focused attentiveness, nonjudgmental awareness of distracting symptoms, and the determination to gently return to a loving, tender gaze. Conversely, it may be advantageous to shift to the "doing" mode, reminiscent of Martha, when Christians are following Jesus through loving action in the outer world, given that "doing" is not inherently problematic. Rather, the "doing" mode creates challenges when it is applied to inner events that cannot be eradicated.

As another example, DBT, originally developed for borderline personality disorder, blends acceptance and change in order to help clients effectively regulate affect (Lynch et al., 2006). In DBT, radical acceptance and behavioral change are both embraced, given that clients with affect regulation difficulties commonly need to change aspects of their current functioning (Lynch et al., 2006). Yet, on the other hand, pursuing a purely change-based agenda can leave clients feeling invalidated because of an ongoing struggle with emotion regulation (Lynch et al., 2006). Because of this, DBT utilizes two change- and two acceptance-based skills modules to teach a variety of new coping strategies (Lynch et al., 2006). Focusing on interpersonal skills, coping strategies for tolerating distress, ways to more effectively regulate overwhelming affect, and mindfulness-based awareness, DBT counselors and therapists help clients to dialectically blend acceptance and action (Lynch et al., 2006). Drawing heavily from mindfulness, DBT clients learn how to notice distressing inner experiences without judging them or reacting to them, fundamentally accepting the parts of their experience they cannot change (Lynch et al., 2006).

With Christian clients, blending acceptance and change is necessary when following Jesus. In terms of recurrent symptoms, many clients struggle to fully eliminate inner distress, which can serve as a distraction to attentively listening to Jesus's teachings. Therefore, radical acceptance, along with the central tenets of mindfulness, seem to parallel Mary's willingness to fully surrender to Jesus's will. Connected to the present moment, firmly planted at Jesus's feet, Mary was able to accept her distracting surroundings, maintaining a loving, attentive gaze upon her instructor as she listened to his teachings. Still, as noted previously, action is also required for Christians. Thus, throughout life, "doing" via servanthood, reminiscent of Martha, will also be necessary, changing the things that need to be changed in order to faithfully follow Jesus.

As one final illustration, ACT employs both acceptance and value-based action to help clients relate to the inner world with more openness and flexibility, while, at the same time, pursuing a set of values that serve as a guide for life (Luoma et al., 2017). In other words, unpleasant thoughts, feelings, sensations, and memories rarely, if ever, lead clients in a life direction that cultivates meaning, purpose, and vitality (Blackledge & Barnes-Holmes, 2009). Instead, the inner world tends to fluctuate, change, wax, and wane (Luoma et al., 2017). Because of this, values, rather than malleable, impermanent inner states, offer a much more reliable road for life, helping clients to create meaning and purpose (Luoma et al., 2017). For ACT clients, values are the "vehicle," but a courageous willingness to live them out, despite recurrent inner pain, is the "motor." Worded differently, clients must be prepared to act, behaviorally speaking, rather than merely developing a set of values as an abstract endeavor (Luoma et al., 2017). By blending acceptance of the inner world and action in the outer world, clients are able to shift the focus from symptom reduction to vital, authentic living (Luoma et al., 2017). Accepting painful thoughts, feelings, sensations, and memories; creating some distance from the reified world of language; recognizing that there is a transcendent, spiritual sense of self beyond impermanent inner states; and staying connected to the present moment helps clients to cultivate psychological flexibility, continuously pushing forward and heading in a valued direction (Luoma et al., 2017).

To draw a parallel with the story of Mary and Martha, Christian clients can learn to accept unpleasant thoughts, feelings, sensations, and memories as they sit at Jesus's feet, just noticing the inner world without getting overwhelmed and continuously shifting their focus back to Jesus as distractions naturally arise. What is more, Christian clients can serve Jesus, similar to Martha, knowing they are in the presence of their Lord and Savior and recognizing they must respond to those in need, similar to the central figure in the parable of the Good Samaritan. Blending hearing and doing, like acceptance and action, can help Christian clients to place Jesus at the center, rather than being bullied around by unpleasant inner experiences and struggling to act because they have lost their way.

In sum, contemporary ACT tends to utilize mindfulness to help clients accept the inner world, focusing on behavioral action in the outer world.[2] Although there are clear similarities between mindfulness (which commonly originates from Buddhism) and contemplation (which commonly originates from Christianity), there are also some differences, explicated below in order to help counselors and therapists offer a faith-based version of acceptance to Christian clients. Above all else, although some of the skills developed within both practices may be similar (e.g., attention, present-moment awareness, acceptance) (Feldman et al., 2007; Knabb et al., 2019, 2021), the point of focus and purpose (i.e., *telos*) may be different (Walsh & Shapiro, 2006). Christian contemplation, for example, is about cultivating a "loving, simple, and permanent attention of the spirit to divine things" (de Sales, 2012) so as to commune with God (Knabb, 2021). Conversely, Buddhist-influenced mindfulness often emphasizes attending to the breath or one of the senses in order to gain insight into the "three marks of existence" and ameliorate suffering (Crane, 2017). What follows, therefore, is a more detailed overview of the similarities and differences, paving the way for a faith-based version of ACT that infuses the acceptance-based processes with Christian contemplation, rather than mindfulness.

Christian Contemplation and Buddhist Mindfulness: Similarities and Differences[3]

In both mindfulness practice, commonly inspired by the Buddhist tradition, and Christian contemplation, captured by Mary's submissive alertness to Jesus, practitioners cultivate sustained, flexible attention by repeatedly shifting to a designated point of focus when they recognize the mind has drifted. In addition, practitioners develop acceptance by relating to thoughts, feelings, sensations, and memories in a nonjudgmental, compassionate, kind, and gentle manner, simply acknowledging when they have been distracted by the inner world, before returning to a predetermined focal point. In other words, the emphasis is on a direct, unmediated experience, rather than being preoccupied with the mind's judgmental, evaluative interpretations of the unfolding moment. Finally, with both methods, clients are firmly rooted in the present moment, rather than engrossed in the past or future. To do this, clients tend to focus on a stabilizing physical experience, like the breath, which helps them to avoid the distractions emanating from an overactive mind. Again, these skills—attention, present-moment awareness, and acceptance (Feldman et al., 2007)—are often present across both practices.

However, foundational differences between Buddhist-influenced mindfulness and Christian contemplation include (a) the intentional point of focus, (b) the *telos*, or end goal, and (c) the individual versus relational nature of the experience. For those practicing mindfulness, attention is commonly drawn in a sustained manner toward the breath, hearing, seeing, feeling, touching, or tasting. In other words, attending to the breath or senses helps practitioners to nonjudgmentally focus on impermanent passing events in the present moment. Over time, this helps clients relate to the inner world in a more passive, noncritical, and flexible way, simply allowing psychological experiences to run their natural course, without having to do anything, other than simply observe them. Indeed, thoughts, feelings, sensations, and memories are viewed as transitory experiences, on equal footing with other impermanent sensory information, such as hearing a bird chirping or a car driving by. As noted by Williams (2008), with the "being" mode, there is a nonjudgmental, present-focused awareness of inner encounters, without a need to change anything. Stated differently, there is no gap that needs to be closed, given that everything is exactly how it is supposed to be in the present moment (Williams, 2008). Discrepancies, to be sure, do not exist between some sort of current and optimal state (Williams, 2008). Ultimately, for mindfulness practitioners, the end goal is the amelioration of suffering, given they are gaining insight into the "three marks of existence" (i.e., life is suffering, everything is impermanent, there is no individual self) (Kok et al., 2013; McCown et al., 2010), and the experience is an individual, not relational, one. (Of course, there has been a more recent emphasis on interpersonal mindfulness in the psychology literature [Pratscher et al., 2019], which will be mentioned repeatedly throughout the book. Still, there is no personal deity in Buddhism, which means the practitioner has no monotheistic God to relate to, as is the case with Christian contemplation.)

122

Embedded within Christian contemplation and inspired in part by Mary's yielding attitude toward Jesus is most certainly attention, present-moment awareness, and acceptance. The focal point, of course, is Jesus, commonly symbolized by the breath or a "prayer word," with surrendering to him as a central aim. Undoubtedly, the end goal of contemplative practice is a deeper communion with God (Knabb, 2021), submitting to his will because he is infinitely loving, wise, and powerful. In other words, because Christians are God's dwelling place, recognizing his active, loving presence in the midst of the ups and downs of life is paramount. Along the way, practitioners are pursuing a relational, not individual, experience, given the God of love is at the center. Step by step, Christian contemplatives are learning to relate differently to inner experiences, given their newfound awareness that God is active and present in the inner world, offering his perfect love from moment to moment. Suffering, as a result, is experienced differently, given practitioners are not alone to struggle with their pain.

Like Mary simply sitting at the feet of Jesus, the end goal is to gaze upon God, recognizing that the purpose of a disciple is to listen to Jesus's teachings and surrender to his will. The breath or "prayer word" serves as a symbolic gesture of consent, rather than an end in and of itself (Keating, 2006). In other words, returning to a short, simple, single-syllable "prayer word" (e.g., "Lord," "God," "love") or the breath helps Christian clients to focus on God, rather than getting pulled away by inner experiences, whether pleasant or unpleasant (Bangley, 2006). Similar to Mary's possible realization that there was nowhere else to be and nothing else to do, Christian practitioners are to submit to God's will, attentively focusing on Jesus from moment to moment through the use of a "prayer word" or the breath. As the attention wanders, Christians are to gently return to the "prayer word" or breath, similar to Mary shifting her gaze back to Jesus after a moment of distraction. Over time, the emphasis is on sitting with Jesus, in silence, recognizing that he is actively and lovingly working in the life of the Christian. In the process, thoughts, feelings, sensations, and memories are neither pursued nor actively discarded, given that Christian contemplatives are seeking a direct experience of God and recognizing that language (and other experiences in the inner world) is inherently limiting, failing to fully capture God's majesty.

An Exercise for Cultivating Hearing and the Mary Mode: Christian Contemplation[4]

The following transcript can be used with Christian clients in order to cultivate the Mary mode of "being," integrating mindfulness and contemplative practice. The skills developed in this exercise include attention, present-moment awareness, and acceptance (Feldman et al., 2007). Yet, unique to Christianity, the point of focus is Jesus and end goal is a loving communion with God (Knabb, 2021; Knabb & Bates, 2020), with the amelioration of suffering as a byproduct of recognizing that the inner world is a dwelling place for God and, thus, Christians are not alone to experience their psychological pain.

Get into a comfortable position with your eyes closed. Sit up straight, with your feet gently touching the floor. Place your palms outward to symbolize your receptivity to God's presence, trusting that he is active during this exercise. Now, begin to recognize that you are breathing. Notice there is nothing you need to do on your part. God has given you the gift of breathing, which you do not need to control in any way. Allow your breathing, which God controls naturally, to symbolize your willingness to simply sit at the feet of Jesus, without needing to do anything. There is nowhere else to be and nothing else to do. Just sitting at the feet of Jesus is all you need in this moment.

Again, just notice your breathing, which represents your consent to Jesus's active, loving presence. Whenever a thought, feeling, sensation, or memory arises, simply acknowledge it, before gently shifting your focus back to your breathing, which captures your willingness to surrender to the love of Jesus in this moment. Each and every time you recognize that your mind has distracted you, gently return your attention to your breathing, capturing your loving gaze upon Jesus.

When you are ready, begin to slowly, softly, gently, and simply recite the word "love" in your mind, allowing it to repeat itself as a symbolic gesture of trustful submissiveness to Jesus's loving presence, letting go of all efforts to control your inner world. As you let the word "love" gently float in your mind, sink deeper and deeper into your loving surrender to God, resting in God's presence and knowing that Jesus is in full control as he ministers to you. There is nowhere else to be and nothing else to do as you sit at his feet. You are firmly planted in this moment with your Lord and Savior, rooted in his loving care. Whatever thoughts, feelings, sensations, or memories arise, simply acknowledge them and return to the word "love" to capture your willingness to listen to Jesus as his disciple. Each time you notice an unpleasant inner experience, relate to it with an attitude of openness and receptivity, recognizing that there is nothing to fear because you are sitting at the feet of Jesus.

As this exercise comes to a close, thank Jesus for his active, loving presence, asking him to remain with you throughout the day. When you are comfortable, you can open your eyes again, allowing this flexible, receptive attitude to continue with you from moment to moment.

The Challenges of Daily Contemplative Practice

Similar to daily mindfulness practice, contemplative practice can be difficult for both beginners and advanced practitioners. Because of this, it is important for faith-based ACT counselors and therapists to normalize the experience that Christian clients may have when getting started. Due to the fast-paced society that many Christian clients live in, asking them to sit in silence and stillness with God for a minimum of 20 minutes per day can be a lot to request. Within the practice, powerful emotions may arise, along with thoughts of doubt, sensations of pain, and memories that conjure up distress, given that Christian clients are no longer using avoidance strategies to distract themselves from inner turmoil. To "stay put," reminiscent of the early desert Christians (Paintner, 2012), means to help Christian clients recognize that consistent contemplative practice typically bears fruit in daily living, rather than during the actual session, given that a deeper awareness of God's active presence is slowly being cultivated, leading to improved psychological flexibility. Therefore, some sort of positive feeling or pleasant inner state is not to be sought as a central aim during the actual practice. In fact, the contemplative literature often mentions the reality of a "dark night of the soul" (John, 2002), sometimes filled with agony and pain, since practitioners are slowly letting go of attachments to this world in order to pursue a deeper communion with God. Above all else, this can be a difficult process and should certainly not be minimized with matter-of-fact descriptions of an inevitably blissful, happy, and enlightened state. As a reminder, the main purpose is to relate differently to inner experiences because there is a newfound recognition that God is dwelling within, not futilely attempt to eradicate them and, thus, get discouraged when the long list of unwanted inner experiences does not go away.

Yet, over time, many Christian clients will begin to enjoy the solitude, silence, and stillness that emanates from sitting at Jesus's feet, with love as their motivation during the ups and downs of daily practice. Along the way, there may be periods of time that do not bear visible, tangible fruit. When this happens, counselors and therapists can continue to encourage Christian clients to simply rest at Jesus's feet, even when experiencing inner discomfort and restlessness, given that the alternative—experiential avoidance—does not work, leading to "pain on top of pain" (Hayes, 2005). For a more detailed discussion of common challenges with contemplative practice, along with ways to effectively respond to roadblocks, see Frenette (2012).

A Technique for Developing Doing and the Martha Mode: Opposite Action

In addition to the aforementioned exercise to help Christian clients shift to the Mary mode during moments of distress, DBT's "opposite action" exercise

(Brodsky & Stanley, 2013) can be modified for Christian clients to follow Jesus, despite unpleasant thoughts, feelings, sensations, or memories. Representing the Martha mode of "doing," this exercise can be used whenever Christian clients struggle with walking with God in love on the road of life. By combining acceptance and action, Christian clients can develop a greater capacity to flexibly navigate the inner and outer worlds, responding to Jesus's teachings and instructions as a faithful disciple.

With "opposite action," an emotion regulation skill within DBT, clients learn to face distressing emotions, rather than trying to avoid them (Brodsky & Stanley, 2013). By engaging in behavior that is the opposite of avoiding, clients are exposed to the distressing emotion, learning that the inner experience will not overwhelm them (Brodsky & Stanley, 2013). Thus, rather than using avoidance as an ineffective means to regulate unpleasant feelings, clients manage difficult inner events by leaning into them, carrying distressing emotions with them as they engage in effective, authentic action.

For Christian clients, following Jesus as his disciple requires loving action, similar to the man who acted in the parable of the Good Samaritan. Although the other characters in the story passed by the wounded man, the main character responded by carrying him to an inn to help him recover. This type of loving action, to be sure, is an important component of Christian living, requiring effective behavior in the face of unpleasant inner experiences.

In counseling and therapy, Christian clients can make a list of small steps to take to follow Jesus's teachings, acting in love, rather than avoidance. For example, if a Christian client is feeling overwhelmed with anxiety, experiencing recurrent thoughts of social rejection when considering helping out in a ministry to greet new congregants at a Sunday church service, the "opposite action" exercise can help them to connect to the unpleasant feeling, acknowledge that they would usually avoid the situation, and follow through with the opposite behavior, asking "What would Jesus do in this situation?"[5] Thus, deciding the direction to take involves following Jesus, recognizing that *he* acts as the guide, rather than avoidance behavior in an attempt to eliminate the distressing inner state. Over time, asking how Jesus would respond, then acting upon this awareness, can help Christian clients to face unpleasant emotions, recognizing distressing affect can "come along for the ride," rather than bully them around.

To conclude, this exercise can assist Christian clients in cultivating the Martha mode of "doing," acting on Jesus's teachings. By acknowledging distressing feelings and acting in an opposite manner, Christian clients are repeatedly exposing themselves to the previously feared emotion and habituating themselves to what was formerly viewed as catastrophic. Sitting with Jesus to accept difficult emotions, along with acting with opposite behavior to serve Jesus, can help Christian clients to authentically live out the Christian life, recognizing the importance of following Jesus as his disciple.

A Clinical Example

Derrick, a 42-year-old, married, White male, presented to therapy because of recurrent depression. Over the past few years, he became increasingly immobile because of arthritis, leading to an inability to work as an electrician. In addition, he was no longer able to play basketball, something he loved to do, and could not go hiking anymore, a hobby he had regularly engaged in since he was a child.

As he lost his ability to work and enjoy physical activities, he became increasingly depressed, struggling with low mood, *anhedonia*, decreased appetite, extreme guilt, low self-esteem, and hopelessness. In fact, his marriage began to suffer as well, with his wife accusing him of "giving up on life." For Derrick, life became meaningless because his identity was intertwined with physical activity. In fact, he began to see himself as "worthless," given that he could not financially provide for his family.

At church, he was no longer able to participate in the weekly basketball league, barely managing to hang out with his friends on the team because of his physical limitations. In therapy, he repeatedly talked about the tremendous sense of loss he felt as he watched others actively living life, knowing that his arthritis would continue to get worse. Indeed, his physician informed him that he would need reconstructive surgery on several joints, leading to an additional sense of hopelessness.

Over the course of about a dozen sessions, Derrick worked with his therapist on learning to sit at the feet of Jesus during moments of hopelessness, fatigue, and low self-esteem, surrendering to God and cultivating present-moment awareness. Rather than feeling hopeless because he could not close the distance between how things were and how he wanted them to be, Derrick began to let go of all expectations about an alternative reality, choosing, instead, to allow things to simply be, exactly how they are, in the present moment. Using the word "love," Derrick practiced sinking into Jesus's loving presence, recognizing that there was nowhere else to be and nothing else to do when he was listening to his Lord and Savior. This "being" mode, reminiscent of Mary's attentive, loving gaze, helped Derrick learn to accept his current situation, finding peace by cultivating an attitude of nonjudgment.

In addition, Derrick worked with his therapist on strategies to embrace the Martha mode of "doing," recognizing that he could take steps toward serving Jesus at his church by setting smaller goals to accomplish. Whenever he felt overwhelmed with hopelessness and sadness, Derrick would ask the question, "What would Jesus do in this situation?" As he began to volunteer in several ministries at his church, he recognized that he could serve, like Martha, in the midst of his hopelessness, slowly habituating himself to his unpleasant inner states. Rather than avoiding life because he could no longer play basketball, Derrick learned to find joy in other activities, especially singing in the church

127

choir, something he never used to believe he could do. Above all else, combining Mary's "being" and Martha's "doing" helped Derrick to live life again, despite continued unpleasant inner experiences, as well as several reconstructive surgeries and an increasing loss of mobility.

Conclusion

Throughout the ages, the story of Mary and Martha has offered a contrast between the contemplative and active life, with many authors highlighting that hearing and doing are two sides of the same coin within the Christian faith. For Christian clients in counseling and therapy, Mary's mode of "being" can help them relate to difficult inner experiences with more openness and flexibility, recognizing that there is nowhere else to be and nothing else to do as they learn from their Lord and Savior. Conversely, Martha's mode of "doing" can help Christian clients to recognize the importance of loving action, serving Jesus despite psychological symptoms that may never fully go away. Combined, acceptance and action can offer Christian clients the opportunity both to learn from Jesus and follow him, flexibly switching between these two modes in daily life, depending on the need. In the next few chapters, the six processes of ACT are explored in more detail, further helping Christian clients with recurrent symptoms to accept the inner world and follow Jesus in the outer world.

Notes

1 For a more detailed review of the teachings of the *Cloud of Unknowing*, see Johnson (2000).
2 Here, it is important to mention that some mindfulness-based therapies in the cognitive behavioral literature seem to rely more overtly on the Buddhist influences of mindfulness than others. For example, although ACT frequently mentions mindfulness when discussing its acceptance-based processes (Hayes et al., 2012), it was not developed with explicitly Buddhist roots (Hayes, 2002), whereas both DBT (Linehan, 2014; Robins, 2002) and MBCT (Crane, 2017; Fennell & Segal, 2011) drew from at least some Buddhist principles in developing their acceptance-based therapies within the cognitive behavioral tradition.
3 See Hayes et al. (2012), Linehan (2014), and Segal et al. (2012) for a discussion of the central tenets of contemporary mindfulness practice within the cognitive behavioral literature, as well as Finley (2004) and Keating (2006) for common characteristics of contemporary contemplative practice within the Christian tradition.
4 This exercise combines recommendations from Keating (2006), Finley (2004), Frenette (2012), Knabb and Bates (2020), and Segal et al. (2012), integrating mindfulness and contemplation for Christian clients.
5 It is worth mentioning, Sheldon's (1899) classic, *In His Steps*, asked this very question, with the fictional character radically living a life devoted to following Jesus based on his answer from moment to moment.

References

Bangley, B. (Ed.). (2006). *The cloud of unknowing: Contemporary English edition*. Paraclete Press.

Bishop, S., Lau, M., Shapiro, S., Carlson, L., Anderson, N., Carmody, J., Segal, Z., Abbey, S., Speca, M., Velting, D., & Devins, G. (2004). Mindfulness: A proposed operational definition. *Clinical Psychology: Science and Practice, 11*, 230–241.

Blackledge, J., & Barnes-Holmes, D. (2009). Core processes in acceptance and commitment therapy. In J. Blackledge, J. Ciarrochi, & F. Deane (Eds.), *Acceptance and commitment therapy: Contemporary theory research and practice* (pp. 41–58). Australian Academic Press.

Brodsky, B., & Stanley, B. (2013). *The dialectical behavior therapy primer: How DBT can inform clinical practice*. Wiley.

Carroll, J. (2012). *Luke: A commentary*. Westminster John Knox Press.

Crane, R. (2017). *Mindfulness-based cognitive therapy: Distinctive features* (2nd ed.). Routledge.

Cutler, D. (2003). *Western mysticism: Augustine, Gregory and Bernard on contemplation and the contemplative life*. Dover Publications, Inc.

de Sales, F. (2011). *Treatise on the love of God: Contemporary English version*. Paraclete Press.

de Sales, F. (2012). *Treatise on the love of God*. TAN Books.

Feldman, G., Hayes, A., Kumar, S., Greeson, J., & Laurenceau, J. (2007). Mindfulness and emotion regulation: The development and initial validation of the Cognitive and Affective Mindfulness Scale-Revisited (CAMS-R). *Journal of Psychopathology and Behavioral Assessment, 29*, 177–190.

Fennell, M., & Segal, Z. (2011). Mindfulness-based cognitive therapy: Culture clash or creative fusion? *Contemporary Buddhism: An Interdisciplinary Journal, 12*, 125–142.

Finley, J. (2004). *Christian meditation: Experiencing the presence of God*. HarperCollins Publishers, Inc.

Frenette, D. (2012). *The path of centering prayer: Deepening your experience of God*. Sounds True, Inc.

Green, J. (1997). *The gospel of Luke*. Wm. B. Eerdmans Publishing Co.

Grudem, W. (1994). *Systematic theology: An introduction to biblical doctrine*. Zondervan.

Hayes, S. (2002). Buddhism and acceptance and commitment therapy. *Cognitive and Behavioral Practice, 9*, 58–66.

Hayes, S. (2005). *Get out of your mind and into your life: The new acceptance & commitment therapy*. New Harbinger Publications, Inc.

Hayes, S., Strosahl, K., & Wilson, K. (2012). *Acceptance and commitment therapy: The process and practice of mindful change* (2nd ed.). The Guilford Press.

John, S. (2002). *Dark night of the soul*. Riverhead Books.

Johnson, W. (2000). *The mysticism of the cloud of unknowing*. Fordham University Press.

Keating, T. (2006). *Open mind, open heart, 20th anniversary edition*. Continuum.

Knabb, J. (2021). *Christian meditation in clinical practice: A four-step model and workbook for therapists and clients*. InterVarsity Press.

Knabb, J., & Bates, M. (2020). "Holy desire" within the "Cloud of Unknowing": The psychological contributions of medieval apophatic contemplation to Christian mental health in the 21st century. *Journal of Psychology and Christianity, 39*, 24–39.

Knabb, J., Vazquez, V., & Pate, R. (2019). 'Set your minds on things above': Shifting from trauma-based ruminations to ruminating on God. *Mental Health, Religion & Culture, 22*, 384–399.

Knabb, J., Vazquez, V., Pate, R., Garzon, F., Wang, K., Edison-Riley, D., Slick, A., Smith, R., & Weber, S. (2021). Christian meditation for trauma-based rumination: A two-part study examining the effects of an internet-based four-week program. *Spirituality in Clinical Practice*. Advance online publication.

Knight, J. (1998). *Luke's gospel*. Routledge.

Kok, B., Waugh, C., & Fredrickson, B. (2013). Meditation and health: The search for mechanisms of action. *Social and Personality Psychology Compass, 7*, 27–39.

Linehan, M. (2014). *DBT skills training manual* (2nd ed.). The Guilford Press.

Luoma, J., Hayes, S., & Walser, R. (2017). *Learning ACT: An acceptance and commitment therapy skills training manual for therapists* (2nd ed.). Context Press.

Lynch, T., Chapman, A., Rosenthal, M., Kuo, J., & Linehan, M. (2006). Mechanisms of change in dialectical behavior therapy: Theoretical and empirical observations. *Journal of Clinical Psychology, 62*, 459–480.

McCown, D., Reibel, D., & Micozzi, M. (2010). *Teaching mindfulness: A practical guide for clinicians and educators*. Springer.

New International Version Bible. (2011). Zondervan. https://www.biblegateway.com/

Paintner, C. (2012). *Desert fathers and mothers: Early Christian wisdom sayings*. SkyLight Paths Publishing.

Pickering, J. (2019). *The search for meaning in psychotherapy: Spiritual practice, the apophatic way and Bion*. Routledge.

Pratscher, S., Wood, P., King, L., & Bettencourt, B. (2019). Interpersonal mindfulness: Scale development and initial construct validation. *Mindfulness, 10*, 1044–1061.

Robins, C. (2002). Zen principles and mindfulness practice in dialectical behavior therapy. *Cognitive and Behvioral Practice, 9*, 50–57.

Segal, Z., Williams, M., & Teasdale, J. (2012). *Mindfulness-based cognitive therapy for depression* (2nd ed.). The Guilford Press.

Sheldon, C. (1899). *In his steps: "What would Jesus do?"* Advance Publishing Co.

Teresa, S. (2002). *Volume two: The complete works*. Burns & Oates.

Walsh, R., & Shapiro, S. (2006). The meeting of meditative disciplines and Western psychology: A mutually enriching dialogue. *American Psychologist, 61*, 227–239.

Williams, M. (2008). Mindfulness, depression and modes of mind. *Cognitive Therapy Research, 32*, 721–733.

6

WATCHING AND ENDURING

Introduction

In this chapter, traditional acceptance and commitment therapy (ACT)[1] strategies within the "opening up" pillar (Harris, 2019, p. 8) are presented, combining the processes of *cognitive defusion* and *acceptance*. Drawing a parallel between these two traditional ACT processes and the Christian contemplative concepts of watchfulness (*nepsis* in Greek) and endurance (*hupomone* in Greek) (i.e., the "watching and enduring" pillar) can allow counselors and therapists to help Christian clients relate to painful inner experiences with more openness and flexibility, rather than futilely attempt to reduce, eliminate, avoid, or distract from unpleasant thoughts, feelings, sensations, and memories. Faith-based ACT exercises and metaphors are offered, including strategies that help Christian clients to view thoughts as passing events, rather than as "facts" that get in the way of value-based living. To "stay with whatever is happening" in the cell (Paintner, 2012, p. 12), a phrase originally used in monastic life to describe solitude with God, is explored to help Christian clients stay in their symbolic cell, that is, the inner world, during moments of distress, inviting God into the experience in order to cultivate compassion, commitment, and devotion. Among other biblical examples, Romans 5 and 1 Peter are explicated for Christian clients to better understand the relationship between suffering, endurance, and following Jesus. Finally, a case example is provided to enhance this faith-based understanding of "opening up," that is, "watching and enduring."

Traditional ACT and Cognitive Fusion

In traditional ACT, clients utilize several acceptance-based strategies to relate to the inner world (e.g., thoughts, feelings, sensations, memories) with more openness and flexibility, leading to a greater ability to employ deeply ingrained values, rather than wavering internal states, as a guide for life. For many clients, language tends to be inherently limiting, given that its use, when carried to an extreme, exacerbates suffering. Certainly, when clients begin to treat language

DOI: 10.4324/9781003181941-7

as a concrete reality, rather than merely an instrument in the service of values, the inner world can get in the way of vigorous, meaningful living. Stated differently, depending too much on the world of words, rather than directly experiencing life, can lead to a pattern of getting "hooked" by language, which paralyzes day-to-day existence. Fusion, thus, involves seeing the world *from* thinking, rather than looking *at* thinking. This *from* versus *at* distinction is very important, given that clients can begin to automatically view deeply engrained, limiting thinking patterns as true, without examining them from a distance to see that they are less than fully objective and accurate.

Common types of thinking patterns that are often unexamined and lead to fusion for clients include rigid rules (e.g., "should" statements), seemingly clever "reasons" to justify avoidance behavior (e.g., "I cannot go to the party because I am depressed"), judgmental statements (e.g., "I am worthless"), ruminating about the past (e.g., "I should have never said that to him"), worrying about the future (e.g., "I am going to lose my job"), and negative self-statements that undermine value-based action (e.g., "I am not smart enough to apply for the job") (Harris, 2019, pp. 27–28; Stoddard & Afari, 2014). Of course, these different categories of thinking tend to get in the way of living out values, resulting in experiential avoidance and an unwillingness to take risks in creating a life that truly matters. In fact, in a state of cognitive fusion, clients tend to overemphasize language as literal, factual, objective, and anchored in reality, rather than as a mere stepping-stone toward value-based action. Unfortunately, many clients struggle to step back and see the proverbial water (i.e., thinking) they are swimming in, similar to a fish that takes for granted it is swimming in the ocean (Hayes, 2005).

For example, a client may have the thought "I'm useless," concluding that this phrase is "true," resulting in a prolonged struggle to apply for an important promotion at work. Over time, this group of letters, constituting repetitive inner dialogue, becomes a concrete reality, preventing the client from connecting to the value of lifelong learning and occupational growth. As another example, clients may utilize language to offer "reasons" for why value-based living is just not possible at a particular moment in time, standing on the "sidelines" of life, to use a sports metaphor, as they watch the game unfold. To offer one more illustration, clients can end up avoiding life because they have labeled inner experiences as "bad," "horrible," or "unfair," rather than relating to inner states directly, with nonjudgment, openness, and curiosity. For a client with depressive symptoms, for instance, they may quickly conclude "I'm depressed," believing that working toward deepening church relationships is just not possible at this point in life, despite a passionate desire to do so.

In ACT, mindfulness exercises, metaphors, and paradoxical interventions are used to untangle clients from language, helping them to recognize that thoughts are mere words, rather than objective truth that blocks value-based action. In other words, the mind may or may not generate accurate commentary. Thus, relating to inner thoughts with more tentativeness and flexibility is a central goal, observing the world of language with a bit more distance in order to act upon heartfelt values, rather than repetitive, inconsistent dialogue generated by the mind. To do so, several steps are taken, including the client "noticing" the thought they are fused with (e.g., recognizing the thinking process altogether), "naming" the thought they are fused with (e.g., "There's 'worrying'"), and "neutralizing" the thought they are fused with, with this third and final step simply involving asking the question, "Will this thought help me to live out my values?" (Harris, 2019, pp. 140–141).

Common ACT exercises to defuse from unhelpful cognitions include repeating words over and over again, saying words in a silly voice or singing words until they lose their power and meaning, and meditative exercises to watch them wander along, like leaves gently floating down a stream. As another popular example, metaphors are used to help clients see the mind as some sort of "word generator," doing its job, rather than acting as a source of objective truth (e.g., "The mind is like a bully with a megaphone") (Hayes, 2005). Finally, placing the phrase "I'm having the thought that …" before the actual thought can help to create some distance between clients' sense of self and the words the mind generates from moment to moment (Harris, 2019, p. 132).

Above all else, cognitive defusion exercises are used to help clients loosen their rigid relationship to language, relating to their thinking patterns with more distance, detachment, and flexibility. In other words, clients are learning to recognize that inner dialogue is not always accurate, and they are less likely to pursue meaningful values when they view thoughts as literal, especially since the world of language can serve as a barrier to effective action. Also, when clients overly rely on language, they tend to utilize labels to evaluate unpleasant inner experiences, leading to added suffering. Undeniably, the common psychological symptoms of low mood and fatigue, when organized together with the label of "depression," can add a dimension of suffering, beyond the initial experience. On the other hand, when clients are able to change the way they view language, pivoting toward value-based action, they begin to recognize that the mind may not always be an ally in the service of vital, vibrant living. Certainly, clients' approach toward the world of language can change from "I'm worthless" to "My active mind is once again generating the thought that 'I'm worthless'" when relating to inner experiences.

Traditional ACT and Experiential Avoidance

As noted in previous chapters, experiential avoidance can help to explain the link between everyday psychological symptoms and problems, conditions, and disorders, with disordered functioning resulting from an unwillingness to experience unpleasant thoughts, feelings, sensations, and memories, rather than the symptoms in and of themselves. For many clients, life is on hold because they are waiting for the symptoms to go away, instead of learning to relate to them with more openness, flexibility, compassion, and kindness. Stated differently, attempting to control the inner world, rather than accepting it, is the culprit. Of course, because many psychological symptoms are recurrent in nature, learning to experience them with an attitude of nonjudgmental willingness may help clients to begin to live life again, instead of spending vital time and energy employing ineffective control or avoidance strategies.

As a result, experiential acceptance in traditional ACT helps clients relate to unpleasant experiences in new ways in order to prevent them from getting in the way of value-based living. Unfortunately, many clients inaccurately view acceptance as some sort of decision to passively give up and lose hope, which is not the case. Indeed, acceptance is about learning to make peace with unpleasant inner states, rather than trying to control them. When clients pursue a control strategy, attempting to fully eliminate psychological pain, they become perpetually distracted from living the life they want. This is especially problematic when avoidance creates "pain on top of pain" (Hayes, 2005, p. 17), meaning that clients not only experience difficult inner states, but also create added pain because of ineffective avoidance strategies, missing out on a life filled with meaning, vitality, and the pursuit of heartfelt values.

Again, acceptance is a way to help clients pursue values in life, rather than fighting against unpleasant inner experiences that may not go away. With acceptance, clients are learning to "acknowledge" when psychological pain is present, "allow" psychological pain to simply run its natural course, and "accommodate" psychological pain by giving it space to exist as a valid part of the human experience (Harris, 2019, pp. 253–254). Common strategies to cultivate the willingness to allow such experiences to be, as they are, include mindfulness exercises, along with the "Curious Child" (e.g., investigating the experience like a "curious child" who has never felt the pain before) and "Passengers on the Bus" (e.g., viewing the inner pain as passengers who freely get on and off a bus, which must continue to drive a predetermined route) metaphors (Harris, 2019, p. 255). Specifically, with the "Curious Child" metaphor, clients are asked to investigate inner experiences with more openness, as if they are an inquisitive child who has never experienced the inner pain before. Like a child who is exploring the world for the first time, clients are asked to relate to their feelings with nonjudgment, describing the experience by naming the shape, color, texture, and size of the emotion. Of course, the purpose of the "Curious Child" metaphor is to help clients let go of their desire to avoid the experience, relating to the distressing emotion in a less judgmental way. By doing this, clients are able to focus on pursing their values, rather than letting unpleasant affective states get in the way of active living.

With the "Passengers on the Bus" metaphor (Harris, 2019, p. 255), clients are asked to imagine they are driving a bus, with individuals getting on and off the bus at each stop. Because the bus is public transportation, even unruly individuals are able to ride. As a result, the bus driver has a decision to make—turn around and argue with the people who are distracting and disruptive, trying to get them off at each stop, or drive their route, recognizing they have a job to do. Every time the bus driver seemingly gets rid of several rude passengers on the bus, more get on because of the nature of public transportation. In other words, everyone is welcome on the bus, even disruptive individuals. As an alternative approach, the bus driver can accept that these insensitive characters will continue to get on the bus, loudly at times, focusing, instead, on effectively driving their route. This metaphor can help clients understand that experiential avoidance does not tend to work in the inner world, given that distress will continue to arise. As a result, an alternative approach involves accepting they are there, even befriending them, relating to wavering affective states with more openness, curiosity, compassion, and kindness.

As one more example, mindfulness meditation, wherein clients employ sustained attention in the here-and-now with an attitude of nonjudgment (Bishop et al., 2004), can be used to cultivate experiential acceptance. With a mindfulness-based approach toward unpleasant inner experiences (e.g., thoughts, feelings, sensations, memories), clients are simply learning to allow the experience to run its natural course, without trying to change it in any way. Over time, clients develop the ability to relate to their inner pain with more curiosity, letting go of the tendency to want to "fix" or "control" the inner world. Common meditations include mindful breathing, wherein clients focus on the breath, gently returning to the air going in and out of the nostrils or abdomen when their attention has shifted, along with mindfulness of emotions, leaning into the affective experience without trying to change it in any way. For example, a client may be asked to allow the experience of anxiety to simply be, without trying to change it, relating to it with nonjudgmental compassion by expanding it in the present moment. By doing this, clients can begin to observe and describe anxiety, without attempting to fight against it, which commonly impairs daily living and undermines value-based action.

In sum, cognitive defusion and acceptance strategies can be employed when clients are overly reliant on the world of language, as well as trying to avoid unpleasant inner experiences, leading to a struggle to live out values. By using the aforementioned strategies and metaphors, clients can learn to relate to inner states with more openness, curiosity, flexibility, compassion, and kindness, pivoting toward value-based action. What follows is a review of contemplative Christianity, building on prior chapters, in order to draw a parallel between making room for unpleasant inner experiences within both traditional and faith-based ACT. After reviewing the Christian contemplative tradition (Foster, 1998), I offer an integrative strategy, including overarching goals, metaphors, techniques, and a case example, to help counselors and therapists more effectively work with Christian clients with recurrent symptoms.

135

Contemplation and Human Suffering: A Christian Perspective[2,3,4]

Sometime around the third century, the life of the Christian *monk* began to take shape in the deserts of Egypt, Arabia, Palestine, and Syria.[5] Christians started moving to the desert to reject the society they came from, including cultural emphases on power and material possessions. By turning to the desert land-scape, these monks sought to cultivate a deeper relationship with God, truly wrestling with matters of existence by letting go of the distracting pursuit of materialistic endeavors and wealth.

Inspired by a variety of biblical figures linked to the desert, including Moses, Elijah, John the Baptist, and Jesus, these early desert emigrants took up resi-dence in caves and other shelters in an effort to grapple with and embrace the difficult terrain of the inner world, inviting God into the process. This yearning for an authentic spiritual encounter, shedding all the proverbial armor that accumulates throughout life, has inspired countless contemplatives over the past 1,700 years, even leading to the development of a formal mystical theology beginning around the fifth century.[6] For these passionate Christians, the desert represents an attitude of facing, even leaning into, the most painful parts of life, rather than avoiding them through distraction, the accumulation of wealth, or other culturally derived strategies to anesthetize life.

The Desert: A Place for Watching and Enduring

The actual location, the desert, symbolizes the stripping away of external pos-sessions and comforts, leading to an experience of total dependence on God and utter vulnerability in the pursuit of a deeper relationship with him. Among other factors, the desert captures the ability to turn inward for spiritual trans-formation and growth. In some ways paralleling the counseling and therapy room in the 21st century, the desert illuminates the courage and bravery that is necessary to welcome unpleasant inner experiences, longing for insight, self-exploration, and, ultimately, the ability to relate to difficult thoughts, feelings, sensations, and memories without attempting to reduce, eliminate, avoid, or distract from psychological pain.

Moreover, many early desert monks firmly believed that demons resided in the desert, consistent with Jesus's experience (Matthew 4:1–11), wherein a bat-tle with temptation took place. It is especially telling that, despite monks' views that demons lived and thrived in the desert, acting as tormenters and haunters, Christians still made the decision to live there (Harmless, 2008). Interestingly, this movement toward, rather than away from, perceived desert demons parallels ACT's experiential acceptance, or embracing painful inner states.[7] Certainly, some monks even seemed to welcome the experience, as revealed by

Abba Evagrius, a fourth-century Egyptian monk, "Take away temptations and no one will be saved" (quoted in Chryssavgis, 2008, p. 38).

As just mentioned, one of the primary examples of this dynamic comes from Jesus's temptation in the desert (Matthew 4:1–11). According to the monastic tradition, monks first learned to use Scripture to fight off the perceived demons of the desert, relying on the repetition of passages from the Bible in order to cultivate silence and stillness (Laird, 2011). Eventually, the repetition of biblical phrases evolved into later, more *apophatic* forms of prayer, such as those in the *Cloud of Unknowing* (Pennington, 1982).

Nonetheless, Jesus used key verses from Deuteronomy and the Psalms to shift his thoughts away from the Devil and focus his mind on God's promises in the Bible (Matthew 4:1–11). In other words, these biblical examples of how Jesus responded to the Devil served as the inspiration for early forms of contemplative practice that still exist today. Selecting a few words from Scripture, monks would repeat them over and over again in an effort to achieve stillness, silence, and inner peace, as well as remind them of God's loving presence.

The Jesus Prayer, for example, is thought to have developed based on these early prayers from Scripture (Harmless, 2004; Laird, 2011). "Lord Jesus Christ, Son of God, have mercy on me, a sinner," which is used in a variety of formats, helps Christians to achieve *hesychia*, or inner silence, stillness, and peace (Harmless, 2008). By employing this prayer, Christians are attempting to avoid being attacked by, or entrenched in, the *logismoi*—eight forms of tempting, obsessive thoughts (Harmless, 2008). As Johnson (1995) revealed, one of the most important contributions of early desert life was the marriage of liturgy and silent prayer, illuminated by the popular monastic saying, "Always a Psalm on the lips: always Christ in the heart" (p. 18). It is worth mentioning, though, these obsessive thoughts were viewed by some early desert Christians as important for spiritual development, to be observed and watched, rather than completely avoided (Laird, 2011). This relationship to thinking, of course, parallels several of ACT's processes, including *cognitive defusion* and *acceptance*.

The Cell: A Symbol for Watching and Enduring

Another interesting development in monastic life involves monks' actual physical location. Referred to as "the cell," monks resided alone in these small rooms, wherein they would practice enduring painful emotions. As Abba Moses, a fourth-century monk, famously stated, "Go, sit in your cell, and your cell will teach you everything" (quoted in Chryssavgis, 2008, p. 41). Although the human struggle with experiential avoidance is rather ubiquitous, the early desert monks purposefully faced their distressing thoughts, feelings, sensations, and memories, enduring them with patience and prayer. To be sure, the reason that monks were able to patiently, calmly, and faithfully endure was because the God of love was also in the cell. Thus, accepting the inevitability of painful thoughts, feelings, sensations, and memories involved staying put, leaning into the experience, and cultivating an awareness of the presence of God, who was literally with them in the midst of pain. Certainly, the experience of the desert cell parallels the notion of experiential acceptance in traditional ACT, which is vital for psychological flexibility.

For Christians in the 21st century, "the cell" symbolizes the inner world, which is filled with distressing thoughts, feelings, sensations, and memories. Yet, the God of love is also active and present, leading to the ability and willingness to persevere despite the occupants of the cell (e.g., perceived demons attacking with *logismoi*).[1] In fact, the imagery of the cell, which represents the inner world, can be especially helpful for Christians struggling with psychological symptoms, given that the task at hand is to "stay put," knowing that God is there to help them endure the pain, offering his perfect love from moment to moment. This image, moreover, provides the psychological space to notice from a safe distance, rather than fuse with, or avoid, inner experiences.

Within the cell, a central focus in monastic life was the use of Scripture (e.g., the psalms) to meditate and cultivate stillness and silence with God (Harmless, 2004). Using biblical passages helped these early desert dwellers to focus their attention on God, rather than distracting, compulsive thoughts or tempting, tormenting demons (Mathewes-Green, 2011). Interestingly, though, some early monks (e.g., Evagrius of Ponticus) emphasized relating to God in a wordless, imageless manner, beyond solely relying on repetitive prayer (Harmless, 2004). Thus, the prayer phrase was eventually used as a stepping-stone toward a deeper relationship with God, beyond mental representations of him, referred to as *apophatic* prayer (Pennington, 1982). Over time, this approach to prayer evolved into more contemporary forms of contemplation, including the suggestions offered by the author of the *Cloud of Unknowing* in the 14th century and the Jesus Prayer currently used in Orthodox Christianity (Pennington, 1982). In either case, this practice seems to parallel mindfulness in the psychology literature, which helps clients to cultivate sustained attention and nonjudgment toward thinking (Bishop et al., 2004), letting go of the tendency to evaluate inner experiences with words and, instead, pursue a direct sensory encounter. Indeed, in the desert terrain, an *apophatic* approach began to take shape, with the desert fathers' sayings and Evagrius of Ponticus's more formal writings on the topic (Harmless, 2004; Lane, 1998).

The Limitations of Language: Mystical Theology and God

In the fifth century, Dionysius wrote *Mystical Theology*, which further developed an *apophatic* theology of God (McGinn, 1991). As opposed to a *cataphatic* theology, which relies on positive statements and language about God to understand him (e.g., attributes and qualities revealed in Scripture), an *apophatic*, or negative, theology suggests that God is beyond mere language and human comprehension (Taylor, 2002). Within this writing, Dionysius, a Syrian monk, instructed a disciple to relate to God beyond words, images, or reason, similar to Moses's experience of meeting God on Mount Sinai, where God appeared as a thick, dense cloud (Exodus 19; Johnson, 1995; McGinn, 1991). For Dionysius, God is ultimately unknowable, similar to Moses's experience of entering a dark cloud; although God dwelled there, Moses could not actually see him (Exodus 19; Johnson, 1995).

Therefore, an *apophatic*, or negative, theology was solidified, which elucidates that God is beyond words, language, images, senses, and reason (Johnson, 1995). In other words, approaching God, like Moses, requires the willingness to let go of prior knowledge (Johnson, 1995). Further popularized by the *Cloud of Unknowing* (Johnston, 2000), written by an anonymous English monk in the 14th century and explored in the previous chapter, this understanding of God's ineffability, captured via a dark cloud that separates humans from complete knowledge of him, seems to resemble, at least in part, an ACT understanding of the limitations of language. Consistent with Dionysius, God is beyond verbally constructed categories, definitions, or other descriptions—at a certain point, words lose their function when approaching God, similar to Moses on the mountain of Sinai.

Watchfulness: The Christian Version of Cognitive Defusion

Considering the limitations of language, watchfulness (*nepsis* in Greek) captures the ability to relate differently to a variety of distracting thoughts, with the Apostle Peter instructing Christians to be "alert and of sober mind" (*New International Version Bible*, 2011, 1 Peter 5:8). This practice appears to parallel ACT's cognitive defusion in the sense that Christians are getting untangled from the thinking process by practicing mental alertness, soberness, vigilance, and awareness. For the early desert monks, inspired by Evagrius's mystical theology on the topic, watchfulness involves a "calm vigilance" in day-to-day experiences, getting to know the patterns of the mind through an intrinsic attentiveness (Paintner, 2012, p. 8).

This approach to the inner world of language, combined with a compassionate grace, helps to identify the eight *logismoi*, or "evil thoughts," to effectively respond to them (Harmless, 2004, p. 322). Evagrius's eight obsessive thoughts, reminiscent of cognitive fusion, include content surrounding gluttony, fornication, money, sadness, anger, apathy (i.e., listlessness, boredom), vanity, and pride (Harmless, 2004). It is worth mentioning that Evagrius's eight *logismoi* correspond to eight virtues—temperance, charity, continence, patience, courage, wisdom, understanding, and prudence—developed in response to the eight patterns of compulsive thinking (see Harmless, 2008). Some of these virtues, along with a more detailed exploration of common *logismoi*, are further explicated in later chapters on value-based living and specific psychological problems, conditions, and disorders.

Nevertheless, for the early desert monks, cultivating interior attentiveness in the cell was a central aim (Chryssavgis, 2008). Through the use of wordless, imageless contemplation, watchfulness can help Christians gently and patiently observe unpleasant thoughts that get in the way of vibrant living, rather than trying to dispute them, resting in God's love and allowing him to do what he will with them (Trader, 2011). As Abba John Colobos revealed,

> I am like somebody sitting beneath a large tree who sees wild beasts and serpents coming at him. When he cannot withstand them, he runs up into the tree and is saved. So it is with me: I stay in my cell and see the evil *logismoi* above me. And when I do not have the strength [to oppose] them, I flee to God in prayer, and am saved from the enemy.
>
> (quoted in Wortley, 2012, p. 195)

Indeed, to watch from a safe distance is possible because God is present, as one of the desert elders accurately elucidated,

> Whether you are sleeping or waking up or doing something else, if God is before your eyes, the enemy can in no way make you afraid. If this *logismos* remains within a person, the power of God remains with him too.
>
> (quoted in Wortley, 2012, p. 208)

To be watchful, with a calm vigilance, focusing on God and practicing God's presence is needed (*hesychia* in Greek), which leads to an inner silence, stillness, and peace (Chumley, 2014; Paintner, 2012). This deeper internal quiet within faith-based ACT is further explored in the next chapter, by way of the Jesus Prayer, paralleling ACT's present-moment awareness process.

Endurance: The Christian Version of Acceptance

In addition to watchfulness (*nepsis* in Greek), endurance (*hupomone* in Greek), which means a hopeful steadfastness, constancy, and patience in the face of suffering, is used approximately 30 times in the New Testament (Barclay, 2000). This word is best captured as a plant that grows despite extreme environmental conditions (Barclay, 2000). This word, moreover, seems to align with ACT's acceptance process, which is the ability to be open, flexible, nonjudgmental, compassionate, and kind toward unpleasant inner experiences. Yet, endurance has an extra element of hope, beyond the neutrality of mere nonjudgment. In other words, Christians can endure because suffering is rooted in an eschatological understanding of God's plan—restoration.

The Book of Revelation illuminates the suffering and persecution first-century Christians were experiencing (Barclay, 2004). However, they were able to "transform even suffering into glory" because they turned their attention to God's kingdom, recognizing that "[Christ] endured to the end, and he can enable those who walk with him to achieve the same endurance and reach the same goal" (Barclay, 2004, p. 47). For followers of Jesus, suffering can have a redemptive quality, given that God is fully present in the midst of pain (Taylor, 2002). As Taylor revealed, suffering redeems because it is a reminder of what Jesus accomplished on the cross, especially God's triumph over evil and death. As a result, in addition to practically helping Christians to relate to difficult private encounters with more openness, endurance offers the hope that suffering with Jesus, in contemplative practice, allows Christians to suffer with endurance, hope, constancy, and a "face to the wind" (Barclay, 2000, p. 145) attitude during life's inevitable adversities.

For early desert monks, "sitting in the cell" and the willingness to endure inner pain was the central aim because the God of love was with them. In fact, at times, the early desert Christians welcomed inner struggles in order to cultivate spiritual growth. As one of the desert elders revealed,

> Just as wax that has not been warmed or softened cannot take the [imprint of the] seal set upon it, neither can a person acquire the strength of Christ unless he has been tried by bouts of toil and sickness.
> (quoted in Wortley, 2012, p. 120)

Faith-Based ACT Goals for Watching and Enduring

When combining the two "opening up" ACT processes of cognitive defusion and acceptance (Harris, 2019, p. 8) with watchfulness (*nepsis* in Greek) and endurance (*hupomone* in Greek) for Christian clients in counseling and therapy, an important goal is to help them relate to inner experiences with more flexibility, recognizing that the God of love is walking with them as they suffer through the bumps and bruises of life. In fact, because God is present from moment to moment, sitting with them in their symbolic cell, enduring inner pain is much more tolerable. Undoubtedly, the willingness to fully embrace the inner world exists because God is active and present, lovingly working in the life of Christian clients in order to help them steadfastly endure.

What is more, because Christian clients are striving to relate to the inner world with more openness, rather than employing control or avoidance, they can pivot toward following Jesus, which is a central aim of the Christian life. Above all else, "opening up" (Harris, 2019, p. 8) is utilized in order to pursue values. For Christians, this means "watching and enduring," leading to a greater willingness to take up their cross and faithfully follow Jesus (Matthew 16:24), that is, walk with God in love on the road of life.

As another goal, Christian clients can learn to endure distressing thoughts, feelings, sensations, and memories because of the hope they have in Jesus, recognizing that they are suffering with the "Suffering Servant" (*New International Version Bible*, 2011, Isaiah 53), who will one day return to restore all things (Revelation 21). In other words, the current suffering that Christian clients are facing, in their symbolic cell, is by no means permanent. Therefore, inner distress (e.g., difficult thoughts, feelings, sensations, and memories) can be endured because it is time-limited, experienced by both Jesus and his followers. Beyond the endurance that comes from an acute awareness that the present world's suffering is impermanent, the contemplation of Jesus's suffering is integral to endurance, given it was an act of love. According to the late contemplative writer Thomas Merton (2005),

> To know the Cross is to know that we are saved by the sufferings of Christ; more, it is to know the love of Christ Who underwent suffering and death in order to save us ... To know all this is to understand something of the Cross, that is: to know Christ. For contemplation is simply the penetration, by divine wisdom, into the mystery of God's love, in the passion and resurrection of Jesus Christ.
>
> (p. 92)

Worded another way, Jesus's loving sacrifice on the cross reveals that there is meaning and purpose in suffering, with God leading the way and God's love at the center. According to the medieval contemplative Teresa of Avila (1980), to follow Jesus means to emulate Jesus, including his suffering:

> I desire to suffer, Lord, all the trials that come to me and esteem them as a great good enabling me to imitate you in something. Let us walk together, Lord. Wherever you go, I will go; whatever you suffer, I will suffer.
>
> (p. 172)

Overall, cultivating a hopeful endurance when working toward "opening up" is vital in faith-based ACT, organically emanating from the contemplation of God's eschatological plan of restoration and Jesus's loving act as the "Suffering Servant" (*New International Version Bible*, 2011, Isaiah 53) as Christians walk with, and attempt to be more like, him.

Finally, Christian clients can strive to trust in God, the author of love, rather than lean on their own understanding (Proverbs 3:5), meaning that the inner world is not treated as always factual. Rather, following Jesus involves trusting in him, including his teachings, guidance, and loving care, instead of the thoughts, feelings, sensations, and memories generated by the less-than-fully-accurate inner world. Similar to Jesus teaching his followers not to worry because God will provide (Matthew 6:25–34), Christian clients can work toward relinquishing their own self-derived control efforts, given that God is infinitely loving, wise, powerful, and present, divine attributes that are trustworthy. Essentially, "opening up" in faith-based ACT involves accepting the inner world with non-judgment in order to follow Jesus in the outer world (i.e., walk with God in love on the road of life), along with cultivating hope and trust in the God of love in the midst of suffering.

Faith-Based ACT Conceptualizations, Metaphors, Descriptions, and Techniques for Watching and Enduring

As a newer development in traditional ACT, the "Choice Point" tool (Harris, 2019) can be employed to quickly conceptualize clients' current struggles. In fact, this useful tool can be collaboratively utilized with the client, working together to better understand their moment-by-moment decisions in life. As revealed in Chapter 4, the "Choice Point" tool involves helping clients to see that they have a decision to make when they are struggling with difficult thoughts, feelings, sensations, memories, situations, and relationships (Harris, 2019). Specifically, they can choose to head toward a life of meaning and purpose, flexibly guided by values, or a life away from meaning and purpose, fused with unhelpful cognitions and reliant upon experiential avoidance as an ineffective coping strategy (Harris, 2019).

In the context of Christian clients' efforts to follow Jesus (i.e., walk with God in love) along the road of life, they have a "Fork in the Road" (adapted from Harris, 2019; Hayes et al., 2012) that they must face when they are struggling with difficult thoughts, feelings, sensations, memories, situations, and relationships, deciding each step of the way if they are going to endure psychological pain and walk with God in love toward his plan or avoid psychological pain and walk alone and away from his plan. Overall, helping Christian clients to recognize that they face this "Fork in the Road" in each unfolding moment of life highlights the urgency of the matter and allows them to, hopefully, decide to walk with God in love toward God's plan for their life. If this is the case, the plethora of "watching and enduring" metaphors, descriptions, and exercises presented in the remainder of this chapter can help them to do so with more confidence and stability. See Figure 6.1 for counselors and therapists to work with Christian clients to fill in the blanks and, thus, succinctly conceptualize the problem and solution to psychological suffering in the human condition, paying particular attention to the "watching and enduring" pillar.

Moving on to metaphors, another strength of traditional ACT involves the wide variety of creative symbols, images, and so forth used to help clients better understand the six processes, applying them to daily living. In fact, metaphors tend to function as one of the building blocks of the thinking process, helping clients to better understand an array of inner and outer events (Siegelman, 1990).

By combining prior experiences with metaphors as "abstract target domains," clients are able to come up with novel ideas, referred to as "abstractive seeing" (Siegelman, 1990, p. 5). To state this process more succinctly, metaphors can allow clients to convert concrete, physical realities to a more abstract, spatial understanding of inner and outer events.

Within the world of traditional ACT, metaphors are stories that help counselors and therapists paint a more vivid picture to deepen clients' understanding of the six processes, offering an experiential way of making sense of ACT (Hayes et al., 1999). Relying less on a linear, logical, fact-based strategy for presenting new material to clients, metaphors bring to life ACT principles in creative ways (Hayes et al., 1999). Certainly, they can assist clients in retaining crucial information, avoiding a heavily language-based, bullet-point format, so

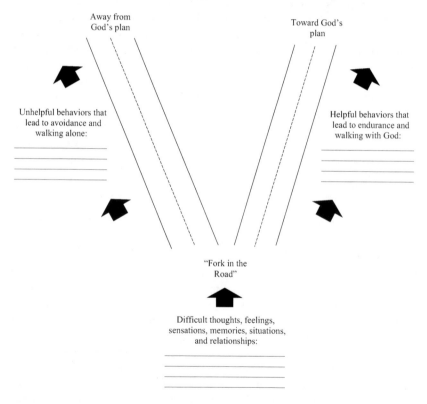

Figure 6.1 The "Fork in the Road" for Christians: "Watching and Enduring." *Note.* Adapted from Harris (2019), Hayes (2019), and Hayes et al. (2012). "Unhelpful" and "helpful" behaviors include those that are overt (i.e., observable, such as walking and talking) and covert (i.e., unobservable, such as thinking and feeling).

clients can immerse themselves in the story and, thus, engage in experiential learning (Hayes et al., 1999).

Interestingly, the Bible also relies heavily on metaphors to convey powerful messages, including information about God's characteristics, God's relationship with humankind, and ways to live in the world. As an example, Jesus referred to himself as the "good shepherd" (*New International Version Bible*, 2011, John 10:1–21), one of the psalmists described God as a "rock" and "fortress" (*New International Version Bible*, 2011, Psalms 62:2), and the Apostle Paul referred to a "potter" and "clay" when describing God's relationship with humankind (*New International Version Bible*, 2011, Romans 9:21). Based on this overlap, counselors and therapists using faith-based ACT can draw from the pages of the Bible to modify many traditional ACT metaphors. Yet, the Bible also uses stories, parables, and teachings to convey important points. Because of this, many traditional ACT metaphors can be adjusted to include biblical stories and teachings for Christians to deepen their awareness of ACT concepts, untangling them from a fused understanding of the inner and outer worlds.

Beyond metaphors, traditional ACT uses experiential exercises to help clients directly connect to unpleasant experiences, allowing clients to let go of purely language-based processing during moments of distress (Hayes et al., 1999). In a similar vein, Jesus relied on experiential learning when engaging with his disciples. Spending several years with Jesus, to be sure, helped his disciples to directly experience Jesus's radical new way of life. Instead of offering some sort of bullet-point list of rules to live by, Jesus famously stated, "Come, follow me" (*New International Version Bible*, 2011, Matthew 4:19). Because of this, for Christians, learning to accept the inner world and follow Jesus in the outer world involves directly experiencing this new way of life, rather than counselors and therapists merely instructing Christian clients on how to do so. Indeed, faith-based ACT can help Christian clients to engage directly with Jesus, instead of learning about following him in an abstract manner that overly relies on language-based processing.

See Table 6.1 for a listing of traditional ACT metaphors and exercises, along with faith-based alternatives for Christian clients, drawing from biblical metaphors, stories, illustrations, and teachings. As the faith-based metaphors and exercises reveal, a foundational adjustment involves placing God at the center, helping Christian clients to endure because God is active and present, walking with them in the midst of their pain. To courageously endure by following Jesus despite inner distress involves the ability to relate to unpleasant thoughts, feelings, sensations, and memories in a new manner, cultivating psychological flexibility along the way as Christians deepen their relationship with God.

In terms of traditional cognitive defusion metaphors, assisting clients in viewing the "mind" as a "Master Salesperson" can be helpful to draw out the idea that the mind is always trying to sell us something, making a variety of promises

Table 6.1 Traditional and Faith-Based ACT Conceptualizations, Metaphors, Descriptions, and Exercises for "Opening Up"/"Watching and Enduring"

	Traditional ACT	Faith-Based ACT
Cognitive defusion		
Conceptualization		
Metaphor	"Choice Point Figure"	"Fork in the Road Figure"
	"The Master Salesperson"	"The False Self"
	"Passengers on the Bus"	"The Judgmental Pharisees"
	"The Family House"	"God's House of Love"
	"The Mind is Like …"	"The Mind is Like the Serpent in the Garden of Eden"
Exercise		
	"Noticing"	Use the Jesus Prayer to simply notice the *logismoi*
	"Clouds in the Sky"	"Hanging Out with Jesus on the Boat"
	"Soldiers in the Parade"	"Walking with Jesus in Jerusalem"
	"Bullying Reframe"	"Talking Back"
	"I'm Having the Thought That …"	"I Will Not Lean on My Own Understanding That …"
	"Replace 'But' with 'And'"	"I Can Do All This Through Him Who Gives Me Strength"
Acceptance		
Conceptualization		
	"Choice Point Figure"	"Fork in the Road Figure"
Description		
	"Make peace with it"	"Make peace with it because I'm walking with Jesus"
	"Let it be"	"Let it be because Jesus is present"
	"Sit with it"	"Sit with it because I'm sitting with Jesus"
Metaphor		
	"Quicksand"	"Approaching God's Throne of Grace with Confidence"/"Be Still"
	"Joe the Bum"	"Judas's Betrayal"
	"'Clean' and 'Dirty' Pain"	"Jonah's 'Pain on Top of Pain'"
Exercise		
	"Normalizing"	"Fully Human Like Jesus"
	"Healing Hand"	"Jesus's Healing Hand"
	"Compassion"	"Jesus's Compassion"
	Mindfulness of feelings	The Welcoming Prayer

Note. Faith-based ACT interventions are adapted from Harris (2019), Hayes (2005), Hayes et al. (2012), Luoma et al. (2017), and Stoddard and Afari (2014).

that might not be fully accurate in order to "get the sale" (Harris, 2109, p. 150). In other words, externalizing the mind can help clients to gain some space between themselves and their thinking patterns (Hayes, 2005). As a Christian alternative, Pennington (2000) suggested that Christians create a "false self" that is organized around "what they have, what they do, [and] what others think of them" (p. 31), drawing upon Jesus's three temptations in the desert to illustrate a pseudo-self that the Devil presented to Jesus (Matthew 4:1–11). Conversely, the "true self" is found only in God, with Jesus modeling this total reliance on God for his identity. Thus, rather than a "Master Salesperson," Christian clients can externalize the mind by referring to it as the "False Self," especially during moments of cognitive fusion and inaction. Thoughts about material possessions, proving self-worth based on accomplishments, and worrying about a personal reputation can be observed, rather than fused with, shifting the focus to an identity in Jesus. Above all else, when Christian clients get stuck in their efforts to follow Jesus, the "False Self" is likely generating statements that bog down active Christian living (e.g., "I cannot follow Jesus because others will reject me").

As another example, Hayes et al. (2012) utilized the "Passengers on the Bus" metaphor, described in a previous section, to help clients better understand the relationship between the inner and outer worlds and their struggle with control. As a Christian equivalent, counselors and therapists working with Christian clients can use the example of the Pharisees, who were commonly following Jesus and questioning his authority and teachings (Mark 8:11; Mark 10:2; Matthew 9:10–13; Matthew 15:1–3). Yet, Jesus had a mission to fulfill, which prevented him from getting sidetracked with endless dialogue and seeds of doubt. Instead, he accepted that they were there, shifting toward accomplishing his divinely inspired task and recognizing that their judgmental words in no way prevented him from healing the sick and ministering to the poor. In essence, for Christian clients, the "mind" can be like "Judgmental Pharisees," constantly attempting to undermine authentic Christian living.

To provide another version of the "Passengers on the Bus" metaphor (Hayes et al., 2012), clients can view their mind like a crowded house, with many different family members (i.e., the "Family House" metaphor). In this house, family members live in the various rooms, share several common living areas (e.g., the kitchen, the dining room, the bathroom), and can sometimes be very loud and selfish, advocating for their own needs, not the needs of the family. Yet, also in this house is a set of family values (e.g., "We will love one another," "We will forgive one another," "We will serve one another," "We will care for one another"), which are framed above the fireplace in the living room for all to see. Therefore, in each moment of the day, a decision needs to be made—will the client follow the agreed-upon family values or give in to the most persuasive voices in the house (i.e., fuse with the arguments that come from the loudest voices), which tend to advocate spontaneous, self-absorbed, highly individualistic needs that conflict with the family's predetermined, selfless, decidedly

147

collectivistic principles for daily living. As a faith-based alternative for Christian clients, the "Family House" metaphor can be slightly altered as the "God's House of Love" metaphor. With this modified metaphor, God is the head of the household, offering his principles for living, built upon his perfect love. With this being the case, will the Christian client allow God to influence every room of the house, which will involve yielding to God's plan, or fuse with the noisy voices from the various family members who are demanding their needs be prioritized? To be sure, if Christian clients are God's dwelling place, then creating a life of meaning and purpose means walking with God in love, slowly and steadily allowing God to take up residence in every room of the house so that God's love can be displayed and God's will can be fulfilled.

Overall, "The Mind is Like …" exercises (Harris, 2019, p. 150) can help clients to relate to thoughts with a bit more distance and flexibility, as in "The mind is like a judgment generator." Again, to offer a Christian version, counselors and therapists working with Christian clients might employ the Creation Story (Genesis 3) to illustrate the mind's struggle to fully see the world through an accurate, godly lens. In other words, "The mind is like the serpent in the Garden of Eden, convincing us to be like God in our own judgments, evaluations, and knowledge of good and evil." By helping Christians to see the limitations of the human mind, at times trying to be like God, rather than dependent on God (Genesis 3),[9] cognitive defusion can occur, wherein Christians treat their own thoughts with less certainty.

Regarding cognitive defusion, like traditional ACT's various "Noticing" exercises (Harris, 2019, p. 150), Christian clients can begin to relate to the *logismoi* (or other distracting thoughts) with more distance and flexibility by practicing the Jesus Prayer. As the Jesus Prayer is repeated, clients continuously attend to the words (i.e., "Lord Jesus Christ, Son of God, have mercy on me, a sinner"), acknowledging the various tempting thoughts, before shifting the focus back to the Jesus Prayer, either with the full (noted above) or a condensed (e.g., "Lord Jesus Christ, have mercy on me," "Lord Jesus, have mercy," "Jesus") version. By repeating the prayer over and over again, sustained attention is cultivated, along with the ability to simply notice distracting thought content, accept its presence, and return to Jesus as the central focus. Over time, Christian clients develop watchfulness over the thinking process (*nepsis* in Greek).

Other traditional ACT exercises to help with cognitive defusion include seeing thoughts like clouds passing in the sky (Harris, 2019), which can be modified for Christian clients. Drawing from the story of Jesus calming the waves when his disciples were in a boat with him on the lake during a storm (Matthew 8:23–27), counselors and therapists can guide Christian clients through an exercise involving imagining that they are on the boat with Jesus, simply watching the wind and waves, which represent passing thoughts. Because Jesus is with them and in control, they can observe what is occurring at sea, rather than getting swept away by the storm.

The "Soldiers in the Parade" exercise (Hayes et al., 2012), a traditional ACT approach to help clients develop cognitive defusion by watching thoughts like observing soldiers marching in a parade, can be modified so that Christian clients imagine they are walking with Jesus in Jerusalem in the first century, with a large crowd following them. As they walk together, a crowd is surrounding them, making comments, asking questions, and so forth. During this time, Christian clients can simply notice the different types of comments and questions that are directed their way, without needing to respond to them or change the direction they are walking in.

Furthermore, consistent with the early desert monks' experience, Christian clients can imagine continuously returning to their symbolic cell—the inner world—watching the emerging temptations of the mind with a calm, sober vigilance, knowing that God is with them. As they repeatedly return to the cell, facing inner experiences instead of avoiding them, they are able to learn to endure, creating some space between themselves and the "occupants" of the inner room they reside in. In fact, one of the early desert Christians, Evagrius of Ponticus (2009), wrote about "talking back" to tempting, compulsive thoughts, employing Scripture, like Jesus (Matthew 4:1–11), to cut off the persuasive suggestions that naturally emanate from the overactive mind. Consistent with traditional ACT's "Bullying Reframe" exercise (Harris, 2019, p. 150), which involves having the client simply reflect on what it is like to be pushed around by a mere thought, rather than living a life of intention, meaning, purpose, and action, Evagrius's "talking back" can help Christian clients to recognize they can disrupt the domineering, bullying human mind with short passages in Scripture (e.g., "Trust in the Lord" [*New International Version Bible*, 2011, Proverbs 3:5], "Commit to the Lord" [*New International Version Bible*, 2011, Proverbs 16:3], "God is love" [*New International Version Bible*, 2011, 1 John 4:16]), reminiscent of Jesus in the desert (Matthew 4:1–11).

Additionally, a common traditional ACT strategy involves helping clients to place the phrase "I'm having the thought that ..." before the actual thought, which allows them to create some distance between themselves and their inner thought content (Harris, 2019, p. 150). As an alternative, Christian clients can draw from Proverbs 3:5, which states, "Trust in the Lord with all your heart and lean not on your own understanding" (*New International Version Bible*, 2011). Integrating the two, Christian clients can place the phrase "I will not lean on my own understanding that ..." followed by the language they are fused with. As an example, a Christian client with depressive symptoms might state "I will not lean on my own understanding that 'I'm worthless,'" helping them to create some space to untangle from this label, which likely has previously led to experiential avoidance. Instead, the Christian client can trust that God is in control, leaning on God's understanding of their self-worth, especially since God created humankind in his image (i.e., the *imago Dei*; Genesis 1:27).

To conclude with cognitive defusion exercises, a popular traditional ACT exercise involves replacing "but" with "and" when describing the relationship between clients' inner struggles and outer behaviors (Hayes et al., 2012). For example, a client may state, "I really want to go to the party, *but* I get very anxious around people." Here, the client is, essentially, fusing with a seemingly "valid" reason for avoiding the party (and corresponding anxiety). On the other hand, inserting "and" in the place of "but" can help clients to defuse from the very reasons that are keeping them stuck from engaging in value-based action, such as "I really want to go to the party, *and* I get very anxious around people." With the latter statement, clients are learning that they can *both* go to the party *and* experience anxiety, rather than seemingly having to choose between the two as a false dichotomy.

For Christian clients, this exercise can be modified to draw upon Philippians 4:13: "I can do all this through him who gives me strength" (*New International Version Bible*, 2011). For instance, a Christian client can replace the statement "I want to follow Jesus, *but* I am depressed" with "I want to follow Jesus, I am depressed, *and* 'I can do all this through him who gives me strength.'" With the former, the Christian client is fusing with a seemingly "valid" reason for avoiding walking with God, whereas the latter involves *both* following Jesus *and* experiencing depression, watching and enduring because God is providing the strength to persevere.

Transitioning to acceptance, Christian clients can employ a range of descriptions to better understand an alternative way to relate to unpleasant inner experiences, accepting, rather than trying to reduce, eliminate, avoid, or distract from, psychological pain. Certainly, Christian clients can utilize traditional ACT language, such as "Make peace with it," "Let it be," or "Sit with it" (Harris, 2019, p. 252), but add in the reason that painful inner states can be endured—Jesus is present (e.g., "Make peace with it because I'm walking with Jesus," "Let it be because Jesus is present," "Sit with it because I'm sitting with Jesus"). Therefore, rather than simply allowing unpleasant inner states to be there for pragmatic reasons—because the alternative leads to an unworkable life—Christians can endure because Jesus, who also suffered, is active and present (Matthew 28:20). To be sure, Jesus empathizes with Christians' weaknesses (Hebrews 4:15) and, thus, is someone who understands the human condition because he faithfully endured, even to the point of suffering a violent death on a cross.

When considering traditional ACT metaphors for acceptance, a range of strategies can be employed to help Christian clients develop an attitude of willingness, rather than control or avoidance. For instance, ACT counselors and therapists commonly use the "Quicksand" metaphor (Hayes, 2005) to help clients recognize that trying to fight against painful inner experiences commonly makes matters worse, similar to attempting to wriggle out of quicksand. Instead, the solution involves staying connected to the quicksand by floating on its surface.

As an alternative for helping Christians with willingness and acceptance, clients can envision "approaching [God's] throne of grace with confidence," given that Jesus the High Priest was tempted in every way and understands human suffering (Hebrews 4:15–16). In other words, Christian clients can visualize walking toward Jesus on his throne. Rather than resisting God's grace, trying to unilaterally eliminate the pain, Christian clients can confidently accept inner distress because God's love is sufficient. To be sure, Christian clients can recognize that Jesus empathizes with them, offering a merciful response. In fact, the Greek word for "mercy" in Hebrews 4:16, *eleos*, means "compassion" (Strong, 2001a, p. 84). Thus, being willing to lean into the experience, reaching out to Jesus the High Priest during moments of suffering, results in Jesus's compassionate reply. Instead of attempting to control the pain through personal efforts, which can make matters worse, Christians can let go of the struggle by choosing to open up to God's outstretched arms on the throne.

Relatedly, Psalm 46:10 famously states, "Be still, and know that I am God" (*New International Version Bible*, 2011). Possibly written to celebrate God's repeated deliverance of the Israelites (Earwood, 1989), the psalmist pointed to God's power and presence in the midst of Israel's turmoil. Interestingly, the Hebrew word for "still" in this passage, *raphah*, can mean to cease striving, abandon, or let go (Earwood, 1989; Strong, 2001b). Just before this verse, in Psalm 46:9, the psalmist mentioned that God has the ability to stop wars and destroy weapons (e.g., bows, spears, shields). Thus, "be still" may have been used in the context of putting down one's arms and stopping all fighting (Earwood, 1989). Overall, the writer seems to have been reminding Israel that God is in control, resulting in the ability to give up futile human efforts because God is serving as a "fortress" (Earwood, 1989). Stated differently, the Israelites were able to set down their weapons, discontinuing the battle because God is sovereign and acting as a stable source of security (Earwood, 1989).

For Christian clients experiencing an inner battle, frequently warring with thoughts, feelings, sensations, and memories that are apparently defeating them, this passage can serve as a reminder that God is sovereign, acting as a "fortress" in spite of difficult inner events. In other words, Christian clients can put down their proverbial weapons, letting go of a unilateral control agenda. Therefore, for Christians with recurrent depression, anxiety, trauma, or relationship distress in the 21st century, to "be still" means to stop all unnecessary, gratuitous striving, which may involve erroneously attempting to get rid of unpleasant inner experiences. Rather, to "be still" means to let go, relinquishing personal control efforts, confidently accepting whatever symptoms arise because God is omnipotent, omnibenevolent, omniscient, and omnipresent. Indeed, because God serves as the ultimate guide for life, offering comfort, strength, and protection, this kind of a battle metaphor can help Christian clients to recognize that God is on their side. Again, Christian clients can confidently drop their metaphorical weapons, focusing on simply "being," rather than "doing."

Another example of an acceptance metaphor in traditional ACT, "Joe the Bum" (Hayes et al., 2012) involves clients envisioning that they are having a party at their home, with the whole neighborhood invited. Because the whole community can come, "Joe the Bum" shows up. He smells, is extremely dirty, and lives behind the local grocery store, distracting the client from socializing with their party guests. Accordingly, the client has a decision to make—accept that "Joe the Bum" is there and will not leave, returning to the party to hang out with the guests, or remain preoccupied with him, arguing with him and trying to get him to leave, to no avail. Of course, the former, rather than the latter, will end up leading to the opportunity to enjoy the party, even though "Joe the Bum" will not depart. This metaphor, certainly, serves as a reminder that clients can live out their values without having to make all of their unpleasant inner experiences go away, especially since fighting with them will ultimately serve as a distraction and fail to achieve the desired result of total elimination of the "nuisance."

As a parallel, in the Christian faith, there are many examples in the gospels that involve Jesus spending time with others, despite their difficult or problematic behavior. Judas Iscariot, for instance, was one of Jesus's 12 disciples, dining with Jesus before betraying him for a handful of coins (Luke 22:1–6; Mark 14:10–11; Matthew 26:15). In this account, Jesus knew that Judas would betray him (John 6:64; Mark 14:18; Matthew 26:25). Even more important, Jesus accepted Judas, who was seated very close to him at the Last Supper, despite his foreknowledge of Judas's betrayal (John 13:27–28). In other words, Judas ate with Jesus, with Jesus accepting that Judas would turn his back on Jesus according to God's divine purpose (Witherington, 2001). As Jesus passed Judas the bread at the Last Supper, his gesture was an act of love, despite what Judas would go on to do (Newbigin, 1982).

Overall, although Jesus was "troubled in spirit," he accepted Judas, given Jesus's submission to God's will. As Milne (1993) revealed, Judas's presence "among the visible company of the disciples throughout the course of Jesus's mission did not prevent the completion of the purpose of the Son, nor the coming of the Spirit, nor the witness of the apostles, nor the going of Jesus to the world through them" (p. 203). For Christian clients, recognizing that "the church is an irreducibly ambiguous company, at once both holy and profane" (Milne, 1993, p. 203) can help them to follow through in their efforts to walk with God in love, despite unpleasant inner experiences. As Jesus elucidated, fulfilling God's purpose is possible even when dining with a betrayer. To draw a parallel with the inner world, although Christian clients may experience unpleasant thoughts, feelings, sensations, and memories, with these inner states firmly seated at the proverbial dinner table of the mind, Christians can continue in their efforts to live out God's will.

To offer an additional illustration for cultivating acceptance, Hayes et al.'s (2012) reference to "clean" versus "dirty" pain can help Christian clients to recognize that suffering involves "pain on top of pain" (Hayes, 2005, p. 17) because of experiential avoidance, rather than pain in and of itself. Within traditional ACT, "clean" pain captures the original symptoms that are causing distress, whereas "dirty" pain constitutes these inner experiences, along with the added pain that results from trying to avoid the "clean" pain. Indeed, many clients would be more than willing to simply accept the original pain if given the choice, especially since suffering results from the combination of pain and the avoidance of pain, leading to an unmanageable life.

For Christian clients, the story of Jonah in the Old Testament may help to illuminate problems that arise from attempting to run from distressing inner experiences, especially in relationship to God. In this narrative, God asked Jonah to travel to Nineveh to share his message (Jonah 1:1–3; Wiersbe, 2002). Yet, Jonah avoided God's plan, running to Tarshish, instead, because he believed God assigned him an impossible task in attempting to save the Assyrians, an enemy of Israel (Jonah 1:1–3; Wiersbe, 2002). For Jonah, his anger over God's compassion for the people of Nineveh led to his desired escape, along with added pain because he ran from God's will. While in the famous fish, Jonah cried out to God while in distress, with God hearing his cries (Jonah 2). Thus, Jonah experienced "pain on top of pain," that is, both "clean" and "dirty" pain (Hayes, 2005, p. 17).

Not only did he struggle with his original anger and doubt toward God, failing to understand (or agree with) God's loving response to those in Nineveh, but he also suffered from added psychological pain because he ran from God's purpose for his life. On the other hand, had Jonah yielded to God's will, sharing his anger with God (rather than attempting to ameliorate his anger through avoidance), he might not have experienced compounded suffering. However, God responded to Jonah with loving compassion, accepting him and restoring their relationship (Wiersbe, 2002). Again, for Christian clients, learning to accept inner pain and cry out to God in the process, rather than running from inner distress, is optimal for value-based living, especially when considering the importance of living out God's will.

In terms of experiential exercises, Harris (2019) offered several traditional ACT interventions, including "Normalizing," "Healing Hand," and "Compassion" (p. 255). With "Normalizing," clients are asked to simply accept their inner experiences as a normal, ubiquitous part of being human, recognizing that inner pain can often result from unmet expectations and disappointments in an imperfect world (Harris, 2019, p. 255). For Christian clients, "Fully Human Like Jesus" can be assigned as an alternative task. Specifically, Christian clients can accept their inner distress, given that Jesus was "fully human in every way" and "suffered when he was tempted" (*New International Version Bible*, 2011, Hebrews 2:17–18), which means he can "empathize with [their] weaknesses" (*New International Version Bible*, 2011, Hebrews 4:15).

As another example, the "Healing Hand" exercise is intended to help clients imagine a gentle, loving hand waving over the inner distress in order to accept it with compassion (Harris, 2019, p. 255). Of course, for Christian clients, Jesus is like a healing doctor (Mark 2:17) and his name is like medicine (Clairveaux, 2012). Thus, Jesus can be the one who waves his "Healing Hand" over the inner wound. As revealed by the medieval contemplative writer Bernard of Clairvaux (2012),

> [The name of Jesus] is a medicine. Does one of us feel sad? Let the name of Jesus come into his heart, from there let it spring to his mouth, so that shining like the dawn it may dispel all darkness and make a cloudless sky ... And where is the man, who, terrified and trembling before impending peril, has not been suddenly filled with courage and rid of fear by calling on the strength of that name ... Was ever a man so discouraged, so beaten down by afflictions, to whom the sound of this name did not bring new resolve?

The purpose of the exercise, though, is not to get rid of the pain. Instead, the intent is to allow it to just be there, knowing Jesus is soothing and comforting the pain with his loving presence.

With the "Compassion" exercise, clients are asked to embrace the inner pain like a vulnerable "crying baby," simply allowing it to be there and displaying an attitude of compassion, gentleness, and kindness (Harris, 2019, p. 255). For Christian clients, rather than embracing a "crying baby," they can imagine Jesus holding their pain, resting in his loving arms. To be sure, the purpose of the exercise is not to make the pain go away, but to recognize that pain is tolerable when Jesus is present.

Finally, rather than employing mindfulness meditation to learn to accept inner experiences with nonjudgment, Christian clients can utilize the welcoming prayer,[10] a variation of centering prayer (Keating, 2006), to relate to emotional pain in a different way. With the welcoming prayer, Christian clients begin by "focusing and sinking into" the unpleasant emotion, simply noticing the experience. Next, Christian clients can "welcome" the emotion, inviting God into the experience, rather than trying to eliminate or avoid it, by literally verbalizing the desire to summon the pain for further exploration (e.g., "Welcome, sadness," "Welcome, anxiety"). For the last step, Christian clients "let go," stating, "I let go of the desire to change the emotion." Undoubtedly, for Christian clients, all of this is possible because God is there, offering his peace, comfort, and love in the midst of emotional suffering.

To wrap up this discussion, the foregoing metaphors and exercises can help counselors and therapists broaden the appeal of traditional ACT strategies, cultivating inner acceptance and flexibility for Christian clients. Of course, the aforementioned examples are only presented tentatively, recognizing that many of them may not be an exact fit with traditional ACT interventions. Indeed, rather than serving as a scholarly, academic explication, the aforementioned adaptations can serve as a starting point, or preliminary guide, so as to help counselors and therapists creatively apply faith-based ACT to Christians in distress.

A central theme, though, embedded within the modified interventions involves Jesus's loving presence, rather than clients employing the exercises in isolation for pragmatic purposes. In other words, because Jesus is actively intervening, offering his loving care, the inner world can be accepted with a hopeful, patient endurance. Similar to the contemplative exercise in the previous chapter, along with the Jesus Prayer elucidated in this chapter, Christian clients can cultivate several contemplative attitudes, including gentleness, acceptance, allowing the experience to simply be, letting go, and resting in God's love (Frenette, 2012). These contemplative strategies are further explored in the next chapter, focusing on the contemplative self (the *nous* in Greek) and practicing God's presence (*hesychia* in Greek). In the meantime, what follows are examples from both Scripture and counseling and therapy to illustrate experiential acceptance for Christians.

The Bible and Enduring

For Christian clients, there are a variety of examples in the Bible to support the notion of experiential acceptance. For instance, in Paul's letter to the Romans (Romans 5:2–4), he mentioned that suffering produces endurance, which cultivates character and hope. In other words, individuals going through adversity are "toughened up" in order to endure life's trials, which result in fortified character (Schreiner, 1998, p. 256). Within this process, the burgeoning character that is produced leads to hope because Christians witness the reality that God is working in their life, changing them until this developmental process is finished (Schreiner, 1998). Here, *hupomone*, or a hopeful, patient steadfastness, is mentioned yet again. For Paul, life's trials lead to endurance, with Christians recognizing that God is producing character in the midst of suffering. Therefore, unpleasant inner experiences can be accepted because God is active in the Christian life.

As another biblical illustration, in Peter's first letter, he indicated that Christians "may have to suffer grief in all kinds of trials" (*New International Version Bible*, 2011, 1 Peter 1:6). In this instance, Peter was reminding his audience that "simultaneous grief and joy [are] normal in the Christian life" (Grudem, 1988, p. 63), with grief resulting from a wide variety of adversities within the fallen human condition. Yet, Christians can still experience joy in the midst of suffering because various trials help them to strengthen their faith in God (Grudem, 1988). In other words, "The trials burn away any impurities in the believer's faith. What is left when the trials have ended is purified, genuine faith, analogous to the pure gold or silver that emerges from the refiner's fire" (Grudem, 1988, p. 64).

For Christian clients, the foregoing passages in Scripture, among others, can help to understand psychological pain and suffering in a different way, recognizing that psychological distress is a normal part of the Christian life. Moreover, Christian clients can find comfort in a wide array of passages that draw attention to the growth and hope that are linked to adversity, especially given that becoming more like Jesus (1 John 2:6; 1 Peter 2:21) is a central goal in the Christian faith. Although the pain of this world may not fully go away, Christians can patiently endure because of the hope they have in God's eventual restoration (Acts 3:21), along with the faith they place in Jesus, the "Suffering Servant" (*New International Version Bible*, 2011, Isaiah 53).

A Clinical Example of Watching and Enduring

Abigail, a 26-year-old, single, Mexican-American female presented to therapy because of recurrent worry from one topic to the next. She reported that she had "always been a worry wart," struggling with catastrophic, doomsday predictions about the future. For Abigail, common sources of worry included paying her bills on time, graduating college, and finding a husband. In fact, she also regularly worried about whether her Christian friends at church liked her, anticipating that they would reject her and ruminating about past conversations that "offended them."

In therapy, the therapist employed a faith-based ACT strategy, given that Abigail reported her Christian faith was central to her life. She indicated that she commonly avoided talking to people at social gatherings because she feared she would be rejected and struggled to apply for a new job, even though her college graduation date was fast approaching. In the first few sessions, her therapist asked her about her futile efforts to avoid worry, rumination, and anxiety, helping her to identify moments of cognitive fusion and experiential avoidance. According to Abigail, she always dreamed of fully devoting herself to following Jesus, serving in some sort of full-time ministry at her church. Yet, her worry and anxiety seemed to sidetrack this heartfelt value, which she had had since childhood when she had interacted with an inspirational youth pastor at a local church.

After identifying common thoughts that she fused with (e.g., "People hate me," "I'll never be able to get hired in full-time ministry"), her therapist began to help her relate to these inner events with more openness and flexibility, using both the Jesus Prayer and a modified "Soldiers in the Parade" exercise. Over time, through repeating the Jesus Prayer (i.e., "Lord Jesus Christ, Son of God, have mercy on me, a sinner"), Abigail was able to focus her attention on Jesus's loving, merciful presence, transitioning toward the prayer whenever her mind began to worry. In the process, she was able to simply observe and acknowledge her worrying thoughts, gaining some distance from them as she pivoted back to the prayer. What is more, she was able to envision herself walking with Jesus in Jerusalem, simply noticing her thoughts as if they were bystanders posing comments and asking questions. As she observed the crowd that surrounded her, which represented her worrying thoughts, she was able to let the crowd be, given she was with Jesus. In fact, as she revealed, the exercise also helped her to feel closer to God, recognizing that he was present in the midst of her distress. These exercises allowed her to "lean not on [her] own understanding," trusting that God had a purpose for her and relying less on her own mind's interpretation of God's will.

Her therapist also helped her relate to her anxiety with more compassion and nonjudgment, ameliorating her tendency to assess her inner distress as "bad." By using the welcoming prayer, she was able to connect to her anxiety, embracing it because God was with her, rather than attempting to avoid it through social isolation and "playing it safe in life." In addition, Abigail's therapist helped her to imagine that she was sitting with Jesus on a boat, similar to Jesus's disciples, with the waves and wind representing her inner pain. For Abigail, recognizing that Jesus was with her on the boat helped her to accept the storms of life, rather than trying to fight against them. Indeed, Abigail began to realize that Jesus was in control, letting go of her tendency to try to eradicate her unpleasant emotions. Instead, she was able to focus on the task at hand, following Jesus and discerning his will for her life.

Conclusion

In this chapter, "opening up" (Harris, 2019, p. 8) was explored, focusing on faith-based ACT strategies to watch the thinking process, rather than getting hooked by it, along with experiential acceptance interventions to cultivate a more hopeful, patient endurance in the face of suffering. For Christian clients, life is by no means free from suffering, as the Bible frequently reveals. Instead, life is about relating to suffering with hope, constancy, and the recognition that inner and outer trials produce character, similar to metal being refined by fire. Above all else, traditional ACT's acceptance and defusion strategies can be utilized in such a way as to allow Christian clients to continue to follow Jesus, despite unpleasant inner experiences. In fact, walking with God in love involves deepening a relationship with him, which is the central focus of the next chapter. Connecting to him in the present moment can help Christian clients in distress to draw strength from this loving relationship, as well as pursue value-based action in the midst of suffering.

Notes

1 Unless otherwise noted, the ACT themes and concepts in this chapter are from Bach et al. (2008), Harris (2019), Hayes (2019), Hayes et al. (2012), and Luoma et al. (2017).
2 In this chapter, I use the term *contemplation*, which I define as a present-moment awareness of God's perfect love (Knabb & Bates, 2020), and briefly review the Christian contemplative tradition (Foster, 1998). Currently, there is not a consensus

in the Christian meditation/prayer/contemplation literature on the use of terminology (e.g., meditation, prayer, contemplation, contemplative prayer, centering prayer, *lectio divina*), given there is often a lack of clear boundaries/dividing lines and formal, operationalized definitions for these practices. For the sake of simplicity, therefore, I primarily draw from the Christian contemplative tradition within this book, which is often (although not exclusively) *apophatic*, in contrast with the long list of *cataphatic* sources on meditation and prayer in Christianity. For a more detailed review of the topic, see Knabb (2021).

3 Here, it is important to note that the collection of *Sayings from the Desert Fathers*, which originated as oral stories (Harmless, 2004), later inspired more formal, theologically oriented writings on contemplation. These comprehensive works, including texts by Evagrius Ponticus and Dionysius, developed into a more organized *mystical theology*, which is defined as an approach to life that involves the expression of God's presence in the context of a particular religion (McGinn, 1991). McIntosh (1998), more precisely, defined Christian mysticism as "a way of grounding all the doctrines of Christianity in God's plan to draw the whole world to Godself in Jesus Christ" (p. 39). It is also worth mentioning that around the turn of the second millennium, the Eastern Orthodox and Roman Catholic Church split, with a second "stream" of mystical theology developing in the East (Johnson, 1995). Although the style of the Jesus Prayer, a central feature of Eastern Orthodox mysticism, dates back to the early desert Christians with the repetition of passages in Scripture (e.g., the psalms), *hesychasm* and the Jesus Prayer are currently associated with the Eastern Orthodox Church, wherein mystical theology is a central focus (Johnson, 1995). Contemporary contemplative approaches, drawn from a rich tradition of mystical theology, include centering prayer (Keating, 2006), Finley's (2004) contemplative writings, and Main's (2006) mantra meditation.

4 Unless otherwise noted, the details on the history of monastic life, the desert landscape, and "the cell" are derived from Burton-Christie (1993), Chryssavgis (2008), Johnson (1995), McGinn (1991), and Paintner (2012).

5 Although *monk* was originally defined as "one who is alone," there have historically been several types of monastic communities, including *cenobites* and *anchorites* (Harmless, 2004, p. 115). Cenobites resided in organized communities, whereas anchorites tended to live life by themselves (Harmless, 2004).

6 For a discussion of Jewish influences on the contemplative movement and Christian mysticism, see McGinn (1991).

7 Some ACT writers use "demon" and "monster" terminology (Harris, 2019; Hayes et al., 2012) as metaphors to refer to the struggle with the inner world, including the tendency to avoid thoughts, feelings, sensations, and memories that are perceived to be frightening. There is certainly an interesting parallel between ACT's symbolic view that "demons" become less scary when clients face them and the early desert monks' desire to confront the literal demons they thought were tormenting and tempting them, similar to Jesus's experience in the desert with the Devil.

8 In the faith-based ACT approach I present in this book, my recommendation is to view the early desert Christians' perceived demonic temptations as symbolic of clients' struggles with the inner world, rather than literal, paralleling ACT's metaphorical use of demon and monster terminology. It is also worth mentioning that some early desert dwellers, such as John Chrysostom, distinguished demonic activity from other causes of mental health problems, including organic origins (Trader, 2011). Yet, many Christian clients believe in a worldview that embraces "spiritual warfare," including a perspective that demons and "the enemy" (i.e., the Devil) tempt them. In fact, a Pew Forum survey from over a decade ago elucidated that 68% of Americans

believe that angels and demons are active and present in day-to-day life (Pew Forum, 2008). Nevertheless, counselors and therapists are reminded to stay within their scope of practice, presenting this material in a symbolic, rather than literal, manner.

9 See Knabb et al. (2010) for a detailed overview of the overlap between the Genesis story of creation and ACT. According to the Lutheran theologian Dietrich Bonhoeffer (1955), Christians continuously struggle with trying to place themselves at the center of the Garden, being like God in their knowledge of good and evil, rather than dependent on God.

10 This description is based on the instructions in Bourgeault (2004, pp. 143–147), which provide a detailed overview of the welcoming prayer, including a discussion of the three major steps and how they relate to centering prayer.

References

Avila, T. (1980). *The way of perfection.* ICS Publications.

Bach, P., Moran, D., & Hayes, S. (2008). *ACT in practice: Case conceptualization in acceptance and commitment therapy.* New Harbinger Publications.

Barclay, W. (2000). *New Testament words.* Westminster John Knox Press.

Barclay, W. (2004). *The revelation of John, volume one.* Westminster John Knox Press.

Bishop, S., Lau, M., Shapiro, S., Carlson, L., Anderson, N., Carmody, J., Segal, Z., Abbey, S., Speca, M., Velting, D., & Devins, G. (2004). Mindfulness: A proposed operational definition. *Clinical Psychology: Science and Practice, 11,* 230–241.

Bonhoeffer, D. (1955). *Ethics.* Touchstone.

Bourgeault, C. (2004). *Centering prayer and inner awakening.* Cowley Publications.

Burton-Christie, D. (1993). *The word in the desert: Scripture and the quest for holiness in early Christian monasticism.* Oxford University Press.

Chryssavgis, J. (2008). *In the heart of the desert: The spirituality of the desert fathers and mothers.* World Wisdom, Inc.

Chumley, N. (2014). *Be still and know: God's presence in silence.* Fortress Press.

Clairvaux, B. (2012). *Commentary on the song of songs.* Jazzybee Verlag.

Earwood, G. (1989). Psalm 46. *Review and Expositor, 86,* 79–86.

Evagrius. (2009). *Talking back: A monastic handbook for combating demons.* Liturgical Press.

Finley, J. (2004). *Christian meditation: Experiencing the presence of God.* HarperCollins Publishers, Inc.

Foster, R. (1998). *Streams of living water: Celebrating the great traditions of Christian faith.* HarperCollins Publishers.

Frenette, D. (2012). *The path of centering prayer: Deepening your experience of God.* Sounds True, Inc.

Grudem, W. (1988). *1 Peter.* Wm. B. Eerdmans Publishing Company.

Harmless, W. (2004). *Desert Christians: An introduction to the literature of early monasticism.* Oxford University Press.

Harmless, W. (2008). *Mystics.* Oxford University Press.

Harris, R. (2019). *ACT made simple: An easy-to-read primer on acceptance and commitment therapy* (2nd ed.). New Harbinger Publications, Inc.

Hayes, S. (2005). *Get out of your mind and into your life: The new acceptance & commitment therapy.* New Harbinger Publications, Inc.

Hayes, S. (2019). *A liberated mind: How to pivot toward what matters.* Avery.

Hayes, S., Strosahl, K., & Wilson, K. (1999). *Acceptance and commitment therapy: An experiential approach to behavior change*. The Guilford Press.

Hayes, S., Strosahl, K., & Wilson, K. (2012). *Acceptance and commitment therapy: The process and practice of mindful change* (2nd ed.). The Guilford Press.

Johnson, W. (1995). *Mystical theology: The science of love*. Orbis Books.

Johnston, W. (2000). *The mysticism of the cloud of unknowing*. Fordham University Press.

Keating, T. (2006). *Open mind, open heart, 20th anniversary edition*. Continuum.

Knabb, J. (2021). *Christian meditation in clinical practice: A four-step model and workbook for therapists and clients*. InterVarsity Press.

Knabb, J., & Bates, M. (2020). "Holy desire" within the "Cloud of Unknowing": The psychological contributions of medieval apophatic contemplation to Christian mental health in the 21st century. *Journal of Psychology and Christianity, 39*, 24–39.

Knabb, J., Ashby, J., & Ziebell, J. (2010). Two sides of the same coin: The theology of Dietrich Bonhoeffer and acceptance and commitment therapy (ACT). *Journal of Spirituality in Mental Health, 12*, 150–180.

Laird, M. (2011). *A sunlit absence: Silence, awareness, and contemplation*. Oxford University Press.

Lane, B. (1998). *The solace of fiery landscapes: Exploring desert and mountain spirituality*. Oxford University Press.

Luoma, J., Hayes, S., & Walser, R. (2017). *Learning ACT: An acceptance and commitment therapy skills training manual for therapists* (2nd ed.). Context Press.

Main, J. (2006). *Word into silence: A manual for Christian meditation*. Canterbury Press Norwich.

Mathewes-Green, F. (2011). *Praying the Jesus prayer*. Paraclete Press.

McGinn, B. (1991). *The foundations of mysticism: Origins to the fifth century*. The Crossroad Publishing Company.

McIntosh, M. (1998). *Mystical theology*. Blackwell Publishing.

Merton, T. (2005). *No man is an island*. Shambhala.

Milne, B. (1993). *The message of John*. InterVarsity Press.

New International Version Bible. (2011). Zondervan. https://www.biblegateway.com/

Newbigin, L. (1982). *The light has come: An exposition of the fourth gospel*. Wm. B. Eerdmans Publishing Co.

Paintner, C. (2012). *Desert fathers and mothers: Early Christian wisdom sayings*. SkyLight Paths Publishing.

Pennington, B. (1982). *Centering prayer: Renewing an ancient Christian prayer form*. Doubleday.

Pennington, B. (2000). *True self/false self: Unmasking the spirit within*. The Crossroad Publishing Company.

Pew Forum. (2008). *U.S. religious landscape survey: Religious beliefs and practices*. Pew Forum on Religion & Public Life.

Schreiner, T. (1998). *Romans*. Baker Academic.

Siegelman, E. (1990). *Metaphor & meaning in psychotherapy*. The Guilford Press.

Stoddard, J., & Afari, N. (2014). *The big book of ACT metaphors: A practitioner's guide to experiential exercises & metaphors in acceptance & commitment therapy*. New Harbinger Publications, Inc.

Strong, J. (2001a). *The new Strong's expanded dictionary of the words in the Greek New Testament*. Thomas Nelson.

Strong, J. (2001b). *The new Strong's expanded dictionary of the words in the Hebrew Bible.* Thomas Nelson.

Taylor, B. (2002). *Becoming Christ: Transformation through contemplation.* Cowley Publications.

Trader, S. (2011). *Ancient Christian wisdom and Aaron Beck's cognitive therapy: A meeting of the minds.* Peter Lang Publishing, Inc.

Wiersbe, W. (2002). *The Bible exposition commentary: Old Testament prophets.* David C. Cook.

Witherington, B. (2001). *The gospel of Mark: A socio-rhetorical commentary.* Eerdmans Publishing Co.

Wortley, J. (2012). *The book of elders: Sayings of the desert fathers.* Cistercian Publications.

7

NOTICING AND SHIFTING

Introduction

In this chapter, the focus is on the traditional acceptance and commitment therapy (ACT)[1] processes of the transcendent self and present-moment awareness, collectively described as the "being present" pillar (Harris, 2019, p. 8), drawing a parallel with the Christian contemplative life and faith-based ACT equivalent—the "noticing and shifting" pillar. Similar to Mary simply sitting at the feet of Jesus, counselors and therapists can help Christian clients to accept difficult thoughts, feelings, sensations, and memories through cultivating a greater awareness of the contemplative self (the *nous* in Greek). This more transcendent, spiritual awareness is similar to the transcendent self in ACT, which is a sense of self for safely viewing painful thoughts, feelings, sensations, and memories with more openness and flexibility. In other words, a common theme involves "flexible perspective taking" (Luoma et al., 2017, p. 163), with Christian clients learning to shift from an earthly to heavenly perspective in the midst of psychological suffering (Burroughs, 2010, 2014; Owen, 2016; Rowe, 1672), with God's love as the foundation.

In addition, traditional ACT's present-moment awareness process is a way for clients to stay connected to each unfolding minute of the day, rather than getting lost in the mind on "automatic pilot" (Segal et al., 2012), preoccupied with the past or future. In other words, for clients, living out their values involves maintaining a sustained, flexible awareness of what is in front of them, in the here-and-now, which resembles practicing God's presence in order to cultivate inner peace, silence, and stillness (*hesychia* in Greek). To be sure, for Christian clients, Jesus instructed his followers to avoid worrying about tomorrow, given that "each day has enough trouble of its own" (*New International Version Bible*, 2011, Matthew 6:34).

Together, these two processes can help Christian clients notice when they are overreliant upon their verbal, content- and language-driven, reasoning self, which can get in the way of following Jesus, then gently shift toward the contemplative self to directly experience the God of love, practice his presence, and cultivate inner quiet, peace, and stillness as they walk with God in love in the

DOI: 10.4324/9781003181941-8

here-and-now. Put another way, Christian clients are learning to notice when they are overly relying on self-derived knowledge, then shift to God-derived love, reminiscent of the pivot from knowledge to love that is exemplified in the famous contemplative writing the *Cloud of Unknowing* (Bangley, 2006).

Also in this chapter, exercises are offered, including contemplative strategies, to help Christian clients develop a deeper relationship with God, a foundational aim in Christianity. With Christian contemplation, or contemplative prayer, which usually involves symbolically focusing on a "prayer word" or the breath, Christians strive to nurture several contemplative attitudes, including surrendering to God's presence, letting go, and the ability to allow inner experiences to simply be (Frenette, 2012). These burgeoning contemplative attitudes can be helpful as Christian clients focus on flexibly following Jesus (i.e., walking with God in love) wherever he would have them go, rather than employing experiential avoidance.

Furthermore, ways to develop the contemplative self are highlighted in order to deepen Christian clients' ability to connect to this newfound "heavenly-mindedness" or "spiritual-mindedness" (Burroughs, 2010, 2014; Owen, 2016; Rowe, 1672) during moments of distress, rather than using experiential avoidance, which keeps them stuck and prevents them from fully following Jesus. Throughout the chapter, examples from the New Testament, writings of contemplative Christians, ACT metaphors, and a case example are offered to help counselors and therapists enhance this portion of faith-based ACT.

Traditional ACT and the Transcendent Self

In traditional ACT, clients are taught that thinking is a "double-edged sword." On one hand, it helps clients to navigate the difficult terrain of an uncertain world. On the other hand, it can lead to clients' suffering, since they can quickly become overly fused with the world of words, blocking effective action. Stated differently, language leads to a more abstract view of reality, rather than a direct sensory experience that unfolds from moment to moment. For many clients, a major struggle involves overly relying on the part of themselves that tends to hold on tightly to stories about the "self," undercutting the pursuit of values. When this happens, clients can lose focus, disconnecting from the self that safely watches the inner world from a distance with curiosity and openness, existing since the formation of consciousness itself.

To distinguish between the immediate thoughts, feelings, sensations, and memories that make up the inner world and sense of self that safely watches these wavering states arise and pass away, ACT differentiates the *verbal self* (i.e., *storied self, thinking self, self-as-content*) from *transcendent self* (i.e., *spiritual self, observing self, noticing self, self-as-context*). Of course, the verbal, thinking self generates thoughts, stories, statements, and other language-based experiences, relying on the mind to judge and narrate the inner and outer worlds. Unfortunately, this

163

evaluative strategy can often get in the way of value-based living, especially when clients tightly grip a narrative that bogs them down. Because the mind can create a variety of stories about who the client is or is supposed to be, effective behavioral activity can be limited, especially when the story is incongruent with a vibrant, action-based life.

Extending back to childhood, humans learn how to create advanced narratives about themselves, starting many sentences with "I am …" before filling in the blanks with unhelpful descriptions. Sometimes, this verbal world can be inherently limiting, especially when clients have experienced abuse, neglect, or other life events that lead to negative conclusions about themselves, including their place in the world. For example, a client who experienced extreme abandonment as a child might conclude, "I am utterly unlovable, which is why my father left me." If this is the case, this narrated story can undermine their efforts to live a life filled with deeply satisfying, intimate relationships that offer support, encouragement, and closeness.

On the other hand, the transcendent, noticing self is a sense of self for perspective taking that is able to watch the inner world unfold from a safe distance, simply observing the wavering, impermanent, language-driven, verbal self unfold from moment to moment. Rather than getting swept away by a stream of thoughts, feelings, sensations, and memories that make up a very limited part of the "river" that is the self, clients can sit on the bank of the river, relating to passing experiences with gentleness, kindness, and curiosity. This sense of self, of course, has existed since clients first experienced conscious reflection, offering a stable lens through which they can watch private events unfold.

In traditional ACT, a variety of exercises are employed to help clients experience the transcendent self, including the "Chessboard" metaphor, wherein clients are asked to think about the game of chess. In the game, the main components are the chess pieces and the board. Many clients, certainly, see themselves as the pieces, whether white or black, with the goal to eliminate the pieces on the other side of the board. For example, the strategy may be for the black pieces, representing positive emotional experiences and pleasant thoughts, to eliminate the white pieces, capturing all of the inner distress that seemingly needs to be eradicated. Yet, the chessboard, which holds all of the pieces in place, can be a safe, permanent location to watch the game unfold, without needing to get pulled into the battle. To be sure, the transcendent self is like the board, a viewpoint from which the inner world can be safely observed, without wrestling with inner events as pieces to be removed, striving to "win" the game. This is especially true when considering that thoughts, feelings, sensations, and memories will continue to arise, leading to the conclusion that beating an opponent (e.g., negative cognitions) through the process of elimination is not possible.

As another traditional ACT example, clients can view themselves like the sky, watching clouds (i.e., the inner world) simply pass by. In this exercise, the goal is to connect to the transcendent self, gently noticing that distressing thoughts, feelings, sensations, and memories tend to come and go, rather than constitute a permanent self. In other words, the "clouds" in the sky are a part of the self, but do not make up the self's entirety. Instead, the sky, which is a vast, open space, holds the clouds, which move to and fro without disturbing the atmosphere.

To summarize, the transcendent self is a sense of self—a perspective or viewpoint—for confidently noticing distressing inner states, with clients recognizing they are more than their thoughts, feelings, sensations, memories, images, stories, and other verbally constructed, language-driven parts of the self. With traditional ACT, the point is to simply watch psychological experiences, rather than becoming overwhelmed by them, so that clients can pivot toward value-based action. To nonjudgmentally observe means to let go of the tendency to rigidly attach to all of the verbal events that clients are convinced constitute the self. Instead, clients can connect to the self that is more than waxing and waning inner states, recognizing there is a large part of them that is not harmed by malleable, impermanent psychological experiences. For this to happen, clients must also maintain an awareness of the present moment, which is explored in the next section.

Traditional ACT and Present-Moment Awareness

In addition to connecting to the transcendent, spiritual self, which is a perspective-taking sense of self for safely noticing, traditional ACT helps clients flexibly anchor themselves to the present moment, leading to intentional, value-based action. When clients overly rely on the world of language, they tend to reify inner experiences, rather than see verbally constructed mental states as a mere tool in the service of values. Because thoughts, feelings, sensations, and memories can get in the way of directly experiencing the world, present-moment awareness is most effective when combined with alertness toward the transcendent self.

With present-moment awareness, clients employ mindfulness skills to directly connect to inner and outer events, commonly relying on sensory experiences, rather than the mind's interpretation of the world. Stated differently, many clients overly rely on the thinking, judging, evaluative mind, leading to "automatic pilot," wherein they are preoccupied with the past or future (Segal et al., 2012). In a sense, if the transcendent self is the spiritual self, which simply notices words, labels, and other evaluative attempts to judge what is happening, then this part of the self must engage directly with the world. For this reason, clients are taught strategies through the use of mindfulness to directly relate to unfolding events, rather than viewing them through the mind's often critical lens. Because now is the only actual time that human beings have, it makes sense that helping clients to operate from the here-and-now would enhance the effectiveness of the other ACT processes, including value-based action, which needs to occur in real time, rather than in the past or future.

With mindfulness meditation, the primary vehicle through which contact with the present moment is pursued, clients develop a sustained, flexible awareness of the here-and-now, employing an attitude of nonjudgment, acceptance, and openness and commonly anchoring themselves to a direct sensory experience, rather than the mind's evaluative lens (Bishop et al., 2004). When these skills are present, clients can begin to design their own mindfulness interventions, such as mindfully watching a sunset, mindfully having a conversation, mindfully breathing, or mindfully eating lunch. Again, the central elements include sustained awareness of the present moment and relating to the inner world with flexibility and openness, neither holding onto nor attempting to eliminate thoughts, feelings, sensations, and memories, even those that are distressing.

Regrettably, many clients mentally "travel" to the past or the future, getting lost in ruminative or worrying thoughts, rather than facing the only time they have—now. Sometimes, this is done to avoid unpleasant inner events (i.e., experiential avoidance); at other times, mental time travel is due to cognitive fusion and rigidly holding on to the "stories" clients have created. Because of this, ACT counselors and therapists are encouraged to continuously help clients stay rooted in the present, especially when clients have drifted to another mental place and time by way of the world of language.

Above all else, contact with the present moment is combined with the transcendent self to relate to inner events with more flexibility, allowing clients to pivot toward value-based action during moments of distress. Employing mindfulness skills helps clients relate differently to previously confining and limiting thoughts, feelings, sensations, and memories with "nonattached awareness" (Germer, 2009, p. 83), with clients realizing that inner events need not get in the way of living a life of vitality and meaning. From a place of compassion, kindness, nonjudgment, curiosity, and openness, clients can stay present, flexibly deciding the direction they would like to take based on intentionality, rather than being bullied around by language, overwhelming feelings, unpleasant sensations, or intrusive memories. What follows is a brief review of traditional ACT's central goal, psychological flexibility, along with its similarities to the main focus of faith-based ACT—walking with God in love. After this discussion, I explore the faith-based ACT versions of the transcendent self and present-moment awareness, before transitioning to faith-based ACT strategies, biblical examples, and a client illustration of "noticing and shifting" in practice.

Psychological Flexibility and Walking with God in Love

For ACT counselors and therapists, helping clients to develop psychological flexibility is the central aim. In fact, all six processes foster a more flexible approach to life, with Hayes et al. (2012) suggesting that rigidity ensues when clients are not engaged with these vital processes. In other words, when clients are overly reliant on the world of language, fusing with verbally constructed labels, stories, memories, and so forth, they can struggle to live out their values, undermining a flexible response to life. What is more, when clients engage in experiential avoidance, they are limiting their ability to choose a valued direction, optimizing a vital, meaningful life.

For many clients, cognitive fusion and experiential avoidance are also linked to an overreliance on the verbal self, drawing from language-based processes to make sense of the world in which they live, along with a distracting preoccupation with the past or future. Once more, when these rigid patterns frequently occur, clients cannot live the life they want, experiencing both "clean" and "dirty" pain (Hayes et al., 2012), or "pain on top of pain" (Hayes, 2005, p. 17). Thus, again, the foundational goal of ACT is to help clients employ the four mindfulness-based processes (i.e., *cognitive defusion, acceptance, the transcendent self, present-moment awareness*) to enhance psychological flexibility, leading to a willingness to endure, acting upon well-defined, deeply meaningful values that emanate from the heart.

For Christian clients, psychological flexibility is also very important, serving as a byproduct of a life devoted to Jesus. Stated differently, life is meaningful when Christians are intimately connected to the Son of God, leading to a flexible ability to follow him in love wherever he would have them go, even during instances of psychological suffering. Of course, following Jesus is a freely chosen decision, rather than a rigid, forced, and coercive effort. As a result, flexibility is built into faith-based ACT, outlined in this book. Yet, for Christians, flexibility is a natural, organic outpouring of a present-moment awareness of God's perfect love (Knabb & Bates, 2020), walking with God in love as they move from justification (i.e., being righteous before, and reconciled to, God because of Jesus), to sanctification (i.e., being like Jesus), to glorification (i.e., being face to face with Jesus) (Grudem, 1994).

As Contemplative Outreach (n.d.), the central hub for the contemplative prayer movement, revealed, contemplation is about "resting in God," a phrase coined by Gregory the Great, and involves "consenting to God's presence and action," ultimately resulting in "opening one's whole being to God" and "divine union." Through the use of a short, simple "prayer word" (e.g., "God," "Jesus," "Lord," "love") to symbolize a willingness to "consent" to God's active presence, practitioners are able to sit at the feet of Jesus, similar to Mary in Luke's gospel (Luke 10:38–42). Indeed, Mary was firmly rooted in the present moment, focusing exclusively on Jesus and letting all other distractions (including her sister's persistent complaints) come and go without pursuing them.

Here, we see that contemplative prayer is primarily focused on "divine union," "resting in God," and "consenting" to God's active presence. Even more, "praying is allowing ourselves to be loved. It is to love in return ... To pray, therefore, is to love" (Jacques, 2001, p. 15). Because of this, rather than psychological flexibility serving as an outcome in and of itself, in this book, faith-based ACT utilizes the Christian contemplative tradition. Within this tradition, *apophatic* prayer is employed to help Christian clients recognize God's active, loving presence, which allows them to more flexibly follow Jesus in the midst of psychological pain and be a dwelling place for God's love, which can be extended to others. Even though their distress may not go away, they can experience a hopeful, patient endurance in knowing that the God of love is with them, yielding to his perfect love in the here-and-now. Phrased in a different manner, Christian contemplative practice is an indirect, relational method for addressing human suffering, helping Christian clients to notice inner distress, then gently and flexibly shift toward a sustained awareness of God's loving presence. Indeed, because God is present, and because focusing on God's love can help nurture Christians as they patiently and steadily walk with him along the road of suffering, a wide variety of difficult thoughts, feelings, sensations, situations, and relationships can be endured. What follows is a further review of the contemplative Christian tradition, focusing specifically on the contemplative self (*nous* in Greek) and practicing God's presence (*hesychia* in Greek), which can serve as vehicles to help Christians deepen their walk with the God of love, enhancing psychological flexibility and leading to value-based action when following Jesus.

The Contemplative Self: The Christian Version of the Transcendent Self

The contemplative self (*nous* in Greek) parallels ACT's transcendent self and represents spiritual intuition, the "eye of the soul," "the eye of the heart," and the human spirit (Coniaris, 1998; Harmless, 2004; Nikodimos, 2015). Within this process, which builds on, and complements, the other three contemplative processes (i.e., watchfulness [*nepsis* in Greek], endurance [*hupomone* in Greek], and practicing God's presence [*hesychia* in Greek]), Christians are aware of an intuitive component to the "self," beyond thoughts, feelings, sensations, and memories. The contemplative self—with the *nous* translated as the intuitive part of the mind that can instantly and experientially know and recognize God, rather than the part of the mind that uses reason, logic, and abstract thought to know about God—is utilized in contemplation (Harmless, 2004). As one of the early desert Christians, Evagrius of Ponticus, revealed, "For knowledge of God, one needs not a debater's soul, but a seer's soul" (quoted in Harmless, 2004, p. 352). Evagrius of Ponticus also noted, "Prayer is the ascent of the [*nous*] to God" (quoted in Harmless, 2004, p. 352).

Ultimately, the contemplative self is the highest form of the self, capturing the *imago Dei* (*New International Version Bible*, 2011, Genesis 1:27), and is used during contemplation (e.g., the Jesus Prayer) to cultivate a deeper, more spiritual, more direct relationship with God (Harmless, 2004). Returning to Evagrius of

Ponticus, the *nous* is the contemplative part of the self that yearns to connect to God in a wordless, imageless prayer state (Harmless, 2004). What is more, both Augustine and Thomas Aquinas differentiated the reason-based mind from the intuitive, spiritual, contemplative mind (Laird, 2006; Smith, 2013). A similar distinction is also drawn within the *Philokalia*—a collection of contemplative writings from the fourth to 15th centuries within the Eastern Orthodox Church— via the *nous*, or "eye of the soul" or "eye of the heart," and *dianoia*, or "thinking mind" or "reasoning mind" (Smith, 2013). In other words, these contemplative writers tended to illuminate the difference between abstract, rational, earthly, and self-derived "head" knowledge and direct, spiritual, transcendent, and God-derived "heart" knowledge, prioritizing the latter as a matter of faith, rather than the former, which is limiting in our efforts to contemplate and experience the God of love (Nesteruk, 2003; Nikodimos, 2015). Interestingly, Mathewes-Green (2011) referred to the *nous* as the "little radio," wherein Christians can directly and intuitively experience God's voice, beyond reason. The *nous* is mentioned several times in the New Testament, including in 1 Corinthians 2:16 in the context of Christians needing to have the "mind of Christ" (*New International Version Bible*, 2011), also referred to as "Christ-thinking" or a "new moral and religious consciousness" (Ridderbos, 1975, p. 228).

For the early desert Christians, this meant a renewing of the mind to become more like Jesus, with prayer serving the dual purpose of protecting the *nous* from compulsive thoughts (e.g., *logismoi*) that pulled them away from God and shifting their focus to him (Nassif, 2012). Although slightly different from the transcendent self within traditional ACT, this understanding of the "mind of Christ" can help to cultivate some distance between a language-based understanding of identity, rooted in the old self (2 Corinthians 5:17), and a transcendent, spiritual self, whose identity is found in Jesus, beyond mere words and images (Coniaris, 1998). Above all else, a Christian understanding of the transcendent self involves Jesus's active presence, fellowshipping with the Christian client and helping to watch over their inner world. Therefore, rather than noticing inner experiences in isolation, Christians have another observer, Jesus, actively collaborating to better understand the inner workings of the mind.

As an overlapping way to understand the contrast between the reasoning self (the *dianoia* in Greek) and contemplative self (the *nous* in Greek), the Puritans, a group of 16th and 17th century English Christians who attempted to apply an orthodox reading of Scripture to all aspects of life, distinguished between "earthly-mindedness" and "heavenly-mindedness"/"spiritual-mindedness" (Burroughs, 2010, 2014; Owen, 2016; Rowe, 1672). Collectively, as the Puritans humbly strived to walk with the God of love from moment to moment, contemplative themes often emerged in their writings (Schwanda, 2012). With "earthly-mindedness," Christian clients are preoccupied with this world, including both positive inner and outer events and negative inner and outer events (e.g., thoughts, feelings, sensations, memories, situations, relationships)

(Burroughs, 2014). What is more, when Christian clients are "earthly-minded," they may be distracted by, and preoccupied with, the past or future, ruminating and worrying because they struggle to trust in God's loving care (Knabb, 2021). With "heavenly-mindedness"/"spiritual-mindedness," Christian clients maintain a more spiritual, transcendent, hopeful, "heavenly" perspective, recognizing that the God of love is active and present in each unfolding moment and will eventually restore all things (Burroughs, 2014).

In agreement, another 17th century writer, the French contemplative François Fénelon (2015), advocated the use of frequent prayer to maintain an awareness of this spiritual perspective:

> Constant prayer is, to keep the heart always right towards God. Strive then, when you come from prayer, not to suffer your mind to be too much entangled with outward things, endeavoring to be totally resigned to the Divine Will; that God may do with you and yours according to his heavenly pleasure relying on him as on a kind and loving Father; and though you be taken up with your outward affairs, and your mind thereby prevented from being actually fixed on him, even then, you will always carry a fire about you that will never go out; but which, on the contrary, will nourish a secret prayer, that will be like a lamp continually lighted before the throne of God.

Here, we see that prayer is the mechanism through which a more transcendent, spiritual perspective can be maintained, communing with God and relying upon God's will to guide daily living.

To summarize, like traditional ACT's transcendent self, faith-based ACT's "heavenly-mindedness"/"spiritual-mindedness" helps Christian clients to notice when they are preoccupied with the time-limited, distracting cares of the world (and corresponding self-derived knowledge), then gently shift toward a more transcendent, hopeful perspective (and corresponding God-derived love), wherein God is at the center to guide them in love toward his final destination—being face to face with him in heaven. This "heavenly" perspective certainly has implications for psychological suffering, given it provides Christian clients with a more flexible vantage point to simply notice the fluctuations of the fallen inner and outer worlds, prior to practicing God's presence so as to achieve a deeper inner stillness, which is the next faith-based ACT process.

Practicing God's Presence: The Christian Version of Present-Moment Awareness

In addition to the contemplative self (the *nous* in Greek), practicing God's presence (*hesychia* in Greek) to achieve inner stillness, silence, and peace is cultivated based on continuously returning to "the cell," mentioned in the previous chapter, and yielding to God's will in the here-and-now. Of course, the symbolic cell captures the inner life for Christian clients, rather than serving as a physical location for monks in a distant land (Harmless, 2004). Described as quietness, surrendering to God's active love, and "a graced depth of inner stillness" (Coniaris, 1998; Harmless, 2004, p. 228), *hesychia* is a deeper, more enduring peace that comes from being in awe of God, beyond words and images. As Abba Poemen, an Egyptian monk who lived in the fourth and fifth centuries, revealed, "Whatever hardship comes upon you, it can be overcome by silence" (quoted in Ward, 2003, p. 173).

The way to develop *hesychia* is through praying with constancy, typically utilizing a brief passage in Scripture or the Jesus Prayer, which emanated from the gospel of Luke, wherein Jesus told the story of the tax collector who shouted, "God, have mercy on me, a sinner" (Harmless, 2004; *New International Version Bible*, 2011, Luke 18:13). Through this experience, monks would fully surrender to God and prevent thoughts and feelings from getting in the way of a direct experience of God's presence. According to Abba Isaiah, "One living in *hesychia* needs these three things: to fear God without ceasing, to intercede with patient endurance, and not to release his heart from being mindful of God" (quoted in Wortley, 2012, p. 19). Consistent with the Jesuit contemplative writer Jean Pierre de Caussade (2008), this fearful, mindful awareness of God also involves being "satisfied" with the here-and-now, "[adoring] God's will in all that comes to us." Combined, this inner stability, attentiveness to God's activity, and acceptance of God's will in each unfolding moment of the day resembles traditional ACT's present-moment awareness, which emanates from mindfulness.

Within both practices, thoughts, feelings, sensations, and memories are observed with flexibility and openness in the here-and-now. Regarding mindfulness, sustained attention may be cultivated by attending to the breath or one of the senses, then gently returning to this point of focus when the attention has drifted, whereas contemplative practice often employs a simple "prayer word" or phrase to focus and settle the mind, cultivate inner stillness, and maintain a loving attentiveness toward God (Jacques, 2001; Laird, 2006), reminiscent of Jesus's use of Deuteronomy and the Psalms to combat the Devil's temptations in the desert (Matthew 4:1–11). In either case, cultivating sustained, flexible, nonjudgmental attention helps to relate to inner experiences with more tentativeness, ameliorating cognitive fusion and experiential avoidance, so that Christians can pivot toward an awareness of God's active, loving presence (e.g., sitting at Jesus's feet).

The Jesus Prayer: An Exercise for Noticing and Shifting[2]

For Christian clients, the contemplative tradition, rather than Buddhist mindfulness, can offer a rich heritage to draw from, especially via the practice of the Jesus Prayer, which focuses on cultivating a deeper relationship with

God through the development of the *nous* and *hesychia*. The Jesus Prayer likely originated with the early desert Christians, who drew from the psalms to focus the mind, as revealed in the previous chapter, and developed mono-logic forms of prayer that emphasized the repetition of a simple, short word or phrase (Goodwin, 1999). Over time, the practice developed by borrow-ing from instances in the gospels that involved individuals asking Jesus for mercy. The term, *mercy*, captures a "cry for help," asking God for compas-sionate empathy in the midst of inner pain. In other words, with the Jesus Prayer, practitioners are inviting Jesus to be with them as they endure difficult thoughts, feelings, sensations, and memories. Like mindfulness, the prayer helps practitioners develop a nonjudgmental, flexible awareness of the pre-sent moment, shedding an overreliance on the mind and the world of words. As an added element for Jesus Prayer practitioners, beyond cultivating flex-ible, nonjudgmental, sustained attention, Christians are attempting to deepen an intimacy with God, which provides them with strength and an awareness of God's loving action.

What follows is a sample transcript of the Jesus Prayer,[3] practiced in a 20-minute block of time and modified for Christian clients struggling with inner distress that leads to cognitive fusion and experiential avoidance:

> Get into a comfortable position. When you are ready, close your eyes. To start the practice, begin to notice the breathing process. Focus on the rising and falling of your abdomen as God gives you your breath as a gift, recognizing that you do not need to control your breathing in any way. Simply notice how air fills your lungs with no added effort, naturally entering and exiting your body.
>
> Now, when you are ready to begin, start to introduce the Jesus Prayer: "Lord Jesus Christ, Son of God, have mercy on me, a sinner." Slowly, gently, and quietly recite the words in your mind, allowing them to penetrate your heart each time you complete the sentence. As you breathe in, say "Lord Jesus Christ, Son of God," surrendering to Jesus's protective, loving care and consenting to him as the Lord of your entire world. Allow these powerful words, "Lord Jesus Christ, Son of God," to remind you of his complete control—Jesus is God's one and only Son, dying for you on a cross. In fact, Jesus is part of the Trinity, intimately united with the Father and Holy Spirit. Just accept this wonderful mystery with an open curiosity, allowing this reality to encourage you and help you to unite with him. Whenever a distress-ing thought, feeling, sensation, or memory arises, simply acknowledge it and gently return to the Jesus Prayer, noticing the experience and confidently reciting Jesus's name again and again.
>
> As you breathe out, gently say "have mercy on me, a sinner," let-ting go of any attempt to cling to or push away your inner distress and

connecting to a profound trust in Jesus's loving care. Simply lean into his compassionate, forgiving nature, resting in his loving arms. In this very moment, there is no other place to be and nothing else to do as you sit at Jesus's feet, focusing entirely on him.

Again, slowly and gently breathe in "Lord Jesus Christ, Son of God" and breathe out "have mercy on me, a sinner," allowing the words to recite themselves. As you further the practice, gently and effortlessly breathing in and out, relinquish the need to achieve any other state, whether holding on to thoughts, feelings, sensations, or memories or trying to push them away. Rather, the Jesus Prayer is simply a way to remember Jesus's active, loving role in your life, which extends to each and every inner experience.

Over and over again, say "Lord Jesus Christ, Son of God, have mercy on me, a sinner." Imagine that you are saying the prayer in your heart, envisioning that you are reciting it within the center of your being, given you are a dwelling place for the God of love. Remember, because you are a dwelling place for God, Jesus is with you in the midst of your most difficult thoughts, feelings, sensations, and memories: "Lord Jesus Christ, Son of God, have mercy on me, a sinner."

Every time you conclude a single recitation of the prayer, "Lord Jesus Christ, Son of God, have mercy on me, a sinner," sink deeper into Jesus's loving care, surrendering your entire being to him as the Lord of your life as you imagine that he is dwelling within you. Just focus on basking in his love, trusting that he will guide you in the present moment, letting go of the need to think about the past or future.

As this prayer concludes, thank Jesus for his forgiving, merciful compassion, asking him to remind you of the Jesus Prayer during moments of inner distress throughout the day.

Faith-Based ACT Conceptualizations, Goals, Metaphors, and Exercises for Noticing and Shifting

A variety of ACT metaphors and exercises can be modified for Christian clients, with the central goal of walking with God in love and being aware of God's active, loving presence, as revealed in Table 7.1. For Christian clients experiencing psychological suffering, connecting to the contemplative self in order to observe the inner world as passing events, watching thoughts, feelings, sensations, and memories with Jesus, is a foundational aim. Also, rather than utilizing mindfulness-based interventions, Christian clients can draw from the rich heritage of the Christian contemplative tradition, working toward practicing God's presence so as to cultivate silence, stillness, and peace via the Jesus Prayer and other contemplative exercises, focusing on spending time with God in solitude and quiet.

Table 7.1 Traditional and Faith-Based ACT Conceptualizations, Metaphors, and Exercises for "Being Present"/"Noticing and Shifting"

	Traditional ACT	*Faith-Based ACT*
Transcendent self		
Conceptualization		
Metaphor	"Choice Point Figure"	"Fork in the Road Figure"
	"The Chessboard"	"Sitting at the Feet of Jesus"
	"Taking Off Your Armor"	"Jesus in the Desert and the True/False Self"
	"The Anthropologist"	"The Mind of Christ"
Exercise		
	Mindfulness	The Jesus Prayer
	"I Can't Possibly …"	"I Can Do All This Through Him Who Gives Me Strength"
	"The Observer"	"Footprints"/"The Owner of the House"
	"Let Yourself Go"	"A New Creation: The Old Has Gone and The New Has Come"
	"Seeing the Self as Part of Something Larger"	"Seeing the Self as Part of the Body of Christ"
Present-moment awareness		
Conceptualization		
Metaphor	"Choice Point Figure"	"Fork in the Road Figure"
	"Dropping Anchor"	"Talking with Jesus at a Wedding"
Exercise		
	"Silent Walking"	"Walking with Jesus"
	"Stepping Into…"	"Practice of the Presence of God"
	"Watching a Movie"	*Lectio divina*
	Mindfully eating a raisin	"Practice of the Presence of God"
	"Free Choice Meditation"	Prayer of the senses
	"Slowing Down"	"Game of Minutes"

Note. Faith-based ACT interventions are adapted from Harris (2019), Hayes (2005), Hayes et al. (2012), Luoma et al. (2017), Segal et al. (2012), Siegel (2010), and Stoddard and Afari (2014).

Overall, with faith-based ACT, Christian clients are starting with traditional ACT, learning to connect to the transcendent self via nonjudgmental, sustained, present-moment awareness. Still, rather than solely enhancing psychological flexibility, Christians are dually developing a deeper relationship with the God of love and more flexible, open posture toward life, which emanates as a byproduct of the contemplative experience. In turn, Christian clients can more effectively follow Jesus, gently noticing the inner world unfold, without getting sidetracked by distressing psychological states.

To conceptualize the "noticing and shifting" pillar within a faith-based ACT perspective, counselors and therapists can modify the "Choice Point" tool (Harris, 2019), relying upon the "Fork in the Road" alternative (adapted from

Harris, 2019; Hayes et al., 2012) to help Christian clients recognize they have a choice to make with each step they take on the road of life. In the context of the "noticing and shifting" pillar, they can walk alone, overly rely on the reasoning self (the *dianoia* in Greek) and get lost on "automatic pilot" (Segal et al., 2012), distracted by a preoccupation with the past or future. Conversely, they can choose to walk with God in love, notice when they are overly relying on the reasoning self (again, the *dianoia* in Greek), shift to the contemplative self (the *nous* in Greek), and practice God's presence (*hesychia* in Greek) so as to maintain a present-moment awareness of God's love, traveling step by step with him. With this "Fork in the Road" adaptation, counselors and therapists are helping Christian clients recognize the salience of "noticing and shifting" throughout the day so as to walk with God in love toward, not way from, his plan for their life. See Figure 7.1 for counselors and therapists to work with Christian clients

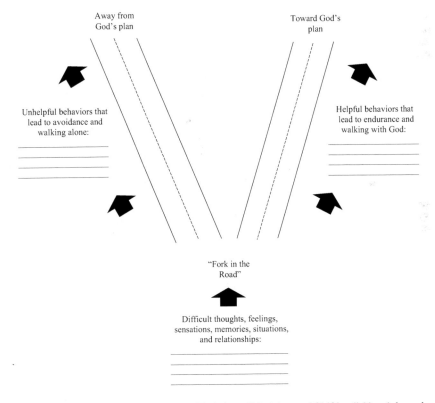

Figure 7.1 The "Fork in the Road" for Christians: "Noticing and Shifting." *Note.* Adapted from Harris (2019), Hayes (2019), and Hayes et al. (2012). "Unhelpful" and "helpful" behaviors include those that are overt (i.e., observable, such as walking and talking) and covert (i.e., unobservable, such as thinking and feeling).

to fill in the blanks and, thus, succinctly conceptualize the problem and solution to psychological suffering within the human condition, paying particular attention to the "noticing and shifting" pillar.

Transitioning to the traditional ACT metaphors, the "Chessboard" metaphor can be modified for Christian clients to better understand the transcendent self, emphasizing the story of Mary and Martha (Luke 10:38–42), reviewed in an earlier chapter. For many Christian clients, life is filled with distractions, similar to Martha's scenario. Of course, Martha's service was not the problem. Rather, her struggle with maintaining an awareness of Jesus prevented her from realizing what was in front of her. Paralleling an overemphasis on the chess pieces, with the goal seemingly to get rid of the "negative" thoughts, feelings, sensations, and memories and preserve the "positive" inner experiences, Martha was attempting to ameliorate her distress with complaints and busyness, which undermined her ability to recognize Jesus's active, loving presence. On the other hand, Mary simply sat at the feet of Jesus, allowing Martha to run around without reacting to her anxious complaints. In fact, Mary apparently continued to sit at Jesus's feet, attentively listening to him as Martha caused a scene by anxiously trying to fix the perceived problem.

For Christian clients, learning to observe with a gentle, present-focused, loving gaze, rather than attempting to eliminate inner pain, is the goal. In other words, Christian clients can work toward envisioning themselves seated with Jesus, allowing environmental distractions (e.g., Martha's complaints) to simply do what they will do, patiently returning to attentively hearing Jesus's message when inner and outer distractions arise. Again, the emphasis is on shifting from getting sidetracked with an anxious, driven need to accomplish, fix, or rigidly and impulsively respond to environmental demands to being present to Jesus and intentionally aware of him, without a need to change anything. The transition is from a "win/lose" mentality to a noticing, calm, and attentive attitude of nonjudgment, simply allowing the present moment to unfold because Jesus is the central focus. This shift, flexibly knowing when to intentionally let go of the need to prepare the meal and clean the house, can occur at any time, similar to a soldier recognizing they can simply walk off the battlefield because the war is over (Hayes et al., 2012). Before concluding this exercise, it is important to reiterate that Martha's service was not the problem. After all, servanthood is a central part of the Christian life, repeatedly emphasized in an earlier chapter. Instead, her distraction from Jesus's active, loving presence, including her efforts to ameliorate her anxiety through complaints and demands, undermined her ability to rest at Jesus's feet, flexibly pursuing what mattered most in the present moment—acting upon her values.

As another example, ACT counselors and therapists commonly use the "Taking Off Your Armor" metaphor, describing a warrior who wears heavy, metal armor to protect themself from battle wounds (Stoddard & Afari, 2014). Yet, because the battle has long since passed, they are now stuck with this layer of protection that undermines their ability to experience a loving embrace, weighed down with a protective shield that no longer serves its purpose. Similar to a client who struggles with cognitive fusion and experiential avoidance, overly relying on the verbal self after a lifetime of trauma, the warrior has a hard time relinquishing the outer shell.

Among Christian clients, the "story" they fuse with may be a false self they have constructed, similar to Pennington's (2000) understanding that Christians can overly rely on a pseudo-identity, emanating from what they do via accomplishments, what other people think of them, and what they have in the form of possessions. For Pennington, Jesus's interaction with the Devil in the desert (*New International Version Bible*, 2011, Matthew 4:1–11) can help to better understand the construction of a false self, like the armor the warrior clung to after the battle was over. In the desert, Jesus was extremely hungry, living without food for 40 days. Indeed, the Devil told Jesus to turn stones into bread, emphasizing what Jesus could accomplish, a central tenet of the false self. However, Jesus famously replied that he would rely on God, rather than "live on bread alone." With Jesus's second temptation, the Devil told Jesus to throw himself off a high ledge so that angels could save him, apparently so that observers could clearly see that Jesus was the Son of God. Still, Jesus replied that he would not put "God to the test." With this example, Pennington (2000) noted that the true self is not wrapped up in what others think. Finally, the Devil offered Jesus the world if Jesus would worship the Devil, but Jesus replied that he would only follow God, suggesting that his identity was bound up in what the Father thought of him, rather than his own possessions. In each of these instances, Jesus rejected the "false self," preferring to find his identity in God. Rather than using the metaphor of a warrior relinquishing unnecessary armor after a long battle, Christians can work toward identifying and shedding the "false self," created based on what they accomplish, what others think of them, and what they have in the form of possessions (Pennington, 2000). In other words, Christian clients are learning to shift from an "earthly-minded" to "heavenly-minded" perspective (Burroughs, 2014).

To offer one final illustration, the "Anthropologist" metaphor is a popular way to contrast the verbal, content-driven and transcendent, noticing self (Stoddard & Afari, 2014). Within this metaphor, clients learn to act like an anthropologist in the study of culture, observing the inner workings of the mind from a distance. Of course, for clients, they are watching the inner world, including their thoughts, feelings, sensations, and memories, rather than a culture from some faraway land. With this exercise, the goal is to cultivate an open, curious, and nonjudgmental attitude toward psychological experiences, recognizing that the inner world can be observed from a safe distance, similar to noticing and documenting a different people group.

With Christian clients, a parallel may involve observing the inner world with the "mind of Christ," rather than the mind of a well-trained anthropologist.

Phrased differently, instead of observing culture from a distance, drawing on a set of skills possessed by a scientist, Christian clients can view the inner world through the lens of Jesus's mind, reminiscent of 1 Corinthians 2:16. When writing to the church at Corinth, the Apostle Paul referenced this phrase to capture God's hidden wisdom (Taylor, 2014), an "attitude" or "outlook" that the quarreling church was to have in order to ameliorate their interpersonal challenges and pursue unity (Ciampa & Rosner, 2010, p. 76). In other words, to have Jesus's mind involves "putting to death selfish ambitions, humbling oneself, and giving oneself to others," emphasizing "self-sacrificing love" (Garland, 2003, p. 102).

Interestingly, Paul clearly stated that he did not utilize "eloquence or human wisdom," determined to "know nothing" but "Jesus Christ and him crucified" when sharing about God to the Corinthians (*New International Version Bible*, 2011, 1 Corinthians 2:1–2), suggesting he relied on the "mind of Christ," rather than his own understanding. Overall, the "mind of Christ" represents a sort of sober watchfulness (Garland, 2003), helping Christian clients to view the inner world from the perspective of Jesus, constituting a dying to the self in order to follow him with self-sacrificial love. Stated differently, rather than getting bogged down with a self-derived story, emanating from the verbal self, Christians are to view themselves from Jesus's perspective, recognizing that a salient requirement in the Christian life is loving acts of service, modeled after Jesus.

Here, we possibly see the marriage of acceptance and action, requiring Christian clients to sacrifice for others, drawing upon biblical teachings, as well as the need to let go of their own stories that get in the way of value-based living. As a visual, Christians can imagine viewing the world through Jesus's eyes, with a special emphasis on loving others, letting go of the tendency to fuse with a story about the self that undermines authentic, effective action in the service of others. Ultimately, to contrast an earthly, self-derived, arbitrary perspective with Jesus's spiritual, Other-derived, heavenly perspective may help Christian clients to take effective, loving action, despite storied mental chatter (e.g., doubts, worries, ruminations).

In terms of experiential exercises to help Christian clients connect to the transcendent self, the Jesus Prayer can be used in place of mindfulness meditation, given that there are several overlapping ingredients. As noted earlier, both help clients to develop sustained, flexible attention, along with nonjudgmental awareness in the present moment, observing the inner world before gently returning to the point of focus. For Christians, though, the purpose is to cultivate a silent stillness with God, maintaining an awareness of the contemplative self to deepen their relationship with him. Because of this, rather than using mindfulness solely for pragmatic purposes (e.g., to ameliorate suffering), Christians can employ the Jesus Prayer to surrender to the God of love during moments of distress, with the added benefit of closeness with, and comfort from, him during instances of suffering.

Another experiential exercise, entitled "I Can't Possibly," helps clients to explore some of the barriers, including fused, storied thinking, that get in the way of effective action (Stoddard & Afari, 2014). In this exercise, clients start with "Because of ..." inserting the inner experience that gets in the way of value-based living, followed by "I can't possibly ..." adding in the value they would like to pursue if the barrier were not present. For Christian clients, this exercise can be modified to reflect their struggle to follow Jesus. Thus, the "I can't possibly ..." statement can be adapted to "I can't possibly follow Jesus ..." Also within this exercise, Christian clients can reflect on Philippians 4:13: "I can do all [things] through [Christ] who gives me strength" (*New International Version Bible*, 2011). In this passage, the Apostle Paul was referring to his "boundless confidence in the ability of Christ to match every situation," given his "vital union" with Jesus (Martin, 1987, p. 180). Therefore, moving from inaction to effective, value-based action involves drawing from the strength of Jesus, which Christian clients can do when fused with unworkable stories that keep them stuck.

For "The Observer" exercise, clients are guided through a lengthy meditation (Hayes et al., 2012, pp. 233–237), with the counselor or therapist focusing on helping the client notice that they are watching the inner world, rather than getting entangled with it. Within this meditative exercise, the client is guided through several life events, including something recent, a situation in adolescence, and an occurrence in childhood, all the while being asked to notice that they are watching the situation unfold as a distant observer. This process is also replicated with thoughts and emotions, with clients being asked to notice that the inner world waxes and wanes. In other words, private events are impermanent, changing from moment to moment during different life events and developmental phases. In sum, the exercise helps clients to recognize that there is a part of them—the transcendent self—that has not changed, despite different thoughts, feelings, sensations, memories, situations, and relationships.

In consideration of Christian clients, a modified version can involve drawing upon the "Footprints in the Sand" poem (Powers, 1993), one of the most famous inspirational writings in the contemporary Christian literature. Within this popular work, the author reflected on a dream, wherein she was walking along a beach, which represented life. During many moments, there were two sets of footprints, representing her relationship with Jesus. Yet, there was only one set of footprints during one of her most painful periods of life, seemingly suggesting that Jesus was not with her during this instance of suffering. However, toward the end of the poem, Jesus responded to her, letting her know that he was carrying her during this moment of adversity.

Here, the poem loosely resembles Hayes et al.'s (2012) "The Observer" exercise. Both involve reflecting on life with a sort of detached, observant watchfulness. Yet, for Christian clients, a salient component of the human condition involves a reflective relationship with Jesus, especially during moments

179

of adversity and suffering. As a result, rather than experiencing the inner world in isolation, Jesus walks with, or carries, Christians during instances of distress. In other words, consistent with the main goal of faith-based ACT, Christian clients are learning to walk with God in love, enduring inner and outer struggles as they travel with Jesus, not alone, along the road of life. Hence, Christian clients can combine "The Observer" with "Footprints" to walk through life, noticing there is a part of them (i.e., the contemplative self) that longs to experience God directly, steadily traveling with Jesus along the beach despite inner and outer events that tend to come and go.

Additionally, counselors and therapists practicing faith-based ACT can utilize Jesus's teaching on a man carefully watching his house:

> Therefore keep watch, because you do not know on what day your Lord will come. But understand this: If the owner of the house had known at what time of night the thief was coming, he would have kept watch and would not have let his house be broken into. So you also must be ready, because the Son of Man will come at an hour when you do not expect him.
>
> (*New International Version Bible*, 2011, Matthew 24:42–44)

In this passage, the house owner carefully watched for the thief, guarding his home with a sober awareness so that he would not be surprised. Similarly, Christian clients can observe the inner workings of the mind, combining an understanding of the contemplative self and watchfulness to employ a calm, attentive vigilance to guard the heart from being overwhelmed by tempting, compulsive thoughts (*logismoi* in Greek) (Coniaris, 1998). Thus, an adapted metaphor might involve imagining that the transcendent self is like a homeowner carefully watching his house, attentive to his inner environment.

To share another illustration, counselors and therapists can utilize the "Let Your Self Go" intervention (Harris, 2009). In this exercise, the counselor or therapist explores with the client all of the "positive" and "negative" statements the client is fused with, asking them to write five of each on an index card. Holding up the card to the client's face (with permission), the counselor or therapist asks the client if they can see life while fused with these statements. Of course, most clients will quickly realize they are distracted by the card, rather than actively attending to the conversation in front of them. During the week in between sessions, clients are asked to carry the card with them, reading over the statements in an effort to defuse from them.

In faith-based ACT, counselors and therapist can modify the aforementioned exercise for Christian clients, turning to Paul's second letter to the Corinthians in the New Testament to help them realize they are a "new creation in Christ" (*New International Version Bible*, 2011, 2 Corinthians 5). In other words, "If anyone is in Christ, the new creation has come: the old has gone, the new is here" (*New International Version Bible*, 2011, 2 Corinthians 5:17). Because of this, God does not "[count] people's sins against them" (*New International Version Bible*, 2011, 2 Corinthians 5:19). Indeed, the false self can be relinquished, with Christian clients defusing from the storied self in order to find their true identity in Jesus. Christians are now "living in vital union with Christ," which has implications for the individual self, the Christian community, and the created order (Comfort & Osborne, 1999, p. 355). To adjust the traditional ACT exercise, Christian clients can write all of the characteristics of the old self they have historically fused with, pulling out the card during the week to remember that "the old is gone" and "the new is here," meaning their identity is no longer found in their own verbally constructed self. Instead, their identity is hidden in Jesus.

As one final traditional ACT exercise for cultivating an awareness of the transcendent self, the "Seeing the Self as Part of Something Larger" exercise is utilized in a group setting to help clients view themselves, including their suffering, as part of, and connected to, a "bigger picture," wherein they are embedded in relationships with others, the environment, the universe, and so forth, not isolated and alone (Luoma et al., 2017, pp. 172–174). First, clients are asked to make contact with their inner world, including their present thoughts, feelings, sensations, and memories (Luoma et al., 2017). Second, clients are asked to recognize that the other people in the room also experience their own thoughts, feelings, sensations, and memories, often in the form of difficult, recurrent inner experiences, just like the client (Luoma et al., 2017). In other words, everyone suffers, and clients are asked to connect to a common humanity, wherein there are both unique and shared instances of suffering (Luoma et al., 2017). Along the way, clients are learning to cultivate greater compassion, kindness, and love toward others, which can be, in turn, applied to themselves when they are suffering (Luoma et al., 2017). Overall, the purpose of this exercise is to develop a greater awareness of the "bigger picture," transcending the verbal, "storied" self in order to connect with others, compassionately, kindly, and lovingly (Luoma et al., 2017).

For Christian clients, the faith-based ACT version of this exercise involves "Seeing the Self as Part of the Body of Christ," shifting from an isolated to communing self. In other words, the famous New Testament metaphor of Jesus being the "head" and Christians being the "body" of the Christian Church, that is, God's established group of believers, can be used to help Christian clients connect to a more spiritual, heavenly perspective (Ephesians 4:12; Romans 12:5). First, Christian clients can be asked to maintain an awareness of their unique, individual thoughts, feelings, sensations, and memories in the present moment, including their inner pain. Second, Christian clients can be asked to reflect on the reality that other Christians suffer, too, beginning with Jesus, the "Suffering Servant" (*New International Version Bible*, 2011, Isaiah 53), then extending to Jesus's disciples and apostles, the early Christian martyrs, the early desert Christians, and other followers of Jesus over the last 2,000 years. Moreover,

Christian clients can be asked to cultivate an awareness of the meta-perspective of the Bible, moving from the creation account to the fall of humankind (and ensuing suffering), to the redemption found in Jesus, to God's eventual restoration of a broken, suffering, isolated world (Wolters, 2005). In the process, Christian clients are pivoting from an earthly-focused, isolated perspective to heavenly- and spiritually-focused, unified perspective, walking with God and others in love as one united "Body." To be more succinct, Christian clients are learning to pivot from an isolating to communing self. From this unified Christian perspective, Christian clients are moving from justification (i.e., being righteous before, and unified with, God because of Jesus), to sanctification (i.e., being more like Jesus), to glorification (i.e., being face to face with Jesus) (Grudem, 1994), doing so with a recognition that they are traveling together with both God and others along the way, not alone, anchored to love as the beginning and ending point.

Transitioning to the traditional ACT process of present-moment awareness, counselors and therapists practicing faith-based ACT can utilize several metaphors and contemplative strategies in place of the technology of mindfulness in order to cultivate sustained attention, nonjudgmental acceptance, and compassion. Of course, the major difference between these two approaches to the inner and outer worlds involves the point of focus, with mindfulness commonly using the breath or senses to experience the world directly and Christian contemplatives seeking a sustained awareness of God's perfect love (Knabb & Bates, 2020).

To begin, Harris (2019) described a metaphor for helping clients to connect to the present moment, referred to as "Dropping Anchor." With this metaphor, clients are asked to envision being in a storm, consistent with their current distress. When clients are overwhelmed, "dropping the anchor" involves connecting to the here-and-now, feeling their feet on the floor and noticing the room they are sitting in. In essence, clients are using the senses, rather than inner experiences (e.g., thoughts, feelings), to directly experience the world, which "anchors" them to the present moment.

As an alternative, Pennington (1982) used the experience of a cocktail party to metaphorically describe centering prayer. Within the party, someone is having an important conversation with a friend, with quite a bit of background noise. Whenever the person is distracted by a sound (e.g., breaking glass, another conversation, the doorbell ringing), they can gently return to the conversation. Of course, reminiscent of an actual cocktail party, there is quite a bit going on in the background (i.e., within both the inner and outer worlds) when engaged in centering prayer. Thus, it is important to notice when one has been distracted by the environment, patiently returning to the conversation at hand.

To modify this metaphor to reflect a loving awareness of Jesus, especially during moments of crisis or distress, Christian clients can envision they have been invited to a wedding. At the wedding, located at Cana in Galilee (John

2:1–11), Jesus is present. During the celebration, the Christian client has the opportunity to converse with Jesus. Certainly, because the event is filled with celebrating guests, there is quite a bit of background noise. Yet, the primary task involves listening to Jesus, fully absorbing this special conversation in the here-and-now. Whenever the Christian client is inevitably distracted with background noise, they can gently return to the present moment, "dropping the anchor" by spending time with Jesus with an attitude of receptivity and openness. Normalizing the Christian client's tendency to get distracted, possibly even overwhelmed, is especially important. After all, the Christian client is at a celebration, with excited people scattered throughout the event. Indeed, this metaphor parallels the task at hand—Christian clients can accept there will commonly be loud noise in the inner world, with unruly guests occupying the space of the mind from time to time. Even so, Christian clients can gently return to a loving, receptive attitude when they notice they have been distracted, taking advantage of this special opportunity to fellowship with Jesus.

Furthermore, "Silent Walking" (Hayes, 2005) helps clients to apply mindfulness to walking outdoors. Within this exercise, clients are asked to walk for ten minutes, simply noticing the chatter of the mind, along with any other events that occur in nature. Whenever the mind is distracted, the goal is to name the experience, such as "bird chirping" or "airplane flying by." Over time, this exercise helps clients to recognize the inner workings of the mind, defusing from the mind's dialogue by simply naming the experience and returning to the direct encounter with nature via the senses.

When working with Christian clients, the aforementioned exercise can be modified when going on a walk, envisioning walking with Jesus (Knabb et al., 2020). To cultivate nonjudgmental, sustained attention and the ability to anchor oneself to the present moment, environmental experiences (e.g., distractions) can be labeled, before returning to the experience of walking silently with Jesus. Above all else, this exercise can help Christians to recognize the nature of the mind, deepening their relationship with God while enjoying his creation.

As another mindfulness exercise, clients can focus on their feelings, employing nonjudgment, compassion, and acceptance to relate to unpleasant inner events with more flexibility and openness. With either "Stepping into Sadness" or "Stepping into Fear" (Siegel, 2010), clients actually attempt to enhance these emotions, embracing them with nonjudgment in order to relate to them in a new way. By learning to accept these ubiquitous feelings with compassionate acceptance (similar to an exposure exercise to habituate the client to distressing inner experiences), clients can shift their focus toward value-based action, ameliorating the tendency to experientially avoid unpleasant inner states.

To offer a modified approach, the medieval monk Brother Lawrence's (2015) instructions for the "Practice of the Presence of God" can help Christian clients to embrace the emotional world, inviting God into the process. Throughout the day, Christian clients can cultivate a greater awareness of God's active, loving presence by "carefully," "deliberately," "gently," and "lovingly" combining their current activity (e.g., washing the dishes, taking out the trash, walking to get the mail) with God's presence, reciting the phrase "My God, I am completely yours" as they accomplish the designated task and yield their emotions to him (Lawrence, 2015, pp. 38, 44). In the process, they can nonjudgmentally accept their inner world, surrendering it to God because he is with them as they complete the given activity. Over and over again, Christian clients can slowly and lovingly complete the task (no matter how large or small), invite God into the process by gently reciting the short phrase, and cultivate a sustained, flexible awareness of the God of love. By dually inviting God into the activity and corresponding emotional experience, Christians can learn that emotions need not overwhelm them or undermine their efforts to follow Jesus, especially because God is present within both the inner and outer worlds. Overall, this exercise parallels mindfulness in many ways, but additionally offers a spiritually sensitive alternative for Christian clients looking to find God's presence in the tasks of daily life and emotional suffering.

To work more effectively with thoughts, clients can employ a strategy presented by Segal et al. (2012) (i.e., "Watching a Movie"), relating to thoughts differently by seeing themselves sitting in a movie theater, watching thoughts like images popping up on the screen. By simply observing their thoughts with nonjudgment, clients can begin to see them as passing events, without getting overwhelmed. Also, clients can learn that thoughts do not inevitably lead to problems, conditions, and disorders. Instead of impulsively reacting to thinking, clients can gently watch the mind do its job—generate a variety of thoughts, with some accurate and some not—without compulsively reacting in a way that undermines value-based living. Over time, clients begin to experience the mental chatter of the mind with more openness and flexibility, ameliorating automatic, rigid, fused responses within the world of language.

As a substitute, Christian clients can use the Jesus Prayer, an *apophatic* form of prayer that de-emphasizes language in order to relate to God directly, beyond words. By repeating the brief prayer in a simple, gentle, steady, and unhurried manner, Christian clients can work toward simply noticing compulsive forms of thinking (*logismoi* in Greek) that get in the way of an awareness of God's active, loving presence. Undoubtedly, Christians drawing from faith-based ACT can continuously notice the mind's thinking patterns, shifting the focus to the Jesus Prayer whenever their attention has drifted.

Moreover, Christian clients can utilize *lectio divina*,[1] a centuries-old form of contemplative practice that emanated from monastic life, to connect to God's Word in the present moment. With *lectio divina*, Christians "prayerfully reflect on the scriptures" (O'Madagain, 2007, p. 115), utilizing passages in the Bible to deepen their intimacy with God. In this practice, Christian clients move through four stages, including reading (*lectio* in Latin), meditating (*meditatio* in

Latin), praying (*oratio* in Latin), and contemplating (*contemplatio* in Latin). First, Christian clients slowly begin to recite a short verse in Scripture, homing in on a few words and staying present to the experience as they pray through the passage, reminiscent of taking a small bite of food (Guigo II, 2012). In this process, they simply notice what emerges, based on reading Scripture from the heart. Second, Christian clients settle into a word or phrase, allowing God to speak to them, without relying on their own efforts to discern the meaning of the phrase, consistent with chewing a small bite of food (Guigo II, 2012). Third, Christian clients engage in a process of prayerful reflection, spontaneously talking to God, based on the needs that arise, and thanking him for this time spent in divine communion, similar to tasting a small bite of food (Guigo II, 2012). Fourth, Christian clients sit in silence with God, resting like Mary sitting at the feet of Jesus, reminiscent of the "being" mode and savoring a small bite of food (Guigo II, 2012).

Continuing with another example, many acceptance-based therapies (Segal et al., 2012) employ an exercise that involves slowly, mindfully eating a raisin so as to experience the senses directly, rather than relying on the mind to evaluate the process. In the exercise, clients hold a raisin, noticing its texture, color, size, and shape and letting go of the tendency to judge the process. Instead, clients act as though they are interacting with a "raisin" for the first time, similar to a curious observer from a distant land. Next, clients place the raisin in their mouth, tasting it and noticing the texture as they slowly chew. Along the way, clients are relating to the experience with openness, nonjudgment, and curiosity, using the process as a way to connect to the present moment, without overly relying on the mind to interpret the unfolding event. Consequently, the practice can be extended to other experiences, whether seemingly important or unimportant, in daily life.

As a faith-based ACT alternative, Christian clients can practice God's presence by "thinking in threes," pairing the experience, psychological reaction to the experience, and God's loving presence in the experience, reminiscent of Brother Lawrence's (2015) "Practice of the Presence of God." For example, when washing the dishes, first, Christian clients can "carefully," "deliberately," "gently," and "lovingly" engage in the activity (Brother Lawrence, 2015), rather than doing so in a hurried manner on "automatic pilot" (Segal et al., 2012). With this first step, Christian clients can directly connect to the experience by relying on the senses, feeling the temperature of the water, hearing the sound of the water and sponge make contact with the dishes, seeing the soap make contact with the dishes, and so forth. Second, Christian clients can recognize God's presence in the activity by pairing washing the dishes with a short phrase, gently repeated interiorly, "God of love, I love you with all my heart" (Brother Lawrence, 2015). Over and over again, Christian clients can simply wash the dishes and repeat this short phrase to God. Third, Christian clients can recognize when any other thoughts, feelings, sensations, or memories have distracted them from washing the dishes with God, then gently return to "thinking in threes." After a designated period of time (e.g., 10 minutes), this activity can be extended to other tasks throughout the day in an effort to cultivate a greater awareness of the contemplative self and practice God's presence in the here-and-now, maintaining present-moment attentiveness to God's perfect love along the way (Knabb & Bates, 2020).

To present another example, ACT clients commonly make use of the "Free Choice Meditation" exercise (Luoma et al., 2017), drawing from mindfulness to gently notice arising sensations with nonjudgment. For example, clients may start by noticing their contact with the chair they are sitting in, transitioning to the breath as a way to anchor them to the present moment. In turn, clients may notice the sounds that arise in their environment, allowing the sensory experience to run its natural course. Whenever the mind begins to wander, clients can simply notice whatever distractions have arisen, compassionately returning to the experience. Overall, this exercise employs the senses, rather than the chattering, judgmental mind, to connect to each unfolding moment.

For Christian clients, an alternative can be the prayer of the senses, developed within the Jesuit spiritual tradition (Fink, 2001; Jackson, n.d.). For Jesuits, there is an understanding that all of creation comes from God, who is active and present in the world (Fink, 2001). In other words, God's loving, attentive action manifests in all of life, even in instances of suffering (Fink, 2001). In the prayer of the senses, drawn from Ignatius's *Spiritual Exercises*, Christians read through a story in the Bible by feeling their way into the account, utilizing the five senses to immerse themselves in the narrative (Endean, 1990).

For example, if Jesus's "Sermon on the Mount" (*New International Version Bible*, 2011, Matthew 5–7) were selected, Christian practitioners would use their sense of touch to experience the hillside they are standing on, sound to hear the birds chirping in the air and the wind blowing on their face, and vision to see the sun reflecting on the Sea of Galilee. Above all else, this exercise helps Christians to have a deeper, felt experience of biblical stories, beyond a merely cognitive endeavor. Paralleling mindfulness meditation, Christians can utilize the senses to connect to the present moment, with the added benefit of experiencing the Bible in a new, expanded way. Of course, this exercise is somewhat different than traditional ACT exercises in that Christian clients are asked to envision themselves within a biblical story, rather than solely connecting to their own experience, as is the case with many transcendent self interventions in ACT.

To offer one final example, traditional ACT employs the "Slowing Down" exercise to cultivate present-moment awareness (Hayes et al., 2012). With this exercise, the counselor or therapist helps the client to slow down the pace of the session to connect to the present moment, focusing on the pace of the session (and corresponding client–counselor/therapist dialogue), as well as the client's unfolding experience. For Christian clients, however, the "Game of Minutes" can be utilized, created by the 20th century Protestant mystic Frank Laubach (2007). In this game, Christian clients can attempt to bring a greater awareness to God's presence in each passing second, focusing the mind on God and inviting him to be with them in their thoughts, feelings, sensations, and memories (Laubach, 2007). To slow down, from a Christian perspective, is to acknowledge all of the ways that the God of love is revealing himself in the here-and-now, even in the middle of psychological pain. Overall, two simple questions to capture God's active, loving presence in the moment involve asking the following: "How is God revealing himself to me right now? How can I keep my focus on him?" Christian clients, in turn, can employ a wide variety of strategies to practice God's presence, including meditating on a short passage in Scripture, offering a short prayer to God, singing a line from a famous hymn to God, or praising God with a simple "Thank you."

In summary, metaphors and exercises in traditional ACT can be modified and adjusted to meet the unique psychological and spiritual needs of Christian clients experiencing prolonged distress. To be sure, a central feature of the Christian contemplative tradition involves cultivating a deeper relationship with the God of love, observing the inner world with gentle passivity, rather than clutching or avoiding distracting thoughts, feelings, sensations, and memories. Combined, ACT and Christianity can offer helpful strategies for allowing Christian clients to connect to the contemplative self (the *nous* in Greek), which relies on God-derived love, not overly rely on the verbal self (the *dianoia* in Greek), which relies on self-derived knowledge. In other words, Christian clients are learning to notice the distinction between the isolating self and communing self, with the latter emphasizing God's active, loving presence. Of course, for Christian clients, the unfolding moment is where God is located, interacting with humankind in a personal, loving manner. As a result, not only can Christian clients employ ACT to connect to each passing instance, pivoting to value-based action to create a meaningful, impactful life, but they can also invite God, the author of love, into the process (*hesychia* in Greek) so as to cultivate a deeper inner peace.

Rather than seeing themselves like the earth at the center of the solar system, with God revolving around them like a distant sun (i.e., geocentrism), Christian clients can draw from the rich contemplative tradition to illuminate the reality that God has always been like the sun at the center (i.e., heliocentrism) (Laird, 2011). In other words, instead of viewing God as "out there," with humans needing to "find him," God has forever been located at the core of the Christian experience, with Christian clients needing to look no further than their center of being to find him. To quote the Medieval contemplative John of the Cross, "The soul's center is God" (Laird, 2011, p. 10). Before concluding the chapter, a case illustration is offered to enhance counselor and therapist understanding of the "be present" (Harris, 2019, p. 8) ACT process, integrated with the Christian faith.

A Clinical Example of Noticing and Shifting

Gary, a married, White male in his mid-40s, presented for outpatient therapy after an inpatient stay for two weeks because of suicidal ideation. Suffering from several depressive symptoms, including low mood, a loss of interest in hobbies, weight loss, and excessive guilt, Gary really began to struggle after his father died. For Gary, life was always difficult, with his mother suffering from debilitating anxiety, leading to her suicide when he was in his early 20s. Experiencing the belief that he could have saved her before she took her life, Gary carried with him a tremendous weight, leading to efforts to numb his pain through heavy drug use.

What is more, Gary took on a job as a traveling salesman in his early 30s, checking out from the world by busying himself with excessive time away from home. Over time, Gary learned to distract himself from the pain through long trips, utilizing alcohol binges and marijuana to forget about his mother's painful death. In fact, Gary continuously struggled to face his inner distress, quite literally running from the pain that emanated from this tragic event.

When his father died shortly before Gary was hospitalized, all of the inner experiences Gary attempted to hide from began to resurface. Faced with overwhelming distress in the here-and-now, Gary fused with a storied self to make sense of what was happening. For Gary, his mother's bouts with anxiety and subsequent suicide were a direct result of his "worthlessness," given that he struggled with his grades in school and had his own behavioral problems as a child. As he grew older, Gary's mind, the "Master Salesman" (Harris, 2019), concluded that he lacked value, leading to efforts to check out from life. Indeed, this strategy of avoidance seemed to work for some time, with Gary always looking forward to the next trip, filled with empty hotel rooms and all-night drinking sessions.

In his relationship with God, Gary also attempted to run. Growing up in the church, Gary found incredible peace and comfort in Sunday school, learning that God loved him and cared for him in a very personal way that he did not experience at home. Yet, as he began to struggle in grade school, feeling a sense of loss in his relationship with his mother because of her mental health challenges, he concluded that God had abandoned him and was punishing him for his perceived failures. Because of this, Gary stopped going to church in his adolescent years, concluding that he was on his own.

During outpatient therapy, Gary's therapist utilized faith-based ACT, given that Gary was "sick of running" and wanted to improve his relationship with God. Therefore, Gary worked on loosening the grip that his storied, verbal self seemed to have on him, practicing the Jesus Prayer to cultivate a calm stillness, as well as allowing his overactive mind to generate thoughts without chasing them or pushing them away. Instead, Gary was able to repeat the powerful words of the Jesus Prayer, learning to relate to the verbal self with more tentativeness and flexibility, recognizing that his identity was found in God. After a few sessions, Gary was able to simply watch the "Master Salesman" (Harris, 2019), concluding that God was with him as his mind continued to generate less than accurate narratives of his life's history.

Also, Gary employed both the prayer of the senses and *lectio divina* in order to have a deeper experience of Scripture, which offered him a way to anchor himself to the present moment, rather than run from inner distress through prolonged road trips and substance abuse. Relatedly, he felt encouraged when viewing his life through the lens of the "mind of Christ," rather than his own verbal, language-based efforts. When therapy concluded, Gary had deepened his relationship with God, learned to observe his inner world without trying to avoid psychological distress, and practiced daily contemplation so as to stay present to God's loving, active care. Although his recurrent depressive symptoms did not fully go away—he continued to notice inner experiences of guilt and doubt about his mother's suicide—he found peace in knowing that God was with him during moments of suffering.

Conclusion

To summarize, Christian clients can draw from traditional ACT, modifying the exercises, strategies, and metaphors to cultivate a deeper relationship with God. Recognizing that the God of love is at the center, Christians can draw from a range of metaphors to tap into the transcendent self, watching the inner world with God. Moreover, nonjudgmentally staying rooted in the present moment can help Christian clients to more effectively follow Jesus. Because of this, the next chapter is devoted to value-based action, combining the last two ACT processes in order to help Christians live a life that is meaningful, guided by intentional behaviors.

Notes

1 Unless otherwise noted, the ACT themes and concepts in this chapter are from Bach and Morgan (2008), Flaxman et al. (2011), Harris (2019), Hayes (2019), Hayes et al. (2012), Luoma et al. (2017), and Strosahl et al. (2004).
2 Unless otherwise noted, the main points in this section are from Mathewes-Green (2009) and Talbot (2013).
3 This guided meditation is based on the central tenets of the Jesus Prayer in Talbot (2013).
4 This discussion is based on the review by O'Madagain (2007).

References

Bach, P., & Moran, D. (2008). *ACT in practice: Case conceptualization in acceptance & commitment therapy*. New Harbinger Publications, Inc.

Bangley, B. (Ed.). (2006). *The cloud of unknowing: Contemporary English edition.* Paraclete Press.

Bishop, S., Lau, M., Shapiro, S., Carlson, L., Anderson, N., Carmody, J., Segal, Z., Abbey, S., Speca, M., Velting, D., & Devins, G. (2004). Mindfulness: A proposed operational definition. *Clinical Psychology: Science and Practice, 11,* 230–241.

Burroughs, J. (2010). *Heavenly-mindedness recommended: In a discourse on Colossians 3:2.* Gale ECCO.

Burroughs, J. (2014). *A treatise on earthly-mindedness.* GLH Publishing.

Ciampa, R., & Rosner, B. (2010). *The first letter to the Corinthians.* Wm. B. Eerdmans Publishing Co.

Comfort, P., & Osborne, G. (1999). *1 & 2 Corinthians.* Tyndale House Publishers, Inc.

Coniaris, A. (1998). *Philokalia. The Bible of orthodox spirituality.* Light & Life Publishing Company.

Contemplative Outreach. (n.d.). *The Christian contemplative tradition.* http://www.contemplativeoutreach.org/christian-contemplative-tradition

de Caussade, J. (2008). *The joy of full surrender: Contemporary English edition.* Paraclete Press, Inc.

Endean, P. (1990). The Ignatian prayer of the senses. *The Heythrop Journal, 31,* 391–418.

Fénelon, F. (2015). *A guide to true peace: A method of attaining to inward and spiritual prayer.* Ichthus Publications.

Fink, P. (2001). Finding God in all things. Jesuit spirituality. *Liturgical Ministry, 10,* 208–210.

Flaxman, P., Blackledge, J., & Bond, F. (2011). *Acceptance and commitment therapy: Distinctive features.* Routledge.

Frenette, D. (2012). *The path of centering prayer: Deepening your experience of God.* Sounds True, Inc.

Garland, D. (2003). *1 Corinthians.* Baker Academic.

Germer, C. (2009). *The mindful path to self-compassion: Freeing yourself from destructive thoughts and emotions.* The Guilford Press.

Goodwin, R. (1999). *Give us this day: The story of prayer.* Lindisfarne Books.

Grudem, W. (1994). *Systematic theology: An introduction to biblical doctrine.* Zondervan.

Guigo II. (2012). *The ladder of monks* (P. Nau, Trans.) [Kindle version]. Amazon.com

Harmless, W. (2004). *Desert Christians: An introduction to the literature of early monasticism.* Oxford University Press.

Harris, R. (2009). *ACT made simple. An easy-to-read primer on acceptance and commitment therapy.* New Harbinger Publications, Inc.

Harris, R. (2019). *ACT made simple: An easy-to-read primer on acceptance and commitment therapy* (2nd ed.). New Harbinger Publications, Inc.

Hayes, S. (2005). *Get out of your mind and into your life: The new acceptance & commitment therapy.* New Harbinger Publications, Inc.

Hayes, S. (2019). *A liberated mind: How to pivot toward what matters.* Avery.

Hayes, S., Strosahl, K., & Wilson, K. (2012). *Acceptance and commitment therapy: The process and practice of mindful change* (2nd ed.). The Guilford Press.

Jackson, C. (n.d.). *Ignatian spirituality.* Jesuit Conference.

Jacques, F. (2001). *I say nothing to him, I love him: Contemplative prayer.* Mediaspaul.

Knabb, J. (2021). *Christian meditation in clinical practice: A four-step model and workbook for therapists and clients.* InterVarsity Press.

Knabb, J., & Bates, M. (2020). "Holy desire" within the "Cloud of Unknowing": The psychological contributions of medieval apophatic contemplation to Christian mental health in the 21st century. *Journal of Psychology and Christianity, 39*, 24–39.

Knabb, J., Pate, R., Sullivan, S., Salley, E., Miller, A., & Boyer, W. (2020). "Walking with God": Developing and pilot testing a manualized four-week program combining Christian meditation and light-to-moderate physical activity for daily stress. *Mental Health, Religion & Culture, 23*, 756–776.

Laird, M. (2006). *Into the silent land: A guide to the Christian practice of contemplation.* Oxford University Press.

Laird, M. (2011). *A sunlit absence: Silence, awareness, and contemplation.* Oxford University Press.

Laubach, F. (2007). *Letters by a modern mystic* (Kindle ed.). Purposeful Design Publications. Amazon.com

Lawrence, B. (2015). *The practice of the presence of God.* (S. Sciurba, Trans.). ICS Publications.

Luoma, J., Hayes, S., & Walser, R. (2017). *Learning ACT: An Acceptance and commitment therapy skills training manual for therapists* (2nd ed.). Context Press.

Martin, R. (1987). *The epistle of Paul to the Philippians: An introduction and commentary.* Wm. B. Eerdmans Publishing Company.

Mathewes-Green, F. (2009). *The Jesus prayer: The ancient desert prayer that tunes the heart to God.* Paraclete Press.

Mathewes-Green, F. (2011). *Praying the Jesus prayer.* Paraclete Press.

Nassif, B. (2012). *Bringing Jesus to the desert.* Zondervan.

Nesteruk, A. (2003). *Light from the East: Theology, science, and the Eastern Orthodox tradition.* Fortress Press.

New International Version Bible. (2011). Zondervan. https://www.biblegateway.com/

Nikodimos. (Ed.). (2015). *Philokalia.* R.P. Pryne.

O'Madagain, M. (2007). *Centering prayer and the healing of the unconscious.* Lantern Books.

Owen, J. (2016). *Spiritual mindedness.* GLH Publishing.

Pennington, B. (1982). *Centering prayer: Renewing an ancient Christian prayer form.* Doubleday.

Pennington, B. (2000). *True self/false self: Unmasking the spirit within.* The Crossroad Publishing Company.

Powers, M. (1993). *Footprints: The true story behind the world's favourite inspirational poem.* Zondervan.

Ridderbos, H. (1975). *Paul: An outline of his theology.* Wm. B. Eerd-mans Publishing Co.

Rowe, J. (1672). *Heavenly-mindedness and earthly-mindedness: In two parts.* Francis Tyton.

Schwanda, T. (2012). *Soul recreation: The contemplative-mystical piety of Puritanism.* Pickwick Publications.

Segal, Z., Williams, M., & Teasdale, J. (2012). *Mindfulness-based cognitive therapy for depression* (2nd ed). The Guilford Press.

Siegel, R. (2010). *The mindfulness solution: Everyday practices for everyday problems.* The Guilford Press.

Smith, A. (2013). *Philokalia: The Eastern Christian spiritual texts.* Skylight Paths.

Stoddard, J., & Afari, N. (2014). *The big book of ACT metaphors: A practitioner's guide to experiential exercises & metaphors in acceptance & commitment therapy.* New Harbinger Publications, Inc.

Strosahl, K., Hayes, S., Wilson, K., & Gifford, E. (2004). An ACT primer: Core therapy processes, intervention strategies, and therapist competencies. In S. Hayes & K. Strosahl (Eds.), *A practical guide to acceptance and commitment therapy* (pp. 31–58). Springer.

Talbot, J. (2013). *The Jesus prayer: A cry for mercy, a path of renewal.* InterVarsity Press.

Taylor, M. (2014). *1 Corinthians: An exegetical and theological exposition of holy scripture.* B&H Publishing Group.

Ward, B. (2003). *The desert fathers: Sayings of the early Christian monks.* Penguin Books.

Wolters, A. (2005). *Creation regained: Biblical basics for a reformational worldview* (2nd ed.). William B. Eerdmans Publishing Company.

Wortley, J. (2012). *The book of elders: Sayings of the desert fathers.* Cistercian Publications.

8

COMMITTING AND FOLLOWING

Introduction

In this chapter, the focus is on the "do what matters" pillar (Harris, 2019, p. 8) in traditional acceptance and commitment therapy (ACT),[1] exploring the values and committed action processes. These processes, which represent the active life for Christians (i.e., Martha serving Jesus in the gospel of Luke), are integrated with Jesus's model of servanthood, self-sacrifice, and suffering, along with Christian virtues, emanating from both the Bible and contemplative Christianity. Collectively referred to as the "committing and following" pillar in faith-based ACT, Christian virtues are explored, rather than the more general term "values," in addition to strategies for Christian clients to engage in committed action in day-to-day living. Examples from Jesus's life are presented to illustrate how Christian clients can pursue God's will, central to the Christian faith, despite suffering and hardship. In addition, the Book of Hebrews is explicated in order to help Christian clients better understand a biblical model of endurance in the face of suffering. Faith-based ACT metaphors and strategies for virtue-based behavioral action are presented for counselors and therapists throughout the chapter, along with a case example to enrich the discussion. Overall, to "do what matters," Christian clients need to have a clear understanding of Jesus's teachings and an attitude of willingness to live them out on this planet.

Traditional ACT and Values

Within traditional ACT, clients learn to defuse from cognitions that get in the way of taking action, along with strategies to accept unpleasant inner experiences (i.e., experiential acceptance). What is more, clients connect to a transcendent self and employ mindfulness to stay rooted in the present moment, nonjudgmentally connecting to life as it organically unfolds. These four mindfulness- and acceptance-based processes allow clients to be more accepting of the inner world, cultivating psychological flexibility in the process.

DOI: 10.4324/9781003181941-9

As clients ameliorate efforts to use control and experiential avoidance in reaction to the pains of life, an alternative strategy needs to be utilized in order to guide daily experiences. Therefore, values, rather than wavering, impermanent inner states (e.g., thoughts, feelings, sensations, memories), can serve as a more trustworthy, principled strategy for engaging life. In fact, several theoretical orientations emphasize "values" language, elucidating the importance of principled living in psychological health (Yadavaia & Hayes, 2009). Among ACT therapists, a compass is commonly used to describe the nature of values, or "chosen life directions" (Luoma et al., 2017, p. 202), capturing taking a certain route, like heading east or west.

In traditional ACT, values are defined more formally as "freely-chosen, verbally constructed consequences of ongoing, dynamic, evolving patterns of activity, which establish predominant reinforcers for that activity that are intrinsic to engagement to the valued behavioral pattern itself" (Hayes et al., 2012, pp. 92–93). To simplify the definition, values involve several key ingredients, including being "principled" and "desired" (i.e., behaviors that clients are passionate about engaging in and standing up for); "global" (i.e., they capture the "big picture," organizing a variety of actions that clients want to pursue under a larger "umbrella" term or concept); and "ongoing" (i.e., they continue to unfold in real time, rather than ending at some point in the near or distant future) (Harris, 2019, pp. 213–214).

Thus, overall, values represent a broader set of behaviors that clients freely choose to live out in an intentional direction, emanating from the heart with a firm zeal and passion because they are profoundly meaningful. Rather than engaging in actions that feel forced or are determined by others, clients connect to a deeper part of themselves, getting excited about these behavioral qualities and personally defining the direction they would like to head in. Indeed, values are by no means an abstract endeavor. Rather, they constitute a proverbial map, emanating from verbally constructed, comprehensive behaviors to guide daily living. In other words, values are intimately linked to present-moment activity, similar to breathing being associated with living.

On the other hand, from a traditional ACT perspective, values are not the same as virtues or morals, given that these terms conjure up evaluations of what constitutes "good" and "bad" behavior. In addition, values are not simply feelings clients have about certain behaviors or needs they tend to express, since these inner experiences wax and wane. Instead, values are deeply ingrained, ongoing actions that clients choose to implement in daily living. Finally, values are not synonymous with goals, which can be completed or crossed off a list, especially because clients continue to pursue values, which have an ongoing quality and are anchored to the present moment.

Surely, values are especially salient in the realm of counseling and therapy because they offer a stable path, directing clients in the midst of suffering and helping them to move forward in a meaningful, intentional way, rather than being blown about by the winds of cognitive fusion and experiential avoidance. To be sure, since values are freely chosen, clients are not simply engaging in fusion all over again. Rather, because they are connected to what matters to them most, acting upon their heartfelt convictions, clients have a litmus test for "workability." In other words, since traditional ACT helps clients to engage in behaviors that are pragmatic, leading to a "rich, full, and meaningful life" (Harris, 2019, p. 2), values are employed as the vehicle for making this happen. Thus, to be flexible means to make moment-by-moment decisions linked to stable values, rather than avoiding life or fusing with unhelpful narratives that keep clients stuck. Above all else, values are important because they are steady, helping clients to accept the ubiquity of suffering in order to find meaning in the midst of psychological pain.

To organize values into a more coherent picture, traditional ACT counselors and therapists commonly employ assessment strategies that involve helping clients to connect to value-based living within a variety of life domains. For example, intimate relationships, family relationships, and work life may be especially important life areas for some clients to pursue firmly held values. On the other hand, physical fitness, community involvement, spirituality, and creative endeavors may be most salient for others. By working from a worksheet that elucidates a dozen or so major life domains, clients are able to organize values under a plethora of overarching headings, rating and prioritizing them in order to discern the most important areas to focus on (Hayes et al., 2012, pp. 311–312).

Because these values are synonymous with principled, continued action, rather than merely serving as an abstract notion, clients must be firmly committed to live them out. In traditional ACT, "willingness" captures a courageous ability to move forward, enduring inner pain and simultaneously acting on values, rather than engaging in cognitive fusion and experiential avoidance, which may have kept clients from fully engaging with life. Like a child who jumps into a pool, rather than repeatedly tipping their toe in the water, committed action has a dichotomous "yes" or "no" quality. Certainly, clients are either living out their values or not, rather than a "sort of," partial pursuit of value-based living. In fact, like the detonation of hand grenades, value-based action is certain, rather than constituting an "almost" quality.

Traditional ACT and Committed Action

As one of the six traditional ACT processes, committed action involves living out the values that clients have identified as meaningful to them. In other words, values without action are merely an abstract endeavor. Given that values are dynamic, action is the other side of the proverbial coin, helping clients to head in an intentional direction and leading to a vibrant, full life. Thus, this process is a crucial ingredient, intimately connected to values within traditional ACT.

195

For clients, identifying values is only the beginning of the process, since action is closely intermingled with what matters most in life. Stated differently, values need to be lived out in the here-and-now, rather than at some later point in time. Because of this, clients need to act upon values in the present moment, placing one foot in front of the other as they combine a verbal, abstract awareness of values with their behavioral manifestation. For certain, traditional ACT has its roots in behaviorism and, thus, focuses heavily on the behavior that emanates from an awareness of how clients want to live. Therefore, traditional ACT is about asking clients what the value looks like, right here and now, when it is implemented.

For example, a client may state that, after a particularly powerful therapy session, he will be more loving toward his wife, viewing this value like heading "east" with a compass. From a traditional ACT perspective, the client needs to immediately take action with behaviors that are involved in being more loving. Over time, the client's willingness to love—a foundational value for most individuals—leads to a pattern of behaviors that are reinforcing, especially if this direction on a compass is meaningful. As the client stumbles, trips, and falls in his pursuit of "being loving," he can readily get back on the road of life, recognizing that the direction he heads in will continue to lead him through obstacles. Yet, for the client, it is extremely empowering to possess a compass to guide his journey, recognizing that his overactive mind will not get him to the peak of the mountain.

Unfortunately, for many clients, life seems to be about pursuing a set of goals in order to be "happy." However, when generating a list of goals, clients can quickly realize there is a large gap between their current and desired state, with goals being "achieved" at some later point in time. When this happens, clients can become increasingly dissatisfied with the present moment, preoccupied with a future that may never come. Because of this, goals are a way to generate change, but need to be anchored to values to serve their ultimate purpose.

After clients have identified values in the major life domains (e.g., family, work, community, spirituality), goals are a way to help clients move forward within the context of values. If values are an overarching way to elucidate desirable, ongoing, meaningful behaviors that enrich life, goals are more precise, pragmatic events to carry out heartfelt values. As an example, a female client might value deepening her relationship with God, emphasizing the spirituality domain of traditional ACT. Embedded in this value-based life direction is a goal involving several more practical events, such as being active in a local church congregation. What is more, the client can take action to pursue this value, meeting this goal by praying daily and attending weekly church services.

Again, the value is the more general principle for guiding life, with the goal acting as a more focused, practical event that moves the client in the chosen direction, likely in the form of an experience that can be checked off a list. In turn, the goal is accomplished by taking specific actions, carrying them out with concrete steps. To summarize this relationship more succinctly, values serve as the compass (e.g., "I need to head east"), with goals constituting events that are to take place to head in a valued direction (e.g., "I need to pass this milestone on the first day of travel") and actions capturing the behavior of walking from one point to another (e.g., "I'll drive my car along this exact route, filling up for gas at this particular gas station").

Finally, within the commitment process, clients need to identify barriers that may get in the way of value-based action. A variety of inner (e.g., thoughts, feelings, sensations, memories) and outer (e.g., situations, relationships) events may come up in life, temporarily sidetracking the client and leading to additional psychological pain. Without a doubt, events in both the inner and outer world can seemingly get in the way of heading in a valued direction. Because of this, traditional ACT counselors and therapists can help clients to identify such barriers in advance, employing the other traditional ACT processes to help clients accept the inner world, rather than resort to cognitive fusion or experiential avoidance. Overall, traditional ACT counselors and therapists can help clients to recognize the importance of accepting that life inevitably comes with barriers. Yet, when they arise, clients can identify them, responding with acceptance, flexibility, and an observing, present-moment awareness, rather than control or avoidance strategies that can keep them stuck.

The traditional ACT processes of values and committed action align quite well with several central tenets within the Christian faith, leading to a "hand in glove" dynamic with faith-based ACT. As a result, next, the story of Mary and Martha is revisited to highlight doing and the active life, before transitioning to virtues within Christianity. Certainly, within traditional ACT, values are freely chosen, personally constructed, global life directions. Yet, within Christianity, virtues are much more precise, intimately linked to the Bible as the sacred text for Christian clients. Because of this, an explication of Christian virtues, rather than a more general emphasis on values, is offered in this chapter, along with a review of the relationship between virtues, compulsive thoughts (*logismoi* in Greek), and passions within contemplative Christianity.

Martha and Action

For Martha, serving Jesus was a central aim (Luke 10:38–42). In fact, in the story of Mary and Martha, Martha's actions involved hospitality, guest preparations, and sacrifice. For the medieval author Thomas Aquinas, both contemplation and action lead to love and charity (Kreeft, 2014). Although, in many instances, contemplation is preferred—given that it focuses on the inner world, extends to the afterlife, fosters contentment, cultivates dependence on God, offers ongoing rest, and increases an awareness of God's divinity—both the contemplative and active life should emanate from a loving charity that is linked to God himself (Kreeft, 2014). Above all else, for Aquinas, loving God in moments of contemplation is intimately connected to loving one's neighbor through acts of charity (Kreeft, 2014). Because of this, the two work together and cannot be divorced from each other in this life (Kreeft, 2014).

With Christian clients, acceptance and action, paralleling the story of Mary and Martha, are two sides of the same coin, with both flowing from the love of God. In moments of contemplation, Christian clients can cultivate acceptance toward unpleasant inner experiences, spending time with God in silence and stillness. Yet, developing a loving attentiveness also leads to acts of charity and service, given that "God is love" (*New International Version Bible*, 2011, 1 John 4:8) and loving others is a foundational goal in the Christian life (Mark 12:31). Within Christian teachings, though, values are typically referred to as virtues, which are explored in the next section.

Biblical Virtues: The Christian Version of Values

As noted previously, values are verbally composed, comprehensive declarations, unilaterally selected by clients and constituting immediate, intrinsically meaningful actions that enrich life (Hayes et al., 2012). On the other hand, "a virtue is a disposition to act, desire, and feel that involves the exercise of judgment and leads to a recognizable human excellence, an instance of human flourishing" (Yearley, 1990, p. 2). To offer a slightly different definition, "virtues are characteristic ways of behaving that make both persons and actions good, and also enable persons to fulfill the purpose of their lives" (Harrington & Keenan, 2002, p. 23). For Harrington and Keenan, the study of virtues focuses on three salient questions: "Who are we? Who ought we to become? How do we get there?" (p. 23). Of course, from a biblical viewpoint, humans are created in God's image (Genesis 1:27), freely choosing to become more like Jesus by following him as a disciple (Matthew 16:24), similar to a student following a rabbi to emulate him and learn from his teachings.

Characteristically, virtues are chosen for their own sake, leading to a plan of action, ameliorating barriers to optimal living (Yearley, 1990). For example, the virtue of courage helps to overcome the human struggle with fear, which undermines effective action (Yearley, 1990). In fact, virtues are evaluative in that they distinguish between different types of behaviors, morally speaking, preferring some and not others (Yearley, 1990). Also, virtues tend to be universal, intimately connected to a given society (Yearley, 1990). To conclude, virtues are usually thought of as traits, embedded within character (Yearley, 1990).

For the medieval theologian Thomas Aquinas, there are four cardinal virtues, including prudence (i.e., wisdom), justice, temperance (i.e., self-control), and fortitude (i.e., courage), along with three theological virtues, namely faith, hope, and charity (i.e., love) (Harrington & Keenan, 2010).[2] The former, for Aquinas, can be cultivated through acting in such a way as to develop habits, whereas the latter emanate from a relationship with God (Harrington &

Keenan, 2010). Before Aquinas, Aristotle also advocated the importance of the cardinal virtues, with "cardinal" translating as "hinge," meaning optimal human functioning "hinges" on these four types of character (Wright, 2010).

On the other hand, in a more contemporary context and drawing from 1 Corinthians 13:13, Austin and Geivett (2012) recently explored the theological virtues, arguing they are highly relevant for Christians living in the 21st century. More specifically, the virtue of faith involves trusting in God, cultivating a deeper relationship with him, and leading to obedience (Austin & Geivett, 2012). Among the faith-based virtues are open-mindedness, wisdom, and zeal (Austin & Geivett, 2012). What is more, hope as a virtue involves focusing on the afterlife, recognizing that Christians can place their trust in God to endure suffering (Austin & Geivett, 2012). Related to hope is contentment and courage, both necessary for vital Christian living (Austin & Geivett, 2012). Finally, love is a foundational Christian virtue, involving compassion, forgiveness, and humility (Austin & Geivett, 2012). Each of these theological virtues embodies excellence of moral character, rather than a feeling state as the source of effective action (Austin & Geivett, 2012).

Wright (2010), too, recently wrote on the topic of Christian virtues, suggesting they are about being human in a unique way, offering character formation, rather than serving as a set of rules for living. For Wright, virtue "is what happens when someone has made a thousand small choices, requiring effort and concentration to do something which is good and right but which doesn't 'come naturally'" (p. 20). In other words, virtue is cultivated when character is "second nature," based on patterns that develop via courageous action. With virtues, habitual patterns of character manifest because individuals are able to relate to their thoughts, feelings, sensations, and memories with a bit more distance, recognizing that virtuous living is more important than being bullied around by wavering, impermanent inner states. These "habits of the heart" are foundational to Christian living, with Wright suggesting that life is about developing "fully formed, fully flourishing Christian character" (p. 31). Among Christians, the development of virtue centers on God, rather than the self, leading to servanthood and self-sacrifice, in that authentic Christian living gives glory to God.

To compare and contrast values and virtues, values are global principles that are chosen by clients, encompassing active, ongoing, present-focused, and desired qualities, not necessarily associated with feelings, needs, morals, or virtues (Harris, 2019, pp. 213–214). In a similar vein, Christian virtues are active, global principles rooted in the present moment, although they also have a future-oriented focus, given that the end result is a fellowship with God in the afterlife that transcends personal preferences. For Christian clients, moreover, rising above personal wants and needs takes place because the central focus is God, rather than the self, whereas values are pursued within traditional ACT because they are intrinsically desired (although not necessarily liked in every moment), varying from client to client. Also, Christian virtues constitute the development of habitual moral character, beyond wavering thoughts, feelings, sensations, and memories. In fact, for Christian clients, virtues are intimately linked to "right" behavior, whereas values within traditional ACT are personally constructed and chosen, separated from evaluations about whether such behaviors are "good" or "bad."

Although some values may be rather common from client to client, traditional ACT counselors and therapists help clients to connect to their *own* freely chosen behaviors. Conversely, virtues are associated with Christian teachings, adopting the cardinal virtues from Aristotle and gleaning the theological virtues from the life, death, and resurrection of Jesus. Finally, similar to the values in traditional ACT, Christian clients are to freely choose to implement these habitual patterns of character formation and by no means forced to do so by some sort of malevolent God or external force. Instead, freely chosen habits of moral character plant seeds, continuing to grow in the afterlife, with Jesus giving his followers a choice to follow him and adopt his teachings (Matthew 16:24).

Moving forward, Christian virtues are integrated into faith-based ACT, including those illuminated in this chapter. In faith-based ACT, I define virtues as moral behaviors that rise above wavering thoughts, feelings, sensations, and memories and are modeled after the life and teachings of Jesus and other New Testament passages. The purpose of virtue-based action for Christian clients involves living a meaningful life devoted to following Jesus (i.e., walking with God in love), giving glory to God, developing character (i.e., sanctification), and planting seeds for the afterlife, leading to a deeper relationship with him. Popular virtues cultivated within the Christian life include love, hope, faith, wisdom (i.e., prudence), justice, self-control (i.e., temperance), and courage (i.e., fortitude). Table 8.1 elucidates seven common Christian virtues, along with definitions and possible behavioral manifestations for Christian clients. It is worth mentioning that in faith-based ACT, virtues are to be lived out, rather than merely viewed in an abstract manner. Thus, a central question for Christian clients is as follows: "How can I live out this virtue in behavioral terms, following Jesus (i.e., walking with God in love) and modeling my life after him?"

Interestingly, the Christian contemplative tradition, too, has much to say about virtue-based living. For the early desert Christians, along with other contemplatives throughout the ages, virtues are a central part of the Christian life, often serving as a response to the tempting, compulsive thoughts that they perceived to be from demons in the desert terrain. What follows is a review of common virtues within contemplative Christianity, along with a discussion of the relationship between virtues, compulsive thoughts (*logismoi* in Greek), and the passions.

Biblical Virtues and Contemplative Christianity

For contemplative monks living in the desert, learning to patiently endure suffering and watch tempting thoughts (*logismoi* in Greek) with a vigilant attentiveness

Table 8.1 Christian Virtues, Definitions, and Behavioral Manifestations in Faith-Based ACT

Christian Virtue	Definition	Behavioral Manifestation
Wisdom	A cardinal virtue; the ability to determine the right path to take; insight and understanding gained from the Bible, prayer, a relationship with God, and interacting with other Christians	A Christian client struggles with depression, leading to social withdrawal and the tendency to cancel a weekly ministry they are leading at their church; yet, they begin to look to the Bible to determine their course of action, resulting in a personal realization that they can love and serve others while still feeling depressed; therefore, they continue to direct their ministry, despite the depressive symptoms, believing God would want them to do so
Justice	A cardinal virtue; positive, good relationships with others; because humans are created in the image of God, everyone deserves dignity and respect	A Christian client experiences social anxiety, leading to a struggle to serve in their church; still, they realize that justice is an important virtue, deciding to volunteer in a ministry devoted to helping abused children because they believe that God desires for them to help the most vulnerable in society
Self-control	A cardinal virtue; related to pleasurable activities, such as food consumption, drinking, and sexual behavior; participating in these activities with the recognition that they do not lead to a fulfilling life on their own, resulting in a more moderate or modest approach; the ultimate goal is a deeper relationship with God, rather than the pursuit of pleasure	A Christian client struggles with generalized anxiety, leading to the tendency to consume alcohol in an effort to numb the psychological pain of recurrent worry and restlessness; however, they recognize that alcohol use will not eliminate their distress, cutting back on their daily use, turning to God in an effort to strengthen their relationship with Jesus Christ
Courage	A cardinal virtue; demonstrating intentional strength, despite psychological pain, including fear; living life based on Jesus's example	A Christian client experiences recurrent panic attacks, leading to the tendency to isolate themselves, fearing they will have another panic attack in public; they are especially preoccupied with being embarrassed, based on a recent experience at a local grocery store that involved being disoriented for several minutes, leading to a perceived humiliating interaction with a store clerk; yet, they courageously decide to continue to attend weekly church service, volunteering in a ministry because they believe that following Jesus in the midst of fear is what they have been called to do on this planet

(Continued)

201

Table 8.1 (Continued)

Christian Virtue	Definition	Behavioral Manifestation
Love	A theological virtue; loving the good of another person, rather than using others purely for personal benefits; God is the perfect manifestation of love	A Christian client struggles with persistent depressive disorder, experiencing low mood most of the time over the past several years; still, they recognize that loving others is a central aim in the Christian faith and, thus, decide to serve as a mentor in their church, spending time with fellow Christians and supporting them in order to serve others like Jesus; they also devote more time to their marriage, believing God has called them to strengthen their relationship with their spouse
Hope	A theological virtue; looking to the future in anticipation of a positive outcome; longing to pursue God as the decisive source of joy and fulfillment	A Christian client struggles with chronic worry, experiencing catastrophic predictions about a doomsday future, including losing their full-time job at church; embracing hope, though, they begin to surrender to God's providence (i.e., protective care), recognizing that their relationship with Jesus is most important; because of this, they are able to continue to minister to others, trusting that God will provide for them because of God's loving care
Faith	A theological virtue; trusting in God, including his assurances in the Bible, because he is benevolent, omnipotent, and offers human beings grace and mercy	A Christian client struggles with major depressive disorder, ruminating in an effort to better understand why they are suffering; yet, they decide to trust in God, rather than rely on their own understanding of depression, which frees them up to follow Jesus, instead of waiting for their depressive symptoms to go away; placing their faith in God, including trusting in God's plans for their future, they decide to read their Bible daily; pray on a daily basis, and attend weekly church service

Note. Adapted from Austin and Geivett (2012).

led to the ability to cultivate a deeper relationship with God. Of course, the behavior through which this uniting love was displayed involved acts of charity, including the love of neighbors (Paintner, 2012). As Paintner revealed, "The desert way will always lead us back to others if we are having an authentic experience of God and of our deepest selves" (p. 110). Within monastic life, monks were known for taking care of those who were struggling with a sickness or illness, offering acts of hospitality as a loving gesture that emanated from a deeper fellowship with God (Paintner, 2012). Rather than focusing on their own self-interests, contemplatives would offer themselves in an effort to resemble Jesus's sacrifice. Among other virtues, patience, humility, prudence, justice, and courage were applied to daily living (Paintner, 2012). The following quote from John the Dwarf, one of the early desert Christians, seems to best capture many of the virtues within the desert path:

> I think it best that a man [sic] should have a little bit of all the virtues. Therefore, get up early every day and acquire the beginning of every virtue and every command of God. Use great patience, with fear and long-suffering, in the love of God, with all the fervor of your soul and body. Exercise great humility, bear with interior distress, be vigilant and pray often with reverence and groaning, with purity of speech and control of your eyes. When you are despised do not get angry, be at peace, and do not render evil for evil. Do not pay attention to the faults of others, and do not try to compare yourself with others, knowing you are less than every created thing.
>
> (quoted in Paintner, 2012, p. 113)

For Iskander (2005), virtues are like a ladder that connects earth and heaven, with each step constituting a behavior that brings Christians closer to God. Amid the list of virtues within the contemplative life, obedience and patience are foundational, with love also capturing moral excellence (Iskander, 2005). With obedience, Christians can search for daily opportunities to yield to God's will. Moreover, patience involves enduring because God is sovereign, recognizing that he will ultimately restore all things. For contemplatives in the desert, the virtues were a way to respond to tempting, compulsive thoughts, which led to the passions, or distractions that undermined an awareness of God's active, loving presence.

Biblical Virtues, Compulsive Thoughts, and the Passions

Evagrius of Ponticus, a fourth-century desert monk, identified eight biblically inspired virtues that desert dwellers were to develop in order to respond to the tempting, compulsive, assaultive, noisy thoughts (*logismoi* in Greek) that interfere with a deeper relationship with God and give way to the passions (Harmless,

2008). These virtues include (a) temperance, charity, and continence to respond to gluttony, fornication, and greed, which, if not noticed and ameliorated, lead to the bodily passions; (b) patience and courage to address sadness, anger, and listlessness, which can give way to the psychic passions; and (c) wisdom, understanding, and prudence, addressing vanity and pride and constituting the rational part of the psyche (Harmless, 2008).

In other words, Evagrius of Ponticus believed that the life of the monk involves resolving a deeper struggle with the passions, courageously facing physical and emotional vulnerabilities, such as insatiable hunger, sexual needs, and the unquenchable desire for more possessions. What is more, monks strived to effectively respond to struggles surrounding sadness and anger in order to achieve a calm, tranquil state, constituting a loving relationship with God (Harmless, 2008). Within the Christian contemplative tradition, passions are "inner wounds" (*pathos* in Greek), meaning "suffering" (Paintner, 2012). In fact, they are commonly viewed as impulses, originating from both the inner and outer worlds, often paralleling an addiction (Cook, 2011). Also, passions are linked to the aforementioned *logismoi*, at times referring to thoughts, feelings, behaviors, and attitudes, serving as a source of recurrent struggle (Cook, 2011). In the *Philokalia*, a collection of spiritual writings in the Eastern Orthodox Church spanning many centuries, passions are associated with both the body and soul (Cook, 2011).

Throughout the years, authors have described passions as "attacking," "enslaving," "tempting," "defiling," "obscuring," and "cunning" (Cook, 2011, p. 68). Among Christian contemplative writings, the passions seem to be indirectly referred to as emotional states through the use of a variety of metaphors, including "storm" and "darkness" associations (Cook, 2011). Although the passions do not exactly align with one psychological process or definition within the 21st-century counseling and therapy literature, they seem to consistently capture habitual, rigid thoughts, feelings, behaviors, and attitudes, a sort of "pathology of the soul," pulling Christians away from an awareness of God's active, loving presence (Cook, 2011; Trader, 2011). Certainly, passions can be conceptualized as either helpful or hurtful for daily functioning, depending on whether they undermine sustained attention on the God of love (Trader, 2011). This understanding parallels traditional ACT's "workability," which views inner experiences in terms of whether they help or hinder the pursuit of values.

Although some authors do not attempt to distinguish passions from the *logismoi* or suggest that they influence one another (see Cook, 2011), others argue the *logismoi* lead to the passions. In other words, the *logismoi* are "a train of thoughts that befog and pollute the mind so that bit by bit it drifts away from reality into a world of fantasy," which are sort of like "seeds of the passions" (Coniaris, 2004, p. 50). In either case, there seems to be a close relationship between tempting, compulsive thoughts and the passions, which can manifest as thoughts, feelings, behaviors, and attitudes.

For the early desert Christians, life was about facing the tempting, compulsive thoughts that were associated with the passions. To be sure, in the desert landscape, monks viewed demons as the source of the *logismoi*, the "energies that scatter our attention" (Paintner, 2012, p. 38), undermining Christians' efforts to cultivate a deeper relationship with God by distracting them from him. Because of this, the Jesus Prayer was commonly employed, using watchfulness (*nepsis* in Greek) to relate differently to these distracting, compulsive thoughts (and passions), watching them without reacting to them so as to practice God's presence and achieve inner stillness (*hesychia* in Greek). In this way, a calm, still, quiet attentiveness helped the early desert monks to focus, instead, on developing key Christian virtues, including love for God and others (Coniaris, 1998).

It is worth mentioning that not all of the early desert Christians viewed the passions as entirely negative, with some suggesting they emanated from God (Paintner, 2012). In fact, from this perspective, passions simply need to be harnessed so that they can guide Christians back to God as the ultimate source. By understanding them and relating to them in a way that ameliorates their controlling, distracting presence, Christians can, ultimately, bring glory to God (Chryssavgis, 2008).

Nevertheless, over time, contemplative practice within desert monastic life aided in addressing the habitual passions, developing virtues, and achieving a calm, tranquil state, culminating with a loving posture that embodies the contemplative life (Harmless, 2008). In other words, these monks began to attain a deeper knowledge of God, moving toward a more contemplative awareness (Harmless, 2008). Evagrius of Ponticus argued that "passionlessness" (*apatheia* in Greek) characterizes someone who gains relief from the eight compulsive thoughts and passions (Harmless, 2008).

Above all else, Evagrius of Ponticus's use of the "passions" terminology helps to better understand the barriers that get in the way of a deeper relationship with God in contemplative practice. Put another way, for the early desert Christians, life was about gaining freedom from the grip of these inner states so as to focus on loving God (Trader, 2011). Of course, thoughts, feelings, sensations, and memories by no means permanently go away in this calm, tranquil state. Rather, through the use of imageless, wordless, continuous prayer, practitioners begin to notice and relate differently to tempting, compulsive thoughts (*logismoi* in Greek) and the passions, utilizing the contemplative self (the *nous* in Greek) to connect to God (Harmless, 2008). By understanding and embracing the passions, contemplatives are able to vulnerably reach out to God, recognizing that he is in control (Chryssavgis, 2008). In Evagrius of Ponticus's lifetime, the early desert Christians commonly used the psalms to deepen their awareness of God, eventually uniting with him in an imageless, wordless state of passionless love (Harmless, 2008).

To summarize, tempting, compulsive thoughts (*logismoi* in Greek) are habitual, distracting thinking patterns that are linked to the passions, which include emotional states and other repetitive patterns of the mind. These inner experiences, which were conceptualized by the early desert monks as both positive and negative and emanating from demonic temptations, have the potential to get in the way of virtue-based living and fellowshipping with God. Similar to cognitive fusion and experiential avoidance, the ways in which Christian clients understand and relate to unpleasant inner experiences can directly affect their ability to follow Jesus (i.e., walk with God in love). Although there does not appear to be a one-to-one correspondence between the *logismoi*, the passions, and a 21st-century understanding of inner psychological processes, the aforementioned contemplative writings can help Christians to understand the need to relate differently to inner pain, deepening their awareness of God's active, loving presence. Certainly, trying to permanently eradicate psychological suffering wastes vital energy that can be used to walk with God in love down the road of life, heading toward his purpose.

Undeniably, through the pursuit of virtues, Christian clients can maintain an awareness of the contemplative self (the *nous* in Greek) and practice God's presence and achieve inner stillness (*hesychia* in Greek) so as to patiently walk with Jesus, culminating in the manifestation of the two greatest biblical commandments—loving God and others (Mark 12:28–31). However, Christian clients must have a willingness to face difficult inner experiences, consistent with the early desert monks' view of the *logismoi* and passions, and the courage to live out Christian virtues. What follows is a review of committed action in the Bible, along with exercises and metaphors for Christian clients to engage in virtue-based living within faith-based ACT.

Following Jesus: The Christian Version of Committed Action

In Scripture, Jesus modeled virtuous living. Thus, Christian clients are to follow him as his disciple, learning from him and living out his teachings. In fact, the Bible elucidates that humankind was created in God's image, with Christian clients commonly striving to become more like Jesus by following his model of self-sacrifice. Although it is unrealistic to behaviorally emulate Jesus in every manner presented in the gospels, there are a variety of ways Christian clients can attempt to replicate Jesus's life, including discerning God's will, living a simple life, letting go of an overemphasis on physical comfort in order to advance the gospel message, and recognizing that suffering is a part of the Christian life (Harrington & Keenan, 2002).

For Christian clients with depression, anxiety, trauma, or relational problems, a common struggle tends to be a preoccupation with the self, attempting to protect the self when in psychological pain (Welsh & Knabb, 2009). For example, with depressive disorders, clients commonly fuse with negative thought content about self-worth, concluding they are unlovable or unworthy. In turn, they may isolate themselves, given the distress they are experiencing, in an attempt to further protect an already vulnerable self. This, too, goes for clients with anxiety disorders, who may avoid unpleasant social encounters in anticipation of some sort of future catastrophe (e.g., being embarrassed in public, losing a job, having a panic attack in front of others). With trauma, moreover, clients may attempt to avoid life because of intrusive memories or other reminders of a distressing traumatic event, believing that experiential avoidance is the solution to navigating a seemingly dangerous world. As another example, clients may fuse with unhelpful thoughts about an intimate partner, which undermines value-based living and the pursuit of love and intimacy with the person closest to them in life. Generally speaking, then, a central focus in counseling and therapy involves helping clients to ameliorate the tendency to overly rely on self-protection, which commonly results in the avoidance of life, in order to thrive in the context of loving, supportive relationships (Welsh & Knabb, 2009).

Interestingly, within the famous "self-emptying" (*kenosis* in Greek; Strong, 2001) passage in Philippians 2:6–7, the Apostle Paul argued that followers of Christ should emulate Jesus's humility: "being in very nature God, [Jesus] did not consider equality with God something to be used to his own advantage; rather, he *made himself nothing* by taking the very nature of a servant, being made in human likeness" (*New International Version Bible*, 2011, italics added). In other words, self-emptying is about letting go of one's own will in order to yield to God's sovereign plan. At the heart of contemplative practice in general (Lane, 1998), as well as centering prayer in particular (Bourgeault, 2004), is a self-emptying attitude of servanthood and surrender, wherein practitioners let go of their attachment to the false self in order to make room for God's desires. Certainly, during moments of contemplation, Christians strive to cultivate an attitude of humility, similar to Jesus's incarnation, relinquishing control, status, and power to accept God's omniscient will.

In a similar vein, in a recent study among college students, I found that "humble detachment" explained the relationship between surrendering to God as a coping skill and repetitive negative thinking (e.g., rumination, worry) (Knabb et al., 2018). Specifically, drawing inspiration from the contemplative writing the *Cloud of Unknowing*, "humble detachment" was defined as

> a detached, flexible, humble ability to (a) let go of the tendency to clutch or push away a preoccupation with inner experiences and the self, and (b) pivot from a preoccupation with the self and inner experiences to a more transcendent awareness of God's active, loving presence.
>
> (p. 172)

As a result, the ability to "humbly detach" may help Christian clients to more confidently watch and endure, notice and shift, and commit and follow as they walk with God in love along the road of life.

With this study in mind, indeed, contemplative practice can help Christian clients to ameliorate the tendency to fuse with a false, storied, rational self (the *dianoia* in Greek) that overly relies on negative thought content about self-preservation, keeping them from serving others through virtue-based living. Among other virtues, humility and love were frequently modeled by Jesus, captured by the self-emptying referred to by the Apostle Paul in Philippians 2:7. This attitude of servanthood—letting go of a recurrent preoccupation with the self to respond to others—dates back to the early desert Christians (Burton-Christie, 1993) and was a central feature of desert life. Attempting to be like Jesus, these desert dwellers strived to detach from a false self, choosing to humbly love both God and others. As Abba Theodore, an early desert monk, revealed, "Humility and the fear of God surpass all the other virtues" (Ward, 2003, p. 154). In fact, humility and self-emptying were often part of an intricate process of cultivating inner stillness and quiet (*hesychia* in Greek) (Ryrie, 2011), explored in an earlier chapter. Pursuing an inner state of humility, self-emptying, and inner stillness, the early desert Christians sought to effectively respond to both the inner and outer worlds (Ryrie, 2011).

In the context of depression, anxiety, trauma, and relational problems, contemplative practice, focused on self-emptying (*kenosis* in Greek), can help Christian clients to ameliorate the tendency to preserve and protect the self, fusing with negative thought content that leads to the avoidance of life. Instead, following Jesus involves emulating his servanthood, self-sacrifice, and humility in the context of loving communities. Rather than overly relying on a storied self ("I'm unlovable because ..."), Christian clients can learn to detach from the often-inaccurate world of language, striving to consent to God's indwelling through *apophatic* prayer. After all, centering prayer is about surrendering to God's loving action, given that God is present at the center, residing within the inner world.

Moreover, Jesus's "Sermon on the Mount" (*New International Version Bible*, 2011, Matthew 5–7) can offer guidance on the behaviors Christians can cultivate in order to be more like him. For example, Jesus suggested that the poor in spirit are "blessed," elucidating that material possessions fail to lead to true happiness and contentment. In fact, Jesus went on to offer a list of characteristics of those who are blessed, including mourning, meekness, longing for righteousness, and showing mercy.

Several virtues seem to dominate in the "Sermon on the Mount," including showing mercy to others, which is central to the Christian faith, especially in the context of God's relationship with humankind and interpersonal interactions between humans (Harrington & Keenan, 2002). Moreover, a "reconciling spirit" appears to be a foundational theme, with Jesus suggesting that peacemakers are blessed (Harrington & Keenan, 2002, p. 73). Finally, hope seems to be especially present in the "Sermon on the Mount," allowing Christians to trust in God and recognize Jesus's eventual restoration of all things (Harrington & Keenan, 2002).[3]

Of course, love is the central virtue in the Christian life, defining God's atoning gift to humankind via Jesus's work on the cross. Also, love captures the "Golden Rule": "So in everything, do to others what you would have them do to you, for this sums up the Law and the Prophets" (*New International Version Bible*, 2011, Matthew 7:12). Indeed, because God first loved human beings, humans, in turn, are able to love others, with Jesus modeling love, servanthood, and self-sacrifice through the incarnation (Tan, 2006). As noted in prior chapters, walking with God in love involves an "outside-in" to "inside-out" process, wherein Christian clients are learning to be more like Jesus (i.e., sanctification) as they follow him home. Gradually, Christian clients are learning to watch and endure the inner world, notice the difference between self-derived knowledge and God-derived love, shift from self-preoccupations to God's active, loving presence so as to achieve and maintain inner peace, and commit to a set of biblical virtues and follow Jesus as the "Great High Priest" wherever he would have Christian clients go.

As the "Great High Priest," Jesus fully lived the human experience, given he was "tempted in every way" (*New International Version Bible*, 2011, Hebrews 4:14–16). As a result, Christians are able to "approach God's throne of grace with confidence," receiving his compassionate mercy during instances of suffering and adversity because Jesus empathizes with what it means to struggle (*New International Version Bible*, 2011, Hebrews 4:14–16). In fact, because Jesus is the "pioneer and perfecter of faith," Christians can look to him to elucidate the direction they should take along the road of life (*New International Version Bible*, 2011, Hebrews 12:1–2). In other words, since Jesus "endured the cross, scorning its shame," he is a perfect example of endurance for Christian clients who are fatigued, exhausted, and uncertain, especially given their battle with recurrent psychological symptoms (*New International Version Bible*, 2011, Hebrews 12:2). As the writer of Hebrews revealed, by looking to Jesus's example, Christian clients can ameliorate weariness, knowing that he faithfully and courageously suffered, dying on a cross to fulfill God's purpose for his life (*New International Version Bible*, 2011, Hebrews 12:3).

In sum, Jesus offered several salient teachings in the "Sermon on the Mount," elucidating the importance of mercy, a spirit of interpersonal reconciliation, hope in God, and the primacy of love. Of course, these key virtues, rather than a more general understanding of personally constructed values, are central for Christian clients attempting to follow Jesus. If virtues are defined as moral excellence and corresponding behaviors—a series of habits that help Christian clients to become more like Jesus—an awareness of them, along with a series of strategies to live them out, is foundational to optimal Christian functioning. What follows, therefore, is a review of several faith-based ACT metaphors and exercises, helping counselors and therapists to work more effectively with Christian clients to follow Jesus in the midst of psychological pain.

Faith-Based ACT Conceptualizations, Goals, Metaphors, Exercises, and Worksheets for Committing and Following

In traditional ACT, a plethora of conceptualizations, metaphors, exercises, and worksheets are utilized, noted in Table 8.2, with the overarching goal of clarifying values, committing to values, and deeply engaging in value-based action for clients struggling with recurrent symptoms. To begin, traditional

Table 8.2 Traditional and Faith-Based ACT Conceptualizations, Metaphors, Exercises, and Worksheets for "Doing What Matters"/"Committing and Following"

	Traditional ACT	Faith-based ACT
Values		
Conceptualization		
Metaphor	"Choice Point Figure"	"Fork in the Road Figure"
	"Compass"	"A Lamp for My Feet, a Light on my Path"
	"Two Kids in the Car"	"Walking with Jesus on the Shore of the Sea of Galilee"/"Parable of the Bags of Gold"
	"Two-Sided Coin"	"James's Teaching on Trials and Perseverance"
	"Path Up the Mountain"	"Trust in the Lord"
Exercise	"Character Strengths"	"Jesus's Character Strengths"
	"Lifetime Achievement Award"	"Well Done, Good and Faithful Servant"
	"Mind-Reading Machine"	"A Person After God's Own Heart"
	"Role Models"	"Fruit of the Spirit"
Worksheet	"Table of Values"	"Table of Virtues"
Committed Action		
Conceptualization		
Metaphor	"Choice Point Figure"	"Fork in the Road Figure"
	"Traveling Partners"	"Jesus's Disciples"
	"Hockey Game"	"Disciples or Pharisees"
Exercise	"Walking the Path"	"Continue Fishing or Follow Jesus"
	"*FEAR* and *ACT*"	"Modified *FEAR* and *ACT*"/"God is Love"
	Interpersonal mindfulness	Four-step model
Worksheet	"Willingness and Action Plan"	"Faith-Based ACT 'Commit and Follow' Plan"

Note. Faith-based ACT interventions are adapted from Harris (2019), Hayes (2005), Hayes (2019), Hayes et al. (2012), Luoma et al. (2017), and Stoddard and Afari (2014).

ACT employs the "Choice Point" tool (Harris, 2019) to help conceptualize the problem and solution, with clients learning that they have a decision to make whenever they experience a difficult thought, feeling, sensation, memory, situation, or relationship. As one option, they can move "toward" a life of purpose, meaning, and vitality, which involves learning to "defuse" from difficult inner experiences and engage in helpful overt (i.e., observable, such as walking and talking) and covert (i.e., unobservable, such as thinking and feeling) behaviors (Harris, 2019). As the second option, clients can move "away from" the life they want, struggling to create meaning and purpose because they are "fused" with unpleasant inner events (e.g., thoughts, feelings, sensations, memories) and engaged in unhelpful overt and covert behaviors (Harris, 2019). In the context of the "doing what matters" pillar (Harris, 2019, p. 8), counselors and therapists can help clients to understand that "moving toward," not "away from," the life they want involves a deliberate, committed effort to follow a set of principles for life, namely, well-defined values. Thus, to move in the direction of values, which are the proverbial building blocks for a meaningful life, "being present," "opening up," and "doing what matters" are all required (Harris, 2019, p. 8). Whether suffering from difficult thoughts, feelings, sensations, or memories, the "Choice Point" tool can help counselors and therapists and their clients to make sense of the inner and outer challenges clients face and need for a new set of behaviors for dually relating differently to psychological pain and living a life of purpose.

As a modified "Choice Point" tool, the faith-based ACT version involves helping Christian clients to recognize the "Fork in the Road" (adapted from Harris, 2019; Hayes et al., 2012) that they are faced with as they place one foot in front of the other on the road of life. In one direction, Christian clients can walk with God in love, endure psychological pain, and live out the plan that he has for them. In the other direction, though, Christian clients can walk alone, avoid psychological pain, and attempt to create a life of purpose on their own. With the latter road, of course, Christian clients are not following Jesus and, thus, are not living out the *telos* of the Christian faith—moving from justification (i.e., being righteous before, and reconciled to, God because of Jesus), to sanctification (i.e., becoming more like Jesus), to glorification (i.e., being face to face with Jesus) (Grudem, 1994). To succinctly conceptualize the current dilemma for Christian clients, when faced with difficult thoughts, feelings, sensations, memories, situations, and relationships in the inner and outer worlds, a set of helpful behaviors is needed (i.e., "watching and enduring," "noticing and shifting," "committing and following") to walk with God in love, endure the inevitable suffering that they will experience in this fallen, broken world, and confidently head home with him. In the context of the "committing and following" pillar of faith-based ACT, Christian clients need a set of moral behaviors to guide life, drawn from God's Word, the Bible, and the life and teachings of their traveling companion, Jesus. See Figure 8.1 for counselors and

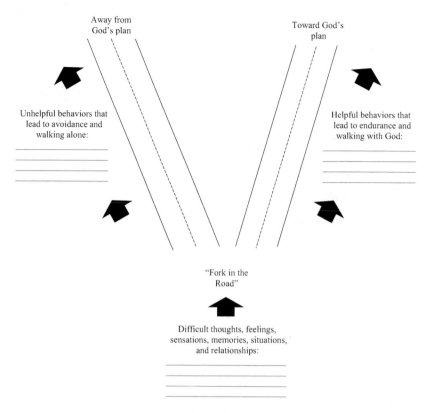

Figure 8.1 The "Fork in the Road" for Christians: "Committing and Following."
Note. Adapted from Harris (2019), Hayes (2019), and Hayes et al. (2012).
"Unhelpful" and "helpful" behaviors include those that are overt (i.e., observable, such as walking and talking) and covert (i.e., unobservable, such as thinking and feeling).

therapists to work with Christian clients to fill in the blanks and, thus, succinctly conceptualize the problem and solution to psychological suffering within the human condition, paying particular attention to the "committing and following" pillar.

Moving on to traditional ACT metaphors, the "Compass" (Harris, 2019) can be presented to help clients understand the ways in which values relate to action. Similar to a compass, values point clients in the right direction, helping them to head down an intentional path, such as east or west. Of course, consistent with a compass, values are never "achieved," meaning clients can continue to walk in a valued direction, rather than crossing a value off a list because it is somehow completed or finished. Consistent with a hiker making use of a compass to head east, a client who values loving relationships can continue to pursue them, despite the obstacles, spending the rest of their life deepening interpersonal interactions on a regular basis.

In a similar vein, many Christian clients commonly utilize passages in Scripture to guide them in life, drawing from wisdom within the Bible, rather than personally constructed values. A popular verse within the Christian tradition, Psalm 119 states, "Your word is a lamp for my feet, and a light on my path" (*New International Version Bible*, 2011, Psalm 119:105). For Christian clients, this verse can be utilized to visualize the role that virtue-based action plays in day-to-day living. In the Christian life, God's Word can serve as a lamp, guiding Christian clients on the right path, illuminating the direction they should take. Consistent with the "Compass" metaphor, following Jesus via virtue-based action involves confidently moving in the direction of God's will, with the Bible serving as the proverbial compass.

As another metaphor, "Two Kids in the Car" (Harris, 2019) involves describing a road trip with two kids in the back seat of a car, both anticipating their arrival at an important destination. The first kid is preoccupied with getting there, thinking about the future. On the other hand, the second kid is rooted in the present moment, looking around and absorbing the thrill of the ride. Indeed, both kids will end up getting to the destination, but one of them has done so in a way that balances the goal ahead with present-moment awareness. Within this metaphor, the focus is on highlighting that the experience (i.e., the pursuit of values in the present moment) should be embraced, rather than merely crossing goals off a list (i.e., getting to the destination).

Likewise, Christian clients may, at times, be preoccupied with achieving some sort of goal, getting to a future destination (e.g., Heaven), rather than following Jesus (i.e., walking with God in love) in the present moment. In other words, within the Christian contemplative tradition, life is about cultivating a deeper relationship with the God of love, which occurs in the here-and-now, rather than some sort of distant future. To modify this metaphor, counselors and therapists can ask Christian clients to envision walking with Jesus on the shore of the Sea of Galilee, with one of his disciples preoccupied with getting to the other side of the lake and the other immersing himself in the experience of fellowshipping with Jesus. Of course, both disciples will eventually get to their destination, whether it is to go with Jesus to heal the sick or teach to a crowd. Yet, one is focused on the most important part of the journey, a relationship with Jesus, while the other is distracted with a future goal.

In faith-based ACT, counselors and therapists can also discuss the "Parable of the Bags of Gold" (*New International Version Bible*, 2011, Matthew 25:14–30) with Christian clients, telling the story of three servants who were entrusted with gold as their master left on a trip. The first two servants "put [their] money to work," generating additional revenue, whereas the third servant hid his money, playing it safe in that he was afraid he would lose the money given to him. Of course, in this famous parable, the lesson seems to be that God entrusts humankind with certain talents and skills, which he hopes humans will utilize while on this planet, rather than "playing it safe." For Christian clients, a big part of following Jesus is making a genuine effort, cultivating a willingness to act, guided by a set of virtues (Barclay, 2001). Conversely, burying the money (i.e., God's blessings), focusing solely on safety and the amelioration of fear, was not the preferred outcome that the master had in mind for his servants (Barclay, 2001).

As another example, the "Two-Sided Coin" metaphor (Greco et al., 2008) can be used to help clients recognize the link between inner pain and values, gaining insight into the notion that psychological struggles help to better understand what matters most in life. As an example, on one side of the coin may be sadness about a lack of intimate relationships, which elucidates the importance of others in a client's life. To be sure, being a loving, committed friend and intimate partner may be an especially salient value, with sadness helping the client to better understand what is missing. Rather than sadness being an unhelpful emotion that needs to be eradicated, it can serve as a signal for the client, pointing to the other side of the coin.

Consistent with this traditional ACT metaphor, the Apostle James suggested that going through a variety of trials, which test Christians' faith, cultivates perseverance (James 1:2). In this passage, *hupomone* is used, meaning a hopeful, constant, patient endurance (Strong, 2001). For Christian clients, suffering within the human condition offers the ability to endure, leading to maturity. Along the way, Christian clients can pursue virtue-based action in order to develop moral excellence, emulating Jesus as their teacher. As a result, Christian clients can view psychological struggles as a "Two-Sided Coin," with psychological pain on one side and endurance, constancy, patience, maturity, and virtue-based action on the other side. By viewing these experiences as intimately linked, Christian clients are better able to embrace psychological pain, knowing that it produces maturity in the Christian life.

To offer one final example, traditional ACT utilizes the "Path Up the Mountain" metaphor (Hayes et al., 2012), which involves helping clients to stay connected to values, not giving up because there are disappointments and setbacks along the way. Like hiking up a long trail toward the top of a mountain, with "switchbacks" that lead the hiker back, forth, up, and down a mountain before reaching the top, clients may experience the "ups and downs" of life, quickly losing hope because they are not seemingly making the progress they had hoped for. Still, from a distance, they are better able to see that the trail that leads toward the top of a mountain will eventually get them there, even though they are walking back and forth, up and down.

Likewise, for Christian clients, the road they are traveling on may be difficult to navigate, with moments of fog, rain, and other environmental distractions. Indeed, they may have the thought that "I'm never going to get there," leading to discouragement and hopelessness. However, according to Scripture, Christian clients are to "Trust in the LORD with all [their] heart and lean not on [their] own understanding; in all [their] ways submit to him, and he will make [their] paths straight" (*New International Version Bible*, 2011, Proverbs 3:5–6). As a result, consistent with traditional ACT's "Path Up the Mountain" metaphor (Hayes et al., 2012), Christian clients can learn to see the path from a distance so as to continue to travel up the mountain when it seems as though they will never get there. What is more, Christian clients have a fellow traveler, Jesus, who is guiding the way and can offer a more transcendent perspective. Therefore, they can "trust in the LORD," not their own navigation system, map, and so forth, who will "make [their] paths straight."

Considering experiential exercises, traditional ACT counselors and therapists can ask clients to think about the types of qualities and strengths they currently possess, along with which ones they want to develop. Also, traditional ACT counselors and therapists commonly ask clients to discuss how they can apply several new character traits to daily living. For Christian clients, this traditional ACT approach can be modified so that they first think about several of Jesus's character strengths, turning to the gospels to make sense of how Jesus lived his life from moment to moment. Rather than identifying abstract qualities of Jesus's behavior, though, Christian clients can attempt to better understand what Jesus's strengths actually looked like as he interacted with others. From there, Christian clients can discuss the ways in which they will apply Jesus's model of love to their own life, such as serving others and forgiving their enemies through concrete actions. Here, it is important for Christian clients to better understand Jesus's approach to living life, drawing out his most salient qualities to emulate. Of course, consistent with traditional ACT, these strengths and qualities must be freely chosen, rather than forced onto the client.

As another example, traditional ACT counselors and therapists commonly employ some sort of metaphor about a funeral or tombstone (e.g., "What do you want your tombstone to eventually say about how you lived your life?") to help clients think about the life they want to live. As a related metaphor that is popular in the traditional ACT literature, clients can imagine that they are receiving a "Lifetime Achievement Award" (Harris, 2019), with everyone they know invited to the event. Because the award is such an honor to receive, friends and family members will have the opportunity to go up on stage and share about the impact the client had on their life. In this exercise, clients are asked to think about what they want loved ones to say (e.g., "He was a loving, compassionate husband who always gave of himself" versus "He played life safe and avoided pain"), which reveals the kind of life they want to live, rooted in deeply meaningful values.

For Christian clients, this traditional ACT exercise can be modified so they envision standing before God, who is reviewing their life with them. Of course, a central aim is for God to state, "Well done, good and faithful servant" (*New International Version Bible*, 2011, Matthew 25:21). Therefore, Christian clients can reflect on the types of virtues they want to live out, anchored to love, in order for

God to make this type of a statement. After all, God has entrusted humankind with certain talents, skills, resources, and abilities, which need to be cultivated and applied to life, rather than buried in a field (Matthew 25). Within this exercise, Christian clients are attempting to connect to what matters most, freely choosing to follow Jesus (i.e., walk with God in love) as their rabbi and teacher.

To offer another illustration, the "Mind-Reading Machine" exercise can be used to help clients understand the role that values play in daily living (Stoddard & Afari, 2014). Within this intervention, clients are asked to envision possessing a machine that reads minds, with the ability to actually read the mind of someone they love. In turn, the traditional ACT counselor or therapist asks the client to think about what types of comments they would like to hear, focusing on the client's strengths, relational qualities, and principles they live by. Asked differently, what does the client *want* to know others are thinking about them, especially in the context of the type of reputation they *want* to possess, assuming that they are living out a set of meaningful values?

Among Christian clients, this traditional ACT exercise can be modified to reflect God's omniscience. In other words, Christian clients can imagine they have the ability to know, maybe just briefly, how God sees them, with the faith-based ACT counselor or therapist asking what they would like to hear. In other words, if they could listen in, what would God say? What would they want him to say? Indeed, from a biblical perspective, many Christian clients would like to be a person "after God's own heart," similar to King David (*New International Version Bible*, 2011, 1 Samuel 13:14). If this is the case, how can they make this happen? How can they follow Jesus in the midst of pain, emulating him during difficult thoughts, feelings, sensations, memories, situations, and relationships? Here, it is important to note that King David was by no means a perfect man, stumbling and falling, to be sure. Yet, he possessed several virtues that are likely admirable in God's eyes, including courage, love, and faith. In fact, David courageously stepped out in faith to face Goliath (1 Samuel 17) and wrote many psalms that captured his love for God (see, e.g., Psalm 18:1).

As one final exercise, traditional ACT employs the "Role Models" technique (Harris, 2019), which asks the questions, "Who do you look up to? Who inspires you? What personal strengths or qualities do they have that you admire?" in order to tap into principles for living (p. 220). As a faith-based ACT alternative, Christian clients can ask what "fruit of the Spirit" (*New International Version Bible*, 2011, Galatians 5:22–23) they want to display in their own life? In other words,

> the nine-fold fruit of the Spirit in Galatians 5:22–23 is a beautiful picture of Jesus. For of course Jesus himself was filled with the Spirit of God, and it is Christ who dwells within us through the Spirit. So the more we are filled with God's Spirit, and the more the Spirit ripens his fruit within us, the more we will become like Christ.
>
> (Wright, 2017, p. 9)

In the Apostle Paul's letter to the Galatians, he stated the following: "But the fruit of the Spirit is love, joy, peace, [patience], kindness, goodness, faithfulness, gentleness, and self-control" (*New International Version Bible*, 2011, Galatians 5:22-23). Combined, the above quotes from Wright (2017) and the Apostle Paul convey that Christian clients are to display these qualities in daily life, which reflect Jesus. Thus, to be a dwelling place for God's love, Christian clients can look to the fruit of the Spirit as a guide. Applied to faith-based ACT, counselors and therapists working with Christian clients can help them to identify how they can display, behaviorally speaking, the aforementioned fruit, beginning with love.

In addition to conceptualizations, metaphors, and exercises, counselors and therapists working from a faith-based ACT perspective can use a modified version of the "Table of Values" handout (Stoddard & Afari, 2014), elucidated in Table 8.3. As the table reveals, Christian clients can list several virtues they want to live out across a variety of life domains, noting the concrete behaviors that will help them to follow Jesus, barriers to virtue-based action,[1] faith-based ACT processes to help them endure in spite of inner obstacles, and specific exercises that can be employed to maintain a present-moment willingness to act. Overall, this handout can be helpful for Christian clients because it offers a visual guide to organize faith-based ACT.

Regarding committed action, ACT counselors and therapists commonly use metaphors to help clients better understand the importance of putting values into practice in the here-and-now, rather than at some later point in time. For example, traditional ACT's "Traveling Partners" metaphor (Stoddard & Afari, 2014) involves describing an important vacation that the client plans on taking,

Table 8.3 Biblical Virtues, Virtue-Based Behaviors, Barriers to Virtues, and Faith-Based ACT Processes, Metaphors, Exercises, and Skills to Address Barriers

	Intimate Partner	Family	Friends	Church	Work	Community	Physical Health	Hobbies
Biblical virtues								
Specific behaviors to live out the virtues								
Barriers to living out the virtues								
Faith-based ACT processes to focus on								
Metaphors, exercises, and skills for balancing acceptance and action								

Note. Adapted from Stoddard and Afari (2014).

with an understanding that the client has been eagerly anticipating the trip for some time. When the client arrives at the bus station, they notice that there is a range of different personality types getting on the bus. Of course, some are pleasant, with good hygiene and polite manners. Yet, many seem to be rather self-focused, engaging in loud, somewhat obnoxious exchanges, with less than stellar hygiene. When the client sees this scenario, they realize there is an important decision to make—go home, canceling the trip in the process, or accept that there will be a variety of individuals they will interact with on the journey, paralleling the ups and downs of the inner world.

In a similar vein, Christian clients can envision being called by Jesus to follow him, dropping their fishing net on the shore of the Sea of Galilee. With this decision, though, comes the realization that Jesus has called others on this journey, too, with some having "annoying" habits, along with hygiene that falls short of an ideal standard. However, the client has a decision to make—follow Jesus (i.e., walk with God in love) and learn to live with the fact that Jesus has called a variety of people to follow him, or go back to fishing, realizing that the opportunity of a lifetime was passed up. Indeed, for Christian clients, the inner world can easily parallel the variation among Jesus's disciples, with a denying Peter, a doubting Thomas, and a betraying Judas. There may also be an anxious disciple, along with disciples who struggle with recurrent sadness, a history of trauma, or relational problems. For Christian clients, the goal is to continue to follow Jesus, learning from him and living out his teachings, despite imperfect inner obstacles.

To present another example, sports metaphors can be helpful to draw a contrast between watching on the sidelines of life and actually playing in the game (Luoma et al., 2017). To offer an illustration, traditional ACT counselors and therapists might describe a professional hockey game, noting how exciting the action is on the ice. As the players skate around, trying to score, there is a sense of urgency and purpose in the arena. Yet, for many clients, they are watching the game from the "cheap seats," barely able to see the game that is unfolding because of their distance from the sporting event. Certainly, this metaphor captures the struggle that clients have with "getting in the game," hesitating to take action because of cognitive fusion and experiential avoidance. Some clients, of course, may say, "I can't play hockey. I don't want to be on the ice." Or, many clients will stay in the "nose-bleed section" of the arena because of a fear of the unknown (e.g., "What if a fight breaks out or I get hurt?"). Still, there can be additional pain, with clients struggling to feel connected to the event, recognizing that watching from afar, although safe, is deeply unfulfilling.

Applying this concept to faith-based ACT, Christian clients can draw a contrast between Jesus's disciples and the Pharisees. In other words, do they want to follow Jesus, experiencing the excitement, fulfillment, and meaning that come from learning from their rabbi? Or do Christian clients want to watch the action unfold, judging from a safe distance, like the Pharisees? For Bonhoeffer (1955), a 20th-century Lutheran theologian, judgment is antithetical to action, with the Pharisees being preoccupied with knowledge of good and evil, at the expense of simple action and love. Therefore, a contrast can be drawn between Jesus's disciples, who were called to love, serve, and share the gospel message, and the Pharisees, who employed knowledge of good and evil and legalism to judge from a cautious, detached position. To be sure, for Christian clients, a central question is as follows: "Will I follow Jesus, engaging in loving action along the way, or stand by from a remote location and critically watch Jesus fulfill his mission?"

To cultivate a deeper awareness of committed action for traditional ACT clients, counselors and therapists can apply the "Walking the Path" exercise (Stoddard & Afari, 2014). In this exercise, the counselor or therapist describes some sort of area in the wilderness, noting that the client is creating a new path as they walk, which can be difficult work, given the thorns, brush, dirt, and other obstacles that are in the way. Off in the distance, however, is a well-worn path, which seems like it would be easier to trek across. Still, this previously trodden trail is all too familiar to the client, given that they have walked on it many times before, leading to behaviors and life events that have kept them stuck. Undoubtedly, this visual exercise helps the client to recognize the importance of continuing to move forward, despite a tendency for the mind to try to convince them that turning around and walking along a previous path is a better use of time and energy.

For Christian clients, faith-based ACT counselors and therapists can guide them through an exercise focused on the decision that Jesus's disciples had to make when they dropped everything they had previously known to follow him. Whether they were fishing on the Sea of Galilee or engaging in some other family trade in the heat of the sun, letting go of the tendency to want to go back to the old way, bravely and courageously moving forward into unknown territory, was the central aim. To be sure, from a Christian perspective, those who let go of their old life will surely find new life when following Jesus (Luke 17:33). Because of this, embracing an attitude of willingness to endure unpleasant inner experiences is foundational, simultaneously following Jesus (i.e., walking with God in love), living out a set of virtues that are anchored to the Bible, and focusing on building moral character that is pleasing to God.

To provide an additional exercise, traditional ACT counselors and therapists frequently use the *FEAR* and *ACT* acronyms to help clients identify barriers to effective action (Hayes et al., 2012). Christian clients can modify these acronyms by integrating their faith. As an example, with *FEAR*, clients commonly fuse with self-derived knowledge (rather than leaning on God for understanding); evaluate inner and outer experiences as "bad" (instead of sitting at the feet of Jesus with attentive nonjudgment); avoid inner and outer experiences (rather than follow Jesus); and offer reasons to explain why they simply cannot fully commit to virtue-based action in the here-and-now, walking away sad like the Rich Young Ruler (Mark 10:17–27).

On the contrary, for *ACT*, Christian clients can accept unpleasant inner experiences, enduring in their symbolic "cell" because the God of love is with them. By doing this, Christian clients can nurture a deeper awareness of God's active, loving presence and commit to a virtue-based direction by following Jesus (i.e., walking with God in love), letting go of prior distractions in order to faithfully follow him. These acronyms can be written down on some sort of small card or paper, with Christian clients carrying it around throughout the week to identify barriers to following Jesus and strategies to continue to walk with the God of love on the road of life.

To be more succinct, as a reminder from the introduction to the book, "love" can be gently repeated within as *the* "prayer word" or short phrase in the Christian life (Laird, 2006), which represents both a willingness to surrender the inner world to God's loving presence and commitment to live a life of virtuous love toward others, with the God of love as the guide. In other words, the *FEAR* and *ACT* acronyms can be condensed to "God is love" (or simply just "love") as an "outside-in" (i.e., justification, or being right before, and reconciled to, God because of Jesus) to "inside-out" (i.e., sanctification, or becoming more like Jesus) process (Grudem, 1994; *New International Version Bible*, 2011, 1 John 4:7–21). With this short word or phrase, Christian clients are practicing shifting from self to Other/other, which is at the core of faith-based ACT, that is, gently pivoting, in love, from a preoccupation with the self (i.e., distracting, self-derived thoughts, feelings, sensations, and memories) to sustained attention on God and others, exemplified by the two greatest commandments (Matthew 22:36–40).

To add a more relational understanding to this process, in the contemporary mindfulness literature, interpersonal mindfulness consists of at least four ingredients in the context of conversations with others, including presence (e.g., being fully engaged in conversations with others in the here-and-now, rather than distracted or preoccupied), an awareness of the self and others (e.g., being fully aware of personal thoughts, feelings, facial expressions, and body expressions, as well as those of others, during conversations), nonjudgmental acceptance (e.g., being accepting and uncritical of others' perspectives and behaviors in conversations, with no desire to change them), and nonreactivity (e.g., being deliberate in slowing down to monitor personal thoughts and feelings, as well as those of others, before responding to others in conversations) (Pratscher et al., 2019). In a recent study among community adults, interpersonal mindfulness was negatively correlated with depression, anxiety, and stress (Pratscher et al., 2019). Although further research is needed on the role that interpersonal mindfulness plays in daily life, including the application of personally derived values to relational exchanges with others, it may hold promise as a strategy for extending some of the more popular traditional ACT values to others (e.g., compassion, kindness). As a faith-based ACT alternative, a four-step model, which combines the six processes of traditional ACT, contemplation, and the story of Mary and Martha in Luke's gospel, can be employed (adapted from Hayes et al., 2012; Knabb, 2021). This model consists of noticing unpleasant inner experiences (e.g., thoughts, feelings, sensations, memories), shifting from an "earthly-minded" to "heavenly-minded" perspective (Burroughs, 2010, 2014; Rowe, 1672), accepting unpleasant inner experiences because the God of love is present, and acting toward others based on a set of biblical virtues as a proverbial road map.

As a quick example, a Christian client with generalized anxiety disorder may struggle with recurrent worry, catastrophizing about the uncertainty of relationships in a fallen, broken world. In this case, the counselor or therapist can work with the Christian client to (a) notice when worry is occurring (e.g., "There's worry"), (b) shift from an "earthly-minded" to "heavenly-minded" perspective with a short "reset" word or phrase from Scripture that reminds the Christian client to pivot from self-derived knowledge to God-derived love (e.g., "God is love"; *New International Version Bible*, 2011, 1 John 4:7–21), (c) accept the worry with a bit more distance because the God of love is present, doing so with a concise self-reminder that emanates from the Bible as God's Word (e.g., "Jesus said not to worry about tomorrow and, instead, focus on today because God will provide"; Matthew 6:25–34), and (d) act in relationships based on Jesus's teachings, not worry (e.g., "Jesus said to 'love one another' [*New International Version Bible*, 2011, John 13:34–35]; therefore, I'm going to invest in other people today, rather than let worry get in the way of being a vehicle for God's love").

In addition to conceptualizations, metaphors, and exercises, traditional ACT counselors and therapists commonly use worksheets to help clients take effective action in the midst of psychological pain. For instance, a modified version of the "Willingness and Action Plan" (Harris, 2009), revealed in Table 8.4, can help Christian clients to better understand the link between biblical virtues, goals, barriers, Scripture, and action. Of course, cardinal and theological virtues emanate from the Bible. Also, the goals are *MAPS* (Chang et al., 2013).

Table 8.4 Faith-Based ACT "Commit and Follow" Plan

Biblical virtues I will rely on to "commit and follow"
    Virtues (biblical)
    Goals (*MAPS*)
    Behaviors (observable)
Inner experiences I will "watch and endure"
    Thoughts
    Emotions
    Sensations
    Memories
Bible verses I will rely on to "commit and follow"
    Jesus's teachings
    Other verses in the Bible

Note. Adapted from Harris (2009).

In other words, they are measurable, meaning they are quantifiable (e.g., "I will exercise three times this week"), attainable (i.e., realistically doable), positive (i.e., phrased as something the client *will* do, rather than *will not* do), and specific (i.e., precise, rather than vague or abstract). In addition, the behaviors are observable activities (e.g., "If I were living out this value and pursuing this goal, what would I notice if I were recording myself with a video camera?"). In sum, worksheets provide a visual aid, helping Christian clients gain insight into important biblical virtues, goals to put the biblical virtues into action, obstacles they will inevitably face, and ways to overcome the roadblocks.

To summarize, a variety of ACT conceptualizations, metaphors, exercises, and worksheets can be modified for Christian clients. Central to this faith-based ACT modification strategy is the awareness that biblical virtues, rather than the more general term "values," are a culturally sensitive alternative for Christian clients, especially because virtues are anchored to both the Bible and Christian tradition. What is more, biblical virtues will naturally emanate from Jesus's life and teachings, given that Christians are to follow him. Yet, some sort of abstract notion of virtues is by no means the end result or goal. Instead, Christian clients must have a willingness to live out the aforementioned biblical virtues, following Jesus in the midst of psychological pain and enduring inevitable suffering. Whether the focus is on adding Jesus to a traditional ACT conceptualization, metaphor, or exercise to help Christian clients imagine Jesus is with them in their pain, Christian clients can begin to head in a virtue-based direction. This, without a doubt, is in contrast to merely gaining insight into a distant, abstract idea about a life devoted to following Jesus. Before concluding this chapter, though, a case example is offered so as to deepen this understanding of virtue-based action in the Christian life.

A Clinical Example of Committing and Following

Helen, a White female in her late 20s, presented to therapy following the painful news that her husband of five years had died in a car accident while drinking and driving. For Helen, life was extremely painful in her adult years, with the "honeymoon phase" of her marriage quickly ending when she learned that her husband had been hiding a serious problem with alcohol. Shocked and hurt by the realization that she "did not know [her] husband anymore," she felt deeply betrayed and fearful that he was hiding other "secrets" as well. Because of this, Helen began to experience heightened generalized anxiety, struggling to come to grips with his concealed life. What is more, she began to lose faith in God, who she believed was absent from her life, given her understanding that her marriage was supposed to be blessed by him.

In their relationship, her husband had become increasingly withholding, leaving for days on end without telling her where he was going. When he would return, he was rather cold and elusive, denying there was an issue they needed to discuss. Over time, Helen's efforts to reach for comfort turned to indifference, given that she simply "could not cry anymore." About three months before his death, she moved out of their house, asking for a separation because she "did not know what else to do."

As soon as she pulled away, her husband began to pursue her, promising that he would stop drinking and pleading with her to go with him to couple therapy, which she agreed to do. In therapy, her husband begged her to return home, making some progress in his own life by remaining sober and seemingly desiring to improve their marriage. Yet, because of her pain, Helen turned down his offer, electing to continue to live alone. One night, a few weeks after she declined to move back home, she got a phone call letting her know he had died in a three-car accident on the freeway, likely as a result of being intoxicated.

In therapy, Helen blamed herself, believing that it was her fault he started drinking again. She also blamed God, who she perceived to be absent from her life, and vowed that she would "never love again," stating that she deserved to be single because she "ruined" her marriage. In her anger, she reported that she could not trust that God would protect her from another "failed" marriage.

As a recurrent struggle after his death, Helen constantly asked herself "What if …" questions, attempting to turn back time to prevent the tragedy from occurring. She also described feeling extremely isolated and alone, with her well-intentioned Christian friends simply offering Bible verses and "clichés" to help, which did not seem to ameliorate a deep sense of loss, guilt, and shame. Because of her inner distress, she stopped going to church, something she used to love to do, avoided praying, given her anger toward God, and discontinued leading a ministry within her congregation.

With the help of her faith-based ACT therapist, Helen began to recognize that she was fusing with a variety of statements, most of which revolved around self-blame and blaming God. Also, she was increasingly avoiding unpleasant emotions through social isolation and hiding from God, fearing she would run into church friends that "did not get it," quickly getting overwhelmed with both anger and sadness. Employing several cognitive defusion and acceptance strategies, along with contemplative prayer, she was able to learn to sit at the feet of Jesus without her mind jumping in to interpret the tragedy, receiving his grace and mercy in her time of need.

What is more, she was able to identify several biblical virtues she wanted to live by, even in the midst of an uncertain future and a grieving process she feared would never end. Thus, she identified hope, love, faith, and courage as particular biblical virtues she wanted to pursue, developing concrete goals and behaviors that would help her to follow Jesus in the midst of her pain. Over time, she was increasingly willing to endure, following Jesus even though she did not know what the future would hold. She started going to church again and volunteering in a ministry and eventually remarried about three years later. Guided by a set of well-defined virtues, she was able to utilize a proverbial map to follow Jesus, slowly grieving a devastating, tragic loss.

Conclusion

In this chapter, the "committing and following" pillar of faith-based ACT was explored, integrating ACT and the Christian faith. For Christian clients experiencing recurrent distress, the cardinal and theological virtues can offer a stable compass, helping them to follow Jesus in the here-and-now, rather than being guided by wavering, impermanent inner states that fluctuate and change from moment to moment. Yet, virtues, or moral excellence (and corresponding moral behaviors), are intimately linked to action, rather than serving as some sort of abstract understanding of the way life *should* be. Because of this, Christian clients must have a willingness to endure the inner pain, faithfully following Jesus, despite a variety of obstacles, reminiscent of Christians in the first-century church. In the remaining four chapters, I review specific ways to conceptualize and treat Christian clients with depression, anxiety, trauma, and relational problems, integrating a traditional ACT and Christian view of the world. Included in the remaining chapters are assessment strategies and a session-by-session discussion for working with these problems, conditions, and disorders in counseling and therapy.

Notes

1　Unless otherwise noted, the ACT themes and concepts within this chapter are from Harris (2019), Hayes (2005), Hayes (2019), Hayes et al. (2012), and Luoma et al. (2017).
2　Interestingly, many of these virtues overlap with "common" values for ACT clients, including courage, persistence, justice, love, and trust (Harris, 2013).
3　These themes, especially mercy and reconciliation, seem to overlap with Harris's (2013) traditional ACT values, including cooperation, generosity, and compassion.
4　Interestingly, several contemplative authors throughout the ages, such as John Cassian, have suggested that proactively envisioning barriers to virtuous living can help to anticipate what may get in the way of moral excellence, responding in a way that emulates Jesus (Trader, 2011).

References

Austin, M., & Geivett, D. (Eds.). (2012). *Being good: Christian virtues for everyday life*. Wm. B. Eerdmans Publishing Co.
Barclay, W. (2001). *The gospel of Matthew: Volume two*. Westminster John Knox Press.
Bonhoeffer, D. (1955). *Ethics*. Touchstone.
Bourgeault, C. (2004). *Centering prayer and inner awakening*. Cowley Publications.
Burroughs, J. (2010). *Heavenly-mindedness recommended: In a discourse on Colossians 3:2*. Gale ECCO.
Burroughs, J. (2014). *A treatise on earthly-mindedness*. GLH Publishing.
Burton-Christie, D. (1993). *The word in the desert: Scripture and the quest for holiness in early Christian monasticism*. Oxford University Press.

Chang, V., Scott, S., & Decker, C. (2013). *Developing helping skills: A step-by-step approach to competency* (2nd ed.). Brooks/Cole.

Coniaris, A. (1998). *Philokalia. The Bible of orthodox spirituality.* Light & Life Publishing Company.

Coniaris, A. (2004). *Confronting and controlling thoughts according to the fathers of the Philokalia.* Light & Life Publishing Company.

Cook, C. (2011). *The Philokalia and mental wellbeing.* James Clarke and Co.

Chryssavgis, J. (2008). *In the heart of the desert: The spirituality of the desert fathers and mothers.* World Wisdom, Inc.

Greco, L., Barnett, E., Blomquist, K., & Gevers, A. (2008). Acceptance, body image, and health in adolescence. In L. Greco & S. Hayes (Eds.), *Acceptance & mindfulness for children & adolescents: A practitioner's guide* (pp. 187–216). New Harbinger Publications, Inc.

Grudem, W. (1994). *Systematic theology: An introduction to biblical doctrine.* Zondervan.

Harmless, W. (2008). *Mystics.* Oxford University Press.

Harrington, D., & Keenan, J. (2002). *Jesus and virtue ethics: Building bridges between New Testament studies and moral theology.* Rowman & Littlefield Publishers, Inc.

Harrington, D., & Keenan, J. (2010). *Paul and virtue ethics: Building bridges between New Testament studies and moral theology.* Rowman & Littlefield Publishers, Inc.

Harris, R. (2009). *ACT made simple. An easy-to-read primer on acceptance and commitment therapy.* New Harbinger Publications, Inc.

Harris, R. (2013). *Getting unstuck in ACT: A clinician's guide to overcoming common obstacles in acceptance and commitment therapy.* New Harbinger Publications, Inc.

Harris, R. (2019). *ACT made simple: An easy-to-read primer on acceptance and commitment therapy* (2nd ed.). New Harbinger Publications, Inc.

Hayes, S. (2005). *Get out of your mind and into your life: The new acceptance & commitment therapy.* New Harbinger Publications, Inc.

Hayes, S. (2019). *A liberated mind: How to pivot toward what matters.* Avery.

Hayes, S., Strosahl, K., & Wilson, K. (2012). *Acceptance and commitment therapy: The process and practice of mindful change* (2nd ed.). The Guilford Press.

Iskander, A. (2005). *Practical spirituality according to the desert fathers.* Saint Mary's Coptic Orthodox Church.

Knabb, J. (2021). *Christian meditation in clinical practice: A four-step model and workbook for therapists and clients.* InterVarsity Press.

Knabb, J., Vazquez, V., Wang, K., & Bates, M. (2018). Unknowing in the 21st century: Humble detachment for Christians with repetitive negative thinking. *Spirituality in Clinical Practice, 5,* 170–187.

Kreeft, P. (2014). *Practical theology: Spiritual direction from Saint Thomas Aquinas.* Ignatius Press.

Laird, M. (2006). *Into the silent land: A guide to the Christian practice of contemplation.* Oxford University Press.

Lane, B. (1998). *The solace of fierce landscapes: Exploring desert and mountain spirituality.* Oxford University Press.

Luoma, J., Hayes, S., & Walser, R. (2017). *Learning ACT: An acceptance and commitment therapy skills training manual for therapists* (2nd ed.). Context Press.

New International Version Bible. (2011). Zondervan. https://www.biblegateway.com/

Paintner, C. (2012). *Desert fathers and mothers: Early Christian wisdom sayings.* SkyLight Paths Publishing.

Pratscher, S., Wood, P., King, L., & Bettencourt, B. (2019). Interpersonal mindfulness: Scale development and initial construct validation. *Mindfulness, 10,* 1044–1061.

Rowe, J. (1672). *Heavenly-mindedness and earthly-mindedness: In two parts.* Francis Tyton.

Ryrie, A. (2011). *The desert movement: Fresh perspectives on the spirituality of the desert.* Canterbury Press Norwich.

Stoddard, J., & Afari, N. (2014). *The big book of ACT metaphors: A practitioner's guide to experiential exercises & metaphors in acceptance & commitment therapy.* New Harbinger Publications, Inc.

Strong, J. (2001). *The new Strong's expanded dictionary of the words in the Greek New Testament.* Thomas Nelson.

Tan, S. (2006). *Full service: Moving from self-service Christianity to total servanthood.* Baker Books.

Trader, S. (2011). *Ancient Christian wisdom and Aaron Beck's cognitive therapy: A meeting of the minds.* Peter Lang Publishing, Inc.

Ward, B. (2003). *The desert fathers: Sayings of the early Christian monks.* Penguin Books.

Welsh, R., & Knabb, J. (2009). Renunciation of the self in psychotherapy. *Mental Health, Religion & Culture, 12,* 401–414.

Wright, C. (2017). *Cultivating the fruit of the Spirit: Growing in Christlikeness.* InterVarsity Press.

Wright, N. (2010). *After you believe: Why Christian character matters.* HarperCollins Publishers.

Yadavaia, J., & Hayes, S. (2009). Values in acceptance and commitment therapy: A comparison with four other approaches. *Hellenic Journal of Psychology, 6,* 244–272.

Yearley, L. (1990). Recent work on virtue. *Religious Studies Review, 16,* 1–9.

9

FAITH-BASED ACT FOR DEPRESSION

Introduction

In the ninth chapter, traditional acceptance and commitment therapy (ACT) processes are applied to depression, covering a theoretical overview of depression, a Christian understanding of depression, Christian contemplative writings on the topic, and faith-based ACT strategies for depression. Because depression is one of the leading sources of disability in the workplace (Goldberg & Steury, 2001), and because residual symptoms and relapse are quite common (Nierenberg et al., 2003; Thase, 2003), the focus is on ways for Christian clients to relate differently to symptoms so as to buffer against additional bouts of depression. In fact, mindfulness-based cognitive therapy (MBCT) suggests that low mood alone does not lead to depression (Segal et al., 2012). Instead, ruminating about the low mood via unhelpful interpretations results in a sort of "snowballing" of depressive symptomatology (Segal et al., 2012). Overall, a central tenet throughout the chapter is that nonjudgmental, compassionate, and kind awareness of Jesus's loving presence can help Christian clients to buffer against future episodes of depression; this, combined with living a life devoted to Christian virtues, can assist Christian clients in embracing the pain of presence and ameliorating the pain of absence (Hayes, 2005).

MBCT for Depression

In MBCT, theorists suggest that recurrent depression stems from catastrophic interpretations of low mood, leading to a sort of "snowball" effect (Segal et al., 2012). In other words, for individuals vulnerable to recurrent depression, unhelpful thinking, including rumination, is employed during moments of low mood, which leads to heightened sadness and additional forms of unproductive thinking (Segal et al., 2012). Because clients experiencing sadness cannot think their way out of the experience, this struggle leads to exacerbated symptoms, turning into major depressive disorder (Segal et al., 2012).

As noted in earlier chapters, MBCT distinguishes the "doing" and "being" modes of the mind, with the "doing" mode creating problems for clients

DOI: 10.4324/9781003181941-10

experiencing low mood, given the emphasis on "fixing" and problem solving, along with the struggle to stay grounded in the present moment (Segal et al., 2012). On the other hand, when in the "being" mode, there is no other place to be and no other state to be achieved, with clients staying firmly grounded in the here-and-now (Segal et al., 2012). As a result, the "being" mode is preferred during moments of low mood, especially since clients' moods will inevitably dip, leading to the need to relate to such inner states with nonjudgment, compassion, and kindness (Segal et al., 2012).

To accomplish this, mindfulness is employed to help clients experience the low mood directly, without the mind jumping in to negatively evaluate the experience (Segal et al., 2012). In turn, clients can simply allow the drop in mood to run its natural course, without leading to the reestablishment of ingrained, unhelpful thinking patterns, generating doomsday scenarios about even mild forms of sadness (Segal et al., 2012). Above all else, cultivating an attitude of open, nonjudgmental compassion and kindness, rather than relying on the ruminative mind to "dig out" of the experience, can help clients to ameliorate depression, given there is no resulting "snowball" effect that leads to relapse (Segal et al., 2012).

Traditional ACT for Depression

In traditional ACT, depression is viewed as a form of experiential avoidance, functioning to circumvent unpleasant inner experiences through escape strategies (e.g., social isolation, low energy level, *anhedonia*) (Batten, 2011; Zettle, 2004). As a milder form of depression, *dysphoria* can actually help clients to let go of efforts to pursue goals that are unattainable, offering rest in order to come up with an alternative, more productive strategy (Zettle, 2007). To be sure, at a certain point, individuals need to protect against the loss of vital energy, with dysphoria serving this purpose, helping clients to avoid making poor, impulsive decisions about how to resolve future problems (Zettle, 2007). Still, when overly relying on this need for rest and restoration, avoidance can get in the way of value-based living.

In addition, clients with depressive symptoms tend to fuse with the world of language—including judgments about unpleasant inner experiences (e.g., low mood)—which exacerbates suffering (Zettle, 2007). Stated differently, when a client experiences a drop in mood, this experience can be catastrophized, leading to a sort of panic, along with attempts to eradicate the low mood through "problem solving." Indeed, traditional ACT refers to this overreliance on language during moments of distress as the "problem-solving mode of mind" (Hayes et al., 2012, p. 56), consistent with MBCT's "doing" mode (Segal et al., 2012). In either case, these efforts to "fix" fail to fully eliminate distressing experiences, leading to a depressive episode and a sense of hopelessness.

Beyond solely evaluating the inner experience of low mood, clients with depression tend to fuse with a variety of other cognitions, including those focused on the future (e.g., "My future is hopeless"), their sense of self (e.g.,

"I'm worthless"), the world in which they live (e.g., "Life is meaningless"), and diagnostic labels (e.g., "I'm depressed") (Batten, 2011). Similar to experiential avoidance, this struggle can get in the way of value-based living, undermining clients' efforts to live a vibrant, meaningful life. In fact, clients with depression may commonly fuse with a verbal, storied self that tells them they are defective, sabotaging attempts to do what truly matters (Zettle, 2007).

In terms of effectiveness, this strategy of experiential avoidance is extremely limited, with clients struggling to relate to inner pain as a ubiquitous, normal part of life. Undoubtedly, *anhedonia* and fatigue can help clients to withdraw from the world for a period of time, avoiding a range of distressing inner states, such as sadness and guilt (Batten, 2011). Yet, this social isolation can undermine the ability to live by a set of action-based values. What is more, this short-term strategy does not permanently eradicate psychological pain. In other words, employing experiential avoidance, relying on the "problem-solving mode of mind," does not work in the long run, getting in the way of value-based living. In fact, Hayes et al. (2012) argued that suicide (or at least recurrent ideation, which is common among clients with depressive symptoms) is the ultimate act of experiential avoidance, with many suicidal clients concluding that the pain of life is not worth enduring.

In traditional ACT, clients learn mindfulness strategies to accept unpleasant inner experiences, defuse from unhelpful cognitions, and connect to the present moment, rather than avoiding symptoms and overly relying on the mind to make sense of them, consistent with MBCT. In a state of cognitive defusion and experiential acceptance, clients can begin to connect to the here-and-now, observing the inner world, rather than ruminating or engaging in attempts to suppress unhelpful thinking (Zettle, 2007). In turn, clients are able to focus on the pursuit of meaningful values, accepting the pain of presence and ameliorating the pain of absence (Hayes, 2005).

Mindfulness and Psychological Flexibility

For both MBCT and traditional ACT counselors and therapists, mindfulness is used to help clients relate to instances of low mood with nonjudgment, flexibility, and openness, rather than overly relying on problem-solving to make sense of the experience (Hayes et al., 2012; Segal et al., 2012). In other words, rather than utilizing the "doing" mode of the mind by trying to close the gap between how things are and how they should be, clients can transition to the "being" mode, rooting themselves in the present moment and nonjudgmentally accepting the experience (Segal et al., 2012). When this occurs, clients are able to allow inner pain to run its natural course, rather than fighting against it through rumination, experiential avoidance, or other strategies that do not work over the long haul.

Although milder versions of depression can be helpful, conserving vital energy in order to make effective decisions (rather than wasting resources when future goals cannot successfully be attained), shutting down for longer periods gets in the way of value-based living (Zettle, 2007). Because of this, mindfulness can help clients to accept the inner world, defusing from unhelpful thought content about the self, the world, and the future (Beck et al., 1979) and letting go of attempts to problem-solve and ruminate, given that low mood cannot be "fixed." Interestingly, in the past decade or so, mindfulness-based approaches have been increasingly explored in the counseling and therapy literature, with promising results for clients with depressive symptoms.

Research on Mindfulness-Based Counseling and Therapy for Depression

Before discussing a Christian understanding of depression, along with faith-based ACT strategies, it is important to note that several meta-analyses have recently elucidated that mindfulness-based approaches are helpful in treating depression. For example, Hofmann et al. (2010) found a medium effect pre- to post-treatment when examining mindfulness as an intervention for mood symptoms across 39 studies, along with a large effect when examining four studies with participants with depressive disorders. Although the meta-analysis focused primarily on *mindfulness-based stress reduction* (MBSR) and MBCT, traditional ACT also uses mindfulness as a central intervention for clients with depression, adding a values component to emphasize value-based action.

Moreover, A-Tjak et al. (2015) examined eight studies on traditional ACT for anxiety/depression, revealing a small effect when comparing traditional ACT with a control condition post-treatment. As another example, Twohig and Levin (2017) explored 36 randomized trials on traditional ACT for depression and anxiety, concluding that "ACT appears to be more efficacious than waitlist conditions and treatment-as-usual, with largely equivalent effects relative to traditional cognitive behavioral therapy" (p. 751). More recently, Bai et al. (2020) examined 18 studies on traditional ACT for depression, revealing a medium effect size when comparing traditional ACT with a control condition post-treatment. Finally, as noted in an earlier chapter, the American Psychological Association (APA) currently lists traditional ACT as having modest research support for treating depression.[1] In addition to a theoretical and empirical understanding of mindfulness-based interventions for depression, a Christian conceptualization of depression can help counselors and therapists to more effectively work with Christian clients in faith-based ACT.

Christianity and Depression

For both MBCT and traditional ACT theorists, depression stems from unhelpful avoidance strategies, with clients unsuccessfully employing the "doing" mode to try to "fix" depressive symptoms (Hayes et al., 2012; Segal et al., 2012).

Unfortunately, this strategy does not tend to work, given that psychological pain is both ubiquitous and unavoidable in life. Thus, mindfulness can help clients to shift to the "being" mode, accepting low mood with nonjudgment in order to allow it to run its natural course without further intensifying the experience by relying on the mind's often inaccurate interpretations (Hayes et al., 2012; Segal et al., 2012).

With Christian clients, the Bible includes countless examples of human suffering, such as instances of loss and sadness (Yarhouse et al., 2005). As a matter of fact, a variety of biblical figures, such as Job and Jeremiah, powerfully articulated their inner distress within the pages of the Bible (Yarhouse et al., 2005). During moments of depression, Christian clients may doubt God's presence or question his existence, isolating themselves, not reaching out to him for comfort (Yarhouse et al., 2005). Coupled with a sense of hopelessness, some Christian clients may actually blame God, assuming that life should be free of penetrating sadness and loss.

In fact, the psychology of religion and spirituality literature has increasingly explored both positive and negative forms of religious coping in response to stressful life events. Specifically, positive forms of religious coping involve collaborating with God, seeking his help, asking him for forgiveness, and attempting to understand how God might be using the situation for spiritual or psychological growth (Pargament et al., 2011). On the other hand, negative religious coping constitutes doubting God's love and availability in the midst of suffering and believing God is using the adversity as a form of punishment (Pargament et al., 2011). Interestingly, in a study among a sample of churchgoing Christians, positive religious coping seemed to buffer the impact that negative life events had on depressive symptoms, with the authors concluding that some Christians may view adversities as a source of growth, emanating from God, with this understanding protecting against a sense of hopelessness and depression (Bjorck & Thurman, 2007). As a more recent study, among a sample of Christian college students, I found that surrendering to God as a form of religious coping was negatively associated with perseverative thinking (Knabb et al., 2018), which reveals that Christian clients may benefit from practicing God's presence within the inner world, which can help with rumination, brooding, worry, and other unhelpful modes of thinking that are often linked to emotional disorders (e.g., depressive, anxiety).

To be sure, Christian clients can certainly find meaning in suffering, yielding to the God of love to illuminate a purpose in the midst of the depressive episode and related repetitive thinking pattern (e.g., rumination) that may be keeping them stuck in life. As Yarhouse et al. (2005) revealed, "We suspect that God ultimately cares more about what he can teach us through depression than about the ways depression can be relieved" (p. 171). Indeed, experiences like depression can allow Christians to reach out to God, relying on his loving care when they do not understand the meaning behind depressive episodes. Similar to many of the lament psalms in the Bible, Christian clients can cry out to God in the midst of pain, trusting in him when the human mind has no satisfactory answer for suffering.

This ability to rest in God's perfect love, of course, can be cultivated through contemplative practice, similar to Mary sitting at the feet of Jesus. Rather than engaging in the "doing" mode, consisting of trying to "fix" instances of low mood (Segal et al., 2012), Christian clients can shift to the "being" mode, surrendering to God's protective care in order to allow the sadness to run its natural course. Although, from a Christian perspective, the fall of humankind has resulted in vulnerabilities like depression (McMinn & Campbell, 2007), Christian clients can find hope in God's active, loving presence, enduring because Jesus modeled virtue-based action in the midst of suffering. To be certain, drawing on Psalm 46, Christians can drop their metaphorical weapons in the midst of battle, ceasing all unnecessary striving and recognizing that God is present, offering protection (Earwood, 1989).

What follows is a review of the early desert Christians' understanding of sadness, weeping, and tears. Although there is not always a one-to-one correspondence between early contemplative authors' understanding of inner distress and a 21st-century conceptualization of depression as a psychological disorder, the following explication can help Christian clients better understand how some of the early desert Christians made sense of painful experiences such as enduring sadness, employing contemplative practice to draw closer to God during moments of suffering. In fact, there have been several recent attempts to explore the overlap between depression and compulsive thoughts (*logismoi* in Greek) (Cook, 2011; MacQuarrie, 2012).

The Contemplative Tradition, Depression, and Metacognition[2]

Among the early desert Christians, two types of *logismoi*, *sadness* and *acedia*, seem to resemble (on at least a general level) the 21st-century experience of depression.[3] For the fourth-century monk Evagrius of Ponticus, sadness involves desire that is frustrated, a "dejection of the soul," which leads to suffering, distraction from contemplation, and a "dulling of the mind" (Cook, 2011, p. 28). Certainly, Evagrius of Ponticus's sadness has been described as both a "devouring lion" and "bound prisoner who cannot run" (Cook, 2011, p. 28). According to Evagrius, contemplation is a central aim, with the *logismoi*, including sadness, distracting from this endeavor. Frequently, the early desert dwellers would experience sadness because of what they gave up in their pursuit of the desert life (Leloup, 2003). To combat sadness, the virtue of joy was cultivated by the early desert Christians. In fact, the early desert monks frequently sought a "spirit of poverty" in response to sadness, meaning that everything in the world is viewed as a gift from God (Leloup, 2003). Rather than holding on to a sense of entitlement, similar to some wealthy, privileged individuals, the early desert monks would cultivate gratitude toward simple blessings, like a meal, shelter, and even existence itself (Leloup, 2003).

As another example, Evagrius of Pontius described *acedia*, the "noonday demon" and "heaviest" of the *logismoi*, as "wind that bends a delicate plant" (Cook, 2011, p. 25; Harmless, 2004, p. 326). In other words, *acedia* involves a "restless boredom," fueled by discouragement and doubt and leading to trouble concentrating (Harmless, 2004, p. 326; Leloup, 2003). Because the early desert Christians spent quite a bit of time in solitude, they needed to combat *acedia* in order to refocus on God's active presence. Interestingly, though, wind can also fortify and strengthen a plant (Harmless, 2004). Hence, this experience was not considered inherently problematic (Harmless, 2004). To combat *acedia*, the virtue of perseverance was pursued among the early desert Christians.

The early desert Christians also mentioned weeping with tears as a way to draw closer to God.[1] Although by no means fully constituting 21st-century depression, connecting to a deeper sense of sadness through the expression of tears helped monks to acknowledge their imperfections before God, relying on his mercy and grace within the desert landscape. In other words, weeping eluci-dates just how frail and vulnerable human beings actually are, with God having compassion for human fragility as humans cry out to him. Through the shedding of tears, Christian clients are able to acknowledge before God that they have "hit rock bottom," so to speak, longing for God's loving response as distractions are stripped away in the barren, dry terrain of the desert. Therefore, paralleling Zettle's (2007) conceptualization of depression as necessary in the short-term, a case can be made that instances of sadness and low mood may help Christian clients reach out to God, relying on his loving, compassionate presence.

Naturally, for the early desert Christians, contemplative practice, along with the cultivation of the aforementioned virtues, was utilized to achieve this aim, with practitioners sitting in solitude with God and recognizing his active, loving presence. Contemplation, to be sure, closely resembles mindfulness meditation, helping Christians to cultivate sustained attention with a "prayer word" (Laird, 2006) in the present moment, letting go of the need to clutch or push away thoughts, feelings, sensations, and memories, including the previously noted *logismoi*. Over time, practitioners learn to gently return to the "prayer word," which symbolizes a loving gaze upon God and willingness to yield to his active, loving presence (Bangley, 2006). For Christian clients with depressive symp-toms, this means shifting from the "doing" mode, reminiscent of Martha, to the "being" mode, sitting at Jesus's feet like Mary (Segal et al., 2012). By doing this, the low mood can run its natural course, as Christian clients surrender to God's loving, protective care and ameliorate the tendency to get stuck in ruminative thinking patterns (Knabb et al., 2018).

It is worth mentioning that both mindfulness and contemplation seem to help practitioners develop metacognitive awareness, or the ability to reflect on the thinking process (Jankowski & Holas, 2014; Williams, 1999). In other words, similar to traditional ACT's transcendent self, clients are able to simply watch inner experiences, such as thoughts, feelings, sensations, and memories, unfold, without attempting to "fix" them. Yet, for Christian clients, this process is also about ameliorating the tendency for the inner world to distract from an awareness of God's active, loving presence, rather than merely for more pragmatic reasons (e.g., reducing suffering, relating differently to psychological symptoms). What is more, contemplative practice is about cultivating a *kenotic* attitude of surrender, pivoting from self-derived knowledge to God-derived love (Bangley, 2006). Nevertheless, because both promote an awareness of the inner world, allowing for some distance and reflection, contemplation can serve as a culturally sensitive alternative to Buddhist-influenced mindfulness for Christian clients. What follows are some additional considerations when working with Christian clients with depressive symptoms in faith-based ACT.

Faith-Based ACT for Depression

Several unique factors may need to be considered when working with Christian clients with depressive disorders (e.g., major depressive disorder, dysthymia). To begin, informed consent needs to be secured, which can look a bit different for Christian clients, especially since some may want to integrate unique practices, such as prayer, into counseling and therapy (Rosenfeld, 2011).[5] Given that client autonomy and self-determination are foundational ethical principles within the mental health field (Rosenfeld, 2011), it is important for Christian clients to lead the way when it comes to their personal faith preferences, including their own interpretation of the role that Jesus plays in their life, with counselors and therapists being especially sensitive to Christian clients' religious worldview. In other words, counselors and therapists should not attempt to practice faith-based ACT if clients do not identify as Christian, are not interested in Christianity's central tenets, or are unsure about their commitment to the Christian faith.

Because of this, in the intake interview, faith-based ACT should be carefully explained so that Christian clients can determine whether they want to utilize the traditional or faith-based version of ACT. Certainly, a collaborative approach should be utilized when implementing faith-based ACT, consistent with other authors' recommendations for integrating religion and spirituality with counseling and therapy (Rosenfeld, 2011). Indeed, if an explanation, metaphor, interpretation of Scripture, etc., does not fit for the Christian client, the faith-based ACT counselor or therapist should model flexibility and curiosity by inquiring about an alternative Christian understanding or example from the Bible.

Also, a variety of assessment instruments, mentioned below in no particular order, can be employed in the first session, attempting to better understand

Christian clients' psychological and spiritual functioning.[6] For depressive symptoms, the Beck Depression Inventory-II (BDI-II; Beck et al., 1996) and Ruminative Responses Scale (RRS; Treynor et al., 2003) can be used, and the Multidimensional Experiential Avoidance Questionnaire (MEAQ; Gamez et al., 2011) can be administered to measure experiential avoidance. In addition, the Brief RCOPE (Pargament et al., 2011) can be employed to measure positive and negative forms of religious coping, as well as the Communion with God Scale (CGS; Knabb & Wang, 2021) to measure Christian clients' relationship with God and the Christian Contentment Scale (CCS; Knabb et al., 2020) to measure their level of inner satisfaction in the midst of psychological suffering.[7] Of course, included throughout the duration of treatment will also be some sort of weekly assessment of suicidal ideation. Within the assessment, counselors and therapists can assess for suicidal thoughts, along with any intent to act on the thoughts and possible means and a plan to carry out the thoughts.[8] If ideation is present, a comprehensive safety plan can be incorporated into treatment, which involves, at minimum, traditional ACT skills to manage ideation, along with a support system and emergency contacts in the event that ideation leads to suicidal intent.

Regarding the role of the counselor or therapist, traditional ACT counselors and therapists can model psychological flexibility and mindfulness in the relationship, demonstrating openness, curiosity, and present-moment awareness within each session (Hayes et al., 2012). For example, the counselor or therapist may notice they have become fused with a certain thought or somewhat overwhelmed with a particular feeling, leading to a sense of distraction in the counseling or therapy room. If this is the case, the counselor or therapist can model psychological flexibility by verbalizing the experience (e.g., "I seem to be getting hooked right now as you share your thoughts"), modeling an open response to their inner world. In other words, there is a sort of togetherness between the counselor or therapist and client, walking side by side, wherein the counselor or therapist acknowledges a less than perfect understanding of the world, relying, instead, on psychological flexibility and values to navigate difficult terrain.

For counselors and therapists employing faith-based ACT, this attitude of open, accepting flexibility also involves modeling *grace*, an undeserved merit or favor God offers to humankind (McMinn, 2008). In turn, counselors and therapists can offer this type of grace to Christian clients, especially in the context of faith-based ACT. Thus, grace can be embedded within traditional ACT's understanding of psychological flexibility, whether the counselor or therapist is extending grace to themselves or the client. Indeed, grace has been offered as a spiritually sensitive version of acceptance in traditional ACT (Hayes et al., 2012).

What is more, when working with Christian clients, rumination is a unique symptom to consider, along with the tendency for clients to fuse with a "flawed," "defective" self (Zettle, 2007, p. 52). Therefore, many Christian clients struggling with depressive symptoms will fuse with unhelpful thought content about themselves, the world, and the future (Beck et al., 1979), treating this inner dialogue as factual. In fact, rumination, as noted previously in this chapter, is often central to depression relapse. As a result, it will be important to identify these types of unhelpful thoughts so as to assist Christian clients in defusing from their storied, false self found outside of the *imago Dei* (Genesis 1:27) and God's mercy and grace. Christian clients' ability to ameliorate leaning on their own self-derived understanding (Proverbs 3:5), employing contemplative practice to submit to God's loving presence within (Keating, 2006), is especially important, cultivating a more open and flexible awareness of the inner world by inviting the God of love into the process. In other words, Christian clients are learning to gently pivot from self-derived knowledge, which is often inaccurate, ruminative, and impermanent, to God-derived love, which is perfect and unchangeable. Along the way, Christian clients are relinquishing their grip on self-preoccupations as they learn to cultivate a more sustained attention on God, walking with him in love as they place one foot after the other on the road of life.

Furthermore, the recurrent nature of depression needs to be taken into account, with Christian clients likely continuing to struggle with depressive symptoms beyond treatment. Of course, from an MBCT perspective, clients can relate differently to these symptoms in the "being" mode, rather than trying to make them go away in the "doing" mode (Segal et al., 2012). To prepare Christian clients for this reality, the story of Mary and Martha (Luke 10:38–42) can be emphasized so as to help them sit at the feet of Jesus during moments of low mood, employing contemplative practice in the place of mindfulness to relate to inner experiences with nonjudgmental compassion. To learn to sit at the feet of Jesus when experiencing depressive symptoms means Christian clients are employing an indirect method (Ware, 2001), rather than directly trying to eliminate depression, noticing when they are preoccupied with difficult thoughts, feelings, sensations, and memories, then shifting toward an awareness of God's active, loving presence.

In addition, a variety of passages in Scripture—such as the lament psalms (e.g., Psalm 142), the Prophet Jeremiah's writings (e.g., Lamentations 1), and the Passion narrative (e.g., John 18–19)—can help Christian clients recognize the ongoing struggle that humankind faces within the human condition. To be sure, Psalm 46 is especially powerful, given that God commanded Jerusalem to "be still" and put down their weapons during battle because God would protect them (Earwood, 1989). Of course, the purpose is to help Christian clients let go of their efforts to reduce, eliminate, avoid, or distract from depressive symptoms, gaining further insight into the recurrent nature of psychological pain. By doing this, Christian clients can pivot toward following Jesus (i.e., walking with God in love).

Moreover, counselors and therapists employing faith-based ACT can explore Christian clients' relationship with God, given that Christian clients may be using negative forms of religious coping (Pargament et al., 2011), which can exacerbate depressive symptoms. In other words, some Christian clients may view God as withholding, punitive, unloving, distant, and so forth, struggling to find him and recognize his presence in the midst of suffering. Because of this, contemplative practice can be especially helpful in allowing Christian clients to simply sit at the feet of Jesus, yielding to his active, loving presence during moments of uncertainty and doubt. By doing this, Christians can begin to make use of positive forms of religious coping, including collaborating with God in response to adversity, along with seeing God's loving response in the midst of pain (Pargament et al., 2011).

Finally, as noted throughout this book, counselors and therapists can use Christian contemplation (e.g., the Jesus Prayer, centering prayer, the welcoming prayer; "love" or "Jesus" as a "reset word," "surrender word," or "prayer word"; see earlier chapters for instructions and citations) in place of mindfulness, given that contemplation is the Christian version of mindfulness-based practice. Also, Christian contemplation may be more fitting because the central aim is an awareness of God's active, loving presence, especially during moments of low mood, when it may seem as though God is distant, absent, or punishing the Christian client in some way. This ability to shift from the "doing" to "being" mode (Segal et al., 2012), relying less on Christian clients' own understanding (Proverbs 3:5), is especially important, given that sitting at the feet of Jesus can allow the low mood to run its natural course, without catastrophizing the experience and, as a result, further intensifying symptoms.

In terms of the structure of each session, after the intake interview, faith-based ACT counselors and therapists can start by reviewing the homework from the previous week, transitioning to a general overview of the chosen faith-based ACT process, including the major goals for each week. After explaining each process, counselors and therapists can turn to using metaphors and exercises to deepen Christian clients' understanding, using contemplative practice in the place of mindfulness. Since traditional ACT is highly experiential, it is important in faith-based ACT to *show* the Christian client, offering them the ability to "try on" the concept, rather than merely *tell* them about ways to balance acceptance and action. To conclude, faith-based ACT counselors and therapists can assign homework for each subsequent session, which usually involves daily contemplative practice (i.e., 20-minute blocks of time, once or twice a day), in addition to other experiential exercises in earlier chapters that help Christian clients to work within a particular faith-based ACT process.

Although there is no exact number of sessions for clients with depressive symptoms, Zettle (2007) offered a detailed overview of a 12-session approach, embedding major goals, a weekly agenda, and techniques into each meeting. This session-by-session guide, of course, can be easily modified to accommodate faith-based ACT, based on the recommended adjustments elucidated throughout this book within traditional ACT's six processes. To provide a quick overview, the first session can focus on securing informed consent, conducting a thorough intake, getting background information on the presenting problem, assessing for suicidality (which will involve some sort of safety plan if ideation is present), and beginning to help the client realize that cognitive fusion and experiential avoidance may be the problem (use of the "Fork in the Road" assessment tool can be helpful, which has been modified from Harris [2019] and Hayes et al. [2012]). During this time, faith-based ACT counselors and therapists can help Christian clients to understand that rumination and the "doing" mode do not typically work when attempting to ameliorate depressive symptoms, with Mary's willingness to sit at the feet of Jesus being the preferred strategy (i.e., the "being" mode) when low mood occurs. Also, drawing a parallel between traditional ACT's experiential acceptance and surrendering to God is important, given that surrender is consistent with the Christian tradition (see, e.g., James 4:7; 1 Peter 5:6–10).

In the second session, cognitive fusion and experiential avoidance are further explored, with willingness and the acceptance process presented to the client. For Christian clients, willingness involves the ability to follow Jesus during instances of low mood, accepting that depressive symptoms are a part of life and help to conserve vital energy. Yet, prolonged inactivity in response to low mood can also tend to keep Christian clients stuck when this strategy is overly relied upon for longer periods. Within faith-based ACT, acceptance parallels Mary sitting at the feet of Jesus (Luke 10:38–42), with *hupomone* capturing the ability to endure with a sense of patience and hope, trusting that God is active and present during moments of low mood. During this session, the welcoming prayer (see earlier chapters for instructions and citations) can be introduced in order to help Christian clients learn to invite God into the pain, shifting from the "doing" to "being" mode in the process.

Within the third and fourth sessions, defusion is further unpacked in order to continue to work with the client on ways to accept the inner world. In these sessions, content surrounding negative views of the self, the world, and the client's future can be explored, highlighting that it is important for the Christian client to avoid leaning on their own understanding in the "doing" mode, letting go of the tendency to overly rely on language when low mood occurs. Instead, Christian clients can focus on relinquishing efforts to let the mind determine who they are and why they are experiencing distress, surrendering their false sense of self to God in order to find the true self in Jesus, which transcends wavering low moods.

In the fifth and sixth meetings, mindfulness is commonly practiced so as to more effectively work with the verbal self, helping the client to defuse from the storied self. For Christian clients, contemplative practice, including centering prayer, the welcoming prayer, and the Jesus Prayer (see earlier chapters for instructions and citations) can be employed, helping them to simply sit at the feet of Jesus, untangling from the false self in order to follow Jesus (i.e., walk with

238

God in love). Within contemplative practice, Christian clients are learning to connect to Jesus in the here-and-now, gently returning to their "prayer word" (Laird, 2006) when they notice the mind has carried their attention away, similar to Mary gazing upon Jesus despite Martha's distractions.

During the seventh through 11th sessions, values are frequently introduced, helping the client to identify meaningful principles to live by, along with goals to get there and the importance of willingness as a way to endure along the way. Of course, for Christian clients, virtues are identified, rather than values, given they are anchored to the Bible. Also, exploring Jesus's teachings can be helpful for Christians to take action, following Jesus in the midst of pain. At this point in counseling or therapy, mindfulness is frequently used to help the client continue to work from all four mindfulness-based processes, with Christian clients using daily contemplative practice in its place.

In the last session, treatment gains are discussed, as are strategies for the Christian client to continue to apply faith-based ACT to daily living. In other words, a central question is as follows: "Given that you might continue to experience low mood, how can you balance sitting at the feet of Jesus with following him in order to live a life that glorifies God and displays his love, even when depressive symptoms are present?" As counseling or therapy is wrapping up, Christian clients are encouraged to think about living a long life, faithfully following Jesus from moment to moment: "I have fought the good fight, I have finished the race, I have kept the faith" (*New International Version Bible*, 2011, 2 Timothy 4:7).

It is also worth mentioning that Harris (2019) presented a plethora of easy-to-use forms for traditional ACT counselors and therapists, including several worksheets for case conceptualization, which can be modified when working with Christian clients. Zettle (2007), too, offered a wide variety of forms for use in treatment, particularly focused on clients with depression. Of course, these forms can be adjusted to embed an awareness of God's active, loving presence into the treatment process, helping Christian clients to think about the ways in which they can follow Jesus in the midst of psychological pain, employing contemplative practice to make this happen.

Essentially, counselors and therapists using faith-based ACT are working with Christian clients with depression to (a) "watch and endure," learning to dually watch depressive rumination with flexibility and endure depressive symptoms because the God of love is present; (b) "notice and shift," learning to dually maintain an awareness of the distinction between "earthly-mindedness" and "heavenly-mindedness" (Burroughs, 2010, 2014; Rowe, 1672) as they shift toward the contemplative self and the God of love by practicing God's presence; and (c) "commit and follow," learning to dually identify a set of biblical virtues (with love as *the* crowning virtue) and follow Jesus (i.e., walk with God in love) as they move from justification (i.e., being righteous before, and reconciled to, God because of Jesus), to sanctification (i.e., being more like Jesus), to glorification (i.e., being face to face with Jesus) (Grudem, 1994).

Above all else, because traditional ACT focuses on six salient processes, rather than a fixed, step-by-step guide, counselors and therapists can decide which process to begin with, given that each process relates to the others and all of them help clients work toward increasing psychological flexibility. Of course, for Christian clients, the central aim is an awareness of God's active, loving presence, with flexibility developing as a byproduct of walking with God in love from moment to moment. In other words, Christian clients with depression are learning an indirect method (Ware, 2001) to gently pivot, over and over again, from a preoccupation with the self (e.g., depressive rumination, negative self-judgments) to a loving awareness of the Other/other, displaying God's love as they confidently walk with God and others on the road of life.

Conclusion

In this chapter, special considerations were presented for counselors and therapists working with Christian clients with depressive symptoms, including a Christian conceptualization of depression and contemplative practice as a substitute for mindfulness meditation. During moments of low mood, Christian clients can sit at the feet of Jesus, shifting from the "doing" to "being" mode in order to let go of the tendency to either escape from or fuse with depressive symptoms. Because rumination is a central struggle, contemplative practice can help Christian clients to foster metacognition, watching the inner world unfold without seeking to change it in any way. Certainly, for Christian clients, contemplative practice can also help to recognize God's active, loving presence, utilizing positive, rather than negative, religious coping in order to buffer against depressive symptoms. Finally, since Jesus endured, Christians, too, can find hope in this experience, recognizing that God is active in the midst of psychological pain, helping them to grow as they pursue moral excellence by way of virtuous living.

Notes

1 See http://www.div12.org/PsychologicalTreatments/treatments.html for a list of evidence-based practices, including traditional ACT for depression.
2 Portions of this section are adapted from Knabb (2012).
3 For a detailed exploration of the *logismoi* and psychological functioning in the 21st century, including similarities and differences, see Cook (2011). See also Burton-Christie (2009) for an explication of Evagrius's writings on sadness.
4 The main points in this paragraph are from Chryssavgis (2008), who offered an overview of the relationship between tears, weeping, silence, the desert landscape, and God among the early desert Christians.
5 For an example of informed consent verbiage for clients with depression using a traditional ACT approach, see Zettle (2007, pp. 158–160).
6 Because these instruments were originally developed for research-related purposes, not necessarily counseling and therapy, they should only be used as brief measures

to get a preliminary understanding of Christian clients' psychological and spiritual functioning.

7 The CGS and CCS are both important because healthy psychological and spiritual functioning in the Christian life involves walking (i.e., communing) with God and experiencing a deeper contentment in him in the midst of depressive symptoms.

8 For a more detailed strategy for assessing suicidal behavior, see Zettle (2007, pp. 204–208).

References

A-Tjak, J., Davis, M., Morina, N., Powers, M., Smits, J., & Emmelkamp, P. (2015). A meta-analysis of the efficacy of acceptance and commitment therapy for clinically relevant mental and physical health problems. *Psychotherapy and Psychosomatics, 84*, 30–36.

Bai, Z., Luo, S., Zhang, L., Wu, S., & Chi, I. (2020). Acceptance and commitment therapy (ACT) to reduce depression: A systematic review and meta-analysis. *Journal of Affective Disorders, 260*, 728–737.

Bangley, B. (Ed.). (2006). *The cloud of unknowing: Contemporary English edition*. Paraclete Press.

Batten, S. (2011). *Essentials of acceptance and commitment therapy*. SAGE Publications Inc.

Beck, A., Rush, A., Shaw, B., & Emery, G. (1979). *Cognitive therapy of depression*. The Guilford Press.

Beck, A., Steer, R., & Brown, G. (1996). *Manual for the Beck depression inventory* (2nd ed.). The Psychological Corporation.

Bjorck, J., & Thurman, J. (2007). Negative life events, patterns of positive and negative religious coping, and psychological functioning. *Journal for the Scientific Study of Religion, 46*, 159–167.

Burroughs, J. (2010). *Heavenly-mindedness recommended: In a discourse on Colossians 3:2*. Gale ECCO.

Burroughs, J. (2014). *A treatise on earthly-mindedness*. GLH Publishing.

Burton-Christie, D. (2009). Evagrius on sadness. *Cistercian Studies Quarterly, 44*, 395–409.

Chryssavgis, J. (2008). *In the heart of the desert: The spirituality of the desert fathers and mothers*. World Wisdom, Inc.

Cook, C. (2011). *The Philokalia and mental wellbeing*. James Clarke and Co.

Earwood, G. (1989). Psalm 46. *Review and Expositor, 86*, 79–86.

Gamez, W., Chmielewski, M., Kotov, R., Ruggero, C., & Watson, D. (2011). Development of a measure of experiential avoidance: The Multidimensional Experiential Avoidance Questionnaire. *Psychological Assessment, 23*, 692–713.

Goldberg, R., & Steury, S. (2001). Depression in the workplace: Costs and barriers to treatment. *Psychiatric Services, 52*, 1639–1643.

Grudem, W. (1994). *Systematic theology: An introduction to biblical doctrine*. Zondervan.

Harmless, W. (2004). *Desert Christians: An introduction to the literature of early monasticism*. Oxford University Press.

Harris, R. (2019). *ACT made simple. An easy-to-read primer on acceptance and commitment therapy* (2nd ed.). New Harbinger Publications, Inc.

Hayes, S. (2005). *Get out of your mind and into your life: The new acceptance & commitment therapy*. New Harbinger Publications, Inc.

Hayes, S., Strosahl, K., & Wilson, K. (2012). *Acceptance and commitment therapy: The process and practice of mindful change* (2nd ed.). The Guilford Press.

Hofmann, S., Sawyer, A., Witt, A., & Oh, D. (2010). The effect of mindfulness-based therapy on anxiety and depression: A meta-analytic review. *Journal of Consulting and Clinical Psychology, 78,* 169–183.

Jankowski, T., & Holas, P. (2014). Metacognitive model of mindfulness. *Consciousness and Cognition, 28,* 64–80.

Keating, T. (2006). *Open mind, open heart, 20th anniversary edition.* Continuum.

Knabb, J. (2012). Centering prayer as an alternative to mindfulness-based cognitive therapy for depression relapse prevention. *Journal of Religion and Health, 51,* 908–924.

Knabb, J., & Wang, K. (2021). The communion with God scale: Shifting from an *etic* to *emic* perspective to assess fellowshipping with the Triune God. *Psychology of Religion and Spirituality, 13,* 67–80.

Knabb, J., Vazquez, V., & Wang, K. (2020). The Christian contentment scale: An *emic* measure for assessing inner satisfaction within the Christian tradition. *Journal of Psychology and Theology.* Advance online publication.

Knabb, J., Vazquez, V., Wang, K., & Bates, M. (2018). "Unknowing" in the 21st century: Humble detachment for Christians with repetitive negative thinking. *Spirituality in Clinical Practice, 5,* 170–187.

Laird, M. (2006). *Into the silent land: A guide to the Christian practice of contemplation.* Oxford University Press.

Leloup, J. (2003). *Being still: Reflections on the ancient mystical tradition.* Paulist Press.

MacQuarrie, D. (2012). *Acedia: The darkness within.* AuthorHouse.

McMinn, M. (2008). *Sin and grace in Christian counseling: An integrative paradigm.* InterVarsity Press.

McMinn, M., & Campbell, C. (2007). *Integrative psychotherapy: Toward a comprehensive Christian approach.* InterVarsity Press.

New International Version Bible. (2011). Zondervan. https://www.biblegateway.com/

Nierenberg, A., Petersen, T., & Alpert, J. (2003). Prevention of relapse and recurrence in depression: The role of long-term pharmacotherapy and psychotherapy. *Journal of Clinical Psychiatry, 64*(Supplement 15), 13–17.

Pargament, K., Feuille, M., & Burdzy, D. (2011). The brief RCOPE: Current psycho-metric status of a short measure of religious coping. *Religions, 2,* 51–76.

Rosenfeld, G. (2011). Contributions from ethics and research that guide integrating religion into psychotherapy. *Professional Psychology: Research and Practice, 42,* 192–199.

Rowe, J. (1672). *Heavenly-mindedness and earthly-mindedness: In two parts.* Francis Tyton.

Segal, Z., Williams, M., & Teasdale, J. (2012). *Mindfulness-based cognitive therapy for depression* (2nd ed.). The Guilford Press.

Thase, M. (2003). Achieving remission and managing relapse in depression. *Journal of Clinical Psychiatry, 64*(Supplement 18), 3–7.

Treynor, W., Gonzalez, R., & Nolen-Hoeksema, S. (2003). Rumination reconsidered: A psychometric analysis. *Cognitive Therapy and Research, 27,* 247–259.

Twohig, M., & Levin, M. (2017). Acceptance and commitment therapy as a treatment for anxiety and depression: A review. *Psychiatric Clinics of North America, 40,* 751–770.

Ware, K. (2001). *The inner kingdom.* St. Vladimir's Seminary Press.

Williams, M. (1999). Metacognition, mindfulness and the modification of mood disorders. *Clinical Psychology & Psychotherapy, 6,* 146–155.

Yarhouse, M., Butman, R., & McRay, B. (2005). *Modern psychopathologies: A comprehensive Christian appraisal.* InterVarsity Press.

Zettle, R. (2004). ACT with affective disorders. In S. Hayes & K. Strosahl (Eds.), *A practical guide to acceptance and commitment therapy* (pp. 77–102). Springer.

Zettle, R. (2007). *ACT for depression: A clinician's guide to using acceptance & commitment therapy in treating depression.* New Harbinger Publications, Inc.

10

FAITH-BASED ACT FOR ANXIETY

Introduction

In this chapter, the six traditional acceptance and commitment therapy (ACT) processes are applied to anxiety, exploring contemporary theories of anxiety; a Christian understanding of worry, uncertainty, and anxiety; Christian contemplative writings on the topic; and a faith-based ACT strategy for anxiety. Because anxiety is future-oriented (e.g., clients are frequently preoccupied with catastrophic, doomsday scenarios unfolding in the future) and research suggests anxiety involves an unwillingness to tolerate uncertainty, special attention is devoted to contemplative strategies to help Christian clients stay connected to Jesus in the present moment, surrendering to God's providence (i.e., "God's continuous, parental care of the world"; Beasley-Topliffe, 2003, p. 230) during moments of doubt, rather than using control or avoidance strategies that do not end up working in the long run. In fact, I conducted a three-part study among Christians that explored surrendering to God's providence, uncertainty, and worry, with results revealing that yielding to God's protective care is linked to less worry, mediated by the ability to accept uncertainty. Of course, from a traditional ACT perspective, anxiety symptoms are not problematic on their own. Rather, experiential avoidance, which includes efforts to get rid of unpleasant anxiety symptoms, can lead to disordered functioning, given that clients are distracted from value-based living.

Traditional CBT for Anxiety

In recent years, traditional cognitive behavioral therapy (CBT) researchers have increasingly investigated the intolerance of uncertainty construct, elucidating its role in anxiety disorders. Originally explored in the context of generalized anxiety (Dugas & Robichaud, 2007), intolerance of uncertainty may be present across depressive and anxiety disorders (Carleton et al., 2012). In fact, in two studies, researchers found higher intolerance of uncertainty scores among participants with panic disorder, social anxiety disorder, and generalized anxiety disorder when compared with nonclinical samples (Carleton et al., 2012; Mahoney & McEvoy, 2012).

DOI: 10.4324/9781003181941-11

More specifically, intolerance of uncertainty, described as a "dispositional characteristic," involves negative views about an uncertain, ambiguous future, with clients believing that uncertainty (a) causes added distress, (b) is unfair, (c) needs to be prevented, and (d) undermines daily functioning (Dugas & Robichaud, 2007, p. 24). When studying intolerance of uncertainty, Sexton and Dugas (2009) uncovered two overarching factors, including negative views about oneself and behavior when faced with uncertainty, along with beliefs about the unfairness of uncertainty. For anxious clients, uncertainty appears to be a central preoccupation, with many individuals struggling to accept that the world is unpredictable and ambiguous and most life events are outside of their control.

When explicating a traditional CBT approach to generalized anxiety, Dugas and Robichaud (2007) suggested there are at least three ways in which intolerance of uncertainty possibly contributes to worry and anxiety. In particular, clients struggling with intolerance of uncertainty may (a) employ catastrophic predictions to understand unknown future scenarios, resulting in worry and anxiety; (b) need a sizeable amount of information when life events are relatively uncertain, leading to worry and anxiety; or (c) lack the confidence to decide a course of action during instances of uncertainty, doubting their ability, which increases worry and anxiety (Dugas & Robichaud, 2007). In each of these possible pathways, clients tend to struggle with the ambiguity of an uncertain future, exacerbating anxiety symptoms.

In response to worry and anxiety, clients commonly attempt to either gain a sense of control over an unknown, uncertain future or attempt to avoid uncertainty altogether (Dugas & Robichaud, 2007). In other words, some individuals may employ various control strategies, such as constantly seeking reassurance and compulsively checking (Dugas & Robichaud, 2007). Conversely, sometimes clients avoid life when dealing with uncertainty, procrastinating, offering "valid reasons" for not taking action, and struggling to follow through with prior commitments (Dugas & Robichaud, 2007). Of course, these control and avoidance strategies do not tend to work, given that uncertainty is a normal, natural part of life and attaining certainty (or avoiding ambiguity) is impossible. Because of this, accepting uncertainty, rather than trying to permanently secure a certain future or avoid an uncertain one, is embedded within a CBT approach to ameliorate generalized anxiety (Dugas & Robichaud, 2007). Interestingly, this preoccupation with an unknown future is consistent with traditional ACT, which suggests that anxious clients struggle to stay connected to the here-and-now, attempting to avoid anxiety and fusing with catastrophic thought content.

Traditional ACT for Anxiety

From a traditional ACT perspective, anxiety is a normal part of life (Eifert & Forsyth, 2005). Experiential avoidance, on the other hand, exacerbates the experience of anxiety, leading to disordered functioning. Consistent with panic disorder, social phobia, and generalized anxiety disorder, many individuals spend a great deal of time trying to reduce, eliminate, avoid, or distract from anxiety symptoms, which seldom works in the long run (Eifert & Forsyth, 2005). In other words, constantly trying to avoid anxiety, rather than the mere presence of anxiety symptoms, gets in the way of living life. Also, overly relying on the world of language, fusing with catastrophic thoughts about the future, is a central struggle for many clients with anxiety disorders (Batten, 2011).

For example, clients struggling with recurrent panic attacks may isolate themselves indoors, fearing they will have another panic attack in public, leading to a diagnosis of panic disorder based on a preoccupation with experiencing additional panic. With panic symptoms, clients may be especially focused on bodily sensations, such as rapid heartbeat. For social phobia, clients may avoid social interactions because of an intense fear of embarrassing themselves, rather than enduring the anxiety when conversing with others. Embedded within this experience is a preoccupation with the self, with clients constantly monitoring their behavior for fear of making a mistake, which will seemingly be noticed and interpreted by others in a negative light. Finally, clients with generalized anxiety may employ control or avoidance strategies to either attain certainty or eliminate uncertainty, leading to impaired daily functioning. For clients with generalized anxiety, worry is commonly employed to eliminate uncertainty, "filling in the blanks" when the future is ambiguous or unknown, given that uncertainty is considered "bad," reflecting negatively on clients' sense of self and behavior.

In each of these instances, clients have the initial symptoms (e.g., physiological symptoms of anxiety, a preoccupation with being embarrassed, excessive worry to attain certainty about the future), along with problematic responses to the symptoms. Thus, although the anxiety of life may never fully go away, clients can relate differently to the experience of uncertainty, worry, and anxiety in order to, instead, pursue meaningful values. As a result, a major part of traditional ACT for anxiety involves normalizing anxiety symptoms, helping clients to let go of ineffective avoidance strategies and pivot toward the pursuit of values (Eifert & Forsyth, 2005).

Unfortunately, in an effort to avoid anxiety, clients may employ unhelpful behavioral strategies, such as checking, seeking reassurance, social isolation, or the avoidance of anxiety-producing situations. In addition, cognitive efforts to avoid anxiety symptoms are commonly used, such as rumination and worry, along with maintaining a prolonged state of hypervigilance to ameliorate being surprised (Orsillo et al., 2004). Although most clients recognize that these efforts have failed to yield the results they are looking for—permanent anxiety elimination—they continue to pursue them, especially given they may experience short-term benefits (Orsillo et al., 2004).

Overlapping with exposure therapy, traditional ACT suggests that the solution to anxiety is to face inner distress, accepting the ubiquity of anxiety as a normal inner state, along with defusing from both catastrophic thinking and reasons to justify the avoidance (Orsillo et al., 2004). Stated differently, clients need to have a willingness to endure the symptoms, ameliorating avoidance strategies because they simply do not work to create a deeply fulfilling, meaningful life. Therefore, traditional ACT counselors and therapists employ cognitive defusion techniques to help clients untangle themselves from catastrophic thoughts about the future; acceptance strategies to relate differently to the inner world; mindfulness to cultivate an awareness of the transcendent self, safely watching anxiety symptoms; and present-moment awareness, given that anxiety is rooted in the future.

Needless to say, because a major component of anxiety disorders involves intolerance of uncertainty, as mentioned previously, this understanding can be integrated into traditional ACT. For example, traditional ACT counselors and therapists can explore clients' views of uncertainty, helping them to identify fused thoughts about an ambiguous future that lead to control or avoidance behaviors that keep them stuck in life. After this, traditional ACT counselors and therapists can help clients with anxiety disorders begin to accept uncertainty via the mindfulness-based processes. In other words, because worry and anxiety are typically future-oriented, grounded in catastrophic, doomsday predictions about an uncertain future, mindfulness meditation can be employed to help clients connect to the present moment. After all, anxiety in the here-and-now is similar to a fish on land—it simply cannot survive because anxiety needs the future like a fish needs water (Wilson & DuFrene, 2010).

Research on Mindfulness-Based Counseling and Therapy for Anxiety

In consideration of empirical support for traditional ACT for anxiety disorders, recent meta-analyses have illuminated that mindfulness is efficacious when working with anxiety disorders. The Hofmann et al. (2010) meta-analysis, mentioned in the previous chapter, revealed a medium effect size pre- to post-treatment when examining mindfulness for anxiety symptoms among 39 studies, as well as a large effect size when investigating seven studies with participants with generalized anxiety, panic, and social anxiety disorders. Despite the fact that these studies commonly utilized mindfulness-based stress reduction (MBSR) or mindfulness-based cognitive therapy (MBCT), traditional ACT practitioners also employ mindfulness, combining mindfulness-based processes with effective action based on a set of well-defined, global, personally chosen values.

In addition, A-Tjak et al.'s (2015) meta-analysis, also mentioned in the last chapter, combined eight studies on traditional ACT and anxiety and depression, elucidating a small effect when comparing traditional ACT with a control group. To offer one more example that was mentioned in the previous chapter, Twohig and Levin (2017) reviewed 36 randomized trials on traditional ACT for depression and anxiety, revealing that "ACT appears to be more efficacious than waitlist conditions and treatment-as-usual, with largely equivalent effects relative to traditional cognitive behavioral therapy" (p. 751). To conclude, the American Psychological Association (APA) currently lists traditional ACT as having modest research support when applied to the treatment of mixed anxiety disorders.[1] When working with Christian clients with anxiety disorders, it may be helpful to first understand a Christian viewpoint in order to apply faith-based ACT in a culturally sensitive manner.

Christianity and Anxiety

From a Christian perspective, the fall of humankind in Genesis 3 inevitably led to the ubiquitous human experience of anxiety, with Adam and Eve worrying about what God's response may be after they ate the forbidden fruit, hiding anxiously in anticipation of his reaction (Yarhouse et al., 2005). Even so, in the New Testament, Jesus taught that Christians should not worry because God will provide for them, pointing to the birds and flowers to highlight God's providential, protective, loving care (Matthew 6:25–34). In other words, because Christians believe that God is omnibenevolent, omnipotent, omniscient, and omnipresent, they can surrender to him, rather than worry about tomorrow, which will not enhance their life in any way. From this perspective, a key ingredient to ameliorating uncertainty, worry, and anxiety is cultivating a state of surrender to God, trusting in his ability to provide because he is in control. Rather than Christian clients relying on their own efforts to attain certainty in response to an ambiguous future, they can let go because God will guide them through life's adversities and trials.

It is worth mentioning that I completed a three-part study on surrendering to God's providence among Christians (Knabb et al., 2017). In the first two studies, I tested and replicated an empirical model of Christian worry, hypothesizing that deeply held, positive beliefs about God's providence would be associated with the ability to surrender control to God, a form of religious coping, during moments of adversity. In turn, the Christian ability to surrender to God would be negatively associated with worry, mediated by the ability to tolerate uncertainty. Stated differently, among Christians, I anticipated that surrendering to God's providence would lead to the amelioration of worry, given that God is perceived to be in control, loving and caring for Christians during moments of uncertainty. Because God is both benevolent and sovereign, Christians can let go of their own efforts to predict the future, consistent with Jesus's teaching (Matthew 6:25–34).

In the first study among college students, this model was empirically supported through path analyses. In addition, with a sample of churchgoers in the community, I was able to replicate these findings, suggesting that anxious Christians may turn to God's providential care, surrendering to him during moments of uncertainty to ameliorate worry. Based on these two studies, I designed an eight-week group therapy model, using contemplative practice (e.g., the Jesus Prayer, centering prayer, the welcoming prayer) to help Christian worriers submit to God's active, loving presence in order to ameliorate uncertainty and worry. Among the pilot sample of Christian adults who reported worrying daily for at least six months, most had either an anxiety or depressive disorder. After eight weeks, findings revealed a reduction in worry, intolerance of uncertainty, and depression, anxiety, and stress, with large effect sizes pre- to post-intervention. Also, there was an improvement in participants' beliefs about God's providence and their ability to surrender to him during instances of adversity, revealing medium effect sizes pre- to post-intervention. Overall, this pilot study offers preliminary support for the aforementioned theoretical model, with contemplation as an intervention for uncertainty, worry, and anxiety.

Consistent with a traditional ACT viewpoint, Christian clients may struggle with anxiety because they are fused with catastrophic predictions about the future, having a hard time accepting the ambiguity of tomorrow. Because of this, a variety of ineffective control or avoidance strategies may be employed, with Christian clients relying on their own efforts to ameliorate suffering. Unfortunately, these strategies seldom work in the long term, leaving Christians exhausted and stuck, given control and avoidance behaviors distract them from following Jesus. Similar to mindfulness, contemplative practice can help Christian clients connect to the present moment, nonjudgmentally accepting the inner world in order to follow Jesus (i.e., walk with God in love), sitting at his feet and surrendering to his providence (i.e., good governance, protective care) (Erickson, 2013). Before exploring several suggestions for working with Christian clients with anxiety symptoms, though, a brief discussion of contemplative writings on the topic is offered.

The Contemplative Tradition, Worry, and Anxiety

Among the early desert Christians, freedom from the worries and cares of the world was a central aim. Moving to the desert landscape, monks attempted to cultivate a deeper awareness of God's loving presence, surrendering control to him, and trusting that he would provide. In their pursuit of a freeing existence, the early desert Christians sought to ameliorate a preoccupation with material wealth and worldly endeavors in order to unreservedly love him. Ultimately, by depending on God, the early Christian contemplatives attempted to relinquish the grip that worry and anxiety had on their lives, detaching from anything that distracted them from God (Burton-Christie, 1993; Chryssavgis, 2008).

For the fourth-century monk Evagrius of Ponticus, worry (*merimna* in Greek) was viewed as one of the most common tempting, compulsive thoughts (*logismoi* in Greek), although not included within his famous list of eight distracting thoughts (Stewart, 2005). According to Evagrius of Ponticus, cultivating a deeper awareness of God's providence is foundational to ameliorating worry, recognizing that God is in control. Stated differently, Evagrius of Ponticus advocated for surrendering worry to God, along with being content, given that worry and anxiety can get in the way of following Jesus (Sinkewicz, 2003).

As Abba Agathon, a fourth-century desert monk, revealed, "Go, cast your powerlessness before God and you shall find rest" (quoted in Burton-Christie, 1993, p. 223). In other words, a starting point for the early desert Christians was the acknowledgment that they were weak, needing God's strength. Above all else, these monks in the barren desert terrain attempted to let go of all worldly attachments in order to focus their attention on God, trusting in his protective, loving care, rather than worrying about tomorrow. Indeed, if Christian detachment is simply defined as "the spiritual disposition, attitude, and practice of letting go of our attachments so that we can root ourselves in God," with "God [becoming] our guide and purpose" (Beasley-Topliffe, 2003, p. 80), these early desert dwellers prioritized detaching from any perceived earthly obstacles in order to practice God's presence on a daily basis. To do this, the early desert Christians employed the psalms, reciting them over and over again as a way to remain attentive to the God of love: "O God, make speed to save me: O Lord make haste to help me" (quoted in Burton-Christie, 1993, p. 126; *New International Version Bible*, 2011, Psalm 69:2). Overall, this desire to relinquish control to God, ameliorating worry in the process, is also captured in an often-overlooked Jesuit contemplative writing from over three centuries ago.

Surrendering to God's Providence: The Christian Version of Acceptance

In addition to the early desert Christians, other contemplative authors have written on suffering and the Christian life. Serving as a source of inspiration, as well as a theological foundation, for my three-part study on surrendering to divine providence as a strategy for Christians to manage chronic worry (Knabb et al., 2017), a Jesuit author wrote a short book almost four hundred years ago that captures this very dynamic. In particular, sometime in the 17th century, Claude de la Colombiere (1980) wrote *Trustful Surrender to Divine Providence*. In this work, he argued that God is sovereign. Because of this, Christians can surrender to him, capturing the secret to peace and happiness along the way.

Like a mother trusting a surgeon to remove a tumor from her child's body, Colombiere (1980) suggested Christians should let go of the tendency to fight against God's plans, recognizing that his benevolent, loving care extends to all of creation. In that God is infinitely wise and active in the world, Christians can submit to God's desires, finding peace in the reality that his design is best (Colombiere, 1980). When concluding this writing, Colombiere offered three recommendations for cultivating a deeper *trust* in God's providence, including recognizing that "nothing escapes his loving watchfulness" (p. 122), leading to the ability to surrender to him. Moreover, Christians can place their *hope* in God's providence, looking to the future to see that God offers his protective love. Finally, Christians can *love* God, appreciating his intentions and actions, even in the midst of trials. In sum, this writing has direct implications for Christian clients with anxiety disorders in the 21st century, given its emphasis on surrender, which parallels mindfulness practice in many ways. For Christian clients, letting go of the struggle with control and avoidance can help to stay rooted in the present moment, maintaining an awareness of God's loving, protective care and ameliorating the tendency to attain certainty because God is sovereign.

The Contemplative Tradition, Anxiety, and Metacognition

As revealed in the last chapter, mindfulness and contemplation seem to overlap in their ability to help practitioners gain a broader awareness of the thinking process, referred to as metacognition. This skill is especially important for Christian clients struggling with anxiety, given the preoccupation with worrying thoughts and doomsday, catastrophic predictions about the future. Being overly reliant on the world of language, caught in a state of cognitive fusion, undermines Christians' efforts to focus on Jesus, learning from him, listening to him, and following him from moment to moment.

Similar to mindfulness, contemplative practice can help Christian clients with uncertainty, worry, and anxiety to nonjudgmentally notice, with compassion and kindness, the inner world, including distressing thoughts, feelings, sensations, and memories that revolve around anxiety-inducing experiences. Focusing on a "prayer word" or phrase (Laird, 2006), Christian clients can learn to consent to God's active, loving presence, recognizing that he is with them during moments of uncertainty and doubt. Added to this nonjudgmental, attentive, loving gazing upon God is the willingness to surrender to him, letting go of control or avoidance strategies that do not work, sitting at the feet of Jesus as an alternative by embracing a *kenotic* attitude.

When the "Martha mode" of the mind (adapted from Segal et al., 2012) is mistakenly applied to inner experiences (as opposed to using "doing" for following Jesus with virtue-based action), Christian clients can erroneously pursue control and avoidance strategies, trying to rid themselves of anxiety through worry, compulsively checking, seeking reassurance, avoiding stressful environments, and isolating from other people. Unfortunately, when this happens, Christian clients are unable to follow Jesus's plan. Within contemplative practice, though, Christian clients are learning to rest at Jesus's feet, anchoring themselves to the here-and-now to gain a deeper awareness of God's active, loving presence. As this happens, Christian clients are able to slowly let go of their futile control or avoidance efforts, which simply do not work. Because God is benevolent and sovereign, Christian clients can trust that he will work

251

things out for good (Romans 8:28), even in the midst of suffering and hardship. Instead, Christian clients can focus their attention on virtue-based action, following Jesus on the road of life. Before concluding this chapter, what follows are several additional considerations when working with Christian clients with anxiety disorders.

Faith-Based ACT for Anxiety

To begin, counselors and therapists using faith-based ACT need to secure informed consent from Christian clients (see the previous chapter for a more detailed discussion). After consent is attained, counselors and therapists can use a range of measures to better understand both Christian clients' anxiety in particular and psychological and spiritual functioning in general, mentioned below in no particular order.[2] For example, the Beck Anxiety Inventory (BAI; Beck et al., 1988) can be used, along with the Penn State Worry Questionnaire (PSWQ; Meyer et al., 1990) and Intolerance of Uncertainty Scale (IUS; Buhr & Dugas, 2002). Moreover, the Multidimensional Experiential Avoidance Questionnaire (MEAQ; Gamez et al., 2011) can be administered to measure experiential avoidance. Furthermore, the Brief RCOPE (Pargament et al., 2011) can be utilized to measure positive and negative forms of religious coping, the Communion with God Scale (CGS; Knabb & Wang, 2021) can be employed to measure Christian clients' relationship with God, and the Christian Contentment Scale (CCS; Knabb et al., 2020) can be given to measure Christian clients' level of inner satisfaction in the middle of psychological suffering.[3] Finally, two subscales can be employed to better understand Christian clients' views on God's providence and surrender as a form of religious coping—the Providence Scale (Lawrence, 1997) and Surrender Scale (Wong-McDonald & Gorsuch, 2000). Overall, this integrative strategy involves a better understanding of both psychological and spiritual functioning, including symptoms of worry, anxiety, intolerance of uncertainty, and experiential avoidance, along with psychospiritual functioning, such as positive and negative forms of religious coping, communion with God, Christian contentment, deeply ingrained beliefs about God's providence, and surrender as a Christian version of religious coping.

In terms of the role of the counselor or therapist, counselors or therapists can refer to the previous chapter for a discussion on a faith-based ACT approach. Of course, it is worth mentioning that counselors and therapists can model a contemplative stance for Christian clients by coming across as nonjudgmental, compassionate, and connected to the here-and-now, aware of God's loving, active presence, even in the midst of anxiety symptoms. In other words, it is important to help Christian clients endure anxiety, in their proverbial "cell," recognizing that God is with them. As a result, Christian clients can yield to God's protective care, rather than trying to control or avoid uncertainty, worry, and anxiety. Above all else, a calm, relaxed engagement with anxious Christian clients is ideal, demonstrating openness and flexibility.

Regarding applying faith-based ACT to Christian clients with anxiety disorders, a central theme involves yielding to God's protective care during moments of uncertainty, worry, and anxiety. Because anxious Christian clients may struggle with accepting an uncertain future, some will have a difficult time staying rooted in the present moment, letting go of attempts to either attain certainty through control or avoid uncertainty through procrastination and related endeavors. With Christian clients, the Bible addresses God's benevolent, sovereign care frequently (e.g., Ephesians 1:11–12; Psalm 103:19; Romans 8:28, 9:21). In fact, as noted previously, Jesus spoke about yielding to God's providence when teaching on worry (Matthew 6:25–34), which means that Christian clients can anchor themselves in the present moment, ameliorating efforts to worry about tomorrow because God will provide for them, consistent with God's care for his creation. Although by no means an easy task, daily dedication can begin to produce results, as revealed in my aforementioned pilot study.

To address intolerance of uncertainty, contemplative practice, rather than mindfulness meditation, can be employed, especially because a central purpose is to surrender to God's active, loving presence through silence, stillness, and the repetition of a "prayer word," which anchors clients to the present moment (Keating, 2006). Consistent with the "being" mode (Segal et al., 2012), "hearing" rather than "doing," and resting at Jesus's feet like Mary, Christian clients can learn through daily contemplative practice that there is nowhere else to be and nothing else to do when they are spending time with the God of love. Because God is in control, Christian clients can let go of their own efforts to attain certainty and predict the future. In fact, reminiscent of Psalm 46, Christians can "be still," ceasing all striving and dropping their metaphorical weapons in the midst of an inner battle because God is loving, powerful, and in control (Earwood, 1989; *New International Version Bible*, 2011).

Related to Christian clients' struggle with uncertainty, worry will likely be a common theme, with many clients worrying about an unknown, ambiguous future. When this is the case, counselors and therapists can focus on the defusion process of faith-based ACT to help Christian clients let go of the tendency to overly rely on language when making sense of both the inner world and outer world (i.e., the future). Consistent with the *apophatic* tradition, Christian clients can use contemplative practice to relate to God in a wordless, imageless state, relinquishing the tendency to fuse with language in an effort to "fix," "problem-solve," or obtain "objective" answers about the future.

Instead, Christian clients can practice patience, attentively sitting at the feet of Jesus and utilizing centering prayer, the Jesus Prayer, or the welcoming prayer to endure anxious inner states, surrendering worry and uncertainty to God along the way. Staying anchored to the present moment, cultivating a deeper awareness of God's active, loving presence, is the central aim, which can be developed via four of the faith-based ACT processes, housed within the "watching and enduring" and "noticing and shifting" pillars. After all, freedom for the early desert Christians involved surrendering to God's protective care, shedding efforts to control their world because God is benevolent and sovereign. In turn, the "committing and following" pillar of faith-based ACT can be emphasized so that Christian clients with anxiety disorders can walk with the God of love on the road of life, doing so with a set of biblical virtues to guide the way.

Furthermore, similar to the previous chapter, counselors and therapists can work with Christian clients to accept the likely reality that anxiety is a chronic experience, helping them to gently return to their loving gaze upon Jesus when they recognize they have been swept away by uncertainty, worry, and anxiety. In other words, an attitude of gentle, compassionate, kind curiosity is being developed, given that Jesus is with them. Instead of catastrophizing about the inner or outer worlds, including panicking about the physiological symptoms of anxiety and worrying about an uncertain future, Christian clients can work toward accepting that the future is impossible to predict and recognizing that God is omniscient, orchestrating each and every step.

Above all else, through contemplative practice, Christian clients can deepen their awareness of God's presence, gaining an appreciation for his active, loving attentiveness. By connecting to this awareness in the present moment, Christian clients are better prepared to respond to anxious inner states with openness and flexibility in order to pivot toward following Jesus, a central aim within faith-based ACT. Using watchfulness strategies, endurance exercises, interventions for cultivating an awareness of the contemplative self, and practicing God's presence so as to achieve a silent, still, and attentive inner state, Christian clients can ameliorate the tendency to overly rely on control and avoidance. Again, rather than using mindfulness to pragmatically relate differently to anxiety symptoms, Christian clients can draw from contemplative approaches to yield to God's protective care.

In consideration of the structure of each session, a general overview can be found in the previous chapter on depression, which will be similar when working with clients with anxiety disorders. To adjust the session content for working with Christian clients with anxiety, the first session can emphasize obtaining informed consent, completing a thorough intake, and attaining background information on uncertainty, worry, anxiety, and control and avoidance strategies. Indeed, Christian clients will likely describe some sort of variation of these challenges as the "presenting problem," with counselors and therapists assisting Christian clients in recognizing that struggling to accept uncertainty is a hindrance to a virtuous life.

Also in this session, use of the "Fork in the Road" assessment tool can be helpful (adapted from Harris, 2019; Hayes et al., 2012), and faith-based ACT counselors and therapists can assist Christian clients in better understanding the relationship between uncertainty, worry, and anxiety, including the idea that surrendering to God's providence can help in letting go of ineffective strategies for attempting to attain certainty via control or avoid uncertainty via procrastination and related endeavors. Therefore, similar to Mary sitting at Jesus's feet, Christian clients can employ contemplative strategies to yield to God's presence.

In the second meeting, unhelpful control or avoidance strategies can be further explored, especially in the context of trying to walk alone on the road of life, apart from God's protective care, with the willingness to endure offered as an alternative. For Christian clients, willingness constitutes following Jesus during moments of uncertainty, worry, and anxiety, accepting that uncertainty and anxiety are a part of the human condition, helping to anticipate future events and take action to resolve problems. Within faith-based ACT, acceptance involves recognizing God's sovereignty, with endurance (*hupomone* in Greek) defined as a patient, steadfast hope, trusting that God is active in instances of uncertainty and doubt. In the second session, the welcoming prayer (Bourgeault, 2004) can be employed to allow Christian clients to invite God into the uncertainty, shifting from the "Martha mode" to the "Mary mode" of the mind when relating to distressing private events (adapted from Segal et al., 2012). Although problem solving and fixing are definitely helpful in many life pursuits, they ultimately distract Christian clients from following Jesus when they are applied to the inner world. Rather, inviting God into the process, yielding to his active, loving presence, can help to relate differently to uncertainty, worry, and anxiety.

In sessions three and four, cognitive defusion is presented to continue to work on ways to relate differently to anxiety. Thus, thoughts about an uncertain future, along with catastrophic, doomsday predictions, can be discussed, with a special emphasis on God's protective care. In other words, instead of trying to control or avoid the world in isolation, Christian clients can let go because God is sovereign, acting in a loving way to work things out according to his plan. Rather than overemphasizing language and unilateral problem-solving strategies, which simply do not work in the long run, Christian clients can use *apophatic* prayer to sit at Jesus's feet during moments of uncertainty, anchor themselves to the present moment, which is where God is located, and let go of leaning on their own understanding (Proverbs 3:5).

For the next two sessions, mindfulness can be utilized to notice the inner world from a safe distance, cultivating an awareness of the difference between the verbal and transcendent self and staying anchored to the present moment. For Christian clients, of course, contemplative practices can be offered as an alternative, culturally sensitive version. During moments of uncertainty, worry, and anxiety, Christian clients can learn to shift from "doing" to "being" (Segal et al., 2012), given that control and avoidance do not typically work. Also, surrendering to God's providence is key, since Jesus taught that worry is to be relinquished because God provides for humans, paralleling his loving care for his creation (Matthew 6:25–34).

In the next five sessions, values can be explored, which offer the ability to identify principles to live by, as well as goals to pursue values on a daily basis. Linked to behavioral action is willingness, given that clients must endure psychological pain to pursue what matters. With Christian clients, though, biblical virtues can be identified in the place of values, since virtuous living is explicated throughout the pages of the Bible, especially in the context of Jesus's teachings. In these sessions, the personhood of Jesus can be further explored, since he exemplifies an ideal blend of acceptance and action, culminating with his awareness of God's loving, active presence.

In the final meeting, strategies for Christian clients to continue to apply faith-based ACT to daily living can be explored, along with potential barriers to following Jesus. An explication of likely roadblocks is especially salient, given that anxiety may continue to arise. When this happens, though, Christian clients can ask a central question: "Given that uncertainty, worry, and anxiety may continue to come up on a daily basis, how can I balance sitting at the feet of Jesus with following him in order to live a life that glorifies God, surrendering my own efforts to control or avoid because he is sovereign?" Similar to what was presented in the last chapter, Christian clients are especially encouraged to think about enduring to the very end, faithfully following Jesus on a daily basis: "I have fought the good fight, I have finished the race, I have kept the faith" (*New International Version Bible*, 2011, 2 Timothy 4:7).

Consistent with the previous chapter's recommendations, Harris (2019) offered a variety of convenient forms for traditional ACT counselors and therapists to use—such as case conceptualization worksheets and other tools to organize session content—which can be adjusted for faith-based ACT. Certainly, most traditional ACT forms can be modified so that an awareness of God's active, loving presence is a central aim. Along the way, Christian clients are (a) "watching and enduring," watching intolerance of uncertainty, worry, and anxiety and enduring uncertainty, worry, and anxiety because the God of love is present; (b) "noticing and shifting," noticing the difference between "earthly-mindedness" and "heavenly-mindedness" (Burroughs, 2010, 2014; Rowe, 1672), shifting toward the contemplative self, and practicing God's presence so as to cultivate a deeper inner peace, stillness, and silence in the midst of uncertainty, worry, and anxiety; and (c) "committing and following," committing to a set of biblical virtues to guide life and following Jesus (i.e., walking with God in love) on the road of life whenever struggling with uncertainty, worry, and anxiety. In that traditional ACT emphasizes six processes, faith-based ACT counselors and therapists can determine which process they would like to start with, especially since each process is linked to the others and they all help clients to improve psychological flexibility. To be sure, for Christian clients with anxiety disorders, watchfulness (*nepsis* in Greek), endurance (*hupomone* in Greek), the contemplative self (the *nous* in Greek), practicing God's presence

256

(*hesychia* in Greek), biblical virtues, and following Jesus all lead to a better grasp of God's active, loving presence.

Conclusion

To wrap up this chapter, a central aim in the Christian life involves faithfully following Jesus, even when the pain of life seemingly gets in the way. Rather than employing control or avoidance strategies, Christian clients can patiently endure, recognizing that God is with them in their proverbial "cell" and actively engaging with them in both the inner and outer worlds. Instead of overly relying on impermanent, wavering inner states to guide life, Christian clients can identify and implement a variety of biblical virtues, which emanate from the life and teachings of Jesus.

Because Christian clients place Jesus at the center of their faith, believing he is the source of life and Son of God (John 1:1, 3:16, 14:6), they can walk with him, listen to him, learn from him, and act on his teachings, reminiscent of value-based action in traditional ACT. In the process, especially in the context of anxiety, Christian clients can apply faith-based ACT strategies to untangle themselves from the world of language, accept inner pain because God is with them, gently notice the inner world from a safe distance, and deepen their awareness of God's active, loving presence through contemplative practice. In turn, accepting the inner world can allow them to focus their time, energy, and attention on the God of love, discerning his will and living a vibrant, meaningful life. Whether Christian clients are stuck because of intolerance of uncertainty, worry, or other symptoms of anxiety, there is hope, since Jesus led the way, offering a stable, reliable path for Christian clients to take.

Notes

1 See http://www.div12.org/PsychologicalTreatments/treatments.html for a list of evidence-based practices, including traditional ACT for mixed anxiety disorders.
2 As noted in the previous chapter, because these instruments were originally developed for research-related purposes, not necessarily counseling and therapy, they should only be used as brief measures to get a preliminary understanding of Christian clients' psychological and spiritual functioning.
3 Consistent with the footnote in the previous chapter, both of these measures are important because healthy psychological and spiritual functioning in the Christian life involves walking (i.e., communing) with God and experiencing a deeper contentment in him in the midst of anxiety symptoms.

References

A-Tjak, J., Davis, M., Morina, N., Powers, M., Smits, J., & Emmelkamp, P. (2015). A meta-analysis of the efficacy of acceptance and commitment therapy for clinically relevant mental and physical health problems. *Psychotherapy and Psychosomatics, 84,* 30–36.

Batten, S. (2011). *Essentials of acceptance and commitment therapy.* SAGE Publications Inc.

Beasley-Topliffe, K. (Ed.). (2003). *The upper room dictionary of Christian spiritual formation.* Upper Room Books.

Beck, A. T., Brown, G., Epstein, N., & Steer, R. A. (1988). An inventory for measuring clinical anxiety: Psychometric properties. *Journal of Consulting and Clinical Psychology, 56,* 893–897.

Bourgeault, C. (2004). *Centering prayer and inner awakening.* Cowley Publications.

Buhr, K., & Dugas, M. (2002). The intolerance of uncertainty scale: Psychometric properties of the English version. *Behaviour Research and Therapy, 40,* 931–945.

Burroughs, J. (2010). *Heavenly-mindedness recommended: In a discourse on Colossians 3:2.* Gale ECCO.

Burroughs, J. (2014). *A treatise on earthly-mindedness.* GLH Publishing.

Burton-Christie, D. (1993). *The word in the desert: Scripture and the quest for holiness in early Christian monasticism.* Oxford University Press.

Carleton, R., Mulvogue, M., Thibodeau, M., McCabe, R., Antony, M., & Asmundson, G. (2012). Increasingly certain about uncertainty: Intolerance of uncertainty across anxiety and depression. *Journal of Anxiety Disorders, 26,* 468–479.

Chryssavgis, J. (2008). *In the heart of the desert: The spirituality of the desert fathers and mothers.* World Wisdom, Inc.

Colombiere, C. (1980). *Trustful surrender to divine providence: The secret of peace and happiness.* Tan Books.

Dugas, M., & Robichaud, M. (2007). *Cognitive-behavioral treatment for generalized anxiety disorder: From science to practice.* Routledge.

Earwood, G. (1989). Psalm 46. *Review and Expositor, 86,* 79–86.

Eifert, G., & Forsyth, J. (2005). *Acceptance & commitment therapy for anxiety disorders: A practitioner's treatment guide to using mindfulness, acceptance, and values-based behavior change strategies.* New Harbinger Publications, Inc.

Erickson, M. (2013). *Christian theology* (3rd ed.). Baker Academic.

Gamez, W., Chmielewski, M., Kotov, R., Ruggero, C., & Watson, D. (2011). Development of a measure of experiential avoidance: The multidimensional experiential avoidance questionnaire. *Psychological Assessment, 23,* 692–713.

Harris, R. (2019). *ACT made simple: An easy-to-read primer on acceptance and commitment therapy* (2nd ed.). New Harbinger Publications, Inc.

Hayes, S., Strosahl, K., & Wilson, K. (2012). *Acceptance and commitment therapy: The process and practice of mindful change* (2nd ed.). The Guilford Press.

Hofmann, S., Sawyer, A., Witt, A., & Oh, D. (2010). The effect of mindfulness-based therapy on anxiety and depression: A meta-analytic review. *Journal of Consulting and Clinical Psychology, 78,* 169–183.

Keating, T. (2006). *Open mind, open heart, 20th anniversary edition.* Continuum.

Knabb, J., & Wang, K. (2021). The communion with God scale: Shifting from an *etic* to *emic* perspective to assess fellowshipping with the Triune God. *Psychology of Religion and Spirituality, 13,* 67–80.

Knabb, J., Frederick, T., & Cumming, T. (2017). Surrendering to God's providence: A three-part study on providence-focused therapy for recurrent worry (PFT-RW). *Psychology of Religion and Spirituality, 9,* 180–196.

Knabb, J., Vazquez, V., & Wang, K. (2020). The Christian contentment scale: An *emic* measure for assessing inner satisfaction within the Christian tradition. *Journal of Psychology and Theology*. Advance online publication.

Laird, M. (2006). *Into the silent land: A guide to the Christian practice of contemplation*. Oxford University Press.

Lawrence, R. (1997). Measuring the image of God: The God image inventory. *Journal of Psychology and Theology, 25*, 214–226.

Mahoney, A., & McEvoy, P. (2012). A transdiagnostic examination of intolerance of uncertainty across anxiety and depressive disorders. *Cognitive Behaviour Therapy, 41*, 212–222.

Meyer, T., Miller, M., Metzger, R., & Borkovec, T. (1990). Development and validation of the Penn State worry questionnaire. *Behaviour Research and Therapy, 28*, 487–495.

New International Version Bible. (2011). Zondervan. https://www.biblegateway.com/

Orsillo, S., Roemer, L., Block-Lerner, J., LeJeune, C., & Herbert, J. (2004). ACT with anxiety disorders. In S. Hayes & K. Strosahl (Eds.), *A practical guide to acceptance and commitment therapy* (pp. 103–132). Springer.

Pargament, K., Feuille, M., & Burdzy, D. (2011). The Brief RCOPE: Current psychometric status of a short measure of religious coping. *Religions, 2*, 51–76.

Rowe, J. (1672). *Heavenly-mindedness and earthly-mindedness: In two parts*. Francis Tyton.

Segal, Z., Williams, M., & Teasdale, J. (2012). *Mindfulness-based cognitive therapy for depression* (2nd ed.). The Guilford Press.

Sexton, K., & Dugas, M. (2009). Defining distinct negative beliefs about uncertainty: Validating the factor structure of the intolerance of uncertainty scale. *Psychological Assessment, 21*, 176–186.

Sinkewicz, R. (2003). *Evagrius of Pontus: The Greek ascetic corpus*. Oxford University Press.

Stewart, C. (2005). Evagrius Ponticus and the "eight generic logismoi." In R. Newhauser (Ed.), *In the garden of evil: The vices and cultures in the middle ages* (pp. 3–34). Pontifical Institute of Mediaeval Studies.

Twohig, M., & Levin, M. (2017). Acceptance and commitment therapy as a treatment for anxiety and depression: A review. *Psychiatric Clinics of North America, 40*, 751–770.

Wilson, K., & DuFrene, T. (2010). *Things might go terribly, horribly wrong: A guide to life liberated from anxiety*. New Harbinger Publications, Inc.

Wong-McDonald, A., & Gorsuch, R. (2000). Surrender to God: An additional coping style? *Journal of Psychology and Theology, 28*, 149–161.

Yarhouse, M., Butman, R., & McRay, B. (2005). *Modern psychopathologies: A comprehensive Christian appraisal*. InterVarsity Press.

11

FAITH-BASED ACT FOR TRAUMA

Introduction

In this chapter, the six traditional acceptance and commitment therapy (ACT) processes are explored in the context of trauma, focusing on cognitive behavioral theories of trauma; a Christian perspective on trauma; Christian contemplative writings on the topic; and a faith-based ACT approach to trauma. In that trauma survivors often employ rumination as a cognitive response to trauma-related intrusive memories and emotional distress, targeting this type of perseverative thinking is a focus of the chapter. What is more, both mindfulness and contemplative strategies are discussed, given that these practices can help clients relate more flexibly to trauma symptoms (e.g., intrusive memories, emotional distress, rumination). Indeed, in recent years, I have conducted original research on trauma among Christian adults, which is presented in this chapter. Overall, faith-based ACT for trauma is about flexibly and nonjudgmentally shifting the attention from trauma-based rumination to contemplating the love of God, employing the Christian contemplative tradition to intentionally and successfully make this pivot.

Traditional CBT for Trauma[1]

In recent years, the cognitive behavioral therapy (CBT) literature has focused on the transdiagnostic construct of rumination for making sense of trauma symptoms and disorders (Ehlers & Clark, 2000; Ehring & Ehlers, 2014). In response to a traumatic event, trauma survivors may struggle with intrusive, vivid memories about the event, such as upsetting images, flashbacks, and nightmares. Given such unwanted memories often cause a sizeable amount of emotional distress because they seem so real in the present moment, trauma survivors may utilize rumination as an ineffective coping strategy, which involves perseverating about the content or experience of the trauma (Smets et al., 2012). In doing so, they might be attempting to avoid the emotional pain that accompanies the intrusive memories, turning, instead, to rumination as a more removed, distant,

DOI: 10.4324/9781003181941-12

overly cognitive coping mechanism (Michael et al., 2007; Steil & Ehlers, 2000). Although this cognitive attempt to distance themselves from the emotional distress that accompanies trauma-related intrusive memories certainly makes sense, it may actually lead to added intrusive memories and emotional pain (Ehlers & Clark, 2000; Ehring & Ehlers, 2014; Michael et al., 2007). Thus, the common rumination strategy of repeatedly asking "why," "what if," and "how" questions about the trauma (e.g., "Why did this happen to me?" "What if it happens again?" "How can I prevent it from happening again?") fails to actually ameliorate the intrusive memories and corresponding emotional distress that are causing so much psychological suffering (Ehlers & Clark, 2000; Ehring & Ehlers, 2014; Michael et al., 2007).

In the last two decades, researchers have attempted to more precisely define rumination, given it can exacerbate psychological suffering across psychological disorders (e.g., depressive, anxiety, trauma-related). In general, rumination is often a passive, perseverative, and unhelpful cognitive attempt to think about past events, the meaning attached to past events, and the current emotions that correspond with past events, with the ultimate aim of achieving perceived control and a sense of distance from psychological pain (Ehlers & Clark, 2000; Ehring et al., 2011; Michael et al., 2007; Smith & Alloy, 2009; Wolkin, 2015). Simply put, rumination is commonly a cognitive form of experiential avoidance.

Based on this understanding—rumination is frequently utilized among trauma survivors as an ineffective cognitive coping mechanism to reduce or eliminate trauma-related intrusive memories and emotional distress—the CBT literature has often turned to mindfulness-based interventions to help trauma survivors relate differently to trauma symptoms. In particular, mindfulness meditation may help trauma survivors to (a) cultivate sustained, flexible attention, shifting from trauma-based memories, emotional distress, and rumination to other avenues of awareness (e.g., the breath, the senses); (b) develop a nonjudgmental, open attitude toward trauma symptoms; and (c) ameliorate the tendency to overly rely on rigid, compulsive, perseverative thinking (e.g., rumination) as an ineffective cognitive coping mechanism for trauma (Lang et al., 2012).

To empirically confirm this theoretical understanding, among a sample of college students, Im and Follette (2016) found that rumination mediated the relationship between the reported number of traumatic events and trauma symptoms, suggesting that individuals who have experienced more trauma occurrences may overly rely on rumination, which, unfortunately, ends up leading to a greater frequency of trauma symptoms. What is more, rumination mediated the relationship between mindfulness and trauma symptoms, which reveals that being more mindful may lead to less rumination, resulting in a lower number of trauma symptoms (Im & Follette, 2016). In a separate study of community trauma survivors, Bishop et al. (2018) found that experiential avoidance mediated the relationship between rumination and trauma symptoms.

Overall, these findings elucidate that rumination may play a key role in trauma-related symptoms and disorders, functioning as a form of experiential avoidance. If this is the case, targeting rumination can be an important way to ameliorate trauma-related symptoms and disorders among trauma survivors. To do so, mindfulness-based approaches may hold promise, given their emphasis on cultivating sustained, flexible, nonjudgmental attention in the here-and-now, which may help trauma survivors relate to intrusive memories and emotional distress with more openness and curiosity, rather than engaging in perseverative rumination, which tends to exacerbate the very symptoms they are trying to avoid.

Intervention-wise, King et al. (2013) conducted a pilot study on *mindfulness-based cognitive therapy* (MBCT) for veterans with *posttraumatic stress disorder* (PTSD). Adapting the eight-week MBCT protocol to target trauma (rather than depressive) symptoms, practitioners engaged in a variety of mindfulness exercises (e.g., mindfully eating a raisin, mindful walking, mindful breathing), with results revealing small to large effect sizes pre- to post-treatment for the MBCT group in the reduction of trauma symptoms (King et al., 2013). Although rumination *per se* was not tracked in this pilot study, the results suggest that mindfulness may hold promise as an intervention for overall trauma symptoms. With this theoretical and empirical foundation in mind, traditional ACT, which is part of the mindfulness-based cognitive behavioral tradition, has been utilized in recent years to target trauma-related symptoms and disorders.

Traditional ACT for Trauma

According to traditional ACT, trauma-related disorders (e.g., PTSD) often involve experiential avoidance, which is the struggle to stay connected to difficult inner experiences, such as thoughts, feelings, sensations, and memories, along with the accompanying behavioral efforts to reduce, eliminate, avoid, or distract from psychological pain (Follette & Pistorello, 2007; Walser & Westrup, 2007). Short-term, experiential avoidance may seem to work for trauma survivors, given they might experience some relief from trauma-related symptoms and experiences in the inner (e.g., intrusive memories) and outer (e.g., environmental triggers) worlds (Follette & Pistorello, 2007; Walser & Westrup, 2007). Yet, over time, experiential avoidance seldom produces lasting results, given trauma survivors are unable to consistently live out their values so as to create a meaningful, vibrant life (Follette & Pistorello, 2007; Walser & Westrup, 2007).

Beyond experiential avoidance, trauma survivors may end up struggling with cognitive fusion, overly relying on the verbal, storied self and dwelling on the past or future. With this type of cognitive entanglement, trauma survivors may actually believe that trauma-related thoughts in the inner world are factual and true in the outer world, which can undermine value-based action (e.g., "No one is safe in this world," "I know I'll be abused again"). What is more, trauma survivors may overly rely on the verbal, storied self, generating a narrative in response to trauma that can get in the way of value-based living (e.g., "I was abused because I'm worthless and unlovable"). Finally, trauma survivors may be preoccupied with the past (e.g., trauma-related memories) or future (e.g., catastrophic predictions about the trauma happening again), which can get in the way of maintaining flexible attention in the present moment so as to live out a set of well-defined values in the here-and-now. Overall, the aforementioned struggles can be addressed with the four mindfulness-based processes of traditional ACT, including cognitive defusion, acceptance, the transcendent self, and present-moment awareness.

In revisiting the definition of mindfulness from previous chapters, the key ingredients include "the self-regulation of attention so that it is maintained on immediate experience" and employing an attitude toward present-moment experiences "characterized by curiosity, openness, and acceptance" (Bishop et al., 2004, p. 232). Stated more succinctly, the skills that are embedded in mindfulness include attention, present-moment awareness, and acceptance (Feldman et al., 2007). In the context of trauma symptoms, trauma survivors can use mindfulness to cultivate sustained, flexible attention in the here-and-now, accepting trauma symptoms (e.g., intrusive memories, emotional distress, rumination) with openness and nonjudgment as they learn to pivot toward the pursuit of value-based living. In other words, when trauma survivors experience intrusive memories and emotional distress and begin to ruminate as an unhelpful cognitive avoidance strategy, they can utilize mindfulness to notice this process with present-moment nonjudgment, openness, and curiosity, then gently shift toward a set of values to guide life, before engaging in committed action to create a life of meaning and purpose. Along the way, they are learning to relate to the inner world with more tentativeness, rather than getting stuck in ruminative avoidance strategies that only end up distracting them from the life they want to live.

Research on Mindfulness-Based Counseling and Therapy for Trauma

In consideration of the mindfulness-based processes of traditional ACT, empirical support has emerged in recent years that suggests mindfulness may be helpful in ameliorating trauma-related symptoms and disorders. For instance, in their review of 18 studies, Hopwood and Schutte's (2017) meta-analysis revealed a medium effect size when examining the impact that mindfulness-based interventions have on reducing trauma symptoms. As another example, Taylor et al. (2020) examined 24 studies on mindfulness-based approaches for trauma, with findings also revealing a medium effect size when investigating the influence that mindfulness has on trauma. Although, to date, no meta-analyses appear to have been published on traditional ACT for trauma-related symptoms and disorders (Bean et al., 2017), based on the aforementioned meta-analytic findings on mindfulness-based interventions, coupled with several publications on traditional ACT applied to trauma (Follette & Pistorello, 2007; Harris, 2021; Walser & Westrup, 2007), traditional ACT appears to hold promise as a comprehensive, process-oriented, mindfulness-based approach for trauma. When working with Christian clients with trauma, of course, it is important to understand a Christian viewpoint on the topic, reviewed in the next section of this chapter.

Christianity and Trauma[2]

According to Christianity, the fall of humankind in Genesis 3 led to suffering entering the world, which includes the inevitable, ubiquitous experience of traumatic events (e.g., car accidents, physical and sexual abuse, the loss of a loved one). When experiencing trauma, a portion of Christian clients may go on to struggle with recurrent, unwanted memories, leading to an overreliance on rumination as an unproductive cognitive avoidance strategy to ameliorate both the original distressing memory and corresponding emotional distress. With rumination, Christian clients may repeatedly ask "why," "what if," and "how" questions in an effort to distance themselves from intrusive, overly vivid memories and related emotional pain, such as "Why did the trauma happen to me?" "What if the trauma happens again?" and "How could I have stopped the trauma from taking place?" (Ehlers & Clark, 2000; Michael et al., 2007). In fact, for Christian clients, rumination may also consist of unhelpful perseverative content about God, such as God's perceived absence during and/or after the trauma (e.g., "Why did God let this happen?" "Why was God not there to protect me?" "What if God is punishing me?") (Exline et al., 2014; Wilt et al., 2017). Unfortunately, combined, this amalgam of ruminative themes, both secular and religious/spiritual, may end up exacerbating the very symptoms Christian clients are attempting to avoid. Because of this, Christian clients might attempt to focus on, or turn to, God with prayer and related forms of religious coping (Pargament et al., 2000).

Yet, without a distinct set of skills to ameliorate this entrenched, unhelpful cognitive pattern of rumination (e.g., getting stuck in repeatedly asking "why," "what if," and "how" questions about the trauma itself or God's role in the trauma), Christian clients may remain stuck in perseverative thinking and struggle to attain the peace and comfort they are seeking from God. Thus, if rumination is simply defined as "the act of thinking deeply about something" (*Oxford Dictionary*, n.d.b), a particular skillset (e.g., attention, present-moment awareness, acceptance; Feldman et al., 2007), anchored to the Christian contemplative tradition, may help with relating differently to trauma symptoms and successfully pivoting from trauma-based rumination to contemplating God. Undoubtedly, if rumination is about pondering a chosen topic in depth and contemplation is defined as "the action of looking thoughtfully at something for a long time" (*Oxford Dictionary*, n.d.a), learning the right set of skills for pivoting from ruminating about the trauma to contemplating the love of God may be necessary for Christian trauma survivors to successfully respond to trauma-related intrusive memories and emotional distress.

With this theoretical understanding in mind, in a recent study of community Christian adults with a history of trauma, I found that trauma-related rumination (e.g., "why," "what if," and "how" questions about the traumatic event; questioning God's availability in the midst of, or following, the traumatic event) was positively associated with attempts to focus on God (e.g., praying to God, focusing on spiritual content) as a form of religious coping, with this relationship mediated by a specific set of mental skills (e.g., attention, present-moment awareness, acceptance) (Knabb et al., 2019). In turn, I completed a two-part randomized trial on Christian meditative and contemplative practices for trauma-based rumination among samples of Christian college and community adults with a history of trauma (Knabb et al., 2021). After completing four weeks of daily Christian meditative and contemplative practices (e.g., Brother Lawrence's [2015] *The Practice of the Presence of God*, the Jesus Prayer) for developing attention, present-moment awareness, and acceptance in response to trauma-related rumination, findings revealed a reduction in rumination, spiritual struggles, content-independent perseverative thinking, and trauma symptoms (small to medium effect sizes), as well as an increase in mindfulness (small to medium effect sizes), for the intervention group.

In line with a traditional ACT viewpoint, Christian clients may struggle with experiential avoidance in response to trauma-related intrusive memories, attempting to use rumination as a cognitive strategy for reducing, eliminating, avoiding, or distracting from emotional distress. Yet, in doing so, they may be unable to create a meaningful, fulfilling life, given they are prioritizing the elimination of pain above following Jesus and carrying out God's will. When this is the case, Christian contemplative practices may help them to successfully pivot from unhelpful ruminations to a present-moment awareness of God's perfect love (Knabb & Bates, 2020). Although the intrusive memories and corresponding emotional distress may not fully go away, they will be walking with the God of love so as to endure with him as they head toward their final destination—being face to face with God in heaven, free from their traumatic experiences and corresponding symptoms in this broken world. Until then, Christian contemplation (and the corresponding skills attached to this practice), rather than mindfulness, can help Christian clients respond differently to some of the inevitable traumas they will experience on this planet, doing so with a greater awareness of the inner workings of the fallen human mind.

The Contemplative Tradition, Trauma, and Metacognition

Consistent with the previous two chapters, mindfulness and contemplation at least partially align in their ability to help practitioners cultivate metacognitive awareness, that is, the crucial human skill of thinking about thinking. In the context of trauma-related symptoms and disorders, Christian clients may end up being preoccupied with intrusive memories and the corresponding emotional distress, searching for a cognitive avoidance strategy. In utilizing rumination, Christian clients might succeed in distracting themselves, short-term. Yet, long-term, they may end up missing out on life, given they are spending their time and energy dwelling on answers to "why," "what if," and "how" questions that may never come.

With the skill of attention, Christian clients can learn to engage in a more sustained, flexible form of concentration, gently pivoting from rumination to an awareness of the God of love whenever they are experiencing intrusive memories and emotional distress. In this process, they are gaining a greater awareness of the thinking process itself, especially unhelpful patterns of repetitive thinking that distract them from the life Jesus has called them to live. Rather than dwelling on the past trauma, moreover, Christian clients can cultivate a greater awareness of God's active, loving presence in the here-and-now, which can help them to walk with God in love on the road of life. In so doing, they are, again, gaining a greater awareness of the thinking process, noticing rumination, then turning to the God of love. Finally, with acceptance, Christian clients can learn to relate differently to trauma symptoms (e.g., intrusive memories, emotional distress), given they are practicing God's presence within the inner world, not unilaterally striving to eliminate psychological suffering with the process of rumination. In other words, they are gaining a more distant, accepting, transcendent awareness of the internal world, simply noticing the inner workings of the mind, not engaging in perseverative rumination as an ineffective avoidance strategy.

To cultivate these three contemplative skills—attention, present-moment awareness, and acceptance—for effectively responding to trauma-based symptoms, a "prayer word" (Laird, 2006) can be utilized. By employing a short "prayer word" or phrase, Christian clients are learning to "reset" whenever they get stuck in perseverative rumination, recognizing that they can endure because the God of love is with them. In other words, they are using an indirect method (Ware, 2001), given they are noticing their trauma symptoms, then slowly pivoting to an awareness of God's presence, not attempting to eliminate the pain. Ultimately, with contemplative practice, the pain does not go away. Rather, Christians have the strength to persevere in knowing that they are a dwelling place for God's love. According to the contemplative author Julian of Norwich (2013), "God is the Creator who dwells in the center of our own being, which is his true home." Indeed, as God takes up residence in every room of Christian clients' proverbial homes, the trauma symptoms no longer have the ability to dictate the direction they take in life. Instead, Christian clients have the metacognitive awareness to simply observe the inner workings of the fallen mind, with God as the trustworthy "head of the house."

Faith-Based ACT for Trauma

As a starting point, counselors and therapists using faith-based ACT need to obtain informed consent from Christian clients (see Chapter 9 for a more detailed discussion). From there, counselors and therapists can use several brief instruments to better understand Christian clients' current psychological and spiritual functioning,[3] including (in no particular order) the Trauma Symptom Checklist-40 (TSCL-40; Briere & Runtz, 1989) to measure trauma symptoms; Responses to Intrusions Questionnaire (RIQ; Clohessy & Ehlers, 1999; Murray et al., 2002; Steil & Ehlers, 2000) to measure trauma-related rumination; Multidimensional Experiential Avoidance Questionnaire (MEAQ; Gamez et al., 2011) to measure experiential avoidance; Responses to Specific Religious/Spiritual Struggles Measure (RSRSSM; Wilt et al., 2017) to measure religious/spiritual struggles; RCOPE (Pargament et al., 2000) to measure a variety of positive and negative forms of religious coping; Communion with God Scale (CGS; Knabb & Wang, 2021) to measure their relationship with God; and the Christian Contentment Scale (CCS; Knabb et al., 2020) to measure their level of inner satisfaction in the midst of psychological suffering.[4] To summarize, this integrative assessment strategy involves better understanding both psychological and spiritual functioning, including trauma symptoms, rumination, and experiential avoidance, as well as religious/spiritual struggles, religious coping, communion with God, and Christian contentment.

Regarding the role of the counselor or therapist in faith-based ACT, counselors or therapists can refer to Chapter 9 for a brief summary. In terms of applying faith-based ACT to Christian clients with trauma-related symptoms and disorders, a central theme involves learning to notice when rumination is being utilized as an ineffective cognitive avoidance strategy, then employ contemplative practice to cultivate attention on God, present-moment awareness of God, and acceptance of God's active, loving presence in the midst of intrusive memories and distressing emotions. To do so, a wide variety of contemplative practices can be utilized, starting with a "prayer word" or phrase (Laird, 2006) to help Christian clients "reset" whenever they recognize they are stuck in perseverative, trauma-related rumination. From there, they can engage in a wide variety of practices, such as the Jesus Prayer, to cultivate a present-moment awareness of God's perfect love (Knabb & Bates, 2020).

From a faith-based ACT perspective, collaborating with Christian trauma survivors involves working from within the three pillars, including "watching and enduring," "noticing and shifting," and "committing and following." With the "watching and enduring" pillar, counselors and therapists are working with Christian clients to cultivate a more watchful, vigilant awareness of trauma-based rumination. Whenever Christian clients get stuck in asking "why," "what if," and "how" questions, they can simply observe them with cognitive flexibility and metacognitive awareness, rather than getting lost in ruminations that do not end up helping them follow Jesus on the road of life. What is more, counselors and therapists are helping Christian clients to endure trauma-related intrusive memories and emotional distress, given that an infinitely powerful, wise, and loving God is with them. Because of this, they can accept the inner world, knowing that they are by no means alone in their proverbial "cell." Instead, God is in control, protecting them and loving them from moment to moment, which means they have a trustworthy traveling companion on the road of life who will be with them whenever dangerous situations arise.

For the "noticing and shifting" pillar, counselors and therapists are working with Christian clients to draw a contrast between "earthly-mindedness" and "heavenly-mindedness" (Burroughs, 2010, 2014; Rowe, 1672). In the context of trauma, "earthly-mindedness" involves getting lost in perseverative rumination, unilaterally attempting to avoid the pain by trying to be omniscient like God, not dependent on God, in knowing answers to the "why," "what if," and "how" questions that organically emanate from the experience of traumatic events. Conversely, "heavenly-mindedness" involves having a more transcendent perspective by surrendering to God, who is at the center of reality. Because God is present, and because God's providential care (i.e., good governance, benevolent protection) (Erickson, 2013) extends to all of creation, Christian clients can learn to trust that God is with them in each unfolding moment, especially instances of danger. This more heavenly perspective also involves seeing a larger story unfolding, with Christian clients playing a salient role in God's plan—although the fall of humankind led to suffering (e.g., traumatic experiences and corresponding symptoms and disorder), God offered his Son to redeem an estranged, broken world, and God will eventually restore all things. As this powerful story takes place, Christian clients are moving from justification (i.e., being righteous before, and reconciled to, God because of Jesus), to sanctification (i.e., becoming more like Jesus), to glorification (i.e., being face to face with Jesus) (Grudem, 1994). Although traumatic experiences are inevitable on this side of heaven, they are by no means a permanent reality. Rather, Christian trauma survivors can confidently walk with the God of love as they become more like him and head to their final destination—to be with him in heaven, with no more trauma-related suffering. To cultivate a more heavenly, spiritual, transcendent perspective, Christian clients can practice God's presence in the midst of difficult inner (e.g., trauma-related intrusive memories, distressing emotions, and perseverative rumination) and outer (e.g., current and future traumatic events, triggers and reminders of prior traumatic events) experiences. To revisit a phrase from the introduction chapter, to "think in threes" means that each situation involves (a) the Christian client, (b) the difficult inner and/or outer experience, and (c) the God of love, who is lovingly guiding, and sovereign over, the process. Like a child who is comforted by a loving, safe parent after a scary fall, emergency room visit, and stitches, Christian clients can learn to "notice and shift" whenever they erroneously believe they are alone on the road of life.

With the "committing and following" pillar, counselors and therapists are working with Christian clients to identify and commit to a set of biblical virtues, derived from Scripture, then take action by following Jesus (i.e., walking with God in love) wherever he would have them go. Unfortunately, with trauma-related symptoms and disorders, the fallen world may seem like an extremely unsafe place, with Christian clients struggling with a variety of reminders of prior traumatic events (e.g., intrusive memories, distressing emotions, environmental triggers). Because of this, a plethora of concrete moral behaviors are needed to guide life, rather than fluctuating trauma-based inner states, with love as *the* crowning virtue for becoming more like Jesus and being a vehicle for displaying God's love.

To summarize, contemplative practice can help Christian clients with trauma-related symptoms and disorders to deepen their awareness of God's active, loving presence, pivoting from perseverative rumination to focusing on God (Knabb et al., 2019). By cultivating this sustained, flexible attentiveness to the God of love in the here-and-now, Christian clients are better prepared to respond to trauma symptoms (e.g., intrusive memories, distressing emotions, perseverative rumination) with openness and flexibility in order to follow Jesus (i.e., walk with God in love), a central aim within faith-based ACT. Using strategies to develop watchfulness, endurance, an awareness of the contemplative self and God's presence, and virtue-based action, Christian clients can ameliorate the tendency to overly rely on cognitive avoidance.

In terms of the structure of each session, a general overview is covered in Chapter 9 on depression, which can also be followed when working with Christian clients with trauma-related symptoms and disorders. To adjust the session content for working with Christian clients with trauma-related symptoms and disorders, the first session can focus on securing informed consent, conducting an intake interview, and obtaining background information on the trauma and related symptoms. Also in this initial session, faith-based ACT counselors and therapists can help Christian clients to better understand the relationship between trauma-related intrusive memories, distressing emotions, and rumination. In other words, although it may be perceived to be helpful, rumination is often a form of cognitive avoidance, which can be a distraction to living a purposeful life and barrier to following Jesus. Indeed, dwelling on "why," "what if," and "how" questions about the trauma, coupled with doubts about God's availability, love, and so forth, can actually end up derailing Christian clients' attempts to create a vibrant, meaningful life. Thus, by employing contemplative practices—which include the cultivation of sustained, flexible attention on God, present-moment awareness of God, and acceptance of God's active, loving presence and providence (i.e., good governance, protective care) (Erickson, 2013)—Christian clients are learning to dually relate differently to unpleasant trauma-related symptoms and draw closer to the God of love. To conclude the first session, the "Fork in the Road" tool can be employed, which has been modified from Harris (2019) and Hayes et al. (2012).

In the second session, Christian clients' ruminative strategy can be further explored in detail, whether the content is secular (e.g., questioning why the traumatic event occurred) or religious/spiritual (e.g., questioning God's availability in the midst of, or subsequent to, the traumatic event). Indeed, the problem of rumination can be discussed in the context of trying to walk alone on the road of life, apart from God's infinite power, wisdom, and love. Ultimately, trauma-based rumination involves Christian clients' unilateral attempts to make sense of the trauma and eliminate trauma-related intrusive memories and distressing moments, outside of their relationship with the God of love.

In sessions three and four, cognitive defusion is often presented to continue to work on ways to relate differently to trauma-based rumination. For Christian clients, though, watchfulness can be explored as a Christian-sensitive alternative, helping Christian trauma survivors to simply observe their mind with flexibility and distance. Rather than overemphasizing language and cognitive avoidance strategies, which do not tend to work in the long-run, Christian clients can use *apophatic* practices (e.g., the Jesus Prayer) to sit at Jesus's feet when struggling with intrusive memories and emotional distress. Also in these two sessions, acceptance can be introduced, with Christian clients learning the faith-based alternative, endurance, for walking with God in the midst of psychological pain. With both cognitive defusion/watchfulness and acceptance/endurance, *apophatic* practices can help Christian clients learn how to accept trauma-based intrusive memories and distressing emotions. In doing so, they are practicing the ability to notice their inner world, then shift toward a more transcendent awareness of Jesus's presence. For example, as they recite the Jesus Prayer over and over again (i.e., "Lord Jesus Christ, Son of God, have mercy on me, a sinner"), they are engaging in an indirect method (Ware, 2001) for maintaining a vigilant watchfulness over the inner world, shifting toward Jesus's name and asking Jesus for his merciful reply in the midst of trauma-related symptoms. In other words, instead of unilaterally and directly attempting to eliminate the trauma-related intrusive memories and emotional distress, they are asking Jesus to be with them, consistent with the metaphor in the introduction chapter about living in a house with noisy roommates. Indeed, although the noisy roommates may continue to persist in obnoxiously shouting their needs, Jesus is asking to take up residence in every room as the "head of the house." When this happens, Christian clients can simply observe the "intrusive memory roommate," the "distressing emotion roommate," and so forth, given Jesus's loving influence extends to the entire living space. The reframe, here, is that life is about recognizing that God is present in the middle of suffering, which means that Christian clients can endure, not attempting to make the inevitable pains of life go away.

For the next two sessions (i.e., sessions five and six), mindfulness is typically utilized to simply notice the inner world with sustained, flexible, nonjudgmental, present-moment attention, developing an open attitude toward trauma-related symptoms along the way. As this process unfolds, trauma survivors are learning to just observe, connecting to the transcendent, not verbal, self. For Christian clients, of course, contemplative practices can be offered as an alternative, culturally sensitive version, cultivating an awareness of the contemplative self by practicing God's presence. When facing intrusive memories and emotional distress, Christian clients can learn to shift from "doing" to "being" (Segal et al., 2012), given that cognitive avoidance, long-term, is not effective in fully eliminating trauma-based inner distress.

In the seventh to 11th sessions, values are commonly discussed in the context of trauma-related symptoms and disorders. In other words, a contrast is made between the traumatic event (and corresponding trauma-related symptoms) and values (i.e., principles for living) serving as a guide for life. With the former, clients may end up ruminating in an effort to avoid distressing memories and emotions, with little to no success and the inability to live a life of meaning and purpose. With the latter, clients are learning to identify and commit to a set of values (e.g., being a loving, kind, and selfless person) that guide life. Of course, when identifying a set of values, a willingness to live them out is necessary, especially since trauma-related symptoms may continue to persist. Yet, in combining the values and committed action processes, trauma survivors are heading in the direction of purpose, even with a trauma-ridden past and uncertain future. Yet, for Christian clients, biblical virtues can serve as a guide for life, such as the fruit of the Spirit (e.g., love, joy, peace, patience, kindness, goodness, faithfulness, gentleness, self-control; *New International Version Bible*, 2011, Galatians 5:22–23). What is more, following Jesus is central, even in a fallen world, filled with the ubiquitous reality of traumatic events (e.g., car accidents, abuse, deaths). To bring these processes together for Christian trauma survivors, the *telos* of life in this broken, fragile, trauma-ridden world can be explored, which is to (a) watch and endure the inner world (e.g., intrusive memories, distressing emotions, perseverative ruminations); (b) notice the difference between an earthly- and heavenly-minded perspective and shift from an overreliance on human-derived knowledge to God-derived love by practicing God's presence; and (c) commit to a set of biblical virtues, derived from God's word as a trustworthy source for optimal living, and follow Jesus, the exemplar who modeled suffering in order to live the life his Father called him to live. To be sure, many of the first-century Christian apostles (as well as other followers of Jesus) likely died martyr's deaths, suffering through the trauma of imprisonment, torture, and, ultimately, execution. Yet, along the way, they walked with the God of love, recognizing that, eschatologically speaking, they were redeemed as they patiently waited for God to restore all things.

In the concluding session of faith-based ACT, a variety of metaphors, exercises, and contemplative strategies can be reviewed, with the aim of discussing

Christian clients' next steps as they travel with Jesus on the road of life. What is more, barriers to following Jesus can be explored with the following question:

> Given I may continue to experience intrusive memories, distressing emotions, and perseverative rumination on a daily basis, how can I balance sitting at the feet of Jesus with following him in order to live a life that glorifies God, surrendering my own efforts to control or avoid because he is infinitely powerful, wise, and loving?

Consistent with the previous two chapters, Christian clients are especially encouraged to think about enduring to the very end, faithfully following Jesus on a daily basis: "I have fought the good fight, I have finished the race, I have kept the faith" (*New International Version Bible*, 2011, 2 Timothy 4:7).

Conclusion

To conclude, following Jesus is foundational to the Christian life, even when experiencing a traumatic event and subsequent trauma-based symptoms. Yet, instead of employing perseverative rumination as a cognitive avoidance strategy, Christian clients can "watch and endure," "notice and shift," and "commit and follow," with the God of love to walk with on the road of life. Worded another way, faith-based ACT for trauma is really a relational approach, anchored to love, with Christian clients learning that they are by no means alone as they endure the inevitable traumas of a broken, fallen world in need of God's redemption and restoration. As David famously declared in the 23rd Psalm,

> The LORD is my shepherd, I lack nothing. He makes me lie down in green pastures, he leads me beside quiet waters, he refreshes my soul. He guides me along the right paths for his name's sake. Even though I walk through the darkest valley, I will fear no evil, for you are with me; your rod and your staff, they comfort me.
> (*New International Version Bible*, 2011, Psalm 23: 1–4)

Ultimately, Christian clients have a "shepherd" and "guide," especially in the "darkest valleys" of trauma, to comfort them and ameliorate the fear that inevitably emanates from the tragedies of life.

Notes

1 Portions of this section are adapted from Knabb et al. (2019).
2 Portions of this section are adapted from Knabb et al. (2019).
3 As noted in the previous two chapters, because these instruments were originally developed for research-related purposes, not necessarily counseling and therapy,

they should only be used as brief measures to get a preliminary understanding of Christian clients' psychological and spiritual functioning.

4 Consistent with a similar footnote in the previous two chapters, these last two measures are important because healthy psychological and spiritual functioning in the Christian life involves walking (i.e., communing, fellowshipping) with God and experiencing a deeper contentment in him in the midst of trauma symptoms.

References

Bean, R., Ong, C., Lee, J., & Twohig, M. (2017). Acceptance and commitment therapy for PTSD and trauma: An empirical review. *The Behavior Therapist, 40*, 145–150.

Bishop, L., Ameral, V., & Palm Reed, K. (2018). The impact of experiential avoidance and event centrality in trauma-related rumination and posttraumatic stress. *Behavior Modification, 42*, 815–837.

Bishop, S., Lau, M., Shapiro, S., Carlson, L., Anderson, N., Carmody, J., Segal, Z., Abbey, S., Speca, M., Velting, D., & Devins, G. (2004). Mindfulness: A proposed operational definition. *Clinical Psychology: Science and Practice, 11*, 230–241.

Briere, J., & Runtz, M. (1989). The trauma symptom checklist (TSC-33): Early data on a new scale. *Journal of Interpersonal Violence, 4*, 151–163.

Burroughs, J. (2010). *Heavenly-mindedness recommended: In a discourse on Colossians 3:2*. Gale ECCO.

Burroughs, J. (2014). *A treatise on earthly-mindedness*. GLH Publishing.

Clohessy, S., & Ehlers, A. (1999). PTSD symptoms, response to intrusive memories, and coping in ambulance service workers. *British Journal of Clinical Psychology, 38*, 251–265.

Ehlers, A., & Clark, D. (2000). A cognitive model of posttraumatic stress disorder. *Behaviour Research and Therapy, 38*, 319–345.

Ehring, T., & Ehlers, A. (2014). Does rumination mediate the relationship between emotion regulation ability and posttraumatic stress disorder? *European Journal of Psychotraumatology, 5*, 1–7.

Ehring, T., Zetsche, U., Weidacker, K., Wahl, K., Schonfeld, S., & Ehlers, A. (2011). The Perseverative Thinking Questionnaire (PTQ): Validation of a content-independent measure of repetitive negative thinking. *Journal of Behavior Therapy and Experimental Psychiatry, 42*, 225–232.

Erickson, M. (2013). *Christian theology* (3rd ed.). Baker Academic.

Exline, J., Pargament, K., Grubbs, J., & Yali, A. (2014). The religious and spiritual struggles scale: Development and initial validation. *Psychology of Religion and Spirituality, 6*, 208–222.

Feldman, G., Hayes, A., Kumar, S., Greeson, J., & Laurenceau, J. (2007). Mindfulness and emotion regulation: The development and initial validation of the Cognitive and Affective Mindfulness Scale-Revised (CAMS-R). *Journal of Psychopathology and Behavioral Assessment, 29*, 177–190.

Follette, V., & Pistorello, J. (2007). *Finding life beyond trauma: Using acceptance and commitment therapy to heal from post-traumatic stress and trauma-related problems*. New Harbinger Publications, Inc.

Gamez, W., Chmielewski, M., Kotov, R., Ruggero, C., & Watson, D. (2011). Development of a measure of experiential avoidance: The Multidimensional Experiential Avoidance Questionnaire. *Psychological Assessment, 23*, 692–713.

Grudem, W. (1994). *Systematic theology: An introduction to biblical doctrine*. Zondervan.

Harris, R. (2019). *ACT made simple: An easy-to-read primer on acceptance and commitment therapy* (2nd ed.). New Harbinger Publications, Inc.

Harris, R. (2021). *Trauma-focused ACT: A practitioner's guide to working with mind, body & emotion using acceptance & commitment therapy.* New Harbinger Publications, Inc.

Hayes, S., Strosahl, K., & Wilson, K. (2012). *Acceptance and commitment therapy: The process and practice of mindful change* (2nd ed.). The Guilford Press.

Hopwood, T., & Schutte, N. (2017). A meta-analytic investigation of the impact of mindfulness-based interventions on post traumatic stress. *Clinical Psychology Review, 57*, 12–20.

Im, S., & Follette, V. (2016). Rumination and mindfulness related to multiple types of trauma exposure. *Translational Issues in Psychological Science, 2*, 395–407.

King, A., Erickson, T., Giardino, N., Favorite, T., Rauch, S., Robinson, E., Kulkarni, M., & Liberzon, I. (2013). A pilot study of group mindfulness-based cognitive therapy (MBCT) for combat veterans with posttraumatic stress disorder (PTSD). *Depression and Anxiety, 30*, 638–645.

Knabb, J., & Bates, M. (2020). "Holy desire" within the "Cloud of Unknowing": The psychological contributions of medieval apophatic contemplation to Christian mental health in the 21st century. *Journal of Psychology and Christianity, 39*, 24–39.

Knabb, J., & Wang, K. (2021). The communion with God scale: Shifting from an *etic* to *emic* perspective to assess fellowshipping with the Triune God. *Psychology of Religion and Spirituality, 13*, 67–80.

Knabb, J., Vazquez, V., & Pate, R. (2019). 'Set your minds on things above': Shifting from trauma-based ruminations to ruminating on God. *Mental Health, Religion & Culture, 22*, 384–399.

Knabb, J., Vazquez, V., & Wang, K. (2020). The Christian contentment scale: An *emic* measure for assessing inner satisfaction within the Christian tradition. *Journal of Psychology and Theology.* Advance online publication.

Knabb, J., Vazquez, V., Pate, R., Garzon, F., Wang, K., Edison-Riley, D., Slick, A., Smith, R., & Weber, S. (2021). Christian meditation for trauma-based rumination: A two-part study examining the effects of an internet-based four-week program. *Spirituality in Clinical Practice.* Advance online publication.

Laird, M. (2006). *Into the silent land: A guide to the Christian practice of contemplation.* Oxford University Press.

Lang, A., Strauss, J., Bomyea, J., Bormann, J., Hickman, S., Good, R., & Essex, M. (2012). The theoretical and empirical basis for meditation as an intervention for PTSD. *Behavior Modification, 36*, 759–786.

Lawrence, B. (2015). *The practice of the presence of God.* (S. Sciurba, Trans.). ICS Publications.

Michael, T., Halligan, S., Clark, D., & Ehlers, A. (2007). Rumination in posttraumatic stress disorder. *Depression and Anxiety, 24*, 307–317.

Murray, J., Ehlers, A., & Mayou, R.A. (2002). Dissociation and posttraumatic stress disorder: Two prospective studies of road traffic accident victims. *The British Journal of Psychiatry, 180*, 363–368.

New International Version Bible. (2011). Zondervan. https://www.biblegateway.com/

Norwich, J. (2013). (M. Starr, Trans.). *The showings of Julian of Norwich: A new translation.* Hampton Roads Publishing Company, Inc.

Oxford Dictionary. (n.d.a). *Contemplation.* https://www.oxfordlearnersdictionaries.com/us/definition/english/rumination

Oxford Dictionary. (n.d.b). *Rumination.* https://www.oxfordlearnersdictionaries.com/us/definition/english/rumination

Pargament, K., Koenig, H., & Perez, L. (2000). The many methods of religious coping: Development and initial validation of the RCOPE. *Journal of Clinical Psychology, 56,* 519–543.

Rowe, J. (1672). *Heavenly-mindedness and earthly-mindedness: In two parts.* Francis Tyton.

Segal, Z., Williams, M., & Teasdale, J. (2012). *Mindfulness-based cognitive therapy for depression* (2nd ed.). The Guilford Press.

Smets, J., Wessel, I., Schreurs, E., & Raes, F. (2012). The interplay between rumination and intrusions in the prediction of concurrent and prospective depressive symptoms in two nonclinical samples. *The Psychological Record, 62,* 777–788.

Smith, J., & Alloy, L. (2009). A roadmap to rumination: A review of the definition, assessment, and conceptualization of this multifaceted construct. *Clinical Psychology Review, 29,* 116–128.

Steil, R., & Ehlers, A. (2000). Dysfunctional meaning of posttraumatic intrusions in chronic PTSD. *Behaviour Research and Therapy, 38,* 537–558.

Taylor, J., McLean, L., Korner, A., Stratton, E., & Glozier, N. (2020). Mindfulness and yoga for psychological trauma: Systematic review and meta-analysis. *Journal of Trauma & Dissociation, 21,* 536–573.

Walser, R., & Westrup, D. (2007). *Acceptance & commitment therapy for the treatment of posttraumatic stress disorder & trauma-related problems: A practitioner's guide to using mindfulness & acceptance strategies.* New Harbinger Publications, Inc.

Ware, K. (2001). *The inner kingdom.* St. Vladimir's Seminary Press.

Wilt, J., Exline, J., Lindberg, M., Park, C., & Pargament, K. (2017). Theological beliefs about suffering and interactions with the divine. *Psychology of Religion and Spirituality, 9,* 137–147.

Wolkin, J. (2015). Cultivating multiple aspects of attention through mindfulness meditation accounts for psychological well-being through decreased rumination. *Psychology Research and Behavior Management, 8,* 171–180.

12

FAITH-BASED ACT FOR RELATIONSHIP DISTRESS

Introduction

In this final chapter, the six traditional acceptance and commitment therapy (ACT) processes are applied to relationship distress with a spouse or intimate partner, focusing on relational problems, a Christian perspective on relational problems, Christian contemplative writings on relational problems, and a faith-based ACT approach to relational problems. Given that humans inevitably rely on relational schemas, or "basic beliefs about the nature of human beings and their relationships" (Tilden & Dattilio, 2005, p. 143), to quickly make sense of their most important interpersonal encounters, this chapter will emphasize the role that these enduring "cognitive structures" (Dattilio, 2010, p. 56) play in relational functioning (Lev & McKay, 2017). More specifically, relational schemas consist of internalized experiences of social interactions with significant others (Baldwin, 1992). In a marriage or intimate relationship, these cognitive templates include a view of self, view of spouse/intimate partner, and "interpersonal script" that helps to elucidate the role that both partners will play in key relational exchanges (Baldwin, 1992).

Because of the salient impact that relational schemas have on a marriage or intimate relationship, in this chapter, interpersonal mindfulness and contemplation are explored so as to offer a set of skills for Christian couples to relate differently to these influential cognitive templates, embedding this discussion within a faith-based ACT approach to couple dysfunction. Ultimately, faith-based ACT for Christian clients with relational distress is about watching and enduring the inner world, creating a bit more distance from unhelpful schemas and related emotions that serve as barriers to a loving, committed relationship with a spouse or intimate partner; noticing the difference between "earthly-mindedness" and "heavenly-mindedness" (Burroughs, 2010, 2014; Rowe, 1672) and shifting toward a greater awareness of the contemplative self by practicing God's presence in key interpersonal exchanges with a spouse or intimate partner; and committing to biblical virtues (with love as *the* crowning virtue) and following Jesus wherever he would have Christian clients go in their relationship with a spouse or intimate partner. Or, put more succinctly,

DOI: 10.4324/9781003181941-13

faith-based ACT for Christian couples is about pivoting from fear to love, with God's love at the center (Blanton, 2013).

Traditional CBT for Relationship Distress

In traditional cognitive behavioral therapy (CBT), counselors and therapists work with clients to identify and change unhelpful automatic thoughts and core beliefs, drawing upon the *cognitive model* along the way. With the cognitive model, the link between thoughts, feelings, and behaviors is heavily emphasized, with an understanding that the varying levels of human cognition (e.g., automatic thoughts, core schemas) have a powerful impact on how humans end up feeling and what they end up doing (Beck, 2020). Automatic thoughts, more specifically, consist of the flow of spontaneous, superficial thoughts and images that often lack precision and are beyond human awareness, whereas core schemas are more deeply embedded and relatively fixed, unchangeable, and enduring beliefs about the self and others that begin to develop in childhood and help people organize and make sense of complex information in their environment (Beck, 2020; Rafaeli et al., 2011). From a traditional CBT perspective, emotional and behavioral problems often stem from distorted, unhelpful automatic thoughts and core schemas, which are targeted in treatment.

Common types of unhelpful cognitions in a marriage or intimate relationship include "selective attention" (e.g., only focusing on a spouse's or partner's perceived mistakes or flaws), "attributions" (e.g., blaming a spouse or partner for the perceived relational problems), and "expectancies" (e.g., predicting a spouse's or partner's negative behavior in a future situation) (Baucom et al., 2008, p. 52). What is more, common types of unhelpful core schemas in a marriage or intimate relationship can often be organized into three higher-level categories, including "helpless" core schemas (e.g., "I'm a failure in this relationship"), "unlovable" core schemas (e.g., "I'm not lovable in this relationship"), and "worthless" core schemas (e.g., "I'm a sinner in this relationship") (Beck, 2020).

From a traditional CBT vantagepoint, automatic thoughts and core schemas can have a sizeable influence on interpersonal functioning in a marriage or intimate relationship, especially when cognitive content is distorted, inaccurate, and unexamined (Baucom et al., 2008). In support of this theoretical understanding, in a study on the relationship between partner schemas and relational functioning, Chatav and Whisman (2009) found that "a greater ratio of positive to positive-plus-negative" partner schemas was linked to a higher level of relational satisfaction among college students in a dating relationship. As this empirical finding reveals, schemas can have a formidable influence on relational functioning.

With this theoretical and empirical understanding in mind, couples treatment approaches in the cognitive behavioral tradition have attempted to target the negative schemas that contribute to relationship distress among spouses and intimate partners. For instance, although schema therapy was originally developed for personality disorders (Rafaeli et al., 2011), it has since been applied to couples (Simeone-DiFrancesco et al., 2015). In schema therapy, more specifically, schemas are defined as "self-defeating emotional and cognitive patterns that begin early in our development and repeat throughout life" (Young et al., 2003, p. 7). Common schemas, from a schema therapy perspective, include abandonment, abuse, shame, isolation, and failure, among others (Simeone-DiFrancesco et al., 2015).

In schema therapy for couples, the counselor or therapist works with the couple to identify the role that early unmet relational needs have played in the development of unhelpful schemas (e.g., abandonment, shame, mistrust), which are typically avoided or carried out in the couple's current relationship (Rafaeli et al., 2011; van Vreeswijk et al., 2014). In turn, the counselor or therapist helps the couple to identify and ameliorate specific "modes," or "predominant emotional states, schemas, and coping reactions that are active for an individual at a particular time" (Rafaeli et al., 2011, p. 47), that may be unhelpful in the relationship (Rafaeli et al., 2011). In other words, each spouse's or intimate partner's schemas, which originally developed in childhood, are triggered in the current marriage or intimate relationship, leading to the expression of a mode, made up of a cognitive, affective, and behavioral response (Simeone-DiFrancesco et al., 2015). As unhealthy schemas and modes are identified and targeted with cognitive and behavioral techniques and interventions, each member of the dyad gradually learns how to respond to their own and the other's needs in a healthy manner (Rafaeli et al., 2011).

As one of many interventions in schema therapy, mindfulness-based conceptualizations and techniques can help couples to cultivate the ability to gain a greater awareness of schemas (i.e., an amalgam of thoughts, feelings, and memories about the self, others, and the world) and modes (i.e., an amalgam of schemas and behavioral responses to schemas) with sustained, flexible, nonjudgmental attention in the here-and-now (van Vreeswijk et al., 2014), rather than automatically getting triggered by schemas, then engaging in unhealthy modes in marriage or an intimate relationship. In fact, in the mindfulness literature, interpersonal mindfulness consists of several ingredients in relational exchanges, including being present and engaged (e.g., in the moment), being aware of the self (e.g., thoughts, feelings) and other person (e.g., nonverbal communication, feelings, intentions), being accepting of the other person (e.g., accepting differing opinions, withholding criticism or judgment), and being nonreactive (e.g., slowing down to be intentional about the words that are spoken, maintaining an awareness of the impact of the words that are spoken on the other person) (Pratscher et al., 2019). In support of the importance of both individual and interpersonal mindfulness in healthy couples functioning, a study of married community adults found a moderate relationship between mindfulness and marital satisfaction (Burpee & Langer, 2005), and a more recent study among married adults in Turkey revealed that interpersonal mindfulness was strongly correlated with marital satisfaction (Deniz et al., 2019). Combined, schema therapy and interpersonal mindfulness can help couples to be more aware of their own, as well as their spouse's or intimate partner's, enduring cognitive, affective, and behavioral patterns so as to maintain a more compassionate awareness of the ubiquitous psychological struggles in life. In fact, in the last few decades, traditional ACT has been applied to couples functioning in an effort to help spouses and intimate partners cultivate psychological flexibility, guided by salient relational values, not wavering inner states (Harris, 2009; Lev & McKay, 2017; Walser & Westrup, 2009).

Traditional ACT for Relationship Distress

In traditional ACT, relationship distress with a spouse or intimate partner often arises when members of a dyad struggle with cognitive fusion and experiential avoidance, leading to the wavering inner world determining the direction they will take in their relationship, rather than a more stable set of values (Harris, 2009; Lev & McKay, 2017; Walser & Westrup, 2009). More specifically, each member of the dyad is often unknowingly influenced by relational schemas—lenses through which they view their most important relationships that consist of core beliefs, stories, and narratives about themselves, the other person, and how their relationship is supposed to operate, which begin to develop in childhood, offer relational coherence and predictability, and, unfortunately, lead to schema-related emotional pain (Lev & McKay, 2017). Because of the emotional pain that emanates from these fairly rigid and ingrained cognitive templates, couples may end up engaging in experiential avoidance, which can undermine the closeness and connection they are longing for and get in the way of pursuing the relational values that can create a meaningful, lasting, more satisfying relational bond (e.g., being a loving, caring, kind, compassionate, generous, or selfless partner) (Lev & McKay, 2017).

Examples of common schemas in a marriage or intimate relationship include abandonment (e.g., being preoccupied with a partner leaving the relationship), mistrust (e.g., being suspicious of a partner's intentions), and shame (e.g., being worried that a partner will be rejecting or unloving) (Lev & McKay, 2017). Once these schemas are triggered, couples may experience a variety of painful feelings, such as sadness, fear, or loneliness with the abandonment schema or inadequacy, defectiveness, or isolation with the shame schema (Lev & McKay, 2017). In turn, couples may engage in a plethora of unhelpful behaviors to avoid the schema-related emotional pain, including being critical, making demands, submitting, clinging, or withdrawing (Lev & McKay, 2017). Over time, each person's schemas, schema-related emotional pain, and schema-related behavioral responses influence the other person's schemas, schema-related emotional pain, and schema-related behavioral responses, to the point where couples struggle to pursue a set of well-defined values that can help to improve and grow their relational bond (Lev & McKay, 2017).

Conversely, healthy relational functioning involves cultivating psychological flexibility, which consists of being mindful of the inner world (i.e., defused from schemas, accepting of schema-related emotional pain, flexibly anchored to the here-and-now [not preoccupied with schemas that emanate from past relational hurts], observant of schemas and schema-related emotional pain with distance and openness) and living out a set of relational values (e.g., being a loving spouse, being a forgiving partner, being a selfless lover) in the outer world, not impulsively and mindlessly reacting to schemas and schema-related emotional pain (Harris, 2009; Lev & McKay, 2017). To date, several studies have emerged on traditional ACT for relationships, including marriages and intimate relationships.

Research on Traditional ACT for Relationship Distress

In a quasi-experimental study among Iranian couples experiencing relational distress, half of the couples were assigned to ten 90-minute sessions of weekly ACT for couples, whereas the other half were assigned to "treatment as usual" (Omidi & Talighi, 2017). Results revealed that, post-intervention, there was a difference between the intervention and control group on marital satisfaction (a small effect size) and quality of life (a large effect size), with the intervention group outperforming the control group (Omidi & Talighi, 2017). In a separate quasi-experimental study on traditional ACT for couples, Iranian couples presenting to divorce court were assigned to either ten hour-long, weekly sessions of ACT or a control group (Abbasi et al., 2017). Results revealed that, pre- to post-treatment, the intervention group reported an increase in well-being and marital satisfaction, both large effect sizes (Abbasi et al., 2017). Finally, in a single-case design among two U.S. couples who were seeking therapy to improve marital satisfaction, both couples received 12 sessions of traditional ACT, with results revealing that both couples reported an increase in marital satisfaction and decrease in marital distress from pre-treatment to the six-month follow-up (Peterson et al., 2009). Although, to date, no randomized trials appear to have emerged on traditional ACT for couples, the aforementioned theoretical and empirical findings support the notion that ACT can be helpful for ameliorating the common distress that emanates from marriages and intimate relationships. For Christian couples, of course, a Christian perspective needs to be taken into consideration, briefly covered in the next section of this chapter.

Christianity and Relationship Distress

According to the *Holman Bible Dictionary* (2016), descriptions of Christian marriage include a "union" and "covenant commitment for a lifetime, second only to [Christians'] commitment to God" (p. 412). In this psychological and spiritual union, Christian spouses have equal worth, given they are created in God's image, and pursue sexual activity, intimacy, and procreation (*Holman Bible Dictionary*, 2016). Indeed, in the first three chapters of Genesis, the Bible reveals that Adam and Eve were created *imago Dei* (i.e., in God's image) to be stewards over God's creation, working together to procreate and take care of the earth (Kostenberger & Jones, 2012).

Yet, with the fall, suffering and brokenness entered the world, which includes pain in the context of marriage (Kostenberger & Jones, 2012). Thus, spouses will inevitably end up bringing earlier relational hurts throughout their lives into the marriage, which create added suffering as they struggle to love both God and one another. Still, placed in the context of the meta-narrative of the Bible—creation, fall, redemption, and restoration (Wolters, 2005)—Christian spouses are called to follow Jesus, given *he* rules over the heavens, earth, church, and marriage (Kostenberger & Jones, 2012). In the process, they are called to love one another as they walk with him, and each other, to their final destination—being face to face with God in heaven (Grudem, 1994; Kostenberger & Jones, 2012). In fact, Christian marriage is a salient vehicle through which Christian spouses can become more like Jesus: "The family, while incomplete and fallen, is still a structure to grow into greater maturity and (ideally) to learn about the person and work of Jesus Christ" (Yarhouse & Sells, 2017, p. 15). As a result, for Christians, marital and intimate relationships are intimately intertwined with holistic health, including psychological, social, and spiritual functioning.

To better understand the impact that Christianity has on marriage, I conducted a study of community Christian couples several years ago in an attempt to elucidate the potential role that religion plays in marital functioning (Knabb, 2014). Findings revealed that anxious God attachment (e.g., being preoccupied with God's availability) for one spouse was negatively correlated with marital adjustment (e.g., healthy marital satisfaction, affectional expression, and cohesion) for both spouses (Knabb, 2014). In other words, one spouse's experience of anxiety in their relationship with God influenced both their own and their spouse's perceived adjustment in the marriage. What is more, vertical faith maturity (e.g., pursuing a closer relationship with God) for one spouse was positively correlated with marital adjustment (e.g., healthy marital satisfaction, affectional expression, and cohesion) for both spouses (Knabb, 2014). Stated differently, one spouse's experience of faith in their relationship with God influenced both their own and their spouse's perceived adjustment in the marriage. Overall, these findings lend support to the notion that religion can have a powerful impact on marriage, which is important to consider when working with Christian couples in faith-based ACT, especially when drawing upon the Christian contemplative tradition for psychological, social, and spiritual change.

The Contemplative Tradition, Relationship Distress, and Metacognition

In *Treatise on the Love of God*, the 16th- and 17th-century contemplative writer Francis de Sales (2011) defined love as "the turning of the heart toward good with a willingness to please" (p. 31). The author went on to state that "an eagerness to please God allows [Christians] to possess God, absorbing the best from him" (de Sales, 2011, p. 32). In other words, this loving desire "makes [Christians] belong to God," "cheerfully [doing] what God wants," with "the soul filled with the goodness of God" (de Sales, 2011, pp. 31–32). Ultimately, as Christians increasingly desire God's love, they are filled with God's love, with no other goal to be pursued (de Sales, 2011). Phrased differently, "[Christians] enjoy the things of God as though they were [their] own" (de Sales, 2011, p. 31).

To dually love God and experience God's love, de Sales (2011) advocated for both meditation and contemplation, with the former consisting of "dwelling on a single thought with great attention" and helping Christians to "discover motivating love" (pp. 44, 46). Through this focused meditation, Christians are storing up God's love, which, in turn, leads to a more general contemplation of God's love, or "an adoring, uncomplicated, and enduring attention of the soul to divine things" (p. 46). Thus, meditation leads to a greater knowledge of God's love, which leads to contemplation and a deeper experience of God's love: "Meditation is love's mother. Contemplation is love's daughter" (de Sales, 2011, p. 47).

This motivation to love God is based on his infinite goodness, whereas the motivation to love others comes from the fact that all humans were created in God's image (de Sales, 2011). Simply put, upon loving their fellow humans, Christians are saying, "This person resembles God" (de Sales, 2011, p. 103). What is more, as *the* crowning virtue, Christians' love influences a wide variety of other biblical virtues (de Sales, 2011), including the remaining fruit of the Spirit: "joy, peace, [patience], kindness, goodness, faithfulness, gentleness, and self-control" (*New International Version Bible*, 2011, Galatians 5:22–23). In essence, "when divine love rules [Christians], it brings into this empire of the heart all of [Christians'] other loves" (de Sales, 2011, p. 127).

Practice-wise, de Sales (2011) advocated for Christians learning to surrender to God's love so they can be guided by God's perfect goodness in their relationships with others. To do so, he encouraged Christians to practice "little prayers" throughout the day, such as "Lord, I am yours," "My God, you are everything to me," and "Jesus, you are my life" (de Sales, 2011, p. 137). With these types of short prayers to God, Christians are learning to yield to God's loving presence within, which can be displayed toward others. As a result, meditating on verses in the Bible that capture God's love (e.g., "God is love"; *New International Version Bible*, 2011, 1 John 4:7–21) can lead to contemplating God's love with a simple "prayer word" (e.g., "love"; Laird, 2006), which can lead to being filled with God's love and extending God's love to others.

In the context of relational distress with a spouse or intimate partner, through contemplative practice, Christian clients are gaining a greater metacognitive awareness of the inner and outer barriers to being a vehicle for God's love; that is, they are learning to notice the schemas, schema-related emotional pain, and schema-related behavioral responses that get in the way of loving both God and their significant other (the two greatest commandments; Matthew 22:36–40). To cultivate this metacognitive awareness, they can employ "love" as their "prayer word," gently pivoting from self to Other/other and self-derived knowledge to God-derived love. Again and again, Christian clients are learning to engage in the "turning of the heart toward good with a willingness to please" (de Sales, 2011, p. 31). In doing so, Christian clients are functioning as a conduit for the fruit of the Spirit to be on full display in their closest human relationship.

Skill-wise, Christian couples engaged in formal contemplative practice are learning to remain still and silent in the outer world, then still and silent in the inner world, which can lead to the ability to be calm in the midst of relational distress throughout the day (Blanton, 2013). What is more, Christian couples engaged in formal contemplative practice are learning to focus their attention on God, which can, in turn, help them to be attuned to their partner, especially when their partner needs their undivided attention (Blanton, 2013). Finally, Christian couples engaged in formal contemplative practice are learning to surrender to God in the present moment, which can help them to be more present to their partner, given they are allowing the present moment to unfold, without being preoccupied with changing it in any way (Blanton, 2013). Over time, when each partner engages in formal contemplative practice on their own (and with God), they are developing a crucial set of skills that they can bring into their relationship with a spouse or intimate partner, with God guiding the way.

In sum, for Christian clients with relationship distress with a spouse or intimate partner, contemplation is key, recognizing that God's love is central. Meditation and contemplation can help to cultivate a greater love for God and others, which leads to the expression of other salient relational virtues, too. Along the way, Christian clients are "practicing divine love" (de Sales, 2011) with a "prayer word" (Laird, 2006) or short prayer throughout the day, which leads to the internalization of God's love, displayed in their relationship with a spouse or significant other. Building on this contemplative understanding of an outside-in to inside-out perspective on Christian love, I now turn to a faith-based ACT perspective on relationship distress, integrating traditional ACT and the Christian contemplative tradition.

Faith-Based ACT for Relationship Distress

Similar to the previous three chapters, counselors and therapists utilizing faith-based ACT with Christian couples need to secure informed consent. In turn, they can employ a range of instruments to further assess Christian couples' psychological and spiritual functioning.[1] For example, they can use the Dyadic Adjustment Scale (DAS) to assess couples' functioning across four dimensions: couples' consensus, couples' satisfaction, couples' expression of affect, and couples' cohesion (Spanier, 1976). Moreover, the RCOPE (Pargament et al., 2000) can be used to measure couples' religious coping; the Communion with God Scale (CGS; Knabb & Wang, 2021) can be utilized to measure couples' relationship with God; and the Christian Contentment Scale (CCS; Knabb et al., 2020) can be employed to measure couples' level of inner satisfaction in the middle of psychological suffering.[2] Overall, administering these measures during the first session can help counselors and therapists to better understand couples' relational and spiritual functioning, including their dyadic adjustment, religious coping, communion with God, and Christian contentment.

With regard to the role of the counselor or therapist in faith-based ACT, counselors or therapists can refer to Chapter 9 for a concise review. When it comes to applying faith-based ACT to Christian couples with relationship distress, a main theme involves identifying problematic relational schemas (e.g., unlovability, worthlessness, helplessness; Beck, 2020) that get in the way of following Jesus, becoming more like him, and serving as a vehicle through which God can display his perfect love in the marriage or intimate relationship. In other words, Christian couples are learning to walk with God in love toward the life he has called them to live, rather than walk alone and away from God's will. In the process, they are learning to recognize the schemas, schema-related emotional pain, and schema-related behavioral responses that undermine the love they are longing for. To do so, Christian couples are engaging in meditative practices to gain a greater knowledge of the role that love plays in their relationship, then engaging in contemplative practices to experience God's love. Consequently, they are bringing this awareness of God's love into the relationship, displaying God's goodness and the remaining fruit of the Spirit (e.g., peace, patience, kindness, goodness, gentleness, self-control; *New International Version Bible*, 2011, Galatians 5:22–23) toward the closest person to them in their life.

In the context of the three faith-based ACT pillars, "watching and enduring" means that Christian couples are learning to simply notice the schema-related narratives that are getting in the way of loving their spouse or significant other, including those that involve themes of abandonment, helplessness, shame, unlovability, and so forth (Beck, 2020; Lev & McKay, 2017). Christian couples are also learning to endure the schema-related emotional pain that emanates from their deeply embedded schemas, rather than engaging in problematic, impulsive, mindless schema-related behaviors (e.g., demanding, criticizing, withdrawing) that prevent them from loving like Jesus loves. In this process, Christian couples are walking with God in love, maintaining the metacognitive awareness that is necessary to observe the fallen inner world with a bit more distance so they can, instead, focus on becoming more like Jesus (i.e., sanctification) in their most important human relationship.

Considering the "noticing and shifting" pillar, Christian couples are learning to notice the difference between "earthly-mindedness" and "heavenly-mindedness" (Burroughs, 2010, 2014; Rowe, 1672), with the former capturing a far too narrow, self-focused perspective on relationships and the latter encompassing a more transcendent, selfless spiritual reality (e.g., God is calling Christian couples to love one another and respond to the other person's needs). Thus, awareness of the contemplative self involves ameliorating the tendency to overly rely on the rational self and, instead, turn to the self that longs to connect directly to the God of love. As Christian couples learn to balance the rational self (the *dianoia* in Greek) with the contemplative self (the *nous* in Greek), they are letting go of the habit of overly leaning on the very relational schemas that are getting in the way of loving like Jesus loves. Put more succinctly, they are learning to "not lean on [their] own understanding" (*New International Version Bible*, 2011, Proverbs 3:5).

To better notice these two selves, Christian couples are practicing God's presence so as to cultivate a deeper, more peaceful inner state, wherein God is active and present at the center, operating from the inside-out to display his perfect goodness toward others. Although schemas, schema-related emotional pain, and schema-related behavioral responses are psychological realities within the fallen human condition, Christian couples can learn to be more observant of the inner world, rather than impulsively acting on the problematic narratives (and, consequently, corresponding emotions and behaviors) that get in the way of following and emulating Jesus in their most important human relationship. By growing a greater awareness of the contemplative self and practicing God's presence, Christians are "letting go of the reins," so to speak, allowing God to lead their marriage or intimate relationship, not unilaterally striving to put their own interests above the interests of their partner.

Finally, with the "committing and following" pillar, Christian couples are learning to identify a set of biblical virtues to guide their marriage or intimate relationship, then commit to living out these moral behaviors as they walk together with God and each other on the road of life. Put another way, rather than viewing walking with God as merely a dyadic endeavor, they can envision a triad, traveling with God and their spouse or significant other as they love him, practice his loving presence, and allow him to take up residence within their entire inner and outer world. Being a conduit for God's love, therefore, involves displaying God's perfect, not their own imperfect, goodness. Along the way, they are displaying the fruit of the Spirit (*New International Version Bible*, 2011, Galatians 5:22–23) toward their spouse or significant other, including peace (e.g., being free from relational conflict with a partner), patience (e.g., accepting the inevitable faults of a partner), kindness (e.g., being considerate and generous toward a partner), gentleness (e.g., being compassionate and tender toward a partner), and self-control (e.g., regulating difficult thoughts, feelings, sensations, and behaviors during conflict with a partner). In so doing, they are prioritizing one of the central goals for marriage—becoming more like Jesus. Ultimately, following Jesus involves walking with him in love wherever he would have Christian couples go, not prioritizing self-interests and unilaterally constructed perceived needs. To become more like Jesus, indeed, involves being a servant like Jesus, emulating Jesus's loving self-sacrifice.

In summary, Christian contemplation can help Christian couples to notice the schemas, schema-related emotional pain, and schema-related behavioral patterns that are getting in the way of following Jesus and being more like him. As they begin to notice these problematic patterns of thoughts, feelings, and behaviors, Christian couples are flexibly developing the ability to be a vehicle through which God's fruit of the Spirit can be displayed, beginning and ending with God's perfect love. Although living in a fallen, broken world certainly means that Christian couples will continue to struggle with relational hurts, they can learn to walk together with the God of love as they travel with him and one another to their final destination—being face to face with God in heaven.

Regarding the structure of each session, a general review can be found in Chapter 9, which can be utilized when working with Christian couples with relationship distress. In collaborating with Christian couples, the first session can include obtaining informed consent, as well as completing an intake interview, which includes getting detailed background information on the couples' relational history and current individual and interpersonal functioning. Also in the preliminary session, counselors and therapists can help Christian couples to better understand the role that schemas play in their unhelpful relational patterns, including the link between schemas, schema-related emotional pain, and schema-related behavioral problems. At this point, counselors and therapists can also introduce the idea that regular contemplative practice can help them to learn to flexibly pivot from such patterns to an awareness of God's active, loving presence. Relatedly, counselors and therapists can help Christian couples to better understand the central role that God's love, as well as the other fruit of the Spirit, plays in healthy couples' functioning. To be sure, by engaging in contemplative practices—which include the development of sustained, flexible attention on God, present-moment awareness of God, and acceptance of God's active, loving presence and providence (i.e., good governance, protective care) (Erickson, 2013; Feldman et al., 2007)—Christian couples are learning to dually relate differently to schema-related thoughts and feelings and draw closer to (and be led by) the God of love. To wrap up the first session, the "Fork in the Road" tool can be utilized, modified from Harris (2019) and Hayes et al. (2012), to help Christian couples contrast the difference between (a) walking with God in love and enduring relational distress with him as they head toward the direction he would have them go, and (b) walking alone and avoiding relational distress as they walk away from his will for their life.

In the second session, Christian couples' schemas can be further explored in detail, including the link between their family-of-origin relational experiences, specific schemas (e.g., abandonment, rejection, unlovability, worthlessness; Beck, 2020; Lev & McKay, 2017), schema-related emotional pain (e.g., sadness, fear, loneliness, shame), and schema-related behavioral patterns (e.g., pursuing/criticizing, withdrawing/shutting down). Along the way, Christian couples are drawing a contrast between the road that leads toward God's plan (i.e., walking with God in love, enduring psychological pain, and loving others like Jesus loves) and the road that leads away from God's plan (i.e., walking alone and avoiding psychological pain). Because schemas cause so much pain in a fallen, broken world, Christian couples are learning to (a) notice their own, as well as their partner's, schema-related vulnerabilities, and (b) relate differently to their own, as well as their partner's, schema-related vulnerabilities. To do so, Christian couples are moving from fear to love (Blanton, 2013; Hayes, 2019), noticing their schema-related pain and shifting toward an awareness of God's active, loving presence.

In the third and fourth session, cognitive defusion and acceptance can be explored, helping couples to gain more distance from the schema-related stories and corresponding emotions and behaviors that can get in the way of living out a set of relational values (e.g., being loving, forgiving, selfless, compassionate, kind, and so forth). For Christian couples, though, watchfulness can be discussed as a Christian-sensitive alternative, helping Christian clients to notice their schemas with a vigilant, flexible attentiveness (e.g., "There's my 'abandonment' schema acting up again"). With the various *apophatic* practices that are housed within the Christian contemplative tradition, Christian couples are learning to let go of their unilateral, self-derived efforts to make sense of their relationship and, instead, rely on God's perfect love, manifesting as the fruit of the Spirit (e.g., love, joy, peace, patience, kindness, goodness, self-control) (*New International Version Bible*, 2011, Galatians 5:22–23) in their moment-by-moment interactions with their significant other. For instance, with a condensed version of the Jesus Prayer (e.g., "Lord Jesus, have mercy"), Christian couples are slowly and gently reciting the prayer, imagining that Jesus is offering his loving kindness from the inside-out (Gillet, 1985). Whenever they notice they are being overly influenced by a problematic schema (e.g., abandonment), which, in turn, leads to problematic schema-related emotional pain (e.g., fear, anxiety) and corresponding behaviors (e.g., criticisms and demands directed at their partner), they can notice these inner and outer experiences, then ever so gently return to the powerful words of the prayer. In essence, they are learning to ask for Jesus's responsiveness in the mist of relationship distress, watching and enduring because he is sovereign over both the inner (e.g., schema-related thoughts, feelings, behaviors, and memories) and outer (e.g., distressing relational interactions) worlds.

In the fifth and sixth sessions, mindfulness can be employed so as to help couples relate differently to the inner world, especially schema-related thoughts, feelings, and memories. By practicing mindfulness meditation, several key skills are being developed (e.g., attention, present-moment awareness, acceptance) (Feldman et al., 2007), which can be helpful for couples in distress. First, couples are cultivating sustained, flexible attention, learning how to pivot from schema-related psychological struggles to another avenue of awareness (e.g., the breath, the senses). Second, couples are developing the ability to anchor themselves to the here-and-now, rather than getting distracted by schema-related thoughts and feelings that emanate from relational experiences in the past or anticipated relational encounters in the future. Third, couples are cultivating acceptance, learning how to relate to schema-related thoughts and feelings with nonjudgment (rather than engaging in experiential avoidance). Along the way, couples can apply these skills to their relationship with their significant other, observing the inner world with a more transcendent, spiritual perspective (i.e., the transcendent self) and maintaining present-moment awareness so they are more engaged with the relationship in front of them.

For Christian couples in distress, they are engaging in contemplative practices so as to cultivate sustained, flexible attention on the God of love, a moment-by-moment awareness of God's active, loving presence, and an acceptance of God's will as they learn to function as a vehicle through which the fruit of the Spirit can be displayed. To engage in the "practice of the presence of God," for instance, Christian couples can learn to repeat a short phrase (e.g., "My God, I am completely yours") as they pair this gentle, simple, interior statement with both an awareness of God and the relational encounter (Lawrence, 2015). With this practice, they are developing the ability to "think in threes" (i.e., viewing all interactions as a triad, with God, the individual, and the activity or other person), recognizing that God is walking with them as they interact with their significant other. Undeniably, maintaining this awareness of the contemplative self has salient implications for Christian couples' functioning, given they are pivoting from self-derived knowledge to God-derived love.

From the seventh to 11th sessions, counselors and therapists can focus on values and committed action, helping couples to draw a clear distinction between being guided by either schemas or values, with the former often getting in the way of the love they are longing for in their most important relationship. The latter, conversely, offers a much more stable "compass reading" (Hayes et al., 2012), given that a set of well-defined principles for living can help them to intentionally cultivate the life they want to live. For Christian couples, of course, the fruit of the Spirit can be focused on, recognizing that Christian clients are a dwelling place for the God of love to work in and through them as they strive to love God and others on this side of heaven.

To integrate and review these three faith-based ACT pillars in the final session, the *telos* for Christians in this fallen, conflict-ridden world, filled with relational distress due to a life filled with an overabundance of interpersonal hurts, is to emulate Jesus's love in their relationship with one another. To do so, Christian couples are striving to (a) watch and endure the inner world (e.g., schema-related thoughts, feelings, and memories); (b) notice two contrasting earthly and heavenly perspectives, shifting from a preoccupation with human-derived knowledge to God-derived love by practicing God's presence; and (c) commit to a set of biblical virtues (e.g., the fruit of the Spirit), derived from God's Word as a trustworthy source for optimal living, and follow Jesus, the "Suffering Servant" (*New International Version Bible*, 2011, Isaiah 53) who experienced pain, suffering, and rejection and, yet, pressed on to self-sacrificially give his life for the world. Although relational pain is inevitable because of the fall of humankind, Christian couples are committing to following Jesus as *the* model of service, self-emptying, and, ultimately, reconciliation.

Conclusion

To conclude both the chapter and book, following Jesus is central to Christian living, even when experiencing psychological pain. Thus, instead of being guided by the fallen, wavering inner world, Christian clients can look to a transcendent source of hope, comfort, and, ultimately, love, functioning as a dwelling place for God's goodness to be on full display as they trek with him along the road of life. Step by step, Christian clients are learning to allow God to live in and through them as they steadily travel to their final destination—being face to face with God in heaven.

My hope is that faith-based ACT can better prepare Christian clients for the long, meandering road ahead, learning to walk with God, talk with God, lean on God, and practice God's presence as they endure this fallen, suffering world. Along the way, my hope is that Christian clients can learn to gently, compassionately, and kindly pivot from fear to love (Blanton, 2013; Hayes, 2019) and self to Other/other, confidently loving God and others as they offer mercy to their fellow traveling companions by saying, like the anonymous desert father who observed another person committing a sin and poignantly declared, "Him today; me tomorrow" (quoted in Wortley, 2012, p. 138). I end this book with the famous contemplative author Frances de Sales's (2011) concluding prayer in the *Treatise of the Love of God,*

Oh, eternal love, my soul desires and chooses you. Come, Holy Spirit. Inflame our hearts with your love. We love or we die. We die and we love. We die to all other loves in order to live Jesus's love.

Notes

1 Consistent with the previous three chapters, given these instruments were originally developed for research-related purposes, not necessarily counseling and therapy, they should only be used as brief measures to get a preliminary understanding of Christian clients' psychological and spiritual functioning.

2 Similar to the footnote in the prior three chapters, the CGS and CCS are important because healthy psychological and spiritual functioning in the Christian life involves walking (i.e., communing, fellowshipping) with God and experiencing a deeper contentment in him in the midst of relationship distress with a spouse or intimate partner.

References

Abbasi, M., Sargahi, S., Bakhtiari, Z., & Alipour, G. (2017). Effect of acceptance and commitment based training on psychological well being and marital satisfaction in divorce applicants couples. *Journal of Research & Health*, *7*, 1146–1153.

Baldwin, M. (1992). Relational schemas and the processing of social information. *Psychological Bulletin*, *112*, 461–484.

Baucom, D., Epstein, N., LaTaillade, J., & Kirby, J. (2008). Cognitive-behavioral couple therapy. In A. Gurman (Ed.), *Clinical handbook of couple therapy* (4th ed., pp. 31–72). The Guilford Press.

Beck, J. (2020). *Cognitive behavior therapy: Basics and beyond* (3rd ed.). The Guilford Press.

Blanton, P. (2013). *Mind over marriage: Transforming your relationship using centering prayer and neuroscience*. Lantern Books.

Burpee, L., & Langer, E. (2005). Mindfulness and marital satisfaction. *Journal of Adult Development*, *12*, 43–51.

Burroughs, J. (2010). *Heavenly-mindedness recommended: In a discourse on Colossians 3:2*. Gale ECCO.

Burroughs, J. (2014). *A treatise on earthly-mindedness*. GLH Publishing.

Chatav, Y., & Whisman, M. (2009). Partner schemas and relationship functioning: A states of mind analysis. *Behavior Therapy*, *40*, 50–56.

Dattilio, F. (2010). *Cognitive-behavioral therapy with couples and families: A comprehensive guide for clinicians*. The Guilford Press.

de Sales, F. (2011). *Treatise on the love of God: Contemporary English version*. Paraclete Press.

Deniz, M., Erus, S., & Batum, D. (2019). Examining marital satisfaction in terms of interpersonal mindfulness and perceived problem solving skills in marriage. *International Online Journal of Educational Sciences*, *12*, 69–83.

Erickson, M. (2013). *Christian theology* (3rd ed.). Baker Academic.

Feldman, G., Hayes, A., Kumar, S., Greeson, J., & Laurenceau, J. (2007). Mindfulness and emotion regulation: The development and initial validation of the Cognitive and Affective Mindfulness Scale-Revised (CAMS-R). *Journal of Psychopathology and Behavioral Assessment*, *29*, 177–190.

Gillet, L. (1985). *On the invocation of the name*. Templegate Publishers.

Grudem, W. (1994). *Systematic theology: An introduction to biblical doctrine*. Zondervan.

Harris, R. (2009). *ACT with love: Stop struggling, reconcile differences, and strengthen your relationship with acceptance and commitment therapy*. New Harbinger Publications, Inc.

Harris, R. (2019). *ACT made simple: An easy-to-read primer on acceptance and commitment therapy* (2nd ed.). New Harbinger Publications, Inc.

Hayes, S. (2019). *A liberated mind: How to pivot toward what matters.* Avery.

Hayes, S., Strosahl, K., & Wilson, K. (2012). *Acceptance and commitment therapy: The process and practice of mindful change* (2nd ed.). The Guilford Press.

Holman Concise Bible Dictionary. (2016). *Marriage.* B&H Publishing Group.

Knabb, J. (2014). A preliminary investigation of the relationship between religion and marital adjustment among Christian adults from a conservative denomination. *Journal of Psychology and Christianity, 33,* 263–276.

Knabb, J., & Wang, K. (2021). The communion with God scale: Shifting from an *etic* to *emic* perspective to assess fellowshipping with the Triune God. *Psychology of Religion and Spirituality, 13,* 67–80.

Knabb, J., Vazquez, V., & Wang, K. (2020). The Christian contentment scale: An *emic* measure for assessing inner satisfaction within the Christian tradition. *Journal of Psychology and Theology.* Advance online publication.

Kostenberger, A., & Jones, D. (2012). *Marriage and the family: Biblical essentials.* Crossway.

Laird, M. (2006). *Into the silent land: A guide to the Christian practice of contemplation.* Oxford University Press.

Lawrence, B. (2015). *The practice of the presence of God.* (S. Sciurba, Trans.). ICS Publications.

Lev, A., & McKay, M. (2017). *Acceptance and commitment therapy for couples: A clinician's guide to using mindfulness, values & schema awareness to rebuild relationships.* New Harbinger Publications, Inc.

New International Version Bible. (2011). Zondervan. https://www.biblegateway.com/

Omidi, A., & Talighi, E. (2017). The effectiveness of marital therapy based on acceptance and commitment on couples' marital satisfaction and quality of life. *International Journal of Body, Mind & Culture, 4,* 46–51.

Pargament, K., Koenig, H., & Perez, L. (2000). The many methods of religious coping: Development and initial validation of the RCOPE. *Journal of Clinical Psychology, 56,* 519–543.

Peterson, B., Eifert, G., Feingold, T., & Davidson, S. (2009). Using acceptance and commitment therapy to treat distressed couples: A case study with two couples. *Cognitive and Behavioral Practice, 16,* 430–442.

Pratscher, S., Wood, P., King, L., & Bettencourt, B. (2019). Interpersonal mindfulness: Scale development and initial construct validation. *Mindfulness, 10,* 1044–1061.

Rafaeli, E., Bernstein, D., & Young, J. (2011). *Schema therapy: Distinctive features.* Routledge.

Rowe, J. (1672). *Heavenly-mindedness and earthly-mindedness: In two parts.* Francis Tyton.

Simeone-DiFrancesco, C., Roediger, E., & Stevens, B. (2015). *Schema therapy with couples: A practitioner's guide to healing relationships.* Wiley.

Spanier, G. (1976). Measuring dyadic adjustment: New scales for assessing the quality of marriage and similar dyads. *Journal of Marriage and the Family, 38,* 15–28.

Tilden, T., & Datillio, F. (2005). Vulnerability schemas of individuals in couples relationships: A cognitive perspective. *Contemporary Family Therapy, 27,* 139–162.

van Vreeswijk, M., Broersen, J., & Schurink, G. (2014). *Mindfulness and schema therapy: A practical guide.* Wiley.

Walser, R., & Westrup, D. (2009). *The mindful couple: How acceptance and mindfulness can lead you to the love you want.* New Harbinger Publications.

Wolters, A. (2005). *Creation regained: Biblical basics for a reformational worldview* (2nd ed.). William B. Eerdmans Publishing Company.

Wortley, J. (Ed.). (2012). *The book of the elders: Sayings of the desert fathers.* Cistercian Publications.

Yarhouse, M., & Sells, J. (2017). *Family therapies: A comprehensive Christian appraisal.* InterVarsity Press.

Young, J., Klosko, J., & Weishaa, M. (2003). *Schema therapy: A practitioner's guide.* The Guilford Press.

INDEX

Page numbers in *italics* represent figures while page numbers in **bold** represent tables.

mercy 172
Merton, Thomas 142
metacognitive awareness 283
metaphors 133, 143–145, **144**, 173, **174**,
    175–187, 189, **210**; "Family House"
    147–148; "God's House of Love" 148;
    "Passengers on the Bus" 134–135, 147;
    "Quicksand" metaphor 150; *see also
    specific metaphors*
Milne, B. 152
mindfulness 82, 88, 97, 118–119, 128n2,
    154, 171, 228–230, 233–234, 263, 288;
    and anxiety 249; Buddhist *vs.* Christian
    88–90, 121–123, 171; Christian 11,
    234; current focus on 10; interpersonal
    220, 278–279; meditations 166, 186,
    261, 288; *vs.* practicing God's presence
    99; *see also* Christian contemplation;
    and rumination 262; using 132–133,
    135, 165, 193, 238, 255, 270
mindfulness-based cognitive therapy
    (MBCT) 37–38, 55–56, 98, 118–119,
    128n2, 236; and anxiety 247–248;
    and depression 227–228, 230; and
    trauma 262
Mindfulness-based counseling 263–264
mindfulness-based stress reduction
    (MBSR) 230, 247–248
"The Mind is Like ..." exercises 148
"mind of Christ," 177–178
"Mind-Reading Machine" exercise 216
modes of mind 118–119
monks 136, 141, 158n5, 171, 203–204,
    232–233, 250
Moo, D. 59
mood, biomedical model 28
mood disorders 23–24
moral behaviors, for guides 269
morals 194
Moses 86–87, 139
Multidimensional Experiential Avoidance
    Questionnaire (MEAQ) 68, 235,
    252, 267
Munkholm, K. 29
Mystical Theology (Dionysius) 138–139

narcissistic personality symptoms 49
"need for treatment" model 47
nepsis 10, 13, **14**, 94, 131, 139–140, 148,
    168, 205, 256
Netherlands 26

New Testament 16, 49, 102; *nous* in 169;
    and psychological pain 8
Niebuhr, Reinhold 91
"Normalizing" exercise 153
"Noticing" exercises 148
Noticing/shifting **14**, **174**, 176, 254, 267,
    269, 272, 285; *see also nous*
nous 10, 13, **14**, 96, 162, 168–170, 187,
    206, 256; *see also* contemplative self;
    transcendent self

"The Observer" exercise 179–180
Old Testament 16, 33, 38; Book
    of Psalms 38–39, 137, 213, 236;
    Jonah 153
"opposite action" exercise 125–126
orthodox Christian beliefs, and
    experiential avoidance 72–73
Ostafin, B. 69

pain, and psychological growth 67
pain of absence 4–5, 87–88, 101, 134,
    167; both/and approach 5, 150; failure
    of 246
pain of presence 3–5, 87–88, 167; and
    avoidance strategies 4, 6; both/and
    approach 5, 150; and following Jesus 7
Paintner, C. 203
panic disorder 24–25, 71–72, 244–246
"Parable of the Bags of Gold" 213–214
Paris, J. 51–52, 62n2
"Passengers on the Bus" 134–135, 147
Passion narrative 8, 46
passions 203–206
pathos 204
"Path Up the Mountain" metaphor
    214–215
Paul (Apostle) 57–58, 99–100, 178–181,
    207; 2 Corinthians 180–181; Letter to
    the Philippians 78–79; Letter to the
    Romans 155
peirasmos 59
Pennington, B. 147, 177, 182
Penn State Worry Questionnaire
    (PSWQ) 252
Pentecostal/Charismatic traditions
    32–33
perfectionism 37
perilypos 59
perseverative thinking 264
Peter (Apostle) 8, 139, 155

Printed in the United States
by Baker & Taylor Publisher Services